Ed Subitzky is a cartoonist, humor writer, and performer. A contributing editor at *National Lampoon* for nearly two decades, he also wrote and performed for *The National Lampoon Radio Hour*. He went on to write and perform for *The David Letterman Show* and *Late Night with David Letterman*. His art and writing have appeared in *The New York Times*, *The American Bystander*, and the *Journal of Consciousness Studies*, among others. He lives in New York City.

Mark Newgarden is a cartoonist known for his novelties (*Garbage Pail Kids*), multimedia projects (from Microsoft to Cartoon Network), and comics (from *Raw* magazine to the award-winning *Bow-Wow* series of children's books). He is the author of *Cheap Laffs: The Art of the Novelty Item* and *We All Die Alone*, a collection of his comics and humor. With Paul Karasik, he co-wrote *How to Read Nancy: The Elements of Comics in Three Easy Panels*, which won an Eisner Award in 2018. Newgarden lives in Brooklyn and teaches at the School of Visual Arts.

THE BEGINNING COMICS!
BY ED SUBITZKY
SON, YOU HAVE FIVE FULL PAGES AHEAD OF YOU!
THAT'S 29 MORE PANELS!
GO OUT AND MAKE THE MOST OF IT! LIVE! LAUGH! ENJOY!
I'VE WASTED FOUR OF YOUR PANELS ALREADY!
GET STARTED ON YOUR GREAT JOURNEY AND GOOD LUCK!

THIS IS A NEW YORK REVIEW COMIC
PUBLISHED BY THE NEW YORK REVIEW OF BOOKS
207 East 32nd Street
New York, NY 10016
www.nyrb.com/comics

Cover design by Joe Kessler

A catalog record for this book is available from The Library of Congress.

ISBN: 978-1-68137-787-2

Printed in South Korea.

10 9 8 7 6 5 4 3 2 1

WOW! SO MANY PANELS, AND ALL FEATURING ME!
I'M GOING TO FIND A GIRL, FALL IN LOVE, AND HAVE STUPENDOUS SEX!
THEN I'M GOING TO GET RICH! AND FAMOUS TOO!
AND I'M NOT GOING TO WASTE ANY MORE PANELS DREAMING ABOUT IT!
ER...HI! MY NAME IS...
MY NAME IS "GET!" "GET LOST!"
UH, NICE WEATHER, ISN'T IT?
WHAT WEATHER, ASSHOLE?

POOR HELPLESS COMICS!

THE CARTOONS (AND MORE) OF ED SUBITZKY

CO-EDITED AND WITH AN INTERVIEW BY
MARK NEWGARDEN

WITH GUEST APPEARANCES BY SUSAN HEWITT AND ANIKA BANISTER

NEW YORK REVIEW COMICS ! NEW YORK

GULP! TWO WHOLE PAGES ARE GONE AND I HAVEN'T FOUND MY DREAM COMPANION YET!
EXCUSE ME, BUT I JUST GOT THIS GREAT STOCK TIP!
IN TWO MORE PANELS, CORNERCO IS GOING TO SPLIT! WE'LL MAKE MILLIONS!
OKAY! I'M IN!
GREAT! SEE YOU SOON!
GASP! IT DIDN'T SPLIT! IT WENT OUT OF BUSINESS!
I'M ALONE... ALONE AND BROKE!

HI! I'M ALONE AND BROKE, TOO! WHY DON'T YOU MARRY ME AND FIND A NICE STEADY JOB?
I GUESS FILLING IN BREAKS IN THE FRAME LINE ISN'T SUCH A BAD OCCUPATION!
I'M SPENDING A WHOLE PANEL TAKING THE GARBAGE OUT!
I'M SPENDING A WHOLE PANEL TRYING TO FIGURE OUT A MICROWAVE DINNER WRAPPER!
THE HELL WITH IT! I'M GOING TO SPEND THE NEXT PANEL DRUNK!
ZZZ...

CONTENTS

INTERVIEW

COMICS, WRITING, & MORE

ACKNOWLEDGEMENTS

ORDER OF APPEARANCES

ONLY ONE MORE PAGE LEFT! AND I HAD SUCH DREAMS AT THE BEGINNING!

NOW I SPEND ALL MY PRECIOUS PANELS JUST THINKING BACK!

THAT FIRST GIRL I MET! MAYBE I SHOULD HAVE SAID, "WHAT'S YOUR SIGN!"

DID I REALLY SPEND A WHOLE PANEL ON THAT STUPID REGRET?

ONLY ONE MORE PANEL LEFT! BOY, AM I GOING TO MAKE THE MOST OF IT!

ON THE OTHER HAND, I THINK THERE'S SOMETHING GOOD ON TV...

THE END

AN INTERVIEW WITH ED SUBITZKY
by Mark Newgarden

1:23 PM on January 6, 2023, at the office of New York Review Books: Mark Newgarden (cartoonist, co-author of How to Read Nancy) *has put together a set of questions for Ed Subitzky, the cartoonist of the hour. Also present: Ed; his wife, Susan Hewitt; NYRC intern Anika Banister; and NYRC editor Lucas Adams. Mark speaks.*

Mark Newgarden: Who is Ed Subitzky?

Ed Subitzky: [*Laughs*] That's a question for the ages. Philosophers have been asking that.

I don't think he's me, for one thing. I'm kind of nerdy, and I'm quite shy with people. I have always loved humor intensely, since I was a young kid. And there's a non-humor side of me that's very important: I'm a huge science buff. I'm always reading a science book of one kind or another. I'm happy to live in an age when we know a little bit. Just a tad! We don't know everything, but we know something. I love philosophy, too. I'm always trying to answer the deep questions.

But people have been trying to answer these questions for millennia! [*Laughs*] I don't think I'm the one who's going to answer them.

MN: What's the most important thing that any reader of this book should know about you? Maybe you just covered it.

ES: I guess the one thing that the reader should know is that I'm a little weird, but I hope I'm weird in a nice and decent way. Back in the 70s, people who liked my work were always disappointed to meet me because I came off as an accountant. In those days, they thought I would have hair out to here, be mumbling strange chants and smoking three joints at once. They expected a really wild *National Lampoon* char-

acter, and all they got was me.[1] Incidentally, that happened to other people at the *Lampoon*. In fact they were all very hardworking publishing people, not what you might expect of them at all.

MN: What kind of a kid were you?

ES: Shy, pretty obedient. I loved drawing and writing. While all the other kids were running around in the yard, I would be pounding at a typewriter or making drawings. It was rough on my parents. It's the story of a kid who loves the arts, but who has blue-collar parents who don't understand that at all. There was nothing wrong with them. They were nice, decent people, but they had no idea how to handle someone like me.

I had a real 50s upbringing in a suburban house, on a tree-lined street, stuff like that. I was the firstborn, with a sister and a brother. My mother was a classic housewife. My father was a glazier. It was a dangerous job. He was always climbing high ladders and trying to avoid being injured by the glass. He didn't want me to take over the glass business.

It's the standard thing of middle-class parents making sacrifices to send their kids to college, wanting their kids to be better off than they are.

MN: Is anybody else in your family creative?

ES: Not at all, no. My sister was a nurse and my brother teaches English in Japan. Nobody but me in the arts. I don't know where it came from.

MN: Did you always know you were funny?

ES: I think, yeah.

[1] *National Lampoon* (1970–1998), an influential American humor magazine.

MN: How did you figure it out?

ES: I used to laugh at my own stuff. [*Laughs*] I'd draw or write something and think, "That looks funny to me." Of course, like with all people of my type, there's a lot of insecurity. "It seems funny—but is it funny? Do I have any talent? Maybe I have no talent at all. Maybe I should be in the glass business."

[*Laughter*]

MN: You still think that?

ES: Oh, yeah... I'm one of those people, when I read something that I wrote in the past—I'm distanced enough from it now that I'll get a chuckle and laugh. If it's something I wrote last week, I'll only see what I think is wrong with it. Where I should have gone with it, and why didn't I change this or that frame when I could, stuff like that.

MN: What sorts of things made the deepest impression on young Ed Subitzky?

ES: *Mad* magazine.[2] Especially the original Harvey Kurtzman ones, with the comic book parodies.[3] I loved those. Those were my lifeline, because it was my first inkling that other people also thought that the suburban life was bullshit.

In my *Mad* worship days, a friend of mine happened to live right across the street from Harvey Kurtzman, and he introduced me. I think I was in my early teens. For me, meeting Harvey Kurtzman was like meeting God. I was nervous as anybody could possibly be. I was stammering, I didn't know what to say. To make matters even worse (or better), who happened to be visiting him at the time but my favorite artist in the whole world, Bill Elder.[4] To be in a room with both Bill Elder and Harvey Kurtzman at the same time—how could this ever happen?

But Kurtzman didn't like my work!

I brought him some work, hoping he'd say, "Wow, this is fantastic." I think he's a wonder-ful person, but I'm not sure he understood that he was looking at the work of a kid. I like to think he was judging it by the same standards he would apply to a real professional coming in to see him. I was appropriately devastated.

MN: Did he tell you to get into the glass business?

[*Laughter*]

ES: No, he was very nice to me. He talked to me a little about how they had basically thrown him off of *Mad* magazine and taken it in a direction he didn't want to go. I think he even got a little teary when he was talking to me.

But while I was growing up, even the later *Mad* were a lifeline for me. A lifeline.

MN: What other kinds of humor were you attracted to?

ES: Oh, TV. I loved the funny TV shows of the time, Ernie Kovacs, Sid Caesar, *I Love Lucy*. I always tended to prefer the weirder and more satirical stuff rather than the straightforward stuff. Oh, and I absolutely adored Bob and Ray on the radio.

MN: Did you follow newspaper comics?

ES: I loved so many of them. In fact, I still do. I subscribe to comic strip services online. I've always adored comics. In addition to the funny ones, I really enjoyed the continuity strips, stuff like *Mandrake the Magician*.

MN: What other comics were you following at the time?

ES: Well, as I grew up, I went through all the standard things. When I was very young, I was reading Walt Disney's comics and stories from Dell Comics. When I got older, I got into Superman, superheroes, all the expected things. One summer, I was staying at my cousin's house for a few weeks, and somehow his father brought home a bunch of DC horror comics that some-

---

[2]*Mad* magazine (1952–), comics and humor magazine, last of the EC line.
[3]Harvey Kurtzman, cartoonist, editor, and founder of *Mad*.
[4]William Elder (1921–2008), illustrator and cartoonist best known for his work for *Mad*.

body had thrown out. The most gruesome ones you can imagine. I spent that summer steeped in the blood of innocent people.

[*Laughter*]

MN: Where did you go to school?

ES: I went to high school in Mount Vernon, then Harpur College at the State University of New York at Binghamton.[5] I was a math major—I had loved math since I was a teenager.

MN: Did you know Art Spiegelman while at Harpur?[6]

ES: Yes, I became friendly with him a little bit. We used to hang out sometimes. I liked his stuff. I did some cartoons for the school newspaper, and if I remember right, Art did something that the local printer refused to print. So they managed to find another printer who'd actually print it. My college was in Binghamton, in a very conservative area. If my memory is correct, the cartoon showed three churches, Christian, Jewish, maybe Muslim, and the hand of God was reaching out of the clouds and giving the finger to all three of them.

MN: Were you reading the early underground comics, when that was a thing—was that a formative part for you at all?

ES: I noticed them, I knew about them. I loved Robert Crumb's work, how could you not?[7] But I never got into that. I never regarded any of the stuff I ended up doing as being part of the underground comics scene. I never thought of it as an area where I could submit my work.

MN: What happened after college? How did you begin your career?

ES: I got out of college, and the only thing I knew was that I loved to write and draw, and I didn't know what to do about that. So I answered every ad for writing that I could find in

The New York Times. One of them was in the advertising business. So the first job I got out of college was writing what people call junk mail. The head of a company I worked for said, "There's no such thing as junk mail, there is only irrelevant mail."

[*Laughter*]

MN: So, you wrote irrelevant mail.

ES: Yeah. That first job I got was for a client, not an ad agency. It was for Moody's Investors Service.[8] I had to write all this financial stuff, but I didn't really know what I was doing. The people would have to correct me. They were decent, nice people there, actually. I lasted about eight months and then I just left. I thought, "This is it for me." The next job I got was at an actual advertising agency, which was very cool. That's what everybody wanted, an agency job. It was this tiny little agency, and I had a very funny, nice boss. He was very good to me.

This is perhaps the most shameful thing I'm going to tell you this afternoon: I have an actual talent for advertising. I'm usually modest, but I'm just going to say it outright: I was damn good at it, to my shock and horror. I ended up staying in a little part of the advertising business outside of the mainstream called direct marketing. For anyone who doesn't know, in direct marketing, the idea is that a person sees the ad, back then they would clip out a coupon and send it in with some money. It amazed me that my stuff was working, and working well. I would write this gibberish, whatever it was, and people out there flipping through a magazine would come across something I wrote, and a minute later they were reaching for their wallet! I said, "This can't be! What am I doing to people?"

[*Laughter*]

I was the only person I ever remember in the advertising business who was concerned about ethics. I was always fighting to be sure things

---

[5]In 1965, Harpur College became State University of New York at Binghamton.
[6]Art Spiegelman (1948–), acclaimed cartoonist and author of *Maus*.
[7]Robert Crumb (1943–), acclaimed cartoonist known for his underground comics.
[8]Investment company founded by John Moody in 1909.

were correct and stuff like that. I was very self-conscious about it. The funny thing about advertising is that, because of legal stuff, the facts are usually accurate. It's what they tell you about the facts that's not so accurate. If they tell you a widget has six flugels in it, it will in fact have six flugels. But when they tell you six flugels will improve your sex life? You ignore that.

MN: You were good at adding the embellishments.

ES: Yeah, I was. I'm ashamed to say it. I was good. But what really mattered to me was when the working day was over, I rushed home and over to the drawing table. That's what mattered.

MN: The advertising wasn't enough.

ES: No, but it paid the rent. As a matter of fact, the *Lampoon* offered me a job as an associate editor. And I had to turn it down because they offered me half of what I was earning at my advertising job, and I didn't think I could hold onto my apartment if I accepted it. Also, the magazine was doing very well then, but I did have a sense that someday the top people who were making it so excellent were going to leave, and then where would I be? I was concerned about that. Whether I made a mistake or not, I'll never know.

MN: So, nine to five, you were writing direct marketing, and there was always a drawing board at home. How did you start transitioning into making work that people know?

ES: I managed to sell a few things before the *Lampoon* stuff. I did know about the *Lampoon* when it was new, and I thought that I would love to be in it if I could. Then one day, I was in a little magazine store and several people came in to ask the news dealer how well the *Lampoon* was selling. It came out while he was talking to them that they were the editors of the *Lampoon*. There was my chance! All I had

to do was tap one of them on the shoulder and say: "Hey, I have a bunch of cartoons and stuff, do you mind taking a look at my work?" But I was too shy. I didn't do it. I let them walk away and I figured that was it, I would never see them again.

MN: How you did get to them?

ES: I was taking an evening course at the School of Visual Arts with Bob Blechman and Charles Slackman and—[9]

MN: I took that class at one point! I was a kid. I dropped out of high school and took that class.

ES: Oh my goodness. Could we have been in the same class at the same time?

MN: Maybe, were you still there in the late 70s?

ES: I took the course again and again, I think it was twelve times.

MN: Twelve times?! Oh my god!

ES: Yeah, I really loved that class.

MN: Maybe you were one of the people who were intimidating me.

[*Laughter*]

ES: Blechman and Slackman were very encouraging to me. They liked what I was doing. One day they came up to me and said, "There's something we want you to try. There's a fine-tip technical pen called a Rapidograph.[10] It's usually used for drawing maps, but we want you to try using that pen and see what happens."

As I started with that pen, I suddenly found my style, or should I say, my non-style. They were so right about the Rapidograph, it was amazing. It was one of the best things they could have done for me.

Anyway, occasionally they would bring in guest speakers, and Michel Choquette, one of

---

[9]Illustrators and cartoonists R. O. Blechman (1930–) and Charles Slackman (1934–2015) taught a humorous illustration course through the 60s and 70s.

[10]Rapidograph is a brand of fine-tip pen, often used for technical and architectural drawings.

the *Lampoon* editors, gave a little talk to the class. He said he was working on a book about the 60s, so Blechman and Slackman made that a class project. Michel liked what I submitted for the book.[11] Luckily, the *Lampoon* offices were only a couple of blocks away from where I worked. When I went there to bring him the artwork, and to talk to him about the piece or whatever it was, the *Lampoon* people were there. Probably they were the same people that I had not talked to at the magazine store that day.

But this time it was an easier circumstance. The fact that I had met them officially gave me the courage, so to speak, to submit some drawings of my own, and they liked them. Michael Gross, who was the editor of the comics section then, accepted them all! The first thing I had published in the *Lampoon* was "Anti-Comics."

MN: Classic.

ES: Nobody would've run that except for the *Lampoon*. Nobody.

---

[11] In the 1970s, Michel Choquette began work on a collection of 1960s cartoons that would eventually become *The Someday Funnies*, published in 2011.

ANTI-COMICS!

HOWEVER, HE WANTED IT WAS TO GO VERY COLD.

HE WANTED WAS INTO TO GO VERY TOWN COLD

INTO TOWN ;

HE WANTED TO GO INTO TOWN; HOWEVER, IT WAS VERY COLD.

THE END

THE BEGINNING OF LIFE

THE FIRST CELL, 10,000,000 B.C.

IT EATS.

IT LOCOMOTES.

IT SHITS.

IT DIVIDES.

IT WALKS THE DOG.

THE END

8 COMICS IN ONE!

by Ed Subitzky

A DIRTY COMIC, A SPORTS COMIC, AN EDUCATIONAL COMIC, A LOVE COMIC, A TRAGIC COMIC, A HUMOR COMIC, A DETECTIVE COMIC, AND A HORROR COMIC!

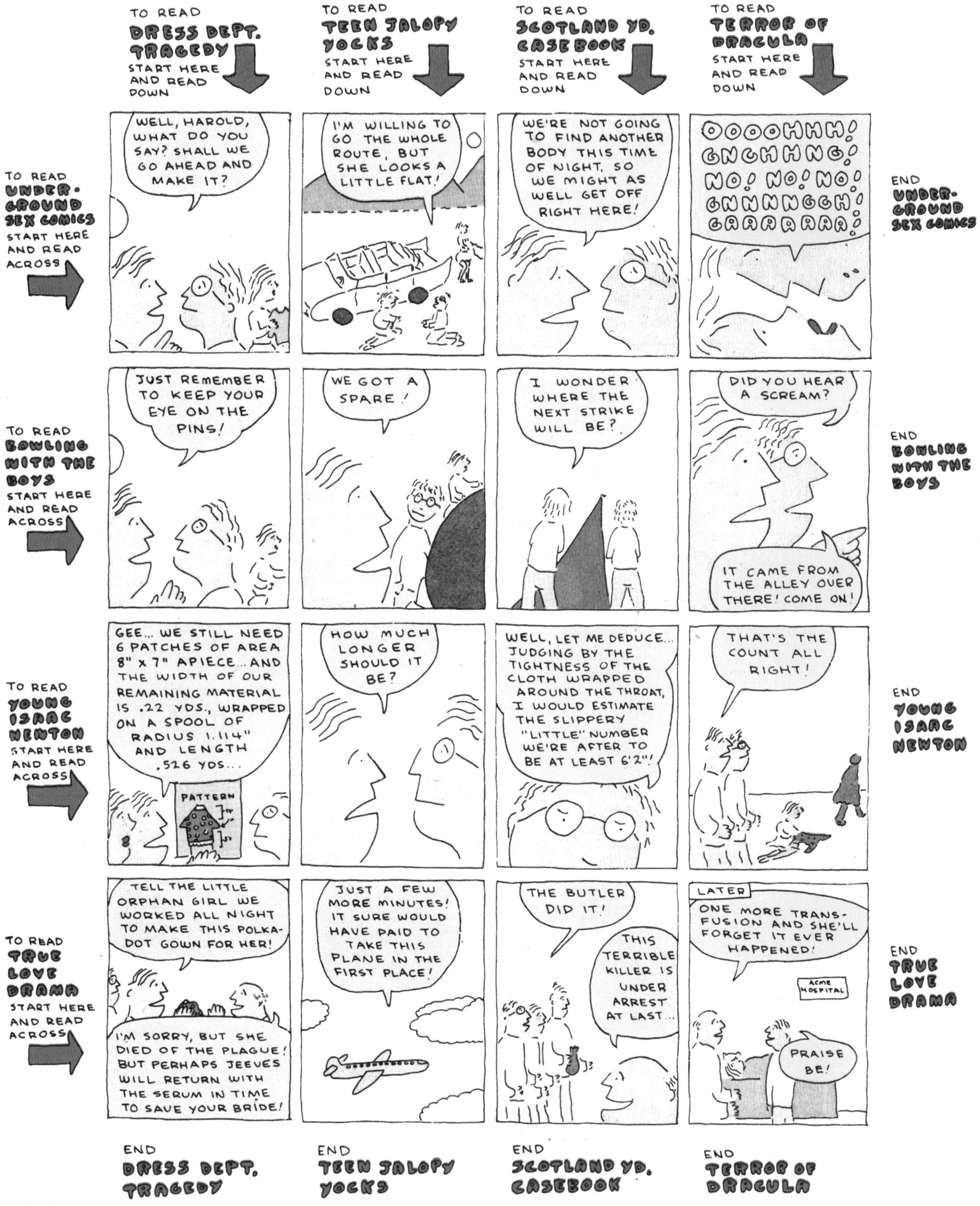

TO READ DRESS DEPT. TRAGEDY START HERE AND READ DOWN
TO READ TEEN JALOPY YOCKS START HERE AND READ DOWN
TO READ SCOTLAND YD. CASEBOOK START HERE AND READ DOWN
TO READ TERROR OF DRACULA START HERE AND READ DOWN
TO READ UNDER-GROUND SEX COMICS START HERE AND READ ACROSS
WELL, HAROLD, WHAT DO YOU SAY? SHALL WE GO AHEAD AND MAKE IT?
I'M WILLING TO GO THE WHOLE ROUTE, BUT SHE LOOKS A LITTLE FLAT!
WE'RE NOT GOING TO FIND ANOTHER BODY THIS TIME OF NIGHT, SO WE MIGHT AS WELL GET OFF RIGHT HERE!
OOOOHHH! GNGHHNG! NO! NO! NO! GNNNNGGH! GAAAAAAA!
END UNDER-GROUND SEX COMICS
TO READ BOWLING WITH THE BOYS START HERE AND READ ACROSS
JUST REMEMBER TO KEEP YOUR EYE ON THE PINS!
WE GOT A SPARE!
I WONDER WHERE THE NEXT STRIKE WILL BE?
DID YOU HEAR A SCREAM?
IT CAME FROM THE ALLEY OVER THERE! COME ON!
END BOWLING WITH THE BOYS
TO READ YOUNG ISAAC NEWTON START HERE AND READ ACROSS
GEE... WE STILL NEED 6 PATCHES OF AREA 8" x 7" APIECE... AND THE WIDTH OF OUR REMAINING MATERIAL IS .22 YDS., WRAPPED ON A SPOOL OF RADIUS 1.114" AND LENGTH .526 YDS...
PATTERN
HOW MUCH LONGER SHOULD IT BE?
WELL, LET ME DEDUCE... JUDGING BY THE TIGHTNESS OF THE CLOTH WRAPPED AROUND THE THROAT, I WOULD ESTIMATE THE SLIPPERY "LITTLE" NUMBER WE'RE AFTER TO BE AT LEAST 6'2"!
THAT'S THE COUNT ALL RIGHT!
END YOUNG ISAAC NEWTON
TO READ TRUE LOVE DRAMA START HERE AND READ ACROSS
TELL THE LITTLE ORPHAN GIRL WE WORKED ALL NIGHT TO MAKE THIS POLKA-DOT GOWN FOR HER!
I'M SORRY, BUT SHE DIED OF THE PLAGUE! BUT PERHAPS JEEVES WILL RETURN WITH THE SERUM IN TIME TO SAVE YOUR BRIDE!
JUST A FEW MORE MINUTES! IT SURE WOULD HAVE PAID TO TAKE THIS PLANE IN THE FIRST PLACE!
THE BUTLER DID IT!
THIS TERRIBLE KILLER IS UNDER ARREST AT LAST...
LATER
ONE MORE TRANS-FUSION AND SHE'LL FORGET IT EVER HAPPENED!
ACME HOSPITAL
PRAISE BE!
END TRUE LOVE DRAMA
END DRESS DEPT. TRAGEDY
END TEEN JALOPY YOCKS
END SCOTLAND YD. CASEBOOK
END TERROR OF DRACULA

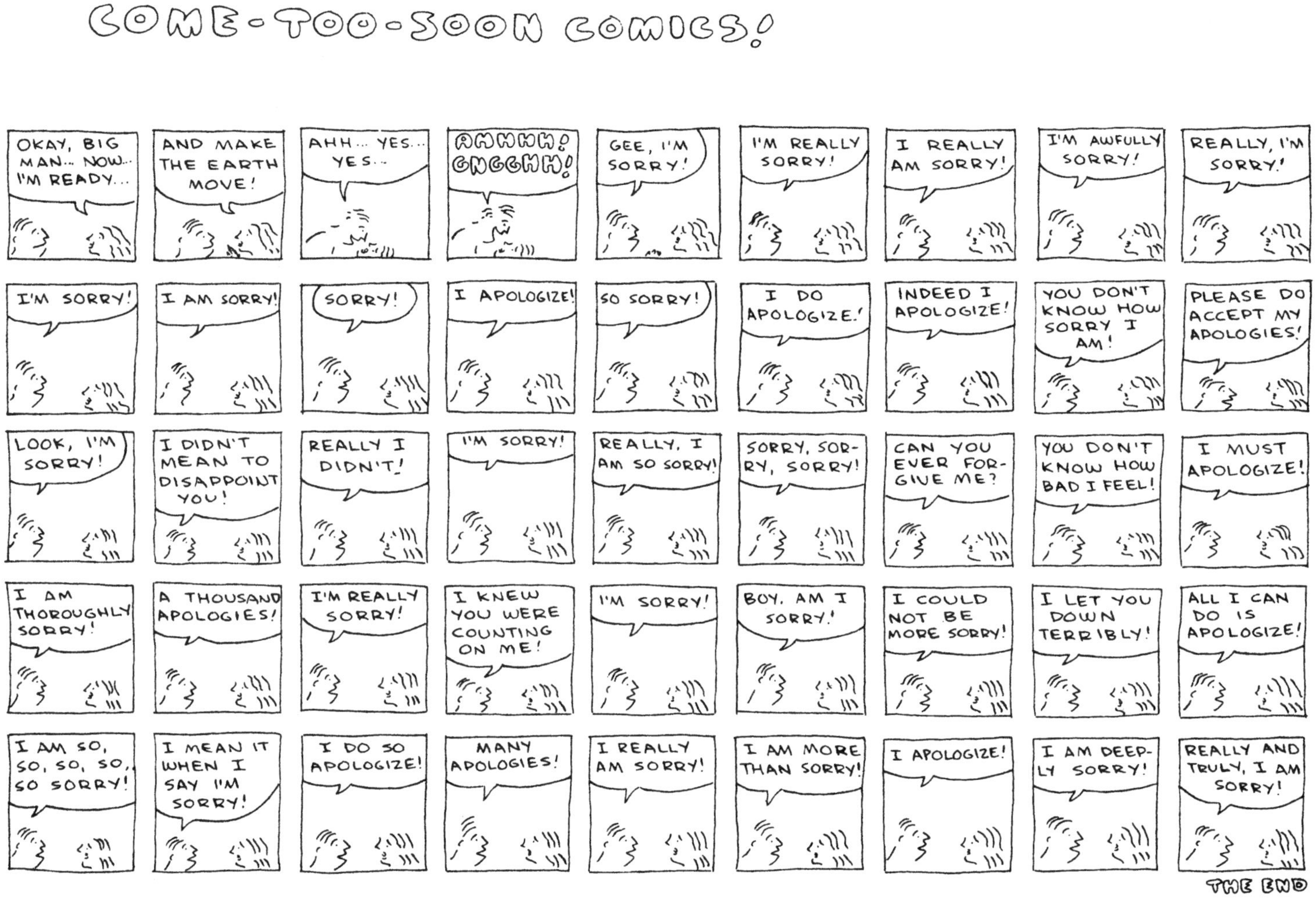
COME-TOO-SOON COMICS!
OKAY, BIG MAN... NOW... I'M READY...
AND MAKE THE EARTH MOVE!
AHH... YES... YES...
AHHHHH! GNGGHH!
GEE, I'M SORRY!
I'M REALLY SORRY!
I REALLY AM SORRY!
I'M AWFULLY SORRY!
REALLY, I'M SORRY!
I'M SORRY!
I AM SORRY!
SORRY!
I APOLOGIZE!
SO SORRY!
I DO APOLOGIZE!
INDEED I APOLOGIZE!
YOU DON'T KNOW HOW SORRY I AM!
PLEASE DO ACCEPT MY APOLOGIES!
LOOK, I'M SORRY!
I DIDN'T MEAN TO DISAPPOINT YOU!
REALLY I DIDN'T!
I'M SORRY!
REALLY, I AM SO SORRY!
SORRY, SORRY, SORRY!
CAN YOU EVER FORGIVE ME?
YOU DON'T KNOW HOW BAD I FEEL!
I MUST APOLOGIZE!
I AM THOROUGHLY SORRY!
A THOUSAND APOLOGIES!
I'M REALLY SORRY!
I KNEW YOU WERE COUNTING ON ME!
I'M SORRY!
BOY, AM I SORRY!
I COULD NOT BE MORE SORRY!
I LET YOU DOWN TERRIBLY!
ALL I CAN DO IS APOLOGIZE!
I AM SO, SO, SO, SO, SO SORRY!
I MEAN IT WHEN I SAY I'M SORRY!
I DO SO APOLOGIZE!
MANY APOLOGIES!
I REALLY AM SORRY!
I AM MORE THAN SORRY!
I APOLOGIZE!
I AM DEEPLY SORRY!
REALLY AND TRULY, I AM SORRY!
THE END

CROSSWORD PUZZLE COMICS!

  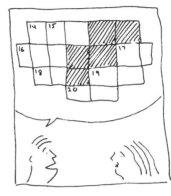 

THE END

ACROSS

1. Conjunction
3. Pronoun
5. Preference
7. Conjunction
8. Oral-genital relation
9. Pronoun
10. Pronoun
11. Expression of disapproval
13. Expression of disgust
14. Correlative
16. Difference between man and woman
17. Conjunction
18. Conjunction
19. Sigh
20. Deep sigh
21. Expression of consent (colloq.)

DOWN

1. Tibetan ox
2. East Indian fruitcake
3. Pelagarian's sister
4. N. African lake
6. Sand dune (var.)
10. Hindu dance
11. Ancestor of Pterydactyl
12. Siberian monastery
14. Caluptusian
15. W. Norfolk mini-park
17. Moon of Narason
19. Peloponnesian mystic

Anika Banister: Can you talk a bit more about the *Lampoon*, for those who aren't familiar with it?

ES: The *Lampoon* had a reputation for being a solid laugh, month after month. Even if you had never heard of it, you're still living in the afterglow right now! They used to call it "sick humor," but the Lampoon changed humor so much that nobody even uses the phrase any more. The *Lampoon* ethos of going after everyone—Republicans, Democrats, prudes, hippies, whatever— that ethos is so embedded into the comedy that it's hard to imagine it was a first when the *Lampoon* hit the newsstand. People— a lot of young men, really— flocked to the *Lampoon* because it was the only magazine that would laugh openly at this sex-crazed, repressed society we were living in. And to look at the nudie cartoons, of course. But the fans really saw it for what it was. The perversions of today are different than fifty years ago, so you have to take the long view, but what was true then is still true now: a sick joke in a sick world is a recipe for a good joke.

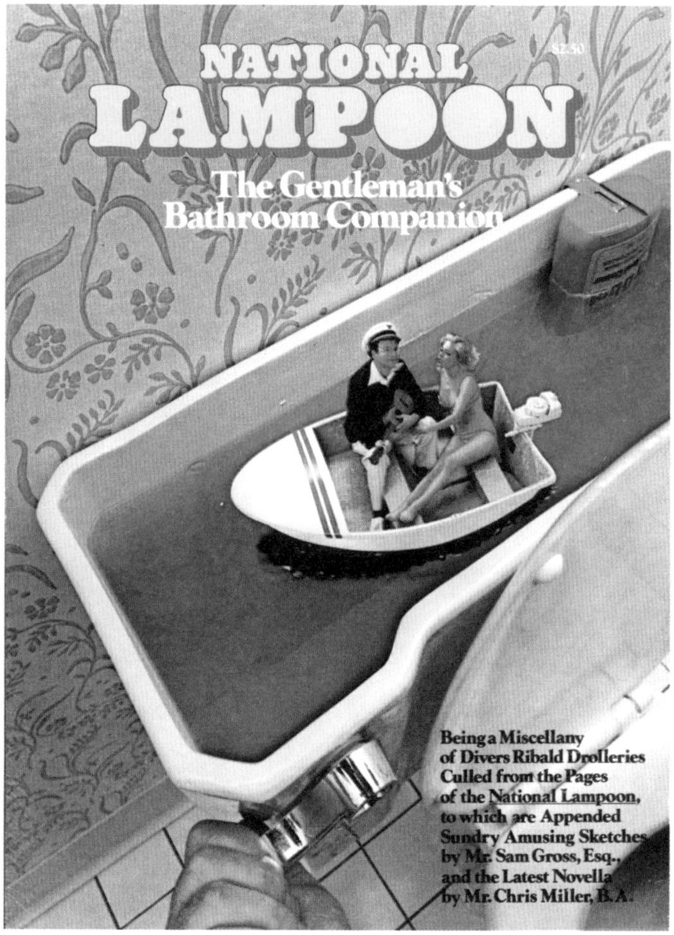
NATIONAL LAMPOON
$2.50
The Gentleman's Bathroom Companion
Being a Miscellany of Divers Ribald Drolleries Culled from the Pages of the National Lampoon, to which are Appended Sundry Amusing Sketches by Mr. Sam Gross, Esq., and the Latest Novella by Mr. Chris Miller, B.A.

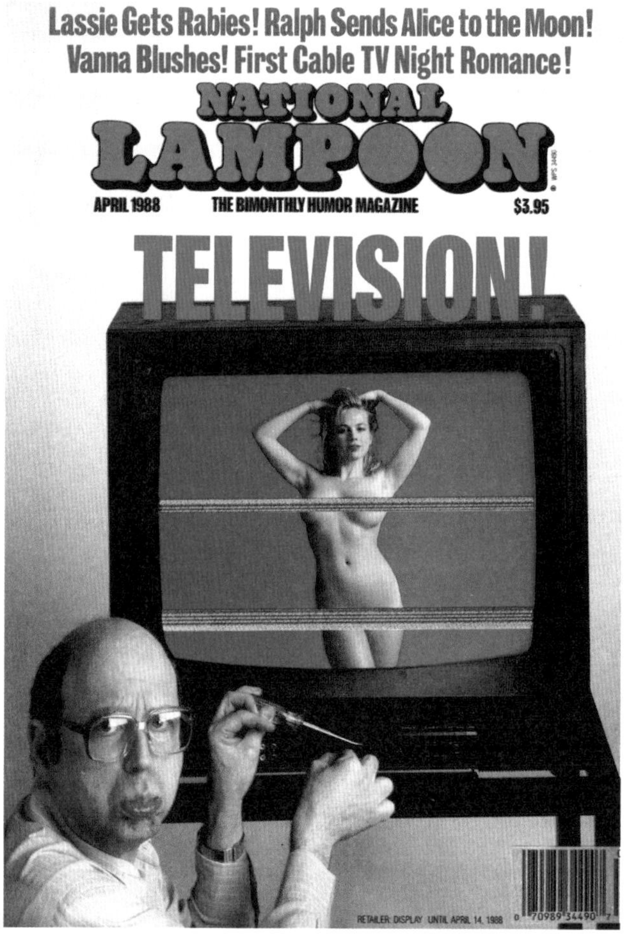
Lassie Gets Rabies! Ralph Sends Alice to the Moon!
Vanna Blushes! First Cable TV Night Romance!
NATIONAL LAMPOON
APRIL 1988
THE BIMONTHLY HUMOR MAGAZINE
$3.95
TELEVISION!
RETAILER DISPLAY UNTIL APRIL 14, 1988

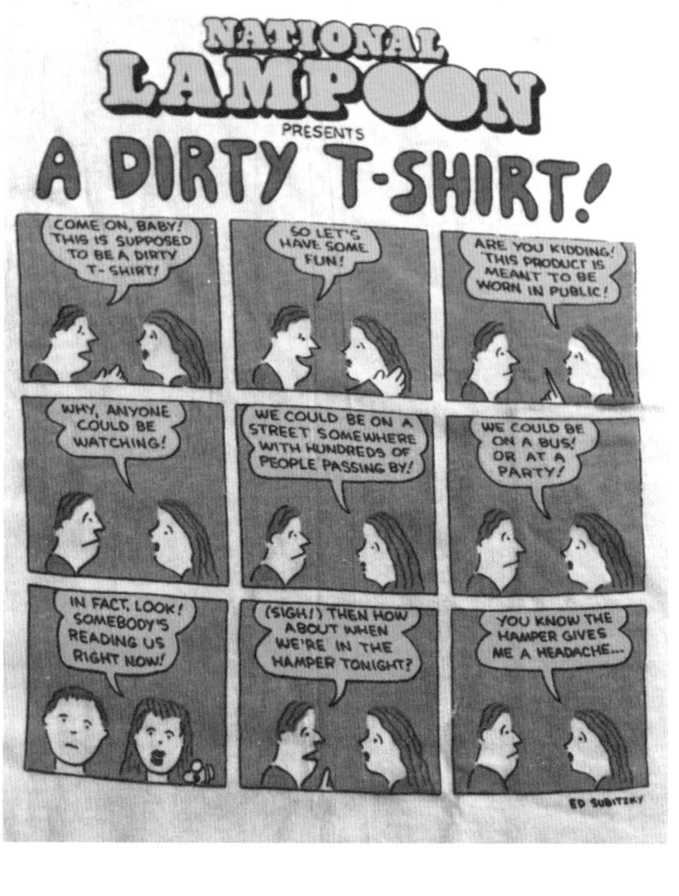
NATIONAL LAMPOON
PRESENTS
A DIRTY T-SHIRT!
COME ON, BABY! THIS IS SUPPOSED TO BE A DIRTY T-SHIRT!
SO LET'S HAVE SOME FUN!
ARE YOU KIDDING! THIS PRODUCT IS MEANT TO BE WORN IN PUBLIC!
WHY, ANYONE COULD BE WATCHING!
WE COULD BE ON A STREET SOMEWHERE WITH HUNDREDS OF PEOPLE PASSING BY!
WE COULD BE ON A BUS! OR AT A PARTY!
IN FACT, LOOK! SOMEBODY'S READING US RIGHT NOW!
(SIGH!) THEN HOW ABOUT WHEN WE'RE IN THE HAMPER TONIGHT?
YOU KNOW THE HAMPER GIVES ME A HEADACHE...
ED SUBITZKY

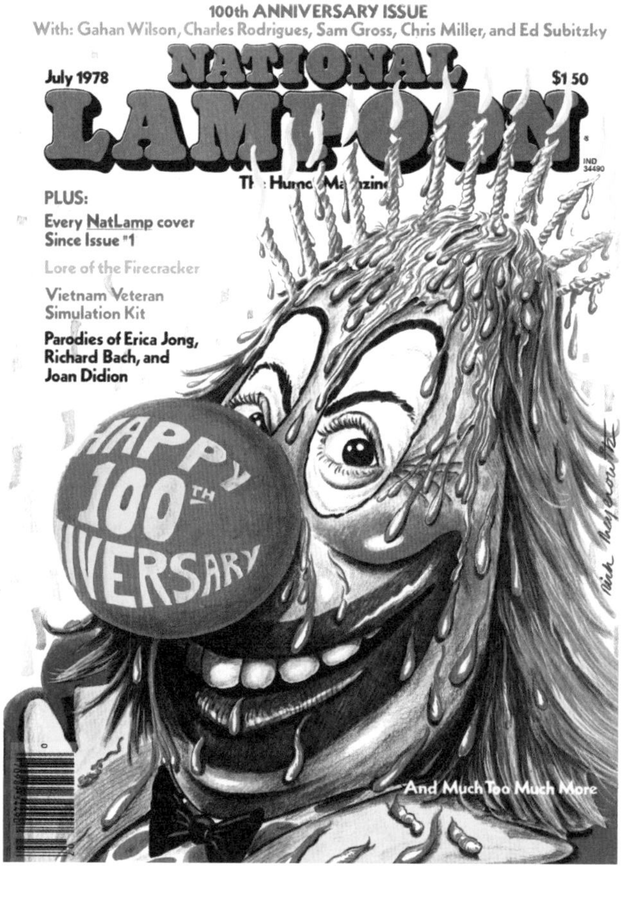
100th ANNIVERSARY ISSUE
With: Gahan Wilson, Charles Rodrigues, Sam Gross, Chris Miller, and Ed Subitzky
July 1978
$1.50
NATIONAL LAMPOON
PLUS:
Every NatLamp cover Since Issue #1
Lore of the Firecracker
Vietnam Veteran Simulation Kit
Parodies of Erica Jong, Richard Bach, and Joan Didion
HAPPY 100TH ANNIVERSARY
And Much Too Much More

NOTE: WE HAVE ALL HEARD OF THE MUCH-PUBLICIZED "SEXUAL REVOLUTION"! HOWEVER, DEEP INSIDE, DON'T YOU REALLY KNOW IN YOUR HEART OF HEARTS THAT YOUR PARENTS AND TEACHERS AND CLERGYMEN WERE REALLY RIGHT ALL ALONG... THAT SEX REALLY IS DIRTY AND DEGRADING, NOT TO MENTION SMELLY? THIS SERIES IS DEDICATED TO GIVING "EQUAL TIME" TO THE ONLY VIEWPOINT THAT CAN SAVE YOUR TARNISHED SOUL....

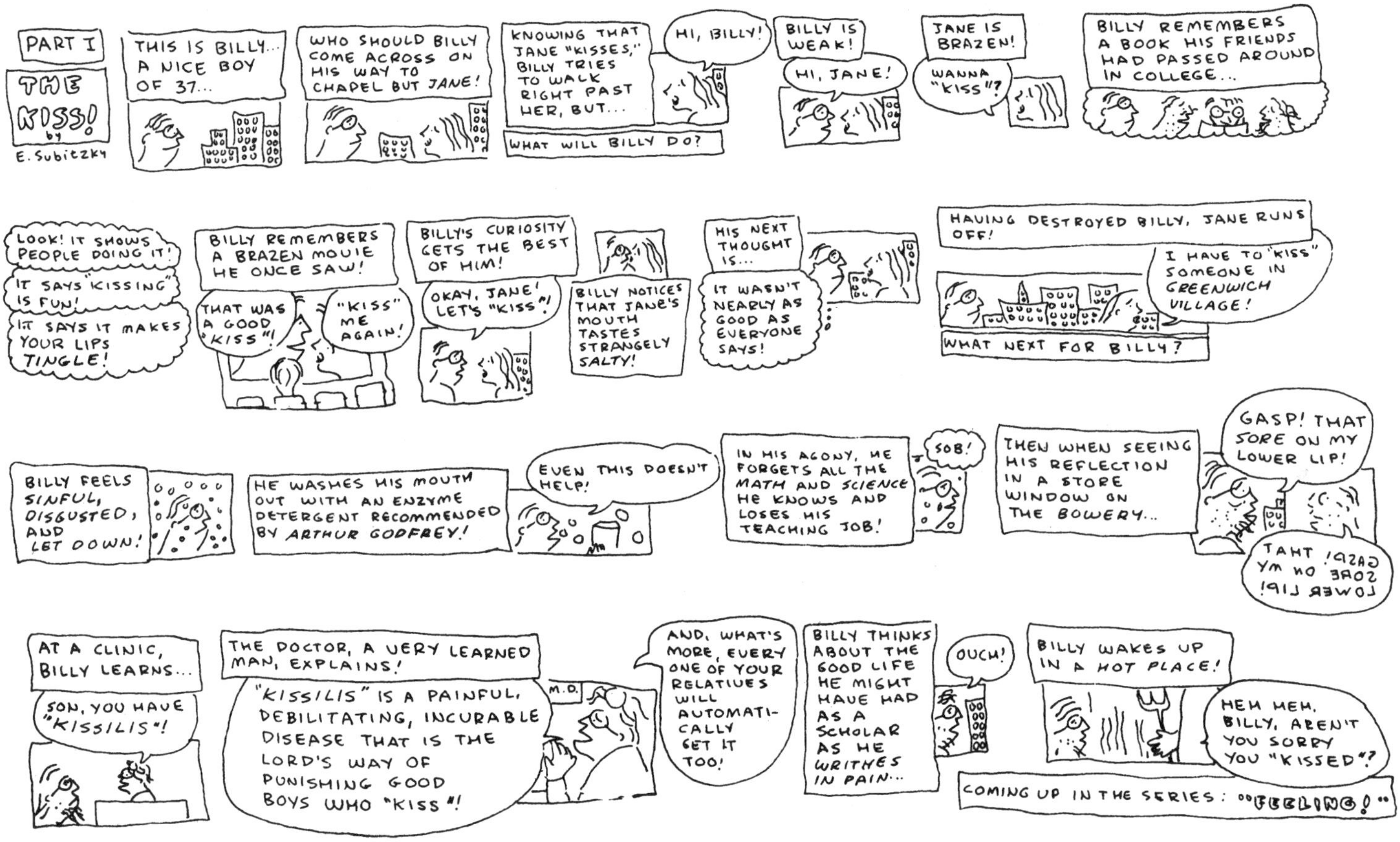

PART I
THE KISS! by E. Subitzky
THIS IS BILLY... A NICE BOY OF 37...
WHO SHOULD BILLY COME ACROSS ON HIS WAY TO CHAPEL BUT JANE!
KNOWING THAT JANE "KISSES," BILLY TRIES TO WALK RIGHT PAST HER, BUT...
HI, BILLY!
WHAT WILL BILLY DO?
BILLY IS WEAK!
HI, JANE!
JANE IS BRAZEN!
WANNA "KISS"?
BILLY REMEMBERS A BOOK HIS FRIENDS HAD PASSED AROUND IN COLLEGE...
LOOK! IT SHOWS PEOPLE DOING IT!
IT SAYS "KISSING" IS FUN!
IT SAYS IT MAKES YOUR LIPS TINGLE!
BILLY REMEMBERS A BRAZEN MOVIE HE ONCE SAW!
THAT WAS A GOOD "KISS"!
"KISS" ME AGAIN!
BILLY'S CURIOSITY GETS THE BEST OF HIM!
OKAY, JANE! LET'S "KISS"!
BILLY NOTICES THAT JANE'S MOUTH TASTES STRANGELY SALTY!
HIS NEXT THOUGHT IS...
IT WASN'T NEARLY AS GOOD AS EVERYONE SAYS!
HAVING DESTROYED BILLY, JANE RUNS OFF!
I HAVE TO "KISS" SOMEONE IN GREENWICH VILLAGE!
WHAT NEXT FOR BILLY?
BILLY FEELS SINFUL, DISGUSTED, AND LET DOWN!
HE WASHES HIS MOUTH OUT WITH AN ENZYME DETERGENT RECOMMENDED BY ARTHUR GODFREY!
EVEN THIS DOESN'T HELP!
IN HIS AGONY, HE FORGETS ALL THE MATH AND SCIENCE HE KNOWS AND LOSES HIS TEACHING JOB!
SOB!
THEN WHEN SEEING HIS REFLECTION IN A STORE WINDOW ON THE BOWERY...
GASP! THAT SORE ON MY LOWER LIP!
GASP! THAT SORE ON MY LOWER LIP!
AT A CLINIC, BILLY LEARNS...
SON, YOU HAVE "KISSILIS"!
THE DOCTOR, A VERY LEARNED MAN, EXPLAINS!
M.D.
"KISSILIS" IS A PAINFUL, DEBILITATING, INCURABLE DISEASE THAT IS THE LORD'S WAY OF PUNISHING GOOD BOYS WHO "KISS"!
AND, WHAT'S MORE, EVERY ONE OF YOUR RELATIVES WILL AUTOMATICALLY GET IT TOO!
BILLY THINKS ABOUT THE GOOD LIFE HE MIGHT HAVE HAD AS A SCHOLAR AS HE WRITHES IN PAIN...
OUCH!
BILLY WAKES UP IN A HOT PLACE!
HEH HEH. BILLY, AREN'T YOU SORRY YOU "KISSED"?
COMING UP IN THE SERIES: "FEELING!"

"Hey Dad, can I have the car tonight?"

BACKGROUND MUSIC COMICS!

BY ED SUBITZKY WITH MUSIC BY KEN LAUFER

A COMEDY-DRAMA-ADVENTURE-MYSTERY-ROMANCE!

INSTRUCTIONS: AS YOU READ EACH PANEL, PLAY THE INDICATED NOTES ON A PIANO OR OTHER INSTRUMENT FOR MAXIMUM MOOD AND DRAMATIC IMPACT!

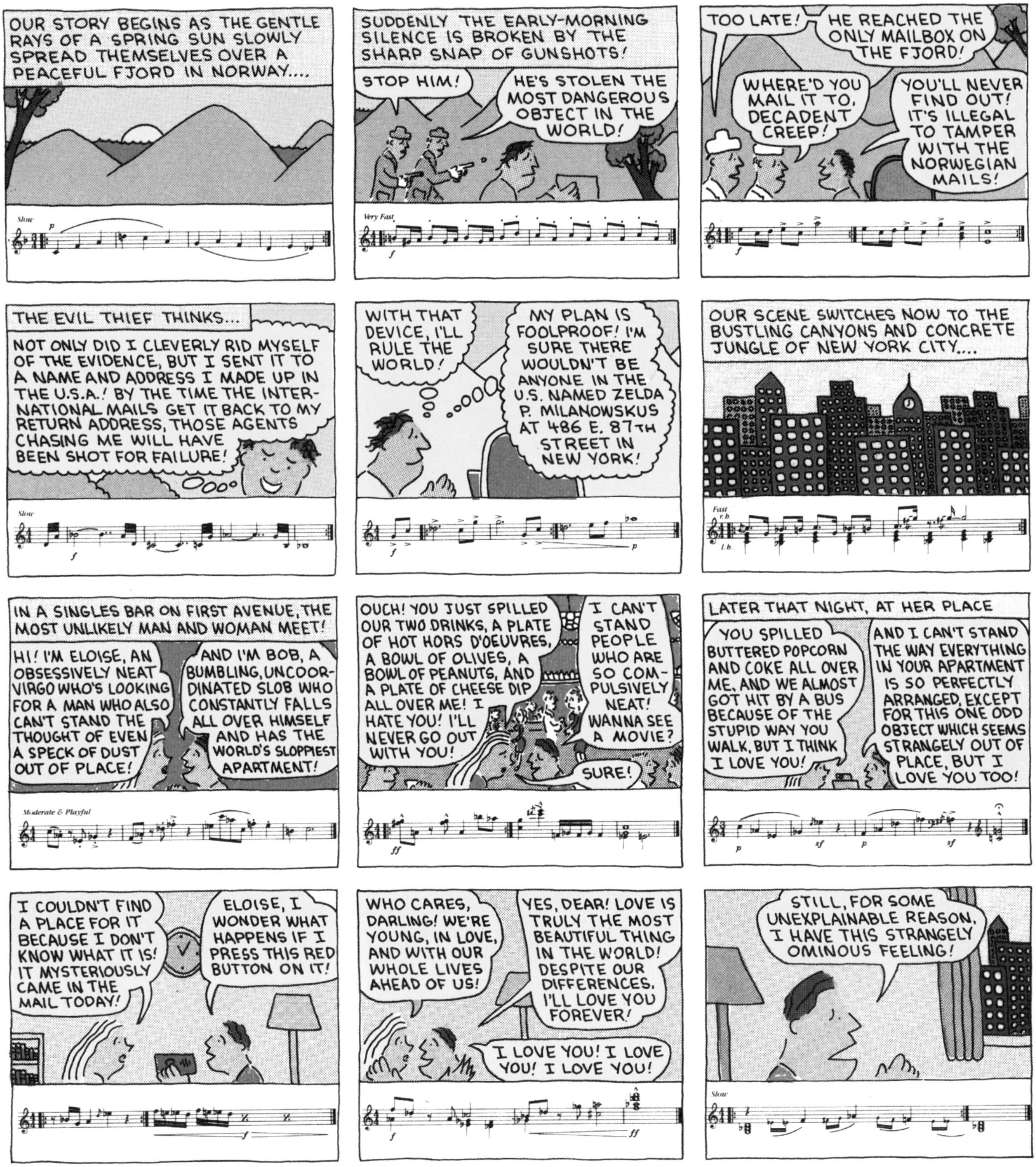
OUR STORY BEGINS AS THE GENTLE RAYS OF A SPRING SUN SLOWLY SPREAD THEMSELVES OVER A PEACEFUL FJORD IN NORWAY....
Slow
SUDDENLY THE EARLY-MORNING SILENCE IS BROKEN BY THE SHARP SNAP OF GUNSHOTS!
STOP HIM!
HE'S STOLEN THE MOST DANGEROUS OBJECT IN THE WORLD!
Very Fast
TOO LATE!
HE REACHED THE ONLY MAILBOX ON THE FJORD!
WHERE'D YOU MAIL IT TO, DECADENT CREEP!
YOU'LL NEVER FIND OUT! IT'S ILLEGAL TO TAMPER WITH THE NORWEGIAN MAILS!
THE EVIL THIEF THINKS...
NOT ONLY DID I CLEVERLY RID MYSELF OF THE EVIDENCE, BUT I SENT IT TO A NAME AND ADDRESS I MADE UP IN THE U.S.A.! BY THE TIME THE INTERNATIONAL MAILS GET IT BACK TO MY RETURN ADDRESS, THOSE AGENTS CHASING ME WILL HAVE BEEN SHOT FOR FAILURE!
Slow
WITH THAT DEVICE, I'LL RULE THE WORLD!
MY PLAN IS FOOLPROOF! I'M SURE THERE WOULDN'T BE ANYONE IN THE U.S. NAMED ZELDA P. MILANOWSKUS AT 486 E. 87TH STREET IN NEW YORK!
OUR SCENE SWITCHES NOW TO THE BUSTLING CANYONS AND CONCRETE JUNGLE OF NEW YORK CITY....
Fast
IN A SINGLES BAR ON FIRST AVENUE, THE MOST UNLIKELY MAN AND WOMAN MEET!
HI! I'M ELOISE, AN OBSESSIVELY NEAT VIRGO WHO'S LOOKING FOR A MAN WHO ALSO CAN'T STAND THE THOUGHT OF EVEN A SPECK OF DUST OUT OF PLACE!
AND I'M BOB, A BUMBLING, UNCOORDINATED SLOB WHO CONSTANTLY FALLS ALL OVER HIMSELF AND HAS THE WORLD'S SLOPPIEST APARTMENT!
Moderate & Playful
OUCH! YOU JUST SPILLED OUR TWO DRINKS, A PLATE OF HOT HORS D'OEUVRES, A BOWL OF OLIVES, A BOWL OF PEANUTS, AND A PLATE OF CHEESE DIP ALL OVER ME! I HATE YOU! I'LL NEVER GO OUT WITH YOU!
I CAN'T STAND PEOPLE WHO ARE SO COMPULSIVELY NEAT! WANNA SEE A MOVIE?
SURE!
LATER THAT NIGHT, AT HER PLACE
YOU SPILLED BUTTERED POPCORN AND COKE ALL OVER ME, AND WE ALMOST GOT HIT BY A BUS BECAUSE OF THE STUPID WAY YOU WALK, BUT I THINK I LOVE YOU!
AND I CAN'T STAND THE WAY EVERYTHING IN YOUR APARTMENT IS SO PERFECTLY ARRANGED, EXCEPT FOR THIS ONE ODD OBJECT WHICH SEEMS STRANGELY OUT OF PLACE, BUT I LOVE YOU TOO!
I COULDN'T FIND A PLACE FOR IT BECAUSE I DON'T KNOW WHAT IT IS! IT MYSTERIOUSLY CAME IN THE MAIL TODAY!
ELOISE, I WONDER WHAT HAPPENS IF I PRESS THIS RED BUTTON ON IT!
WHO CARES, DARLING! WE'RE YOUNG, IN LOVE, AND WITH OUR WHOLE LIVES AHEAD OF US!
YES, DEAR! LOVE IS TRULY THE MOST BEAUTIFUL THING IN THE WORLD! DESPITE OUR DIFFERENCES, I'LL LOVE YOU FOREVER!
I LOVE YOU! I LOVE YOU! I LOVE YOU!
STILL, FOR SOME UNEXPLAINABLE REASON, I HAVE THIS STRANGELY OMINOUS FEELING!
Slow

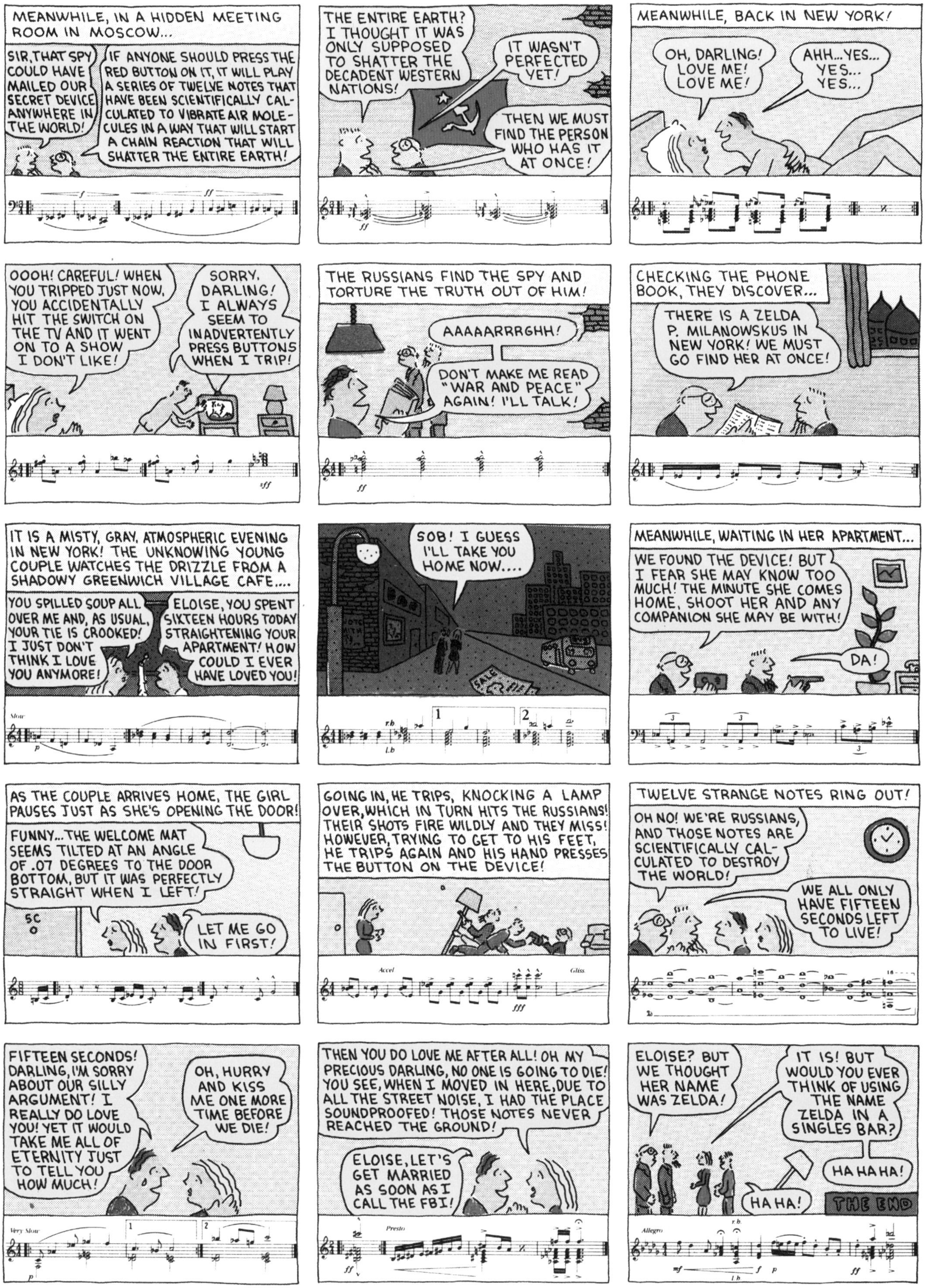
MEANWHILE, IN A HIDDEN MEETING ROOM IN MOSCOW...
SIR, THAT SPY COULD HAVE MAILED OUR SECRET DEVICE ANYWHERE IN THE WORLD!
IF ANYONE SHOULD PRESS THE RED BUTTON ON IT, IT WILL PLAY A SERIES OF TWELVE NOTES THAT HAVE BEEN SCIENTIFICALLY CALCULATED TO VIBRATE AIR MOLECULES IN A WAY THAT WILL START A CHAIN REACTION THAT WILL SHATTER THE ENTIRE EARTH!
THE ENTIRE EARTH? I THOUGHT IT WAS ONLY SUPPOSED TO SHATTER THE DECADENT WESTERN NATIONS!
IT WASN'T PERFECTED YET!
THEN WE MUST FIND THE PERSON WHO HAS IT AT ONCE!
MEANWHILE, BACK IN NEW YORK!
OH, DARLING! LOVE ME! LOVE ME!
AHH...YES... YES... YES...
OOOH! CAREFUL! WHEN YOU TRIPPED JUST NOW, YOU ACCIDENTALLY HIT THE SWITCH ON THE TV AND IT WENT ON TO A SHOW I DON'T LIKE!
SORRY, DARLING! I ALWAYS SEEM TO INADVERTENTLY PRESS BUTTONS WHEN I TRIP!
THE RUSSIANS FIND THE SPY AND TORTURE THE TRUTH OUT OF HIM!
AAAAARRRGHH!
DON'T MAKE ME READ "WAR AND PEACE" AGAIN! I'LL TALK!
CHECKING THE PHONE BOOK, THEY DISCOVER...
THERE IS A ZELDA P. MILANOWSKUS IN NEW YORK! WE MUST GO FIND HER AT ONCE!
IT IS A MISTY, GRAY, ATMOSPHERIC EVENING IN NEW YORK! THE UNKNOWING YOUNG COUPLE WATCHES THE DRIZZLE FROM A SHADOWY GREENWICH VILLAGE CAFE....
YOU SPILLED SOUP ALL OVER ME AND, AS USUAL, YOUR TIE IS CROOKED! I JUST DON'T THINK I LOVE YOU ANYMORE!
ELOISE, YOU SPENT SIXTEEN HOURS TODAY STRAIGHTENING YOUR APARTMENT! HOW COULD I EVER HAVE LOVED YOU!
Slow
SOB! I GUESS I'LL TAKE YOU HOME NOW....
MEANWHILE, WAITING IN HER APARTMENT...
WE FOUND THE DEVICE! BUT I FEAR SHE MAY KNOW TOO MUCH! THE MINUTE SHE COMES HOME, SHOOT HER AND ANY COMPANION SHE MAY BE WITH!
DA!
AS THE COUPLE ARRIVES HOME, THE GIRL PAUSES JUST AS SHE'S OPENING THE DOOR!
FUNNY... THE WELCOME MAT SEEMS TILTED AT AN ANGLE OF .07 DEGREES TO THE DOOR BOTTOM, BUT IT WAS PERFECTLY STRAIGHT WHEN I LEFT!
5C
LET ME GO IN FIRST!
GOING IN, HE TRIPS, KNOCKING A LAMP OVER, WHICH IN TURN HITS THE RUSSIANS! THEIR SHOTS FIRE WILDLY AND THEY MISS! HOWEVER, TRYING TO GET TO HIS FEET, HE TRIPS AGAIN AND HIS HAND PRESSES THE BUTTON ON THE DEVICE!
Accel
Gliss
TWELVE STRANGE NOTES RING OUT!
OH NO! WE'RE RUSSIANS, AND THOSE NOTES ARE SCIENTIFICALLY CALCULATED TO DESTROY THE WORLD!
WE ALL ONLY HAVE FIFTEEN SECONDS LEFT TO LIVE!
FIFTEEN SECONDS! DARLING, I'M SORRY ABOUT OUR SILLY ARGUMENT! I REALLY DO LOVE YOU! YET IT WOULD TAKE ME ALL OF ETERNITY JUST TO TELL YOU HOW MUCH!
OH, HURRY AND KISS ME ONE MORE TIME BEFORE WE DIE!
Very Slow
THEN YOU DO LOVE ME AFTER ALL! OH MY PRECIOUS DARLING, NO ONE IS GOING TO DIE! YOU SEE, WHEN I MOVED IN HERE, DUE TO ALL THE STREET NOISE, I HAD THE PLACE SOUNDPROOFED! THOSE NOTES NEVER REACHED THE GROUND!
ELOISE, LET'S GET MARRIED AS SOON AS I CALL THE FBI!
Presto
ELOISE? BUT WE THOUGHT HER NAME WAS ZELDA!
IT IS! BUT WOULD YOU EVER THINK OF USING THE NAME ZELDA IN A SINGLES BAR?
HA HA HA!
HA HA!
THE END
Allegro

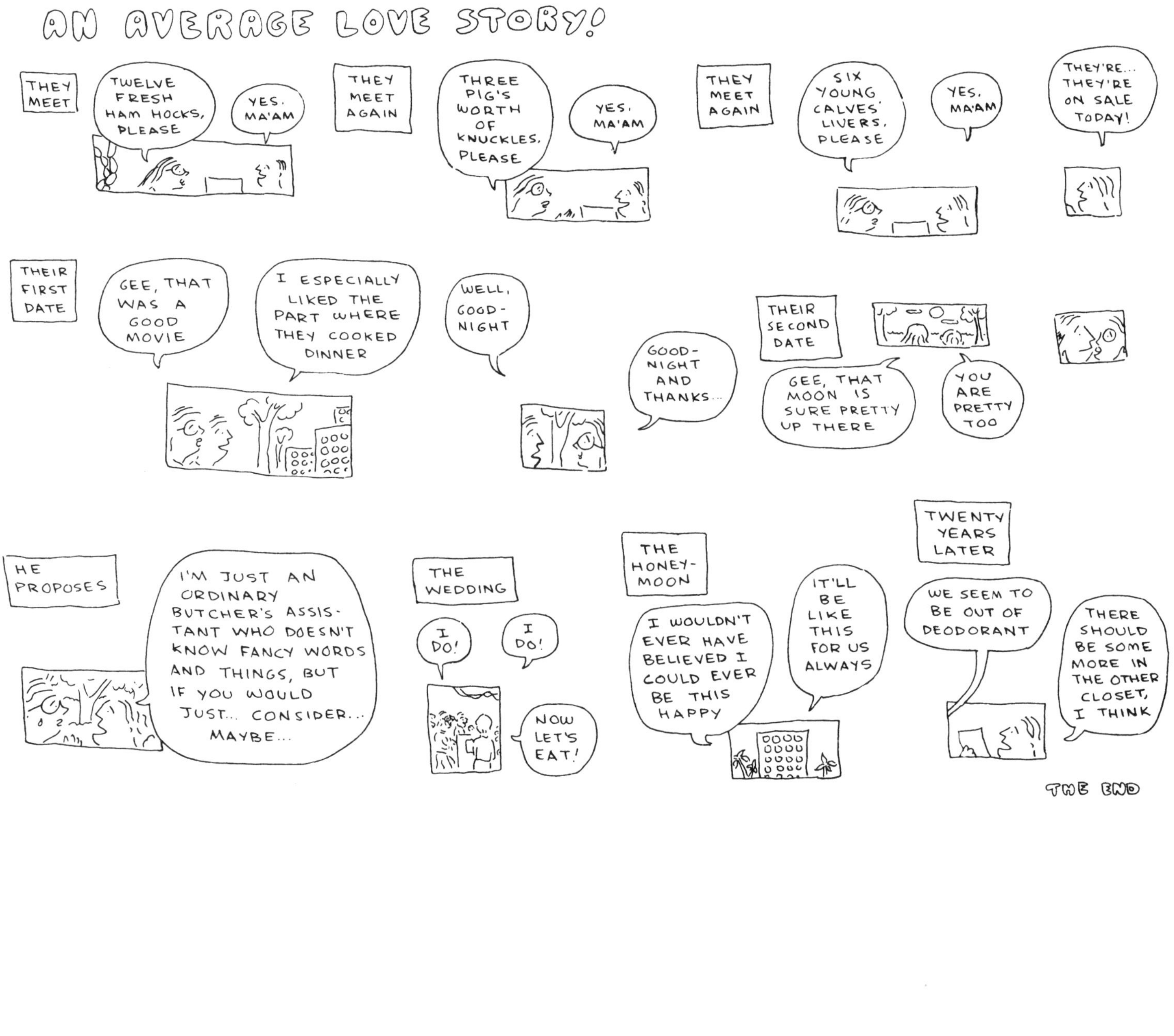
AN AVERAGE LOVE STORY!
THEY MEET
TWELVE FRESH HAM HOCKS, PLEASE
YES, MA'AM
THEY MEET AGAIN
THREE PIG'S WORTH OF KNUCKLES, PLEASE
YES, MA'AM
THEY MEET AGAIN
SIX YOUNG CALVES' LIVERS, PLEASE
YES, MA'AM
THEY'RE... THEY'RE ON SALE TODAY!
THEIR FIRST DATE
GEE, THAT WAS A GOOD MOVIE
I ESPECIALLY LIKED THE PART WHERE THEY COOKED DINNER
WELL, GOOD-NIGHT
GOOD-NIGHT AND THANKS...
THEIR SECOND DATE
GEE, THAT MOON IS SURE PRETTY UP THERE
YOU ARE PRETTY TOO
HE PROPOSES
I'M JUST AN ORDINARY BUTCHER'S ASSISTANT WHO DOESN'T KNOW FANCY WORDS AND THINGS, BUT IF YOU WOULD JUST... CONSIDER... MAYBE...
THE WEDDING
I DO!
I DO!
NOW LET'S EAT!
THE HONEY-MOON
I WOULDN'T EVER HAVE BELIEVED I COULD EVER BE THIS HAPPY
IT'LL BE LIKE THIS FOR US ALWAYS
TWENTY YEARS LATER
WE SEEM TO BE OUT OF DEODORANT
THERE SHOULD BE SOME MORE IN THE OTHER CLOSET, I THINK
THE END

HOT SEX PORNO COMICS!
HI! ACTUALLY, THIS ISN'T HOT SEX PORNO COMICS! THAT WAS JUST A TRICK TO GET YOU TO READ THIS!
THIS IS REALLY HYPNO COMICS! LOOK CLOSELY AT THIS CIRCLE!
YOU CANNOT STOP... YOUR CURIOSITY DRIVES YOU ON... YOU ARE GETTING SLEEPY... SLEEPY...
YOU ARE NOW IN MY POWER COM-PLETELY! YOU WILL OBEY ALL MY INSTRUCTIONS! YOU WILL SEND ALL OF YOUR MONEY TO THIS MAGAZINE!
WHEN YOU SEE THE WORDS "THE END," YOU WILL WAKE UP AND REMEMBER NOTHING THAT HAS HAPPENED TO YOU!
THE END

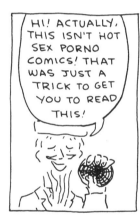

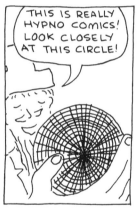

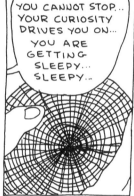

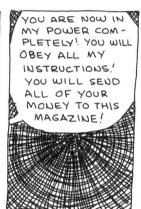

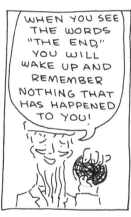

MÖBIUS STRIP COMICS!

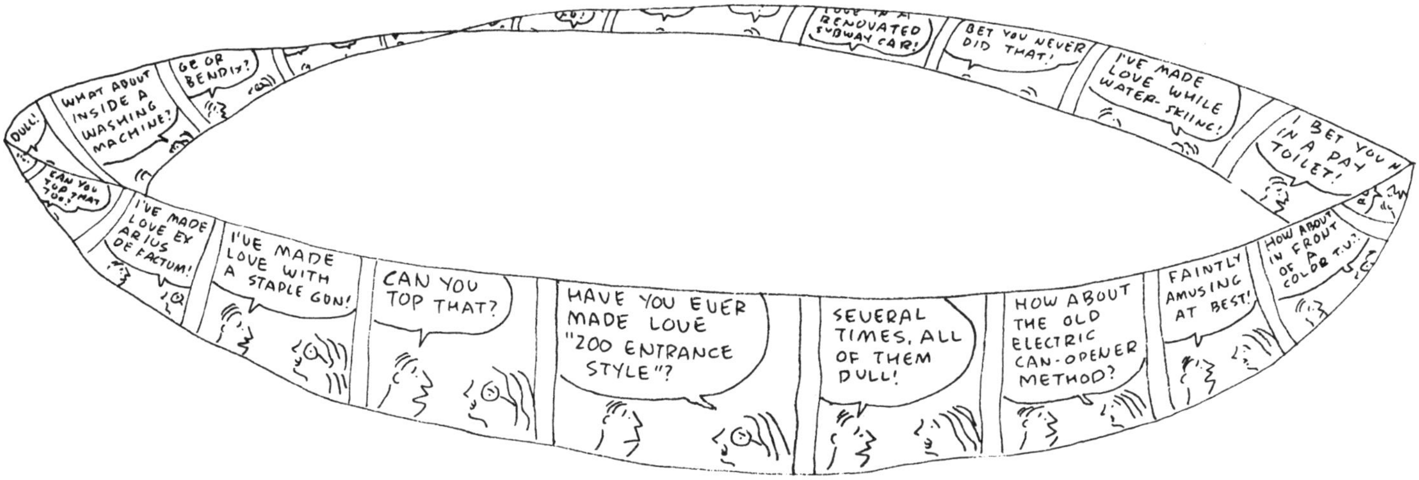

I'VE MADE LOVE WITH A STAPLE GUN!
CAN YOU TOP THAT?
HAVE YOU EVER MADE LOVE "ZOO ENTRANCE STYLE"?
SEVERAL TIMES, ALL OF THEM DULL!
HOW ABOUT THE OLD ELECTRIC CAN-OPENER METHOD?
FAINTLY AMUSING AT BEST!
HOW ABOUT IN FRONT OF A COLOR T.V.?
I BET YOU N
IN A PAY TOILET!
I'VE MADE LOVE WHILE WATER-SKIING!
BET YOU NEVER DID THAT!
RENOVATED SUBWAY CAR!
GE OR BENDIX?
WHAT ABOUT INSIDE A WASHING MACHINE?
DULL!
CAN YOU TOP THAT TOO?
I'VE MADE LOVE EX ARIUS DE FACTUM!

POTBOILER COMICS!
A COMPLETE CHEAP NOVEL IN HALF A PAGE!
PART I
CHAPTER I
ON SKID ROW, A SEEDY-LOOKING BUM IS THROWING UP, WHEN...
OH NO! THAT PRETTY YOUNG WOMAN IS ABOUT TO BE HIT BY A RUNAWAY GARBAGE TRUCK!
BUM OR NOT, I'VE GOT TO SAVE HER!
CH. 2
AS A REWARD, SHE TAKES HIM TO DINNER!
MY NAME IS JEANETTE!
MINE IS ELLIOT! AND GEE! WITH YOU, I HAVEN'T THROWN UP FOR A WHOLE HALF HOUR!
CH. 3
THEY SHARE LIFE'S STORIES!
ME, I'M JUST AN OLD-FASHIONED, SIMPLE, KINDHEARTED GIRL LOOKING FOR THE RIGHT MAN!
ME, I'M A SCIENTIFICALLY INCLINED ZITHER PLAYER! WHEN I INVENTED A NEW KIND OF "LASER-ZITHER," THEY LAUGHED ME OUT OF THE ZITHER SOCIETY AND I BECAME A BITTER HOBO!
WHY... MY GRANDFATHER, OLD MAN "NOTES," HEADS AN INTER-NATIONAL SYMPHONY ORCHESTRA! MAYBE HE CAN DO SOMETHING FOR YOU!
CH. 4
SO ELLIOT BIDS GOOD-BYE TO HIS BEST FRIEND, AN ALCOHOLIC EX-NEUROSURGEON NAMED JONES!
I KILLED MY DOG ONCE, AND GAVE UP MY PRACTICE FOREVER!
CH. 5
ELLIOT BECOMES A SMASH HIT AND HE AND JEANETTE ARE MARRIED!
JUST THINK, ELLIOT! LITTLE ME, MARRIED TO THE WORLD'S MOST FAMOUS SYMPHONY PLAYER! BUT PROMISE ME YOU'LL ALWAYS REMAIN UNSPOILED AND FAITHFUL, LIKE I AM!
OF COURSE, MY DARLING! NOW EXCUSE ME! I SEE A GIRL SCOUT WHO'S SELLING COOKIES TO AID THE POOR!
PART II
CH. 6
NICE DAY, GRANDPA "NOTES"!
INDEED! YOU KNOW, SON, HAVE YOU EVER THOUGHT ABOUT ENTERING POLITICS?
POLITICS?
YES! THE SYMPHONY ORCHESTRA COULD USE A GOOD CONTACT IN THE U.S. GOVERNMENT, AND THE PUBLIC KNOWS AND LOVES YOU!
CH. 7
DARLING, I KNOW THE ELECTION IS TOMORROW, BUT DO YOU THINK IT'S RIGHT TO SMEAR YOUR OPPONENT BY CIRCULATING THESE FALSE DOCUMENTS ALIGNING HIM WITH A SECRET GROUP OF CHILD-MOLESTING HOMOSEXUALS FROM RED CHINA!
HONEY, DON'T YOU UNDERSTAND! THIS IS POLITICS!
FOR PRESIDENT
OH, ELLIOT, YOU NEVER SPOKE THIS WAY BEFORE! SOMETIMES I WISH I HAD NEVER TAKEN YOU OFF SKID ROW!
CH. 8
ELLIOT WINS THE ELECTION! ONE DAY, IN THE WHITE HOUSE...
WHY, THAT NEW FEMALE PAGE LOOKS FAMILIAR! AND SHE'S HEADING TOWARDS ELLIOT'S BEDROOM!
JEANETTE FOLLOWS HER...
AH!
MORE! YES!
OH NO! IT'S THE GIRL SCOUT HE ONCE BOUGHT THE COOKIES FROM! SHE'S OBVIOUSLY AN UNSCRUPULOUS LITTLE SOCIAL CLIMBER WHO READ THAT HE BECAME PRESIDENT!
CH. 9
IN SHOCK AND DESPERATION, JEANETTE WANDERS AIMLESSLY AROUND...
FUNNY I SHOULD LAND ON SKID ROW!
EXCUSE ME, MISS, GOT A QUARTER FOR A CUP OF COFFEE?
WHY, JONES, THE EX-NEURO-SURGEON!
HMMM... LET ME SEE THAT FUNNY GREEN BLOTCH ON YOUR FOREHEAD!
PART III
CH. 10
IT'S TRUE, GRANDPA "NOTES"! IN CONJUNCTION WITH TOP-SECRET PENTAGON DATA, I REALIZED THAT MY ZITHER EQUATION CAN BE TRANSMUTED INTO A "VIBRATION" BOMB THAT CAN WIPE OUT A CONTINENT IN SECONDS!
CALL AN INSTANT MEETING OF THE U.N.! TELL THEM I WANT TO BE DICTATOR OF THE WORLD!
NO! I SHOULD NEVER HAVE BROUGHT YOU INTO POLITICS! I MUST STOP YOU!
OW! YOU'VE BROKEN MY CONDUCTING ARM!
YOU'LL NEVER APPEAR IN FRONT OF AN ORCHESTRA AGAIN, YOU OLD FOOL!
CH. 11
ELLIOT IS NOW DICTATOR OF THE WORLD!
BUT, YOUR GLORY, YOU ALREADY HAVE 10,000 GIRL SCOUTS LIVING HERE!
I WANT 20,000! 30,000! 60,000!
BUT YOU'RE MARRIED! TO MY GRAND-DAUGHTER!
WHY, THAT'S RIGHT! BUT I HAVEN'T SEEN HER IN MONTHS! HIRE DETECTIVES TO TRACK HER DOWN!
CH. 12
JEANETTE – AND HER COMPANION – ARE BROUGHT TO HIM...
MY ONE-TIME BEST FRIEND!
(SOB!) I CONFESS! JONES AND I ARE HAVING AN AFFAIR! BUT IT DOESN'T MATTER! I HAVE AN INCURABLE NEUROLOGICAL DISEASE!
ONCE, I WOULD HAVE BEEN THE ONLY DOCTOR TO BE ABLE TO SAVE HER! BEFORE I TOOK TO DRINK!
SUDDENLY ELLIOT CRIES...
YOU MUST SAVE HER! YOU MUST!
IF YOU RENOUNCE YOUR DICTATOR-SHIP OF THE WORLD AND RETURN IT TO NORMAL INTERNATIONAL ORDER, I MIGHT BE LESS UPSET BY CIRCUMSTANCES AND GIVE UP DRINKING!
CH. 13
WEEKS LATER, ON SKID ROW...
DARLING, NOW THAT I'M NOT DICTATOR OF THE WORLD, ALL OF THE GIRL SCOUTS HAVE LEFT ME, AND ANYWAY I'M PURE AND DECENT AGAIN! MARRY JONES IF YOU MUST, BUT KNOW I'LL ALWAYS LOVE YOU!
OH, MY DARLING! JONES KILLED HIMSELF THIS MORNING! HE SAID HE HAD TO JOIN HIS DOG!
THE END

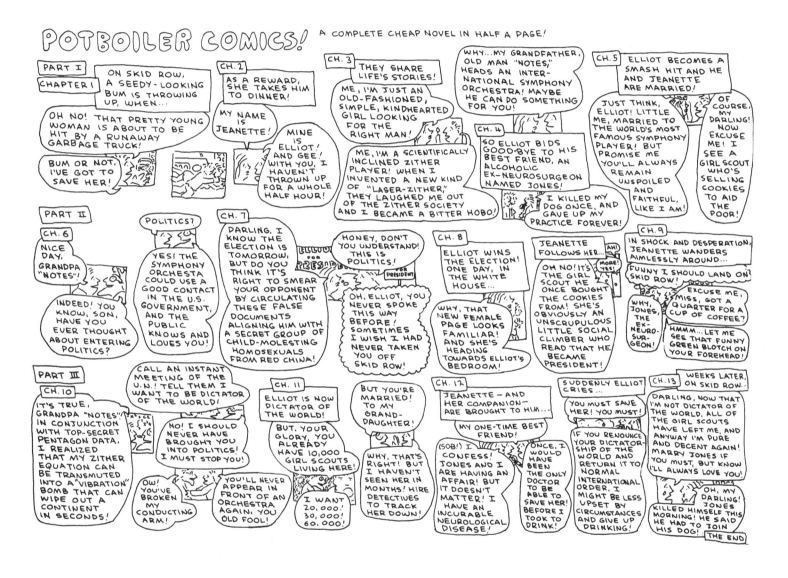

SOCIALLY REDEEMING SEX COMICS!

BY ED SUBITZKY

THE TAWDRIEST, MOST EXPLICIT, MOST VIOLENT, MOST DISGUSTING SEX COMIC EVER WRITTEN — BUT PERFECTLY LEGAL BECAUSE EVERY OTHER PANEL DISCUSSES IMPORTANT SOCIAL, PHILOSOPHICAL AND SCIENTIFIC ISSUES!

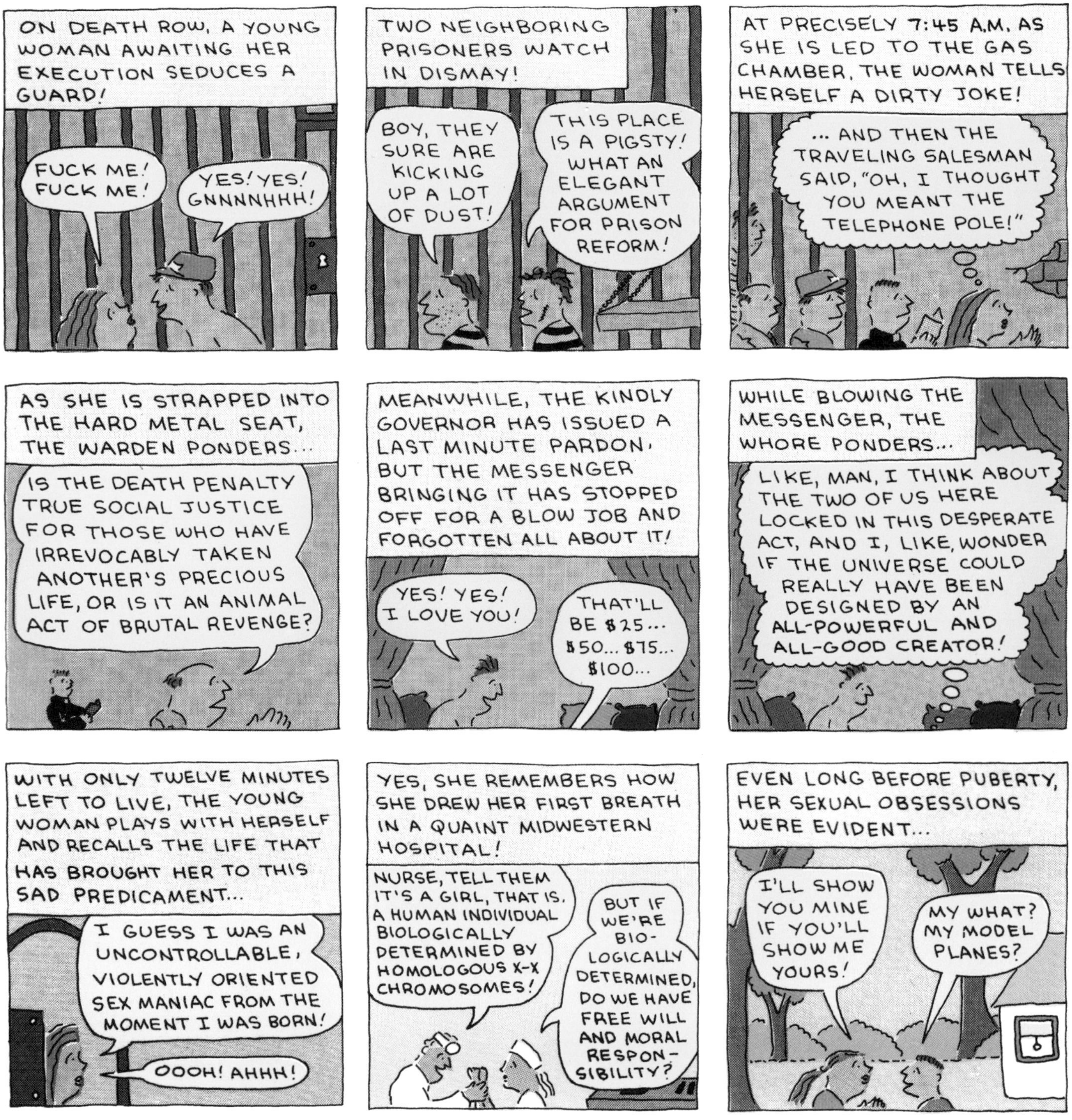
ON DEATH ROW, A YOUNG WOMAN AWAITING HER EXECUTION SEDUCES A GUARD!
FUCK ME! FUCK ME!
YES! YES! GNNNNHHH!
TWO NEIGHBORING PRISONERS WATCH IN DISMAY!
BOY, THEY SURE ARE KICKING UP A LOT OF DUST!
THIS PLACE IS A PIGSTY! WHAT AN ELEGANT ARGUMENT FOR PRISON REFORM!
AT PRECISELY 7:45 A.M. AS SHE IS LED TO THE GAS CHAMBER, THE WOMAN TELLS HERSELF A DIRTY JOKE!
... AND THEN THE TRAVELING SALESMAN SAID, "OH, I THOUGHT YOU MEANT THE TELEPHONE POLE!"
AS SHE IS STRAPPED INTO THE HARD METAL SEAT, THE WARDEN PONDERS...
IS THE DEATH PENALTY TRUE SOCIAL JUSTICE FOR THOSE WHO HAVE IRREVOCABLY TAKEN ANOTHER'S PRECIOUS LIFE, OR IS IT AN ANIMAL ACT OF BRUTAL REVENGE?
MEANWHILE, THE KINDLY GOVERNOR HAS ISSUED A LAST MINUTE PARDON, BUT THE MESSENGER BRINGING IT HAS STOPPED OFF FOR A BLOW JOB AND FORGOTTEN ALL ABOUT IT!
YES! YES! I LOVE YOU!
THAT'LL BE $25... $50... $75... $100...
WHILE BLOWING THE MESSENGER, THE WHORE PONDERS...
LIKE, MAN, I THINK ABOUT THE TWO OF US HERE LOCKED IN THIS DESPERATE ACT, AND I, LIKE, WONDER IF THE UNIVERSE COULD REALLY HAVE BEEN DESIGNED BY AN ALL-POWERFUL AND ALL-GOOD CREATOR!
WITH ONLY TWELVE MINUTES LEFT TO LIVE, THE YOUNG WOMAN PLAYS WITH HERSELF AND RECALLS THE LIFE THAT HAS BROUGHT HER TO THIS SAD PREDICAMENT...
I GUESS I WAS AN UNCONTROLLABLE, VIOLENTLY ORIENTED SEX MANIAC FROM THE MOMENT I WAS BORN!
OOOH! AHHH!
YES, SHE REMEMBERS HOW SHE DREW HER FIRST BREATH IN A QUAINT MIDWESTERN HOSPITAL!
NURSE, TELL THEM IT'S A GIRL, THAT IS, A HUMAN INDIVIDUAL BIOLOGICALLY DETERMINED BY HOMOLOGOUS X-X CHROMOSOMES!
BUT IF WE'RE BIO-LOGICALLY DETERMINED, DO WE HAVE FREE WILL AND MORAL RESPON-SIBILITY?
EVEN LONG BEFORE PUBERTY, HER SEXUAL OBSESSIONS WERE EVIDENT...
I'LL SHOW YOU MINE IF YOU'LL SHOW ME YOURS!
MY WHAT? MY MODEL PLANES?

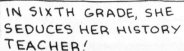

IN SIXTH GRADE, SHE SEDUCES HER HISTORY TEACHER!

WE SHOULDN'T BE DOING THIS! DON'T YOU KNOW THAT MORAL DECAY WAS A SIGNIFICANT CONTRIBUTING FACTOR TO THE DECLINE AND FALL OF ROMAN CIVILIZATION?

AFTERWARDS, IN TOTAL DISGRACE, THE MAN SLITS HIS WRISTS AND BLEEDS A LOT!

YECCCH! I THINK I'M GOING TO BE SICK! LUCKILY, I'LL BE DEAD IN A SECOND!

AT THE FUNERAL, THE SCHOOL SCIENCE TEACHER WONDERS...

COULD THERE BE A SOUL AND AN AFTERLIFE... OR ARE MENTAL PROCESSES JUST MANIFESTATIONS OF COMPLEXLY INTERACTING PHYSICAL MOLECULES WHICH CANNOT MAINTAIN STRUCTURED RELATIONSHIPS AFTER DEATH?

IN RETRIBUTION, SHE GETS AN "F" IN DEPORTMENT! HER PARENTS GET ANGRY AND SHE BURNS THE HOUSE DOWN!

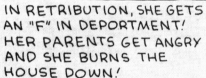

AT LEAST THEIR PET HAMSTER ESCAPED!

BUT THE FAMILY DIED IN UNSPEAKABLE AGONY!

THE FIREMEN OBSERVE...

BOY, WAS THIS A CASE OF ATOMS COMBINING VIOLENTLY WITH O_2 IN THE SURROUNDING AIR FOR COMPLETE COMBUSTION!

YES, AND THANK GOODNESS H_2O MOLECULES ARE POLAR!

AT NINETEEN, AFTER BEING CAUGHT SHOPLIFTING IN AN EROTIC BOOKSTORE, SHE IS THROWN OUT OF TOWN!

BUT I WAS GOING TO RETURN IT AS SOON AS I CAME!

A LIKELY STORY!

TO GET TO NEW YORK, SHE HOPS A FREIGHT TRAIN, WHICH IS A LOCOMOTIVE DEVICE ULTIMATELY DEPENDANT UPON NEWTON'S FIRST, SECOND AND THIRD LAWS OF MOTION, WITH RELATIVISTIC CORRECTIONS NOT NECESSARY!

ON THE WAY, JUST FOR FUN, SHE HAS SEX WITH A BULLDOG!

FOR A MOMENT, I ACTUALLY LOVED YOU! CIGARETTE?

ARF!

SHE ARRIVES PENNILESS IN NEW YORK CITY AND CAN'T EVEN FIND WORK AS A PROSTITUTE!

GEE, I WISH MORE UNITED STATES BUSINESSES WOULD ADOPT JAPANESE-STYLE MANAGEMENT TECHNIQUES AND SO GET OUR ECONOMY MOVING ONCE AGAIN!

AFTER ROBBING A BANK, KILLING THE GUARDS, AND SHOOTING SEVERAL INNOCENT, PREGNANT BYSTANDERS...

OOPS! SORRY!

OOOPS!

BY COINCIDENCE, SHE BUMPS INTO A YOUNG MAN WHO FALLS MADLY IN LOVE WITH HER AND THINKS...

ARE COINCIDENCES REALLY MEANINGLESS INSTANCES OF QUANTUM-MECHANICAL UNCERTAINTY, OR DO THEY REFLECT SOME DEEPER PURPOSE OF A BASICALLY DETERMINISTIC UNIVERSE?

ONE DAY SHE BEATS THE YOUNG MAN WITH A LEATHER BUGGY WHIP AND HE DISCOVERS HE LOVES IT!

SOB! HOW COULD A GOOD, CLEAN ASPIRING POLITICIAN LIKE ME STOOP TO THIS LEVEL!

MORE! MORE! MORE!

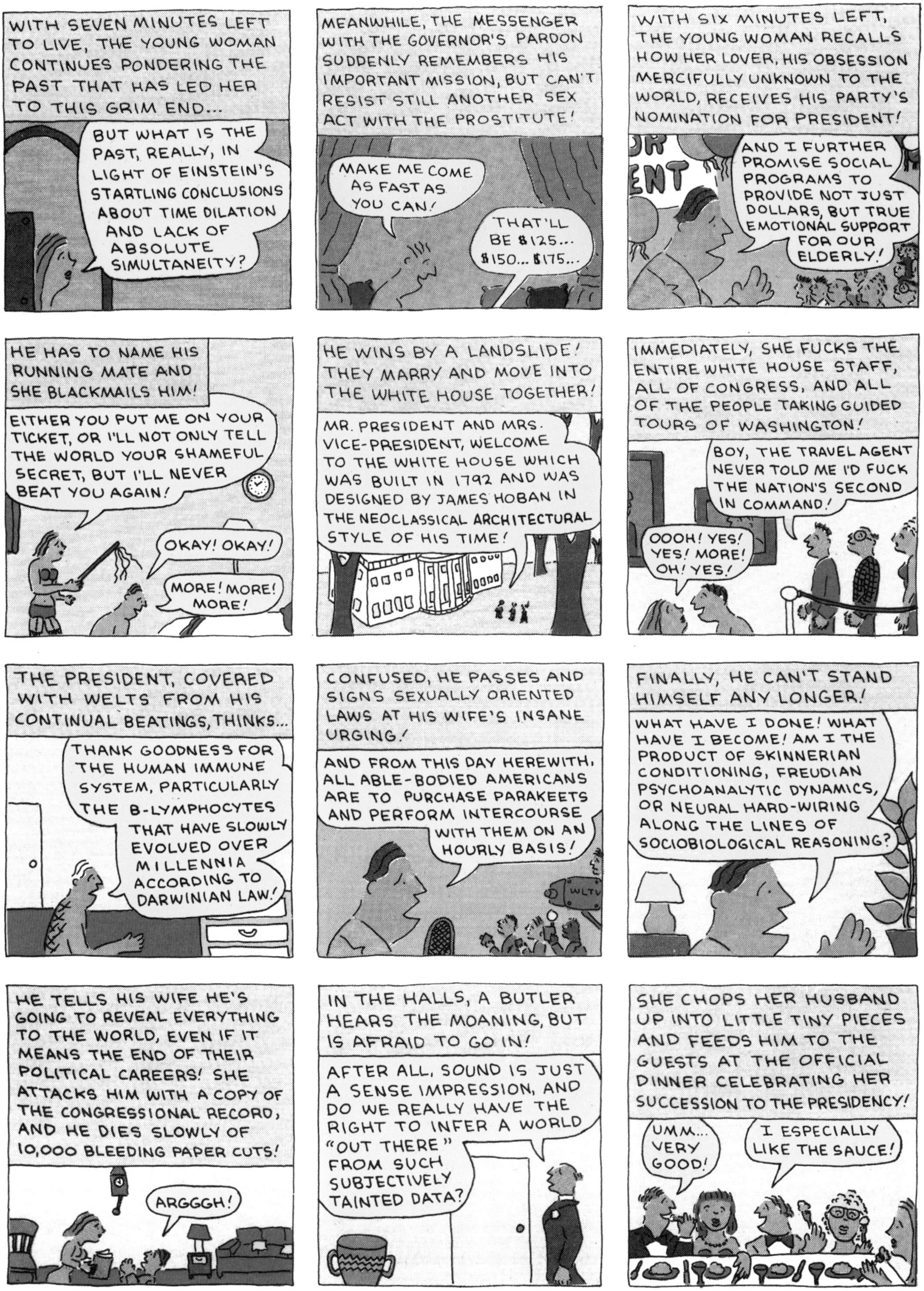
WITH SEVEN MINUTES LEFT TO LIVE, THE YOUNG WOMAN CONTINUES PONDERING THE PAST THAT HAS LED HER TO THIS GRIM END...
BUT WHAT IS THE PAST, REALLY, IN LIGHT OF EINSTEIN'S STARTLING CONCLUSIONS ABOUT TIME DILATION AND LACK OF ABSOLUTE SIMULTANEITY?
MEANWHILE, THE MESSENGER WITH THE GOVERNOR'S PARDON SUDDENLY REMEMBERS HIS IMPORTANT MISSION, BUT CAN'T RESIST STILL ANOTHER SEX ACT WITH THE PROSTITUTE!
MAKE ME COME AS FAST AS YOU CAN!
THAT'LL BE $125... $150... $175...
WITH SIX MINUTES LEFT, THE YOUNG WOMAN RECALLS HOW HER LOVER, HIS OBSESSION MERCIFULLY UNKNOWN TO THE WORLD, RECEIVES HIS PARTY'S NOMINATION FOR PRESIDENT!
AND I FURTHER PROMISE SOCIAL PROGRAMS TO PROVIDE NOT JUST DOLLARS, BUT TRUE EMOTIONAL SUPPORT FOR OUR ELDERLY!
HE HAS TO NAME HIS RUNNING MATE AND SHE BLACKMAILS HIM!
EITHER YOU PUT ME ON YOUR TICKET, OR I'LL NOT ONLY TELL THE WORLD YOUR SHAMEFUL SECRET, BUT I'LL NEVER BEAT YOU AGAIN!
OKAY! OKAY!
MORE! MORE! MORE!
HE WINS BY A LANDSLIDE! THEY MARRY AND MOVE INTO THE WHITE HOUSE TOGETHER!
MR. PRESIDENT AND MRS. VICE-PRESIDENT, WELCOME TO THE WHITE HOUSE WHICH WAS BUILT IN 1792 AND WAS DESIGNED BY JAMES HOBAN IN THE NEOCLASSICAL ARCHITECTURAL STYLE OF HIS TIME!
IMMEDIATELY, SHE FUCKS THE ENTIRE WHITE HOUSE STAFF, ALL OF CONGRESS, AND ALL OF THE PEOPLE TAKING GUIDED TOURS OF WASHINGTON!
BOY, THE TRAVEL AGENT NEVER TOLD ME I'D FUCK THE NATION'S SECOND IN COMMAND!
OOOH! YES! YES! MORE! OH! YES!
THE PRESIDENT, COVERED WITH WELTS FROM HIS CONTINUAL BEATINGS, THINKS...
THANK GOODNESS FOR THE HUMAN IMMUNE SYSTEM, PARTICULARLY THE B-LYMPHOCYTES THAT HAVE SLOWLY EVOLVED OVER MILLENNIA ACCORDING TO DARWINIAN LAW!
CONFUSED, HE PASSES AND SIGNS SEXUALLY ORIENTED LAWS AT HIS WIFE'S INSANE URGING!
AND FROM THIS DAY HEREWITH, ALL ABLE-BODIED AMERICANS ARE TO PURCHASE PARAKEETS AND PERFORM INTERCOURSE WITH THEM ON AN HOURLY BASIS!
WLTV
FINALLY, HE CAN'T STAND HIMSELF ANY LONGER!
WHAT HAVE I DONE! WHAT HAVE I BECOME! AM I THE PRODUCT OF SKINNERIAN CONDITIONING, FREUDIAN PSYCHOANALYTIC DYNAMICS, OR NEURAL HARD-WIRING ALONG THE LINES OF SOCIOBIOLOGICAL REASONING?
HE TELLS HIS WIFE HE'S GOING TO REVEAL EVERYTHING TO THE WORLD, EVEN IF IT MEANS THE END OF THEIR POLITICAL CAREERS! SHE ATTACKS HIM WITH A COPY OF THE CONGRESSIONAL RECORD, AND HE DIES SLOWLY OF 10,000 BLEEDING PAPER CUTS!
ARGGGH!
IN THE HALLS, A BUTLER HEARS THE MOANING, BUT IS AFRAID TO GO IN!
AFTER ALL, SOUND IS JUST A SENSE IMPRESSION, AND DO WE REALLY HAVE THE RIGHT TO INFER A WORLD "OUT THERE" FROM SUCH SUBJECTIVELY TAINTED DATA?
SHE CHOPS HER HUSBAND UP INTO LITTLE TINY PIECES AND FEEDS HIM TO THE GUESTS AT THE OFFICIAL DINNER CELEBRATING HER SUCCESSION TO THE PRESIDENCY!
UMM... VERY GOOD!
I ESPECIALLY LIKE THE SAUCE!

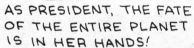

AS PRESIDENT, THE FATE OF THE ENTIRE PLANET IS IN HER HANDS!

THE EARTH IS FINALLY MINE... INCLUDING ALL SEVEN MAJOR TECTONIC PLATES WHICH DRIFT GRADUALLY OVER MILLENNIA AND CAUSE THE DEVELOPMENT OF MIDOCEAN RIDGES AND OTHER GEOLOGICAL FEATURES!

HER BLOOD LUST BOILING AT AN UNCONTROLLABLE PITCH, SHE FINDS THAT SHE CANNOT REACH ORGASM UNLESS SHE H-BOMBS A FOREIGN CITY!

AMERICA TODAY RAINED NUCLEAR WARHEADS ON COPENHAGEN FOR NO APPARENT REASON!

YES! OH YES! AGGGGGH!

IN BETWEEN, SHE GOES TO MOVIES, CHEWS POPCORN NOISILY, AND MAKES OBNOXIOUS, IF VALID, CRITICAL COMMENTS!

IN MY OPINION, THE CINEMA, LIKE ALL ART FORMS, MUST ACHIEVE ITS EFFECTIVENESS THROUGH A COHERENT STRUCTURE INTEGRATING PLOT, CHARACTER, AND EMOTION!

CONCERNED PEOPLE EVERYWHERE TRY TO STOP HER, BUT THE HANDS OF THE COURTS ARE TIED!

WE KNOW SHE'S RESPONSIBLE FOR MILLIONS OF DEATHS, BUT WE JUST CAN'T GET ANY DIRECT EVIDENCE!

AND SHE KEEPS BURNING ALL OUR BUILDINGS DOWN!

DECLARING HER FREE ONCE AGAIN, THE JUDGE WONDERS...

HAVE WE GONE SO FAR IN PROTECTING THE RIGHTS OF OUR CITIZENS THAT WE FAIL TO PROTECT THEIR RIGHT TO SAFETY AND SECURITY FROM VIOLENT CRIMINALS?

FINALLY, HER SEXUAL PERVERSIONS REACH A PEAK WHERE SHE CAN ONLY REACH ORGASM DURING A WORLDWIDE NUCLEAR WAR!

I'LL BOMB MOSCOW... THEY'LL RETALIATE... LIFE ON EARTH WILL BE WIPED OUT... BUT I'LL COME!

AS THE MISSILES HEAD TOWARDS MOSCOW, A TOP GOVERNMENT SCIENTIST THINKS...

STRANGE HOW THE WORLD WILL END IN A THERMONUCLEAR MAXIMIZATION OF ENTROPY, SO UNLIKE THE MINIMAL CONDITION OF ENTROPY EMERGING FROM THE ORIGINAL "QUARK SOUP" AFTER THE BIG BANG!

WHEN SUDDENLY, IN THE COURTS, A MAN RUSHES IN...

I'M A FIREMAN FROM THE TOWN WHERE SHE WAS BORN, AND LOOK! I'VE GOT EVIDENCE! THE HAMSTER FINALLY DIED OF SMOKE POISONING!

PRAISE BE! ARREST HER AND CALL OFF THE MISSILES AT ONCE!

MEANWHILE, IN A FOREST OUTSIDE OF WASHINGTON, A TREE FALLS WHEN NO ONE IS THERE, AND MAY OR MAY NOT MAKE A SOUND!

IN THE GAS CHAMBER, THE YOUNG WOMAN'S MIND COMES BACK TO THE PRESENT! JUST AS THE CYANIDE PELLETS ARE ABOUT TO FALL INTO THE ACID, SHE TEARS OFF HER CLOTHES!

AT LEAST I CAN DIE LIKE A CENTERFOLD!

SUDDENLY THE GOVERNOR'S MESSENGER RUSHES IN WITH THE PARDON!

EVEN THOUGH I'VE ARRIVED AT THE VERY LAST MOMENT, YOU MUST STILL STOP THE EXECUTION BY THE BASIC ORDER-RELATION INHERENT IN THE NUMERICAL CONTINUUM!

THE SHOCK OF A SECOND CHANCE MAKES HER REALIZE THE ERROR OF HER WAYS!

REMEMBER... TO ERR IS HUMAN, TO FORGIVE IS DIVINE EVEN THOUGH I'M STILL NAKED WITH MY TITS SHOWING!

THE END

MN: Were you intimidated at all by the *Lampoon* crowd?

ES: Oh, totally intimidated by every one of them. I mean, they were absolutely brilliant—pure humor geniuses. I couldn't believe that I was working with people like Henry Beard, Michael O'Donoghue, and Brian McConnachie.[12] I mean, what do they have to do with me? I was pretty amazed by it all.

MN: Did they give you a sense of what they wanted from you early on?

ES: No... no, what was amazing about the *Lampoon* was—when a person came around, if they liked you, they used you. And if they didn't like you, they had nothing to do with you. But in my case they actually took everything I gave them and ran with it, without any changes at all. That's unheard of in publishing, I know. I know!

I'd hand a piece in and then I'd see it in print. In fact, my earlier pieces, I would ink them in before anyone had even seen them. No submitting pencil sketches or anything. They would take what I gave them and use it. They were amazing people. No focus grouping, no talk about target audience. If we think this is funny, it goes in the magazine.

MN: What was the *Lampoon* culture like? And how did it impact you and your work?

ES: It didn't impact me at all! I was never on staff, so I missed a lot of it. I know there were a lot of feuds. Big, huge feuds that often involved one person's perception that another person stole their girlfriend, or something like that. There were people who would hardly talk to each other over stuff like that. Even if I had been there, I never would've gotten involved with it. But as I keep telling people, what you had there was a bunch of super professional, hardworking publishing people. They had deadlines, they had X number of blank pages to fill each issue, and they would work hard at it.

---

[12]Henry Beard (1945–), Michael O'Donoghue (1940–1994), and Brian McConnachie (1942–) were all early and major contributors to the *Lampoon*.

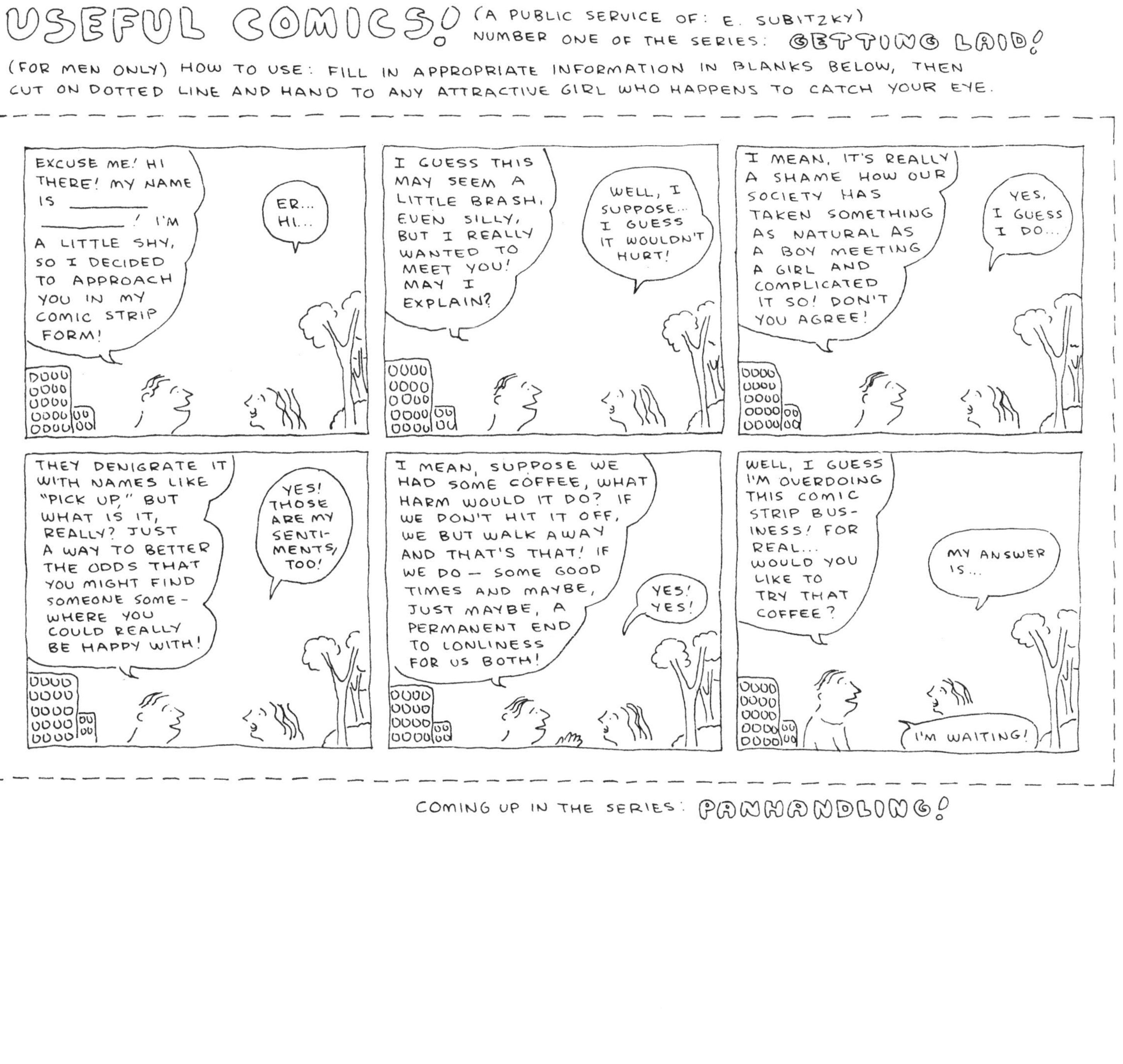
USEFUL COMICS!
(A PUBLIC SERVICE OF: E. SUBITZKY)
NUMBER ONE OF THE SERIES: GETTING LAID!
(FOR MEN ONLY) HOW TO USE: FILL IN APPROPRIATE INFORMATION IN BLANKS BELOW, THEN CUT ON DOTTED LINE AND HAND TO ANY ATTRACTIVE GIRL WHO HAPPENS TO CATCH YOUR EYE.
EXCUSE ME! HI THERE! MY NAME IS ________ ________! I'M A LITTLE SHY, SO I DECIDED TO APPROACH YOU IN MY COMIC STRIP FORM!
ER... HI...
I GUESS THIS MAY SEEM A LITTLE BRASH, EVEN SILLY, BUT I REALLY WANTED TO MEET YOU! MAY I EXPLAIN?
WELL, I SUPPOSE... I GUESS IT WOULDN'T HURT!
I MEAN, IT'S REALLY A SHAME HOW OUR SOCIETY HAS TAKEN SOMETHING AS NATURAL AS A BOY MEETING A GIRL AND COMPLICATED IT SO! DON'T YOU AGREE!
YES, I GUESS I DO...
THEY DENIGRATE IT WITH NAMES LIKE "PICK UP," BUT WHAT IS IT, REALLY? JUST A WAY TO BETTER THE ODDS THAT YOU MIGHT FIND SOMEONE SOMEWHERE YOU COULD REALLY BE HAPPY WITH!
YES! THOSE ARE MY SENTIMENTS, TOO!
I MEAN, SUPPOSE WE HAD SOME COFFEE, WHAT HARM WOULD IT DO? IF WE DON'T HIT IT OFF, WE BUT WALK AWAY AND THAT'S THAT! IF WE DO — SOME GOOD TIMES AND MAYBE, JUST MAYBE, A PERMANENT END TO LONLINESS FOR US BOTH!
YES! YES!
WELL, I GUESS I'M OVERDOING THIS COMIC STRIP BUSINESS! FOR REAL... WOULD YOU LIKE TO TRY THAT COFFEE?
MY ANSWER IS...
I'M WAITING!
COMING UP IN THE SERIES: PANHANDLING!

BACKWARDS COMICS!

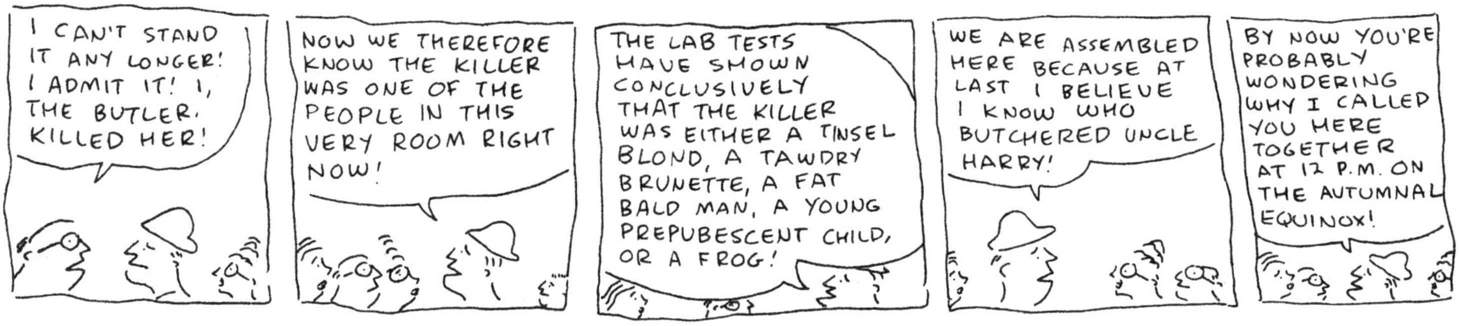
I CAN'T STAND IT ANY LONGER! I ADMIT IT! I, THE BUTLER, KILLED HER!
NOW WE THEREFORE KNOW THE KILLER WAS ONE OF THE PEOPLE IN THIS VERY ROOM RIGHT NOW!
THE LAB TESTS HAVE SHOWN CONCLUSIVELY THAT THE KILLER WAS EITHER A TINSEL BLOND, A TAWDRY BRUNETTE, A FAT BALD MAN, A YOUNG PREPUBESCENT CHILD, OR A FROG!
WE ARE ASSEMBLED HERE BECAUSE AT LAST I BELIEVE I KNOW WHO BUTCHERED UNCLE HARRY!
BY NOW YOU'RE PROBABLY WONDERING WHY I CALLED YOU HERE TOGETHER AT 12 P.M. ON THE AUTUMNAL EQUINOX!

ORIGAMI COMICS!

HAROLD! I DEMAND TO KNOW! IS IT TRUE THAT YOU HAVE NAMED A RHINOCEROS IN YOUR DIVORCE SUIT AGAINST ME?
I WAS HOPING WE MIGHT BE ABLE TO KEEP THIS CIVILIZED, MARSHA!
BESTIALITY ONE OF YOUR THINGS NOW?
SODOMY, NECROPHILISM AND MOUTH-TO-MOUTH RESUSCITATION!
SHOW ME!
SHALL I DEMONSTRATE WITH A
ENOUGH!
THE END

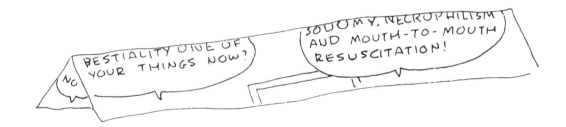

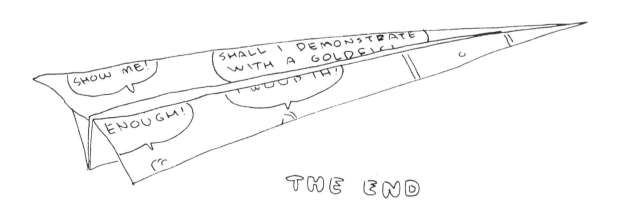

FEELIES COMICS!

ALMOST AS GOOD AS THE REAL THING!
SIMPLY FOLLOW DIRECTIONS UNDER SPECIFIC PANELS

HI THERE, BABY! WANNA KISS?

SURE!

MMMMMM!

DIRECTIONS:
PLACE LIPS ON
PAGE WHERE
INDICATED
BY ARROW

THAT WAS GREAT! WANNA PET?

WHY NOT!

AHHHHHH!

DIRECTIONS:
PLACE FINGERS
ON PAGE WHERE
INDICATED
BY ARROWS

REALLY SOMETHING ELSE! WANNA MAKE LOVE?

OKAY...

AHH! MORE! OO!
YESYES! AHH!
GMGRRRR!

DIRECTIONS:
PLACE LIPS,
FINGERS, ETC.,
ON PAGE
WHERE IND.
BY ARROWS

BABY, YOU ARE TOUGH! CIGARETTE?

YEAH. THANKS!

DIRECTIONS:
PLACE LIPS
ON PAGE
WHERE
INDICATED
BY ARROW

MN: So how did you branch out from comics and drawings to the written pieces?

ES: I had always wanted to try a written piece. I started by submitting one terrible print piece for them. It was just awful. I won't even talk about it, it was so wrong. But then Henry Beard said, "Why don't you try another print piece and base it on one of your comic strips, like 'Backwards Comics'?" So I went home, pounded out "Do Not Reveal the Trick Beginnings," and submitted it. And they liked it! They just weren't sure they should give it so much space in the magazine. I have to admit—I know most people know me for the cartoons, but I do enjoy the print pieces.

    I have always loved writing as much as I have loved drawing. I was anxious to see if I could get some of my writing in there, and I did, luckily. I had quite a few writing pieces, if I remember right.

MN: No other cartoonist ever went that route there. You were the sole cartoonist to transition into written stuff—you even edited an issue!

HOW I SPENT MY SUMMER

I'm really glad for this chance to be able to tell you what happened to me over the summer, because I did some really great things you'll be interested in. For the first part of the summer, I didn't do much. I just stayed around the house and looked out the window from my favorite chair. But then one night, my friend and I got together and before we knew it we found ourselves saying, "Hey, why don't we go on a cross-country trip!" It all happened just like that, as spur-of-the-moment as can be. The next day we were off and packing and, let me tell you, neither of us had any idea of the kinds of adventures that were waiting for us along the way! I even met this real nice girl in Yellowstone National Park and my friend and I went to this burlesque show in Arizona, with a live woman on the stage who took off her things. But I'll tell you about that later, when I come to it.

The first thing we did was to rent a car, a really nifty brand-new Chevrolet with air-conditioning and a radio, and let me tell you, we felt proud as can be just to be seen driving in something like that. We piled our suitcases on the back seat, although some of them had to go in the trunk, and we were on our way! My friend is good with maps and things, and he plotted us a route that took us almost straight West.

We could actually see Chicago from Interstate 97, which is one of the greatest roads I've ever been on in my life. It was straight and long and there was plenty of room for lots and lots of cars. And they kept it really clean, with no trash or candy wrappers on the shoulders. If you ever want to try a really great road, I can't recommend it too highly. I should be honest with you and tell you I'm not exactly sure it was Interstate 97. It might have been Interstate 87 or even 77, but I am sure it had a 7 in it.

Anyway, from this road, you could really see Chicago from the distance, and they have some super tall buildings there. I could even see the Sears building, which is world-famous. Like a tall gaping needle, it rose from the pristine stillness of the plains and dared to stab the heavens with its bold insistence. It took me a good while to think that up, but those are the best words I found yet for describing the Sears building to people who haven't gone across country like I have.

The next day was pretty uneventful. We just drove. We also ate at a Howard Johnson's and we stopped for gas. Once I had to go to the men's room, so we had to pull into a gas station when we didn't need gas. I went right up to the owner and said, "Sir, I'm from out of state and I thought perhaps you might not mind if I used your men's room for a moment." "Sure!" he replied with a big, friendly grin and he pointed me to this little room in the back. It turned out to be kind of greasy and they didn't have any toilet paper, so I had to use some old newspaper that was lying on the floor. It's too bad, because it was a local newspaper with lots of interesting news about the area and I would have liked to bring it back as a souvenir.

As we got further West, the scenery really began to change. In one spot, there were these big purple cliffs all over the place. I took lots of pictures of them and all the other things I saw, but it turned out I'd forgotten to put a fresh battery in my camera, so none of the pictures came out. So I've done a bunch of little drawings instead. My Aunt Maggie says I draw real good, and that some of my drawings look even better than the real thing. She should know, because she and my uncle once went on a cross-country trip, too. Of course, that was when he was still alive, but the truth is I never liked him very much, although I know it's not very nice to say that kind of thing about a dead person. Anyway, here's one of me standing beside the funny cliffs.

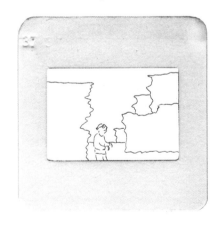

After we finished with the funny cliffs, my friend and I stopped in this little town for dinner. I don't remember its exact name, but if you ever want to go there too, it began with an A and it was somewhere near Wisconsin. We had some steak, and it was easily the best steak I ever had, because that's real steak country around there. I ordered mine well done, but my friend likes his rare. We didn't argue about it, though, because each of us believes in live-and-let-live. In fact, for the most part we got along pretty good, even though we did have one big fight near the end of the trip. I'll tell you about it later, when I come to it.

After we finished eating, I happened to notice this really keen game room right next door to the restaurant. I think they called it Playland. They had some of the best pinball machines I'd ever seen, and I was just about to get my first free game when all of a sudden this local kid comes up to me. "Hey," he says, "bet you a quarter for highest score." Those might not be his exact words, but they're as close as I can remember. I said okay, then we began to play. Some of his friends came around to watch and my friend watched, too. I won by a lot of points and he even said I was one of the best pinball players he'd ever come across but that he accidentally forgot to bring his quarters. He had a lot of pimples. I told him not to worry about it and asked him what the weather was like in this neck of the woods. "It can get pretty cold in the winter," he said. Then he said he would mail me the quarter and he asked me for my name and address, but when I gave it to him, I lied.

Next we got on another really interesting highway. It had a lot of trees on the side, as you can see.

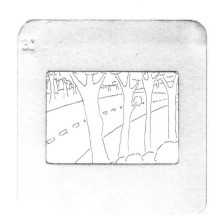

By the time we reached our exit, we could see the Rocky Mountains in the distance!

I took lots and lots of pictures in the Rockies. In fact, I think I was starting to annoy my friend because I kept making him stop the car every time the lighting changed. Boy, were those Rockies big! They were even more impressive than the whole Sears building, that's how big they were. In fact, I had to work really hard to come up with good words for the Rockies. I hope you like them. Steel-edged and mighty, rising starkly from the pristine plains, they dared, with their stony arrogance, to pierce even the highest of cloud.

Here's one of me and my friend together standing in front of one of the Rockies. If you're wondering how I took it, I put the camera on the hood of the car and used the self-timer. Most photographers neglect their self-timers, but not me!

Then we left the Rockies and had to do a lot of driving to stay on schedule. By this time, though, I'd gotten really natural at asking gas station men if I could use their men's rooms. At the beginning, I was a little shy, but after a while you learn that people are just people anywhere you go. I did run into one guy in Idaho who was a little nasty, but I told him my father owned a gas station too and that I could appreciate the kinds of problems

he had each day. I made it up, but it worked. I'd also gotten good at being able to tell which gas stations were clean inside. For example, say there were four or even five gas stations at an intersection. I'd give them one quick lookover and just like that tell my friend, "That one." He admitted I really amazed him sometimes.

In fact, often stopping off at gas stations turned out to be very educational. It really gives you a chance to meet the local people. Some of the gas station men would have these neat girlie calendars on the walls, and then I would make a joke about how the calendars around there were even better than the scenery, and they would really laugh. I always test out my jokes that way and then, if they get a lot of laughs, I remember them and tell them later on to the same kind of person in the same kind of situation.

Also, in one gas station in Minnesota, there was this old guy hanging around and he told me that the town I was in had some of the biggest pine cones in the whole world. At first I didn't believe him, but then he took me out back to see a pine tree and he stood on a chair with a broom and knocked off one of the pine cones. Sure enough, that thing was almost as big as a football! Since you didn't get to see it, you might not believe me when I tell you either, but just you take a look at this picture.

That's not trick photography you're seeing there. No sir, that pine cone was really that big! The old man even told me I could keep it to show all my friends at home how his town had the biggest pine cones in the world. I thanked him again and again until my friend began to honk the horn and I had to excuse myself. One day, though, I accidentally ran over the big pine cone when I was backing out of a motel. But in case you ever want to visit that town and see its pine cones for yourself, the name begins with a K or an L. I don't remember the rest of it, but there aren't that many towns in Minnesota.

Speaking of motels, we stayed in some really nice ones along the way. Here's one of the more modern ones. I think it was in the state of Washington, and it even had a sunlamp in the bathroom. In fact, I bet I'm the only person you've ever known who's actually set foot in the state of Washington. Not Washington, D.C., where a lot of tourists go, but the state of Washington that isn't so far from Alaska!

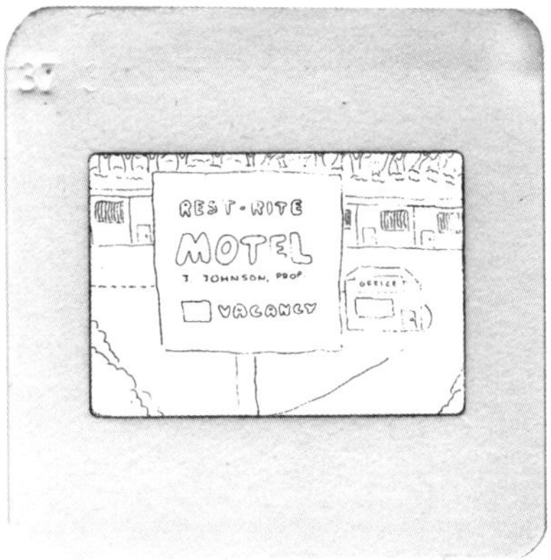
REST-RITE
MOTEL
J. JOHNSON, PROP.
VACANCY
OFFICE

One thing I noticed about sleeping with people in motels is that you really learn their bad habits. For example, I found out that my friend hardly ever brushed his teeth. I told him what my dentist said about brushing every day and how important it was to fight Mr. Tooth Decay, and it looked like we might have an argument about it, but we didn't. He also snored a lot, and one night he rolled off the bed. I also think he sometimes touched himself down below before we went to sleep, but I shouldn't say something like that unless I'm absolutely sure.

After we hit—that means drove into—the state of Washington, we began to go southward down the coast. That was good because, for one thing, it gets warmer. In Oregon, we saw some real California redwoods. And let me tell you, they were something. When I was a kid, I used to think the maple tree in front of our house was just about the biggest tree in the whole world, but those redwoods even made that maple tree look like nothing! I made a joke about how long it would take to climb one if you had a lion chasing you, and I made it loud enough so the other tourists around us could hear and they all laughed. There was this girl near us who was about my age, and she laughed too, but she wasn't the one I met. Even my friend laughed a little, and he isn't the kind of person who laughs more than once a week.

Since you've never seen redwoods before, you can't possibly imagine how tall they look. Even a picture can't give you too good an idea, but just look at the size of that thing compared to me.

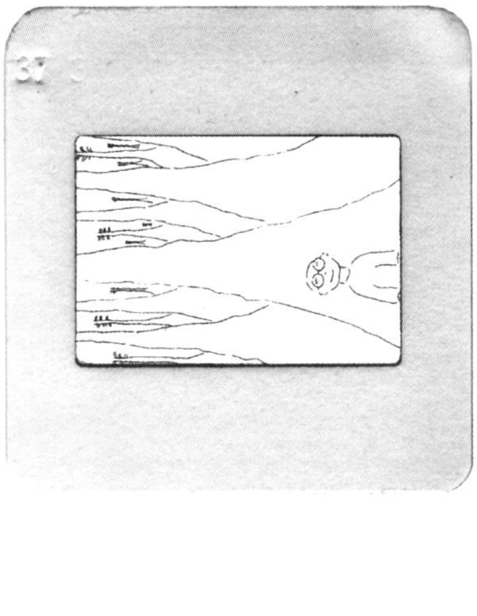

I've tried to come up with a good way of describing the redwoods, too. The best I could do was this. Tall and majestic, their woody shapes climb like slim needles up from the pristine landscape, daring to prick the very bottoms of the sky.

After we saw the redwoods, we got on a road that wasn't so good. It twisted and turned a lot, and once it felt like the Chevy was going to fall right off the side of a cliff and into the ocean. I was afraid for what my parents and the people at the rent-a-car place would think.

Actually, though, the Pacific is a very pretty ocean. The cliffs alongside it, even though they're dangerous to drive on, are pretty too. There are beaches everywhere, and lots of pretty girls stand around on them in really small bathing suits. On one beach, it even looked like the girls were swimming without their suits, but it was far away and we couldn't be sure. We stopped at one of those lookouts where they have those telescope-machines, and I got a little excited and I was going to put a dime in to see if they really did have all their clothes off. But my friend told me to calm down and not to waste the money, so we just went back to the car.

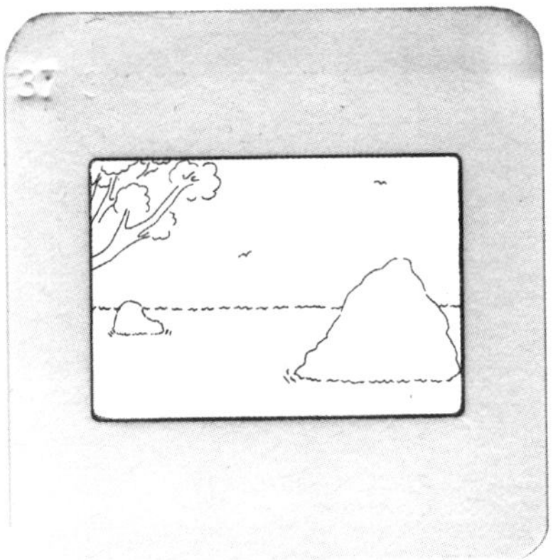

This is a picture of the Pacific. I didn't try to find any words for it, because I'm only good at finding words for things that are tall and go-up and down, not things that are wide and far across.

After we saw the Pacific, we headed inland and it got very hot. In fact, in one place the radio said the temperature was over one hundred degrees. I wanted to try to fry an egg on the sidewalk, but my friend told me that would make us look like tourists, so I dropped the idea. Anyway, we hadn't taken any eggs with us. But let me tell you, you really do sweat a lot when the temperature gets that high. In fact, one day my armpits got so wet and sticky I had to take my shirt off and go around in just an undershirt. And here's the picture to prove it!

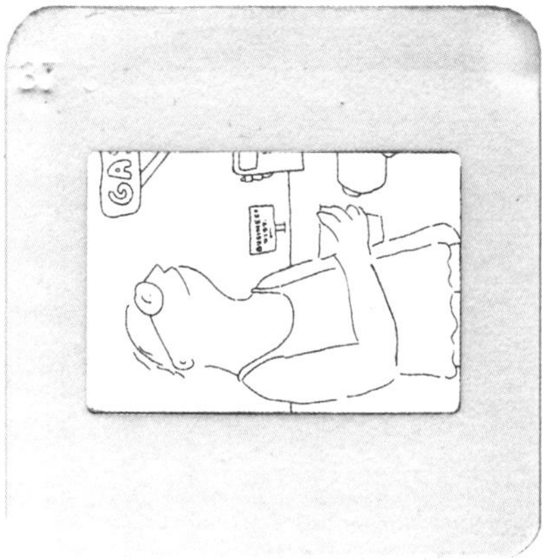

Our next stop was Yellowstone National Park. This is where I meet the girl I told you about, but I'll come to that in a moment. My friend and I wanted to see Old Faithful go off, and while we stood around and waited we each had hot dogs. I put lots of mustard and sauerkraut on mine, but he took his plain. I was almost going to tell him that all the other people could tell what state we were from because of the license plate on our car, and because of him they would think our state had the kinds of people who took their hot dogs plain. But I didn't want to start an argument, so I held back my tongue.

Then someone announced that it was almost time and this big crowd of people gathered around to watch Old Faithful go off. I was glad to see that Old Faithful reached very high in the sky because I knew I would be able to find good words for it. Here they are. Tall and streaming, its underground hissing waters bursting from the subterranean darkness into the egg-frying sunlight, it shot starkly up from the pristine stillness of the plains and dared scorch the very bottoms of the clouds with its steam-laden dragon breath.

While Old Faithful was going off, there was this really pretty girl standing right beside me. She had long blonde hair and a really sweet face and she looked about my age. A few minutes before, I had noticed her getting something from a car that had a New Jersey license plate, which is the state right next to mine. The crowd was really packed, so our shoulders were almost touching. As Old Faithful went off, everyone went oooooooh and ahhhhhhhhhh and I said to her, "It's really something, isn't it?" She said, "Yeah." Then I said, "In steaming splendor does it now shoot up from the pristine stillness of the plain." I was going to ask her how she liked living in New Jersey, but I realized she would figure out that I'd been watching her get in and out of the car. Then Old Faithful turned back off and the crowd began to thin out and she waved to some tall guy who was coming over with two ice-cream cones, and he put his arm around her and they went to the car together and got in. I think they must have been on their honeymoon or something. Anyway, it was nice to meet a girl like her on my vacation.

Here's one of my friend standing just in front of the spot where Old Faithful goes off.

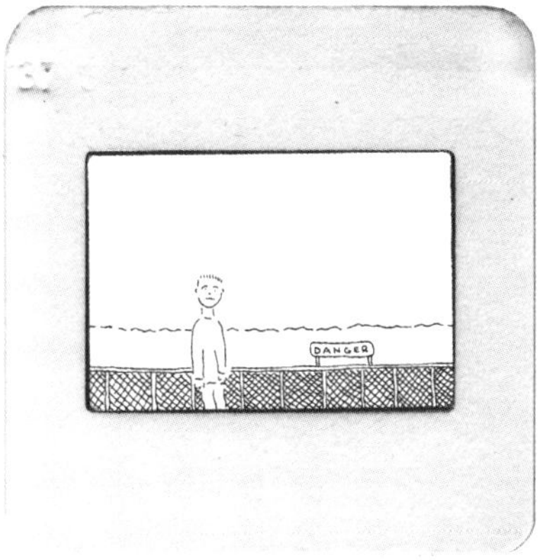
DANGER

That night, when we stopped off in a motel near Old Faithful, was when my friend and I had our argument. I guess part of the reason I was in a bad mood was that, when we pulled into our parking space, I noticed that the girl's car was parked right beside us. At least, I think it was the same car, because it had the same color dice hanging over the dashboard and it had a license plate from New Jersey. I could hear all this laughing and giggling coming through the walls, so I figured they must be doing it.

My friend checked our schedule—he was always doing things like checking our schedule—and he told me we'd have to skip a place because we'd fallen behind. He said he didn't want to skip Las Vegas because another friend had told him they had some really good burlesque shows there, but I told him I wanted to go to Disneyland instead. Since I was a little kid, I've always dreamed of going to Disneyland, especially to see the magic castle and the midgets who walk around dressed like Mickey Mouse. In fact, before I agreed to the trip, I made it very clear to my friend that we had to stop at Disneyland or I wouldn't go with him, and he said okay.

So I got really angry at him and I told him that, where I come from, a promise is a promise, especially a promise to a friend. Finally, he said we could flip a coin. I'm usually lucky at flipping coins, so I went along with him. I called heads for Disneyland and tails for Las Vegas, but the coin came up tails. Then I got really sad, so my friend agreed to go to Disneyland anyway and the argument ended.

In the morning, I got up extra early and looked through the window because I thought maybe I could see the girl leave her room and then I could hurry outside and say something like didn't I remember seeing her at Old Faithful. After all, it was possible that the guy she was traveling with could have been her brother or something, and it wouldn't have been the first time I was wrong about some noises I'd heard. But it turned out she got up even earlier than I did, because her car was already gone and I've never seen her again even though I've taken several rides through New Jersey. My friend woke up and asked me why I'd gotten up so early just to look out the window and I made a joke about how this was the day they were moving Mount Rainier down south on a big truck, and it was just going by. He didn't laugh so I've never told it again.

Let me tell you, Disneyland was even better than I imagined. If you ever get the chance to go there, you really should. The Mickey Mouse men looked just like the real Mickey Mouse, and the magic castle was even better than it used to look at the beginning of the TV show when Tinkerbell flew across it. In fact, I made up some of the best words for it. I hope you like them. Tall and gleaming, stark and gaunt, its multifaceted surfaces reflecting the afternoon sun with a frenzied and yet an innocent delight it rose from the pristine plains and pierced the very heavens with its silvery affirmation of the fantasy joys of childhood.

Now comes one of my favorite pictures. I took it at a sign in Disneyland that said it was a good spot for taking a picture, and, boy, was that sign right!

After Disneyland, it was time to head back to home and hearth, so we pointed the Chevy east. That's when we ran into the worst danger of the whole trip.

We were on this dry, dusty road somewhere in the desert when all of a sudden the car came to a dead stop and we realized we'd run out of gas. I guess it was my fault because I was the one who was supposed to keep track of the gas that day, and I apologized lots of times to my friend. Finally, he told me it was all right. We sure were scared, though. We could see some dark storm clouds looming on the horizon and they really looked menacing. The guidebook made a point of warning that we were in tornado country and, since you've never been in tornado country yourself, you can't possibly know how we felt.

Lucky for us, though, this old truck just happened to come along down the road. This real nice old man and woman were driving it, and they had a lot of hens in the back. They took us to this gas station that must have been at least thirty miles away, and to pass the time they told us these really interesting stories about their son who had grown up to become a teacher and what it had been like during the war. They even invited us back with them for a home-cooked dinner, but we didn't have time. At the gas station, a man in a tow truck and dungarees drove us back to the car with a pail of gas. He didn't say much because he was chewing gum, and we had to pay him a lot of money. But we really felt relieved when the car started up and we felt even more relieved when we realized that the clouds had been moving in the other direction all along.

That night, when we stopped at a motel in a small town in Arizona, my friend still wasn't talking to me much. I mean, he would be polite and answer me when I asked him something, but he wasn't really starting conversations. I decided that maybe I hadn't been fair to him after all, so, right in front of him, I took out the phone book and started looking up to see if there were any burlesque places in town. He asked me what I was doing, then he smiled a little and told me you couldn't find that kind of thing in the phone book, but maybe if we took a walk through the business section we'd come across a place. He got really happy and talkative now, and so the two of us went out to look. I didn't like to leave my camera in the motel room, so I took it with me.

It turned out all we could find was this one tiny bar with a sign on the window that said GIRLS–GIRLS–GIRLS, so we went inside. It was very dark and there were some real cowboys sitting around and smoking. I wish you could have seen them yourself, they looked just like the ones we'd seen back in Frontierland. In the back of the room, we saw this tiny stage and we sat down at a table right in front of it. The owner came over and my friend, who knows more about these kinds of things than I do, ordered us some beers. I've never really liked the taste of beer, so I purposely sipped mine slowly. Soon all the other tables around us began to fill up, mostly with old men who chewed a lot. Then suddenly the curtains opened and we could see this woman standing there and behind her was a man at a piano. He started to play and right away the woman began to take off her clothes. I could see that my friend was really enjoying himself, but I kind of felt a little funny about looking, especially on our way home. But soon she had all her clothes off and I couldn't help but look. I would have taken pictures, but I was afraid I wasn't allowed to. In case you ever get around there and you're looking for that kind of a place, though, here's a picture I took of the outside.

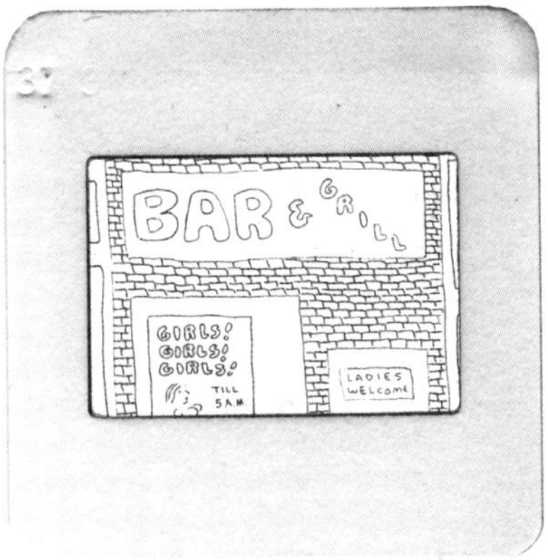
BAR & GRILL
GIRLS! GIRLS! GIRLS!
TILL 5AM
LADIES WELCOME

Let me tell you, you'll never see a show anywhere that's anything like it.

After we got back to the motel, my friend said thanks for going with him and he called me his buddy again. I felt real good.

On the way back east, we saw some pretty sights, too. In particular, I was really impressed by this very tall radio antenna we passed in Tennessee.

It was something to see all right, and after the trip I had to spend a long time trying to find words for it. Sleek and slender, a needle of voices and music and time checks, it rose from the pristine plains and split asunder the very dusk itself with a cacophony of blinking red lights.

I hope you don't mind, but the radio antenna will have to be the last picture I show you, because after that I ran out of film and my friend wouldn't let me stop to buy any more.

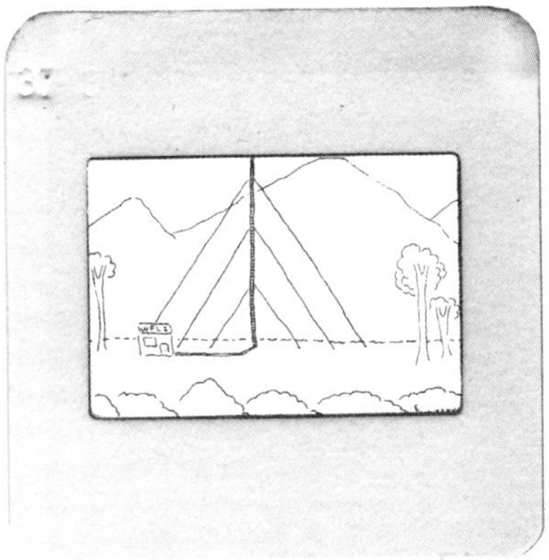

So that was my vacation. We came home safe and tired, but we were glad we went because we knew we'd had a really special experience and a good time, too. We'd learned a lot about our country and its people and we'd seen a lot of things we'd never seen before and may never see again. After a while, we even started to make jokes about the way we'd gotten angry at each other and my friend told me that it turned out he'd really enjoyed Disneyland after all, especially the Haunted House. He even admitted he'd noticed the girl with the blonde hair too and was hoping that someday he could marry someone just like her.

I hope that someday you, too, have the chance to have a summer like I did. It wasn't always easy and I guess, if you ever do get a chance to go all around the country, it won't always be easy for you, either. But just yesterday I was telling somebody that you only live once and, if you don't mind, I think I'll leave you with those words, too. Because it was sure the kind of summer that memories are made of and I know that, years from now when I'm old and grey, I'll still be thinking of what I did this summer.

MN: In your opinion what's the funniest thing in the book?

ES: The funniest thing in the book? I think it's either "Saturday Nite on Antarius!" or the print piece "How I Spent My Summer."

SATURDAY NITE ON ANTARIUS!

(THE PLANET WITH 12 DIFFERENT SEXES)

by E. Subitzky

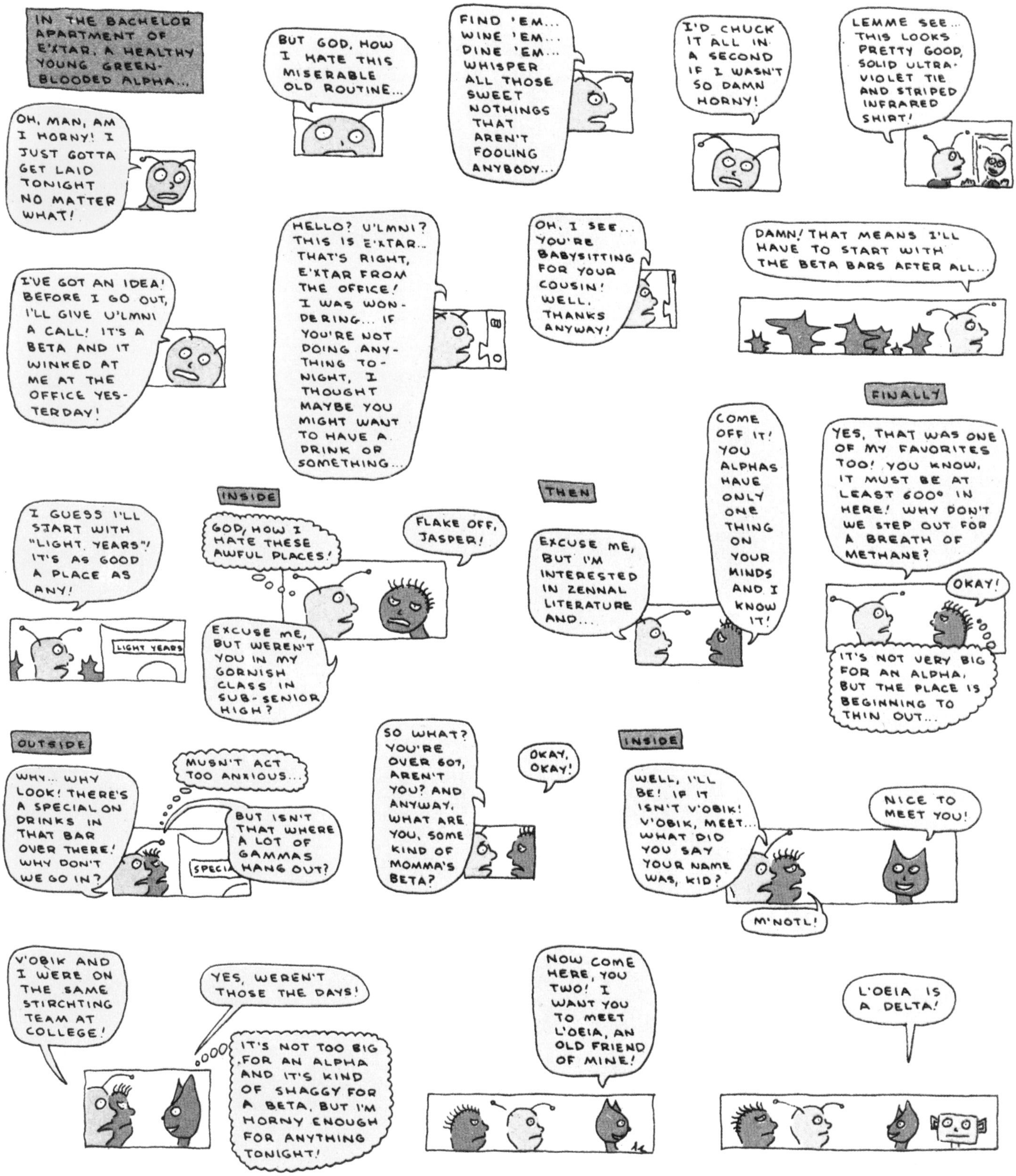

IN THE BACHELOR APARTMENT OF E'XTAR, A HEALTHY YOUNG GREEN-BLOODED ALPHA...
OH, MAN, AM I HORNY! I JUST GOTTA GET LAID TONIGHT NO MATTER WHAT!
BUT GOD, HOW I HATE THIS MISERABLE OLD ROUTINE...
FIND 'EM... WINE 'EM... DINE 'EM... WHISPER ALL THOSE SWEET NOTHINGS THAT AREN'T FOOLING ANYBODY...
I'D CHUCK IT ALL IN A SECOND IF I WASN'T SO DAMN HORNY!
LEMME SEE... THIS LOOKS PRETTY GOOD, SOLID ULTRA-VIOLET TIE AND STRIPED INFRARED SHIRT!
I'VE GOT AN IDEA! BEFORE I GO OUT, I'LL GIVE U'LMNI A CALL! IT'S A BETA AND IT WINKED AT ME AT THE OFFICE YESTERDAY!
HELLO? U'LMNI? THIS IS E'XTAR... THAT'S RIGHT, E'XTAR FROM THE OFFICE! I WAS WONDERING... IF YOU'RE NOT DOING ANYTHING TONIGHT, I THOUGHT MAYBE YOU MIGHT WANT TO HAVE A DRINK OR SOMETHING...
OH, I SEE... YOU'RE BABYSITTING FOR YOUR COUSIN! WELL, THANKS ANYWAY!
DAMN! THAT MEANS I'LL HAVE TO START WITH THE BETA BARS AFTER ALL...
I GUESS I'LL START WITH "LIGHT YEARS"! IT'S AS GOOD A PLACE AS ANY!
LIGHT YEARS
INSIDE
GOD, HOW I HATE THESE AWFUL PLACES!
EXCUSE ME, BUT WEREN'T YOU IN MY GORNISH CLASS IN SUB-SENIOR HIGH?
FLAKE OFF, JASPER!
THEN
EXCUSE ME, BUT I'M INTERESTED IN ZENNAL LITERATURE AND...
COME OFF IT! YOU ALPHAS HAVE ONLY ONE THING ON YOUR MINDS AND I KNOW IT!
FINALLY
YES, THAT WAS ONE OF MY FAVORITES TOO! YOU KNOW, IT MUST BE AT LEAST 600° IN HERE! WHY DON'T WE STEP OUT FOR A BREATH OF METHANE?
OKAY!
IT'S NOT VERY BIG FOR AN ALPHA, BUT THE PLACE IS BEGINNING TO THIN OUT...
OUTSIDE
WHY... WHY LOOK! THERE'S A SPECIAL ON DRINKS IN THAT BAR OVER THERE! WHY DON'T WE GO IN?
MUSN'T ACT TOO ANXIOUS...
BUT ISN'T THAT WHERE A LOT OF GAMMAS HANG OUT?
SPECIA
SO WHAT? YOU'RE OVER 601, AREN'T YOU? AND ANYWAY, WHAT ARE YOU, SOME KIND OF MOMMA'S BETA?
OKAY, OKAY!
INSIDE
WELL, I'LL BE! IF IT ISN'T V'OBIK! V'OBIK, MEET... WHAT DID YOU SAY YOUR NAME WAS, KID?
M'NOTL!
NICE TO MEET YOU!
V'OBIK AND I WERE ON THE SAME STIRCHTING TEAM AT COLLEGE!
YES, WEREN'T THOSE THE DAYS!
IT'S NOT TOO BIG FOR AN ALPHA AND IT'S KIND OF SHAGGY FOR A BETA, BUT I'M HORNY ENOUGH FOR ANYTHING TONIGHT!
NOW COME HERE, YOU TWO! I WANT YOU TO MEET L'OEIA, AN OLD FRIEND OF MINE!
L'OEIA IS A DELTA!

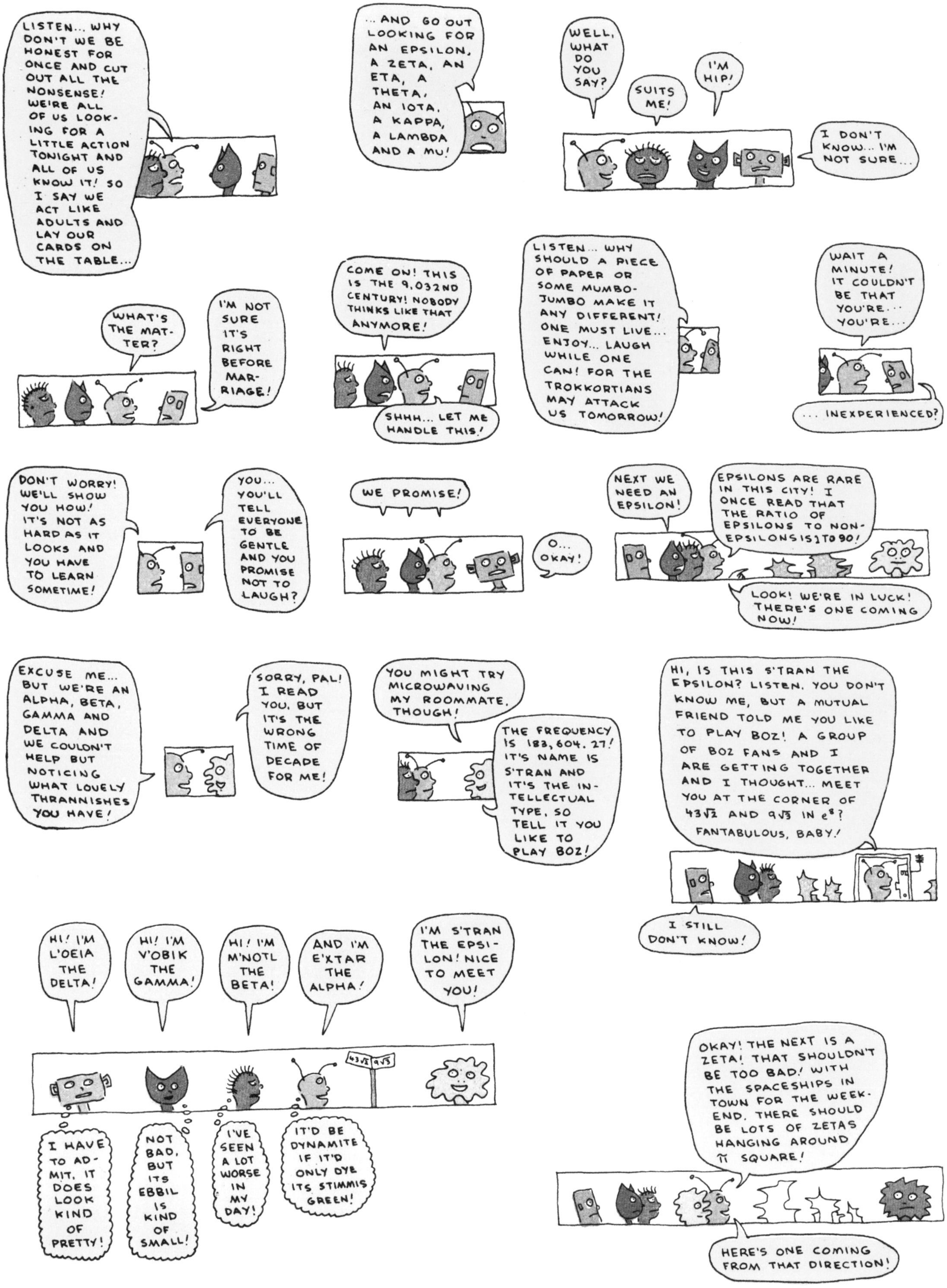
LISTEN... WHY DON'T WE BE HONEST FOR ONCE AND CUT OUT ALL THE NONSENSE! WE'RE ALL OF US LOOKING FOR A LITTLE ACTION TONIGHT AND ALL OF US KNOW IT! SO I SAY WE ACT LIKE ADULTS AND LAY OUR CARDS ON THE TABLE...
...AND GO OUT LOOKING FOR AN EPSILON, A ZETA, AN ETA, A THETA, AN IOTA, A KAPPA, A LAMBDA AND A MU!
WELL, WHAT DO YOU SAY?
SUITS ME!
I'M HIP!
I DON'T KNOW... I'M NOT SURE...
WHAT'S THE MATTER?
I'M NOT SURE IT'S RIGHT BEFORE MARRIAGE!
COME ON! THIS IS THE 9,032ND CENTURY! NOBODY THINKS LIKE THAT ANYMORE!
SHHH... LET ME HANDLE THIS!
LISTEN... WHY SHOULD A PIECE OF PAPER OR SOME MUMBO-JUMBO MAKE IT ANY DIFFERENT! ONE MUST LIVE... ENJOY... LAUGH WHILE ONE CAN! FOR THE TROKKORTIANS MAY ATTACK US TOMORROW!
WAIT A MINUTE! IT COULDN'T BE THAT YOU'RE... YOU'RE...
...INEXPERIENCED?
DON'T WORRY! WE'LL SHOW YOU HOW! IT'S NOT AS HARD AS IT LOOKS AND YOU HAVE TO LEARN SOMETIME!
YOU... YOU'LL TELL EVERYONE TO BE GENTLE AND YOU PROMISE NOT TO LAUGH?
WE PROMISE!
O... OKAY!
NEXT WE NEED AN EPSILON!
EPSILONS ARE RARE IN THIS CITY! I ONCE READ THAT THE RATIO OF EPSILONS TO NON-EPSILONS IS 1 TO 90!
LOOK! WE'RE IN LUCK! THERE'S ONE COMING NOW!
EXCUSE ME... BUT WE'RE AN ALPHA, BETA, GAMMA AND DELTA AND WE COULDN'T HELP BUT NOTICING WHAT LOVELY THRANNISHES YOU HAVE!
SORRY, PAL! I READ YOU, BUT IT'S THE WRONG TIME OF DECADE FOR ME!
YOU MIGHT TRY MICROWAVING MY ROOMMATE, THOUGH!
THE FREQUENCY IS 183,604.27! IT'S NAME IS S'TRAN AND IT'S THE INTELLECTUAL TYPE, SO TELL IT YOU LIKE TO PLAY BOZ!
HI, IS THIS S'TRAN THE EPSILON? LISTEN, YOU DON'T KNOW ME, BUT A MUTUAL FRIEND TOLD ME YOU LIKE TO PLAY BOZ! A GROUP OF BOZ FANS AND I ARE GETTING TOGETHER AND I THOUGHT... MEET YOU AT THE CORNER OF 43√2 AND 9√3 IN e⁸? FANTABULOUS, BABY!
I STILL DON'T KNOW!
HI! I'M L'OEIA THE DELTA!
HI! I'M V'OBIK THE GAMMA!
HI! I'M M'NOTL THE BETA!
AND I'M E'XTAR THE ALPHA!
I'M S'TRAN THE EPSILON! NICE TO MEET YOU!
43√2
9√3
I HAVE TO ADMIT, IT DOES LOOK KIND OF PRETTY!
NOT BAD, BUT ITS EBBIL IS KIND OF SMALL!
I'VE SEEN A LOT WORSE IN MY DAY!
IT'D BE DYNAMITE IF IT'D ONLY DYE ITS STIMMIS GREEN!
OKAY! THE NEXT IS A ZETA! THAT SHOULDN'T BE TOO BAD! WITH THE SPACESHIPS IN TOWN FOR THE WEEKEND, THERE SHOULD BE LOTS OF ZETAS HANGING AROUND π SQUARE!
HERE'S ONE COMING FROM THAT DIRECTION!

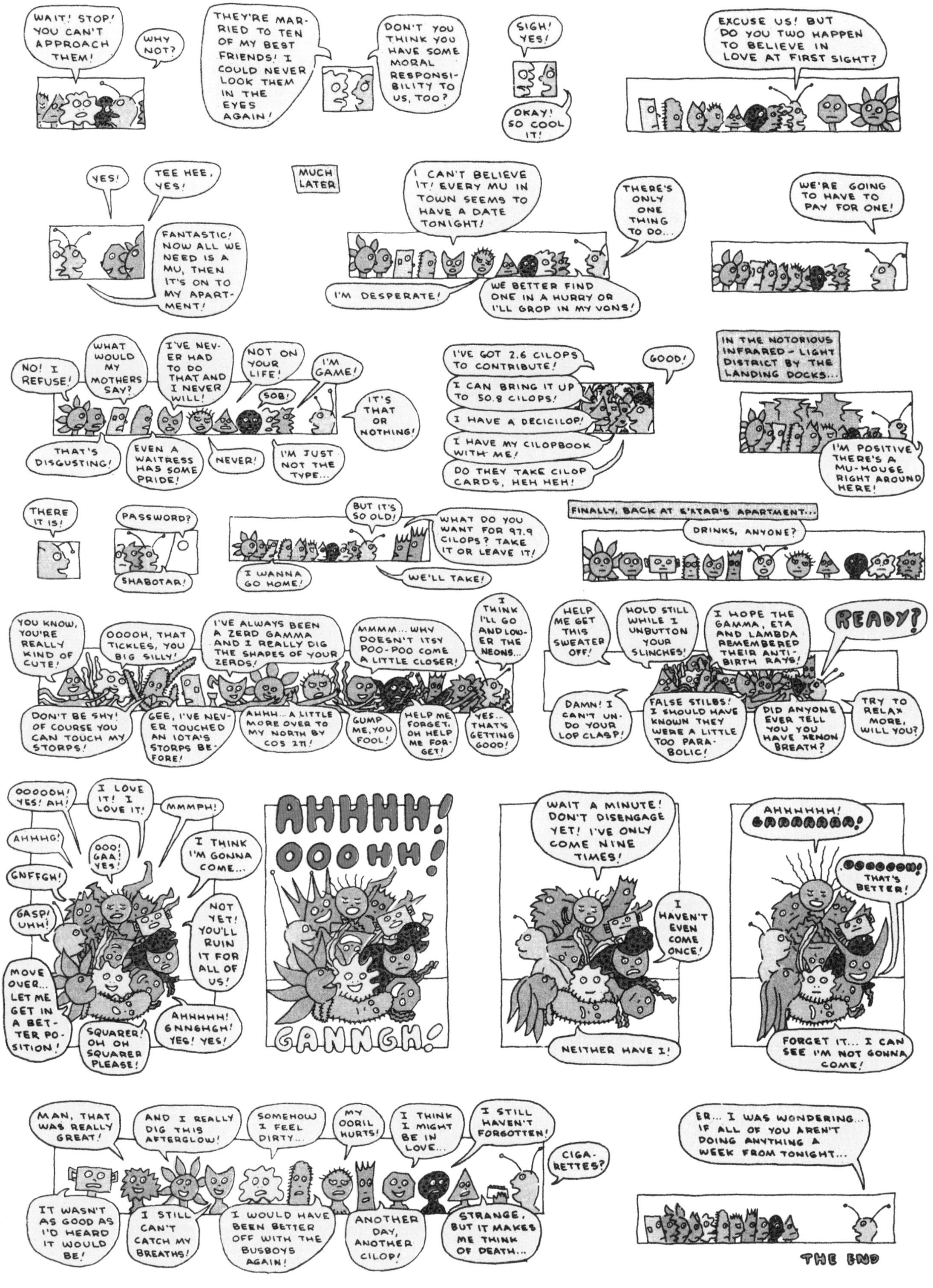

WAIT! STOP! YOU CAN'T APPROACH THEM!
WHY NOT?
THEY'RE MARRIED TO TEN OF MY BEST FRIENDS! I COULD NEVER LOOK THEM IN THE EYES AGAIN!
DON'T YOU THINK YOU HAVE SOME MORAL RESPONSIBILITY TO US, TOO?
SIGH! YES!
OKAY! SO COOL IT!
EXCUSE US! BUT DO YOU TWO HAPPEN TO BELIEVE IN LOVE AT FIRST SIGHT?
YES!
TEE HEE, YES!
FANTASTIC! NOW ALL WE NEED IS A MU, THEN IT'S ON TO MY APARTMENT!
MUCH LATER
I CAN'T BELIEVE IT! EVERY MU IN TOWN SEEMS TO HAVE A DATE TONIGHT!
I'M DESPERATE!
WE BETTER FIND ONE IN A HURRY OR I'LL GROP IN MY VONS!
THERE'S ONLY ONE THING TO DO...
WE'RE GOING TO HAVE TO PAY FOR ONE!
NO! I REFUSE!
WHAT WOULD MY MOTHERS SAY?
I'VE NEVER HAD TO DO THAT AND I NEVER WILL!
NOT ON YOUR LIFE!
SOB!
I'M GAME!
IT'S THAT OR NOTHING!
THAT'S DISGUSTING!
EVEN A WAITRESS HAS SOME PRIDE!
NEVER!
I'M JUST NOT THE TYPE...
I'VE GOT 2.6 CILOPS TO CONTRIBUTE!
I CAN BRING IT UP TO 50.8 CILOPS!
I HAVE A DECICILOP!
I HAVE MY CILOPBOOK WITH ME!
DO THEY TAKE CILOP CARDS, HEH HEH!
GOOD!
IN THE NOTORIOUS INFRARED-LIGHT DISTRICT BY THE LANDING DOCKS...
I'M POSITIVE THERE'S A MU-HOUSE RIGHT AROUND HERE!
THERE IT IS!
PASSWORD?
SHABOTAR!
BUT IT'S SO OLD!
I WANNA GO HOME!
WHAT DO YOU WANT FOR 97.9 CILOPS? TAKE IT OR LEAVE IT!
WE'LL TAKE!
FINALLY, BACK AT E'ATAR'S APARTMENT...
DRINKS, ANYONE?
YOU KNOW, YOU'RE REALLY KIND OF CUTE!
OOOOH, THAT TICKLES, YOU BIG SILLY!
I'VE ALWAYS BEEN A ZERD GAMMA AND I REALLY DIG THE SHAPES OF YOUR ZERDS!
MMMM... WHY DOESN'T ITSY POO-POO COME A LITTLE CLOSER!
I THINK I'LL GO AND LOWER THE NEONS...
DON'T BE SHY! OF COURSE YOU CAN TOUCH MY STORPS!
GEE, I'VE NEVER TOUCHED AN IOTA'S STORPS BEFORE!
AHHH... A LITTLE MORE OVER TO MY NORTH BY COS 2π!
GUMP ME, YOU FOOL!
HELP ME FORGET, OH HELP ME FORGET!
YES... THAT'S GETTING GOOD!
HELP ME GET THIS SWEATER OFF!
HOLD STILL WHILE I UNBUTTON YOUR SLINCHES!
I HOPE THE GAMMA, ETA AND LAMBDA REMEMBERED THEIR ANTI-BIRTH RAYS!
READY?
DAMN! I CAN'T UNDO YOUR LOP CLASP!
FALSE STILBS! I SHOULD HAVE KNOWN THEY WERE A LITTLE TOO PARABOLIC!
DID ANYONE EVER TELL YOU YOU HAVE XENON BREATH?
TRY TO RELAX MORE, WILL YOU?
OOOOOH! YES! AH!
I LOVE IT! I LOVE IT!
MMMPH!
AHHHG!
OOO! GAA! YES!
I THINK I'M GONNA COME...
GNFFGH!
GASP! UHH!
NOT YET! YOU'LL RUIN IT FOR ALL OF US!
MOVE OVER... LET ME GET IN A BETTER POSITION!
SQUARER! OH OH SQUARER PLEASE!
AHHHHH! GNNGHGH! YES! YES!
AHHHH! OOOHH!
GANNGH!
WAIT A MINUTE! DON'T DISENGAGE YET! I'VE ONLY COME NINE TIMES!
I HAVEN'T EVEN COME ONCE!
NEITHER HAVE I!
AHHHHHH! GRRRRRRR!
OOOOOOH! THAT'S BETTER!
FORGET IT... I CAN SEE I'M NOT GONNA COME!
MAN, THAT WAS REALLY GREAT!
AND I REALLY DIG THIS AFTERGLOW!
SOMEHOW I FEEL DIRTY...
MY OORIL HURTS!
I THINK I MIGHT BE IN LOVE...
I STILL HAVEN'T FORGOTTEN!
CIGARETTES?
IT WASN'T AS GOOD AS I'D HEARD IT WOULD BE!
I STILL CAN'T CATCH MY BREATHS!
I WOULD HAVE BEEN BETTER OFF WITH THE BUSBOYS AGAIN!
ANOTHER DAY, ANOTHER CILOP!
STRANGE, BUT IT MAKES ME THINK OF DEATH...
ER... I WAS WONDERING... IF ALL OF YOU AREN'T DOING ANYTHING A WEEK FROM TONIGHT...
THE END

REVERSE CENSORSHIP COMICS!

(FOR PEOPLE WHO ARE ONLY INTERESTED IN THE GOOD PARTS)

[redacted] SON OF A BITCH! [redacted] FUCK?
[redacted] FELT UP!
[redacted] BITCHES [redacted] SHIT!
[redacted] ASS!
[redacted]

THE END

MN: Can you describe your personal approach to making comics?

ES: Well, I'm one of those people who hardly ever think of my work when they're not doing it. I've always had the feeling, when I do my comics, that it's not really me who is doing them. That they've already been planted on a chip in my brain and that I'm just the conduit to getting them out onto paper. I can't say I don't ever redo and rewrite, but I think I don't do it as often as some other people do.

MN: It's like automatic writing.[13]

ES: I never consciously structure anything. I never say this should be the beginning, this should be the end. That's how my advertising was, too. I would write these long ads very quickly because they would just come out of me.

MN: With very little or no revision. Wow.

ES: Very little or no revision. Especially the comics. The print pieces I did some revision on. As a matter of fact, there's a funny story about "How I Spent My Summer." In the days before word processing, you handed in a manuscript, and if you wanted to make any last-minute changes, you wrote them down right on the manuscript page. So when I submitted the story "How I Spent My Summer," I had crossed out a section because I didn't think it worked. It wasn't like I had deleted it on a computer somewhere and no one would ever know about it; Brian McConnachie, who was in charge of the issue, could see the cross-out, and he said, "Ed, I like this. I want you to keep this in." That was the only time the *Lampoon* ever edited my work. And that was to put something back in.

MN: Anti-editing!

ES: [*Laughs*] Anti-editing!

---

[13]Automatic writing is the psychic ability to produce written work without conscious intent.

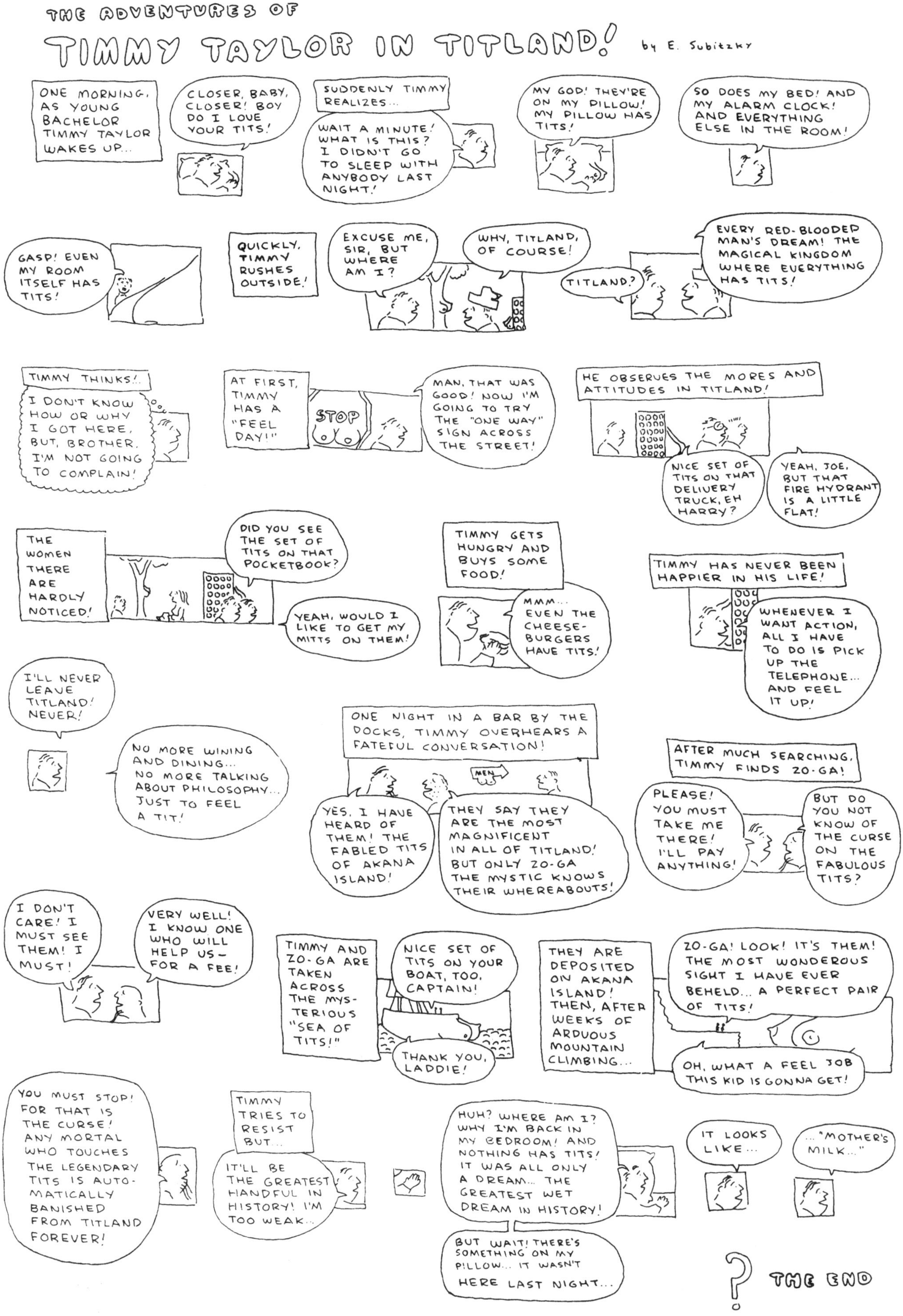
THE ADVENTURES OF
TIMMY TAYLOR IN TITLAND!
by E. Subitzky
ONE MORNING, AS YOUNG BACHELOR TIMMY TAYLOR WAKES UP...
CLOSER, BABY, CLOSER! BOY DO I LOVE YOUR TITS!
SUDDENLY TIMMY REALIZES...
WAIT A MINUTE! WHAT IS THIS? I DIDN'T GO TO SLEEP WITH ANYBODY LAST NIGHT!
MY GOD! THEY'RE ON MY PILLOW! MY PILLOW HAS TITS!
SO DOES MY BED! AND MY ALARM CLOCK! AND EVERYTHING ELSE IN THE ROOM!
GASP! EVEN MY ROOM ITSELF HAS TITS!
QUICKLY, TIMMY RUSHES OUTSIDE!
EXCUSE ME, SIR, BUT WHERE AM I?
WHY, TITLAND, OF COURSE!
TITLAND?
EVERY RED-BLOODED MAN'S DREAM! THE MAGICAL KINGDOM WHERE EVERYTHING HAS TITS!
TIMMY THINKS!
I DON'T KNOW HOW OR WHY I GOT HERE, BUT, BROTHER, I'M NOT GOING TO COMPLAIN!
AT FIRST, TIMMY HAS A "FEEL DAY!"
STOP
MAN, THAT WAS GOOD! NOW I'M GOING TO TRY THE "ONE WAY" SIGN ACROSS THE STREET!
HE OBSERVES THE MORES AND ATTITUDES IN TITLAND!
NICE SET OF TITS ON THAT DELIVERY TRUCK, EH HARRY?
YEAH, JOE, BUT THAT FIRE HYDRANT IS A LITTLE FLAT!
THE WOMEN THERE ARE HARDLY NOTICED!
DID YOU SEE THE SET OF TITS ON THAT POCKETBOOK?
YEAH, WOULD I LIKE TO GET MY MITTS ON THEM!
TIMMY GETS HUNGRY AND BUYS SOME FOOD!
MMM... EVEN THE CHEESE-BURGERS HAVE TITS!
TIMMY HAS NEVER BEEN HAPPIER IN HIS LIFE!
WHENEVER I WANT ACTION, ALL I HAVE TO DO IS PICK UP THE TELEPHONE... AND FEEL IT UP!
I'LL NEVER LEAVE TITLAND! NEVER!
NO MORE WINING AND DINING... NO MORE TALKING ABOUT PHILOSOPHY... JUST TO FEEL A TIT!
ONE NIGHT IN A BAR BY THE DOCKS, TIMMY OVERHEARS A FATEFUL CONVERSATION!
MEN
YES, I HAVE HEARD OF THEM! THE FABLED TITS OF AKANA ISLAND!
THEY SAY THEY ARE THE MOST MAGNIFICENT IN ALL OF TITLAND! BUT ONLY ZO-GA THE MYSTIC KNOWS THEIR WHEREABOUTS!
AFTER MUCH SEARCHING, TIMMY FINDS ZO-GA!
PLEASE! YOU MUST TAKE ME THERE! I'LL PAY ANYTHING!
BUT DO YOU NOT KNOW OF THE CURSE ON THE FABULOUS TITS?
I DON'T CARE! I MUST SEE THEM! I MUST!
VERY WELL! I KNOW ONE WHO WILL HELP US - FOR A FEE!
TIMMY AND ZO-GA ARE TAKEN ACROSS THE MYS-TERIOUS "SEA OF TITS!"
NICE SET OF TITS ON YOUR BOAT, TOO, CAPTAIN!
THANK YOU, LADDIE!
THEY ARE DEPOSITED ON AKANA ISLAND! THEN, AFTER WEEKS OF ARDUOUS MOUNTAIN CLIMBING...
ZO-GA! LOOK! IT'S THEM! THE MOST WONDEROUS SIGHT I HAVE EVER BEHELD... A PERFECT PAIR OF TITS!
OH, WHAT A FEEL JOB THIS KID IS GONNA GET!
YOU MUST STOP! FOR THAT IS THE CURSE! ANY MORTAL WHO TOUCHES THE LEGENDARY TITS IS AUTO-MATICALLY BANISHED FROM TITLAND FOREVER!
TIMMY TRIES TO RESIST BUT...
IT'LL BE THE GREATEST HANDFUL IN HISTORY! I'M TOO WEAK...
HUH? WHERE AM I? WHY I'M BACK IN MY BEDROOM! AND NOTHING HAS TITS! IT WAS ALL ONLY A DREAM... THE GREATEST WET DREAM IN HISTORY!
BUT WAIT! THERE'S SOMETHING ON MY PILLOW... IT WASN'T HERE LAST NIGHT...
IT LOOKS LIKE...
..."MOTHER'S MILK..."
?
THE END

TORTURE THE CHARACTERS COMICS!

BY ED SUBITZKY
COLORING: B. SCHUBECK

LETS YOU, THE READER, CHANGE PEOPLE'S DESTINIES AND RUIN LIVES!

DIRECTIONS: READ ONLY ONE BALLOON IN EACH PANEL! WHENEVER YOU WANT TO TEMPORARILY RAISE FALSE HOPES FOR THE CHARACTERS, READ THE YELLOW BALLOON IN A PANEL! WHENEVER YOU WANT TO PLUNGE THE CHARACTERS INTO DESPAIR, READ THE BLUE BALLOON IN A PANEL! AS YOU PROCEED ONWARD THROUGH STRIP, JUMP BACK AND FORTH BETWEEN YELLOW AND BLUE (HAPPINESS AND DESPAIR) AS MUCH AS YOU WANT, WHENEVER YOU WANT!

BOY, DO I FEEL GOOD! NOTHING LIKE A GOOD NIGHT'S SLEEP!
I DIDN'T SLEEP TOO WELL LAST NIGHT! HOPE I'M NOT COMING DOWN WITH THE FLU!
MY HOROSCOPE SAYS TODAY WILL BE ONE OF THE HAPPIEST DAYS OF MY LIFE!
HMM... MY HOROSCOPE SAYS, "BETTER LOOK BEHIND YOU TODAY!"
GEE, MAYBE I'LL FALL IN LOVE TODAY! I'VE ALWAYS WANTED TO FALL IN LOVE!
SHIT, I SHOULDN'T TAKE HOROSCOPES TOO SERIOUSLY, ANYWAY!
THE SUN IS OUT AND IT'S WARM! GREAT DAY FOR A WALK IN THE PARK!
THE SUN IS OUT, BUT IT'S FUCKING COLD FOR THIS TIME OF YEAR!
OH, LOOK! A TEN DOLLAR BILL! WOW!
DAMN IT! I STEPPED IN GREAT DANE SHIT!
I'M FAMISHED! WHY DON'T I EAT IN THAT CHARMING LITTLE CAFÉ!
I'M FAMISHED! THAT RESTAURANT LOOKS LIKE A DUMP, BUT I'LL HAVE TO TAKE MY CHANCES!
GOOD AFTERNOON, SIR! MAY I TAKE YOUR ORDER, IF YOU PLEASE!
WHAT'LL IT BE, MAC? COME ON! I AIN'T GOT ALL FUCKING DAY!
WHAT DO YOU KNOW! FOR THE REASONABLY LOW PRICE, THIS QUICHE IS REMARKABLY GOOD!
THIS LOUSY SWILL TASTES LIKE I THREW UP IN IT! MAYBE I ALREADY DID!
HMM... THAT GIRL OVER THERE IS CUTE, AND I'M POSITIVE SHE LOOKED MY WAY!
THAT GIRL OVER THERE IS CUTE, BUT SHE REFUSES TO EVEN GLANCE AT ME!
GOD, I COULD EVEN FALL IN LOVE WITH HER!
GOD, I COULD EVEN FALL IN LOVE WITH HER!
I'VE GOT TO MEET HER! EXCUSE ME, MISS...
I'VE GOT TO MEET HER! ER... AH... EXCUSE ME... ER, UM, MISS...
I WAS WONDERING... MAYHAP YOU WOULD LIKE TO ACCOMPANY ME TO THE ART MUSEUM ACROSS THE WAY?
I... ER... UM, THAT IS... UHH... MAYBE... ER... ART MUSEUM... ACROSS WAY... UH... UMMM... ER, THAT IS... WELL, I... I, UM, LIKE... YOU KNOW...
GOSH! I THINK I AM IN LOVE WITH HER! SHE'S SO WARM AND ALIVE!
GOSH! I THINK I AM IN LOVE WITH HER, BUT SHE LOOKS A LITTLE PALE!
I LOVE YOU! I KNOW I'VE ONLY KNOWN YOU FOR A FEW HOURS... BUT I LOVE YOU!
I LOVE YOU! I KNOW I'VE ONLY KNOWN YOU FOR A FEW HOURS... BUT DO YOUR HANDS ALWAYS TREMBLE THIS WAY?
I LOVE YOU, TOO! I TREMBLE WITH LOVE!
I LOVE YOU, TOO! GASP! I CAN'T BREATHE!
IMAGINE, SO MUCH IN LOVE YOU'RE EVEN BREATHLESS! LET'S GO RIGHT DOWN FOR OUR BLOOD TESTS AND BE MARRIED AT ONCE!
NOW YOU'RE TURNING BLUE! I BETTER GET YOU TO A DOCTOR!
I'M HAPPY TO TELL YOU THERE'S NOTHING WRONG! IN FACT, YOU SHOULD BOTH LIVE TO 100!
I'M SORRY, BUT SHE HAS AN INCURABLE FORM OF THE PLAGUE! BY BEING WITH HER, YOU HAVE IT, TOO! IN FACT, NOW I HAVE IT! WE'RE ALL GOING TO DIE!
WE INTERRUPT THIS PROGRAM FOR A SPECIAL ANNOUNCEMENT! AN UNEXPECTED CURE FOR THE RECENT PLAGUE HAS BEEN FOUND!
RADIO
WE INTERRUPT THIS PROGRAM FOR A SPECIAL ANNOUNCEMENT! A SUDDEN INCURABLE PLAGUE IS RAVISHING MILLIONS, AND ANYONE COULD CATCH IT AT ANY TIME!
I NOW PRONOUNCE YOU MAN AND WIFE!
ACCEPT THESE LAST RITES, MY CHILDREN! CURE OR NO CURE, YOU BOTH CAUGHT SUCH A SEVERE FORM OF THE PLAGUE THAT YOU'RE GOING TO DIE ALMOST AT ONCE! PEACE BE WITH YOU!
NEXT!
I'M SO GLAD THEY FOUND A CURE FOR EVEN THE SEVEREST FORM OF THE PLAGUE! NOW WE CAN HAVE A WORRY FREE HONEYMOON HERE IN HAWAII! I JUST HOPE-- HEH HEH-- WE HAVE SOME TIME BEFORE DINNER!
YIPES! WE BOTH CAUGHT A SPECIAL, INCURABLY SEVERE FORM OF THE PLAGUE! HOW MUCH TIME DO WE HAVE LEFT?
WE HAVE ABOUT TWO HOURS, DARLING!
WE HAVE ABOUT TEN MINUTES, DARLING!
IT CAN BE AN ETERNITY! LET'S MAKE THE MOST OF IT!
LET'S MAKE THE MOST OF WHAT LITTLE TIME IT IS!
O.K., MY LOVE! I'M READY!
WAIT! DID YOU HEAR SOMEONE SHOUT SOMETHING?
SIX O'CLOCK AND ALL IS WELL!
FIRE!
DARLING, I GOT SO HOT, BUT YOU MANAGED TO EXTINGUISH MY FLAMES PERFECTLY! NOW WHY DON'T WE HURRY OUT FOR A LAST DIP AT THE NEARBY BEACH! MAYBE WE'LL CATCH THE SUNSET!
LOOK! THE WHOLE PLACE IS ON FIRE!
BEAUTIFUL! LUCKY WE JUMPED DOWN INTO THIS SUNSET WATER AT JUST THE RIGHT MOMENT!
GASP! A SUDDEN, FRESH FIRE, AND WE'RE BEING ENGULFED BY THE FLAMES!
DARLING, LISTEN TO THAT ANNOUNCEMENT ON A DISTANT RADIO!
SCIENTISTS HAVE DISCOVERED AN AMAZING RAY THAT INSTANTLY CURES ALL DISEASES AND PLAGUES, EVEN THE SEVEREST, AND ALSO SOLVES THE WORLD'S FAMINE AND ENERGY PROBLEMS, AND ALSO PUTS OUT ALL FIRES AT ONCE! THE WORLD IS BEING BATHED IN THIS RAY NOW!
SCIENTISTS REPORT A SUDDEN SHIFT IN THE ORBIT OF THE SUN, AND PRAY THAT IT SETS NORMALLY TONIGHT!
LOOK, DARLING! THE SUN IS SETTING NOW! HOW BEAUTIFUL! I SUDDENLY FEEL SO CONTENT! YOU AND I MAY BE JUST TWO PEOPLE, BUT SOMEHOW I FEEL THIS IS THE START OF A GOLDEN AGE OF PEACE AND JOY FOR ALL MEN!
LOOK! THE SUN IS OUT OF ITS ORBIT AND APPROACHING US! IT'S NOT ONLY THE END OF US, BUT OF ALL LIFE ON EARTH!
THE END

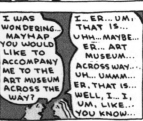

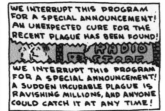

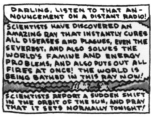

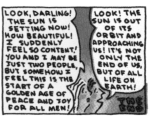

STRIPTEASE COMICS!

CIGARETTE?
HI THERE! LET'S MAKE IT!
OOOOOOOH! THAT'S GOOD!
I'M EXHAUSTED!
CIGARETTE?
HI THERE! LET'S MAKE IT!
O.K., BUT HURRY!
OOOOOOH! THAT'S GOOD!
I'M EXHAUSTED!
CIGARETTE?
HI THERE! LET'S MAKE IT!
O.K., BUT HURRY!
OOOOOOH! THAT'S GOOD!
I'M EXHAUSTED!
CIGARETTE?

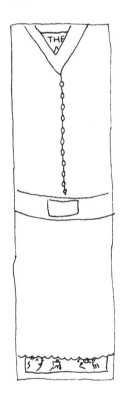

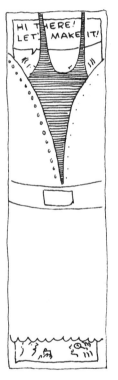

COINCIDENTAL JUXTAPOSITION COMICS!
GREAT WEATHER! GOOD DAY FOR A PIC-NIC ET I'D SAY!
WHY EVEN TO MY VAL- ET IT'S BEAUTIFUL!
EVEN SOMEONE NORMALLY AS NASTY AS DR. FU C MANCHU WOULD SMILE!
EVEN A COLLORATURA ORDINARILY KNOWN AS A HIGH C KING WOULD HIT HIGH A!
WELL THEN LET'S GRAB THE BULLS BY THE HORNS!
COME ON! WE'LL HIT THE BEACHES TOO!
MAYBE I CAN EVEN BORROW MA'S PRETTY BEACH BLANKET!
WE'LL GO WHERE THERE'S NOTHING TO DIS-TURB AT, I ON MY BLANKET AND YOU ON YOURS!
FAR OUT!
TO A T!
IT ALL SOUNDS AS EX-CITING AS CAN BE! WE'LL BUY SOD-AS!
IT WILL BE A TRULY UNUS-UAL AND PLEASANT AFTERNOON! BUT ITS LATE! O MY! WE'D BETTER HURRY!
THE END!

MN: What did you want to be when you grew up?

ES: Ah, a movie director! If you had asked eighteen-year-old me what I would be if I had a choice, I would have said a movie director. But I realized I don't have the talent or personality for that. As a kid I used to run around with a movie camera making monster movies. I would make my sister, brother, and grandmother wear masks and run around the yard like crazy, and I would film them and edit them like crazy.

But if you had asked me about number two, right behind movie director would have been cartoonist.

MN: You hit number two. That's pretty good.

CINEMA EAST
SCHEDULE

TITLES	9:37
"WELL, GOODNIGHT HELEN."	9:41
"'NIGHT, MARGE."	9:42
SCREAM	9:43
"WAIT A MINUTE, MARGE. DID YOU HEAR SOMETHING?"	9:44
"JUST THE WIND, I GUESS."	9:46
SCREAM	9:47
"THERE IT GOES AGAIN!"	9:49

CINEPLEX COMICS!

SIX DIFFERENT COMICS — BUT, FOR THE PRICE OF THIS MAGAZINE, YOU'RE ONLY ALLOWED TO READ ONE!

COMIC #1	COMIC #2	COMIC #3	COMIC #4	COMIC #5	COMIC #6
"BIFF AND BOFFO"	"FAMILY FROLICS"	"LIZARDER"	"WIFE OF MY LIFE"	"ALLISON ANDERSON"	"AND FRIES TO GO"

DUH! HEY, BIFF, HOW COME YOU CAN'T COMPARE APPLES AND ORANGES?	DAD, IS GOD A UNION MEMBER? 	THIS IS A HOLDUP, MAC! REACH! 	HONEY, HAVE YOU SEEN MY FAVORITE CHAIR? 	DARLING, MARRY ME NOW! 	THAT GUY COMES IN HERE EVERY DAY AND ORDERS A "NEW WORLD ORDER" SHAKE! 
I GIVE UP! HOW COME? 	WHY DO YOU ASK, SON? 	STOP OR I'LL LOWER YOUR BODY TEMPERATURE! 	I ACCIDENTALLY GAVE IT TO THE JUNK MAN! 	ARE YOU SURE IT'S NOT MY SISTER YOU'RE REALLY IN LOVE WITH? 	A NEW WORLD ORDER SHAKE? 
DUH! 	WELL, YOU ONCE TOL' ME THAT HE MAKES THE SNOWFLAKES... 	YOU CAUGHT THE CROOKS, LIZARDER! 	SO I GUESS IT'S IN THE CITY DUMP! 	DARLING, A MAN WITH AMNESIA CAN NEVER BE SURE OF ANYTHING! 	YES! EVERY FLAVOR KNOWN TO MANKIND... 
IT'S BECAUSE I ATE 'EM ALL! 	AN' HE TAKES THE SUMMER OFF! 	YES... BUT WAS IT TO HELP THE PUBLIC OR TO BE FED ANOTHER FLY? 	I HOPE IT LOOKS GOOD NEXT TO THE SOFA! 	WHAT IF I... IF I TOLD YOU WE'RE ALREADY MARRIED? 	BUT HOLD THE BROCCOLI! 

54

LAW OF THE UNIVERSE # 8,407

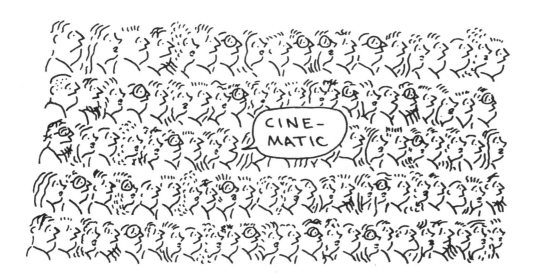

If you put enough people in a theatre lobby, sooner or later one of them will say the word "Cinematic".

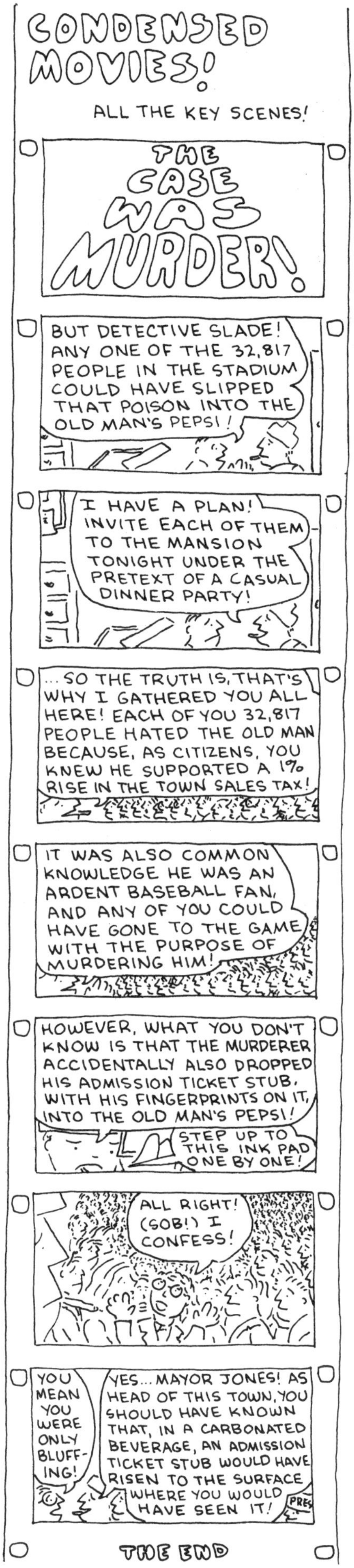
CONDENSED MOVIES!
ALL THE KEY SCENES!
THE CASE WAS MURDER!
BUT DETECTIVE SLADE! ANY ONE OF THE 32,817 PEOPLE IN THE STADIUM COULD HAVE SLIPPED THAT POISON INTO THE OLD MAN'S PEPSI!
I HAVE A PLAN! INVITE EACH OF THEM TO THE MANSION TONIGHT UNDER THE PRETEXT OF A CASUAL DINNER PARTY!
... SO THE TRUTH IS, THAT'S WHY I GATHERED YOU ALL HERE! EACH OF YOU 32,817 PEOPLE HATED THE OLD MAN BECAUSE, AS CITIZENS, YOU KNEW HE SUPPORTED A 1% RISE IN THE TOWN SALES TAX!
IT WAS ALSO COMMON KNOWLEDGE HE WAS AN ARDENT BASEBALL FAN, AND ANY OF YOU COULD HAVE GONE TO THE GAME WITH THE PURPOSE OF MURDERING HIM!
HOWEVER, WHAT YOU DON'T KNOW IS THAT THE MURDERER ACCIDENTALLY ALSO DROPPED HIS ADMISSION TICKET STUB, WITH HIS FINGERPRINTS ON IT, INTO THE OLD MAN'S PEPSI!
STEP UP TO THIS INK PAD ONE BY ONE!
ALL RIGHT! (SOB!) I CONFESS!
YOU MEAN YOU WERE ONLY BLUFF-ING!
YES... MAYOR JONES! AS HEAD OF THIS TOWN, YOU SHOULD HAVE KNOWN THAT, IN A CARBONATED BEVERAGE, AN ADMISSION TICKET STUB WOULD HAVE RISEN TO THE SURFACE WHERE YOU WOULD HAVE SEEN IT!
THE END

BEING AT THE MOVIES COMICS!

BY ED SUBITZKY

JUST LIKE A REAL EVENING OUT – COMPLETE WITH PEOPLE WHO SIT IN FRONT OF YOU SO YOU CAN'T SEE AND TALK SO YOU CAN'T HEAR!

INSTRUCTIONS: SIMPLY TAKE YOUR SEAT! THE MOVIE'S ABOUT TO BEGIN!

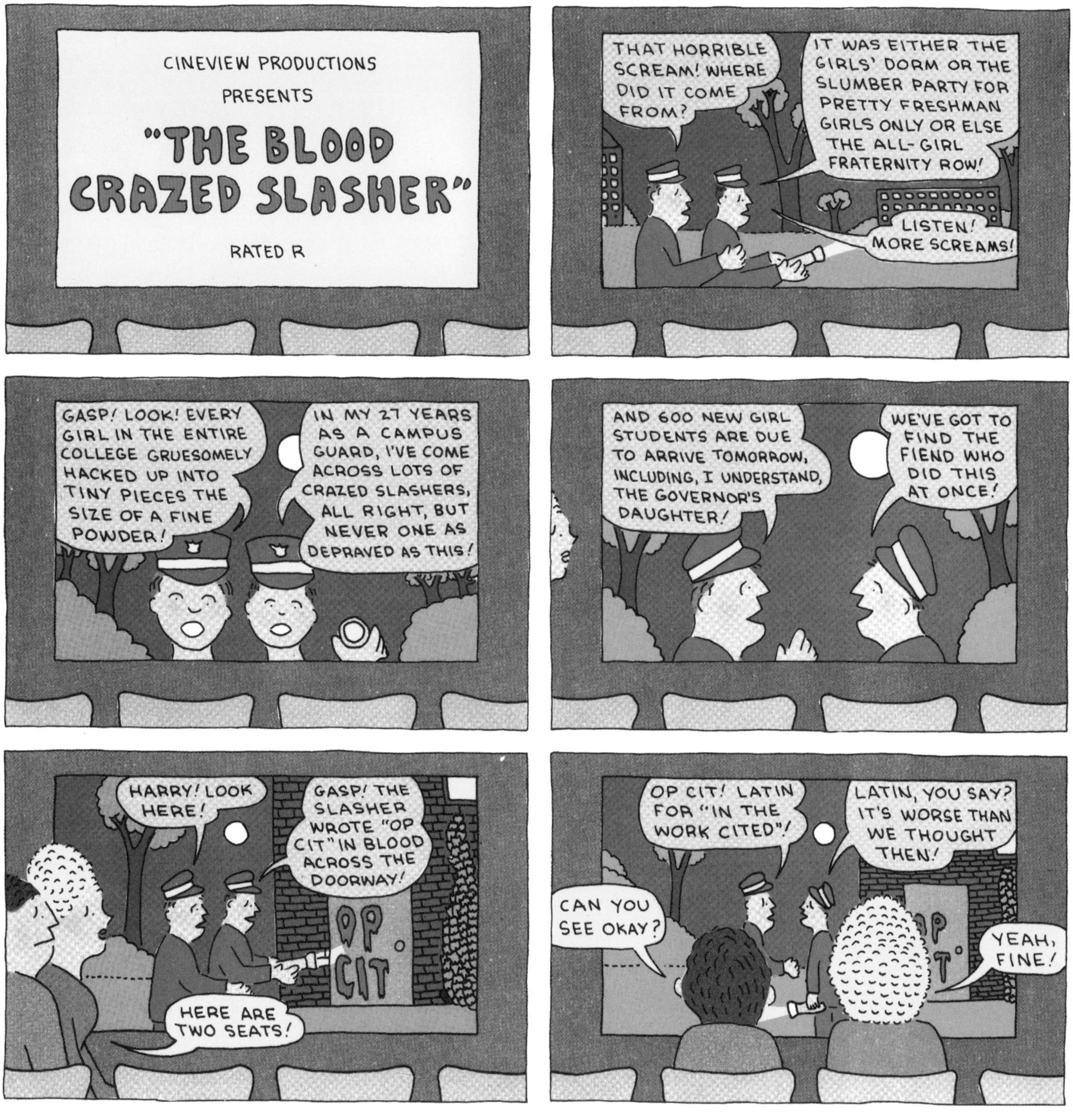

CINEVIEW PRODUCTIONS
PRESENTS
"THE BLOOD CRAZED SLASHER"
RATED R
THAT HORRIBLE SCREAM! WHERE DID IT COME FROM?
IT WAS EITHER THE GIRLS' DORM OR THE SLUMBER PARTY FOR PRETTY FRESHMAN GIRLS ONLY OR ELSE THE ALL-GIRL FRATERNITY ROW!
LISTEN! MORE SCREAMS!
GASP! LOOK! EVERY GIRL IN THE ENTIRE COLLEGE GRUESOMELY HACKED UP INTO TINY PIECES THE SIZE OF A FINE POWDER!
IN MY 27 YEARS AS A CAMPUS GUARD, I'VE COME ACROSS LOTS OF CRAZED SLASHERS, ALL RIGHT, BUT NEVER ONE AS DEPRAVED AS THIS!
AND 600 NEW GIRL STUDENTS ARE DUE TO ARRIVE TOMORROW, INCLUDING, I UNDERSTAND, THE GOVERNOR'S DAUGHTER!
WE'VE GOT TO FIND THE FIEND WHO DID THIS AT ONCE!
HARRY! LOOK HERE!
GASP! THE SLASHER WROTE "OP CIT" IN BLOOD ACROSS THE DOORWAY!
OP CIT
HERE ARE TWO SEATS!
OP CIT! LATIN FOR "IN THE WORK CITED"!
LATIN, YOU SAY? IT'S WORSE THAN WE THOUGHT THEN!
CAN YOU SEE OKAY?
YEAH, FINE!

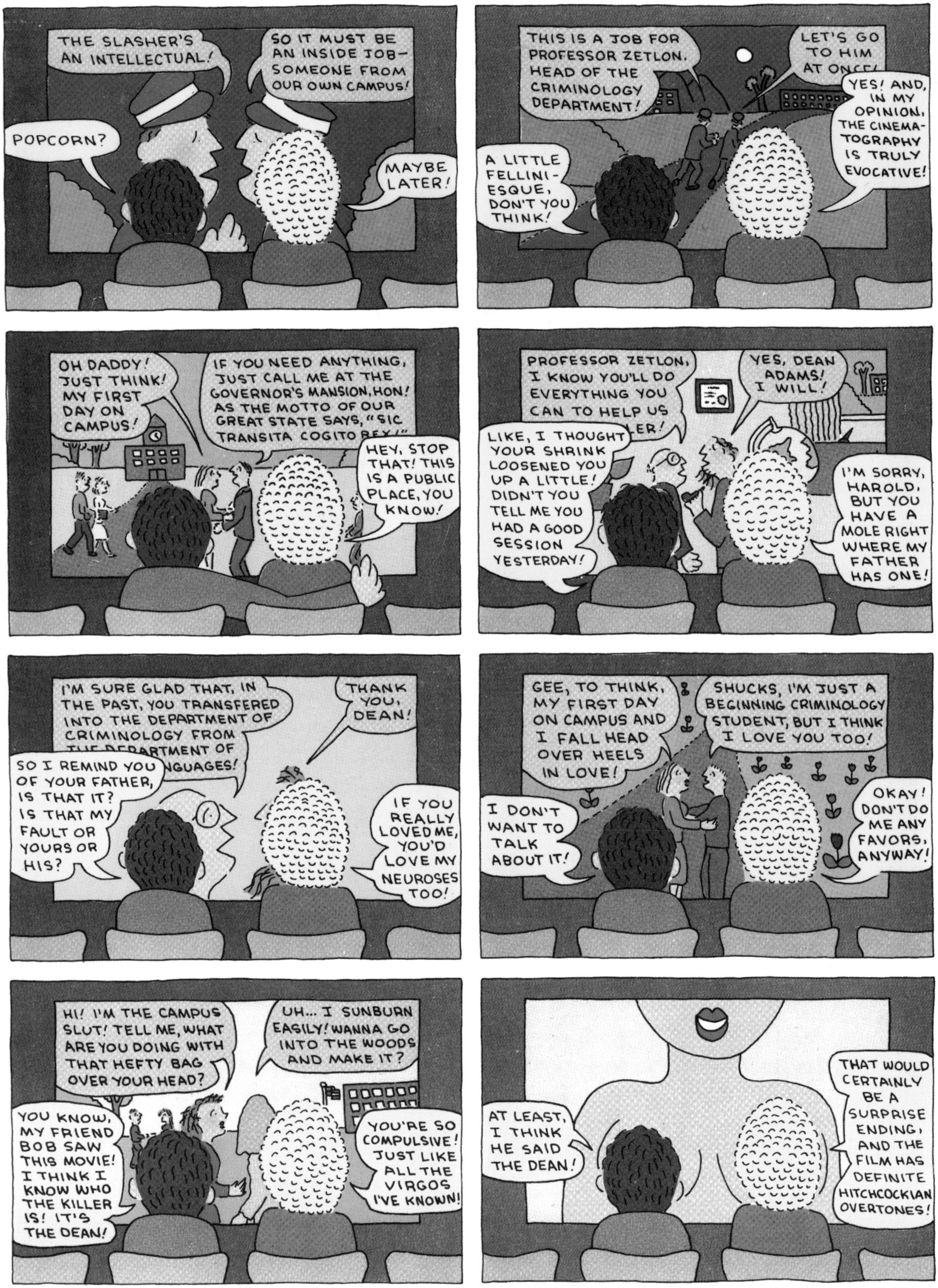
THE SLASHER'S AN INTELLECTUAL!
SO IT MUST BE AN INSIDE JOB— SOMEONE FROM OUR OWN CAMPUS!
POPCORN?
MAYBE LATER!
THIS IS A JOB FOR PROFESSOR ZETLON, HEAD OF THE CRIMINOLOGY DEPARTMENT!
LET'S GO TO HIM AT ONC
A LITTLE FELLINI-ESQUE, DON'T YOU THINK!
YES! AND, IN MY OPINION, THE CINEMATOGRAPHY IS TRULY EVOCATIVE!
OH DADDY! JUST THINK! MY FIRST DAY ON CAMPUS!
IF YOU NEED ANYTHING, JUST CALL ME AT THE GOVERNOR'S MANSION, HON! AS THE MOTTO OF OUR GREAT STATE SAYS, "SIC TRANSITA COGITO REX!"
HEY, STOP THAT! THIS IS A PUBLIC PLACE, YOU KNOW!
PROFESSOR ZETLON, I KNOW YOU'LL DO EVERYTHING YOU CAN TO HELP US
LER!
YES, DEAN ADAMS! I WILL!
LIKE, I THOUGHT YOUR SHRINK LOOSENED YOU UP A LITTLE! DIDN'T YOU TELL ME YOU HAD A GOOD SESSION YESTERDAY!
I'M SORRY, HAROLD, BUT YOU HAVE A MOLE RIGHT WHERE MY FATHER HAS ONE!
I'M SURE GLAD THAT, IN THE PAST, YOU TRANSFERED INTO THE DEPARTMENT OF CRIMINOLOGY FROM
NGUAGES!
THANK YOU, DEAN!
SO I REMIND YOU OF YOUR FATHER, IS THAT IT? IS THAT MY FAULT OR YOURS OR HIS?
IF YOU REALLY LOVED ME, YOU'D LOVE MY NEUROSES TOO!
GEE, TO THINK, MY FIRST DAY ON CAMPUS AND I FALL HEAD OVER HEELS IN LOVE!
SHUCKS, I'M JUST A BEGINNING CRIMINOLOGY STUDENT, BUT I THINK I LOVE YOU TOO!
I DON'T WANT TO TALK ABOUT IT!
OKAY! DON'T DO ME ANY FAVORS, ANYWAY!
HI! I'M THE CAMPUS SLUT! TELL ME, WHAT ARE YOU DOING WITH THAT HEFTY BAG OVER YOUR HEAD?
UH... I SUNBURN EASILY! WANNA GO INTO THE WOODS AND MAKE IT?
YOU KNOW, MY FRIEND BOB SAW THIS MOVIE! I THINK I KNOW WHO THE KILLER IS! IT'S THE DEAN!
YOU'RE SO COMPULSIVE! JUST LIKE ALL THE VIRGOS I'VE KNOWN!
AT LEAST, I THINK HE SAID THE DEAN!
THAT WOULD CERTAINLY BE A SURPRISE ENDING, AND THE FILM HAS DEFINITE HITCHCOCKIAN OVERTONES!

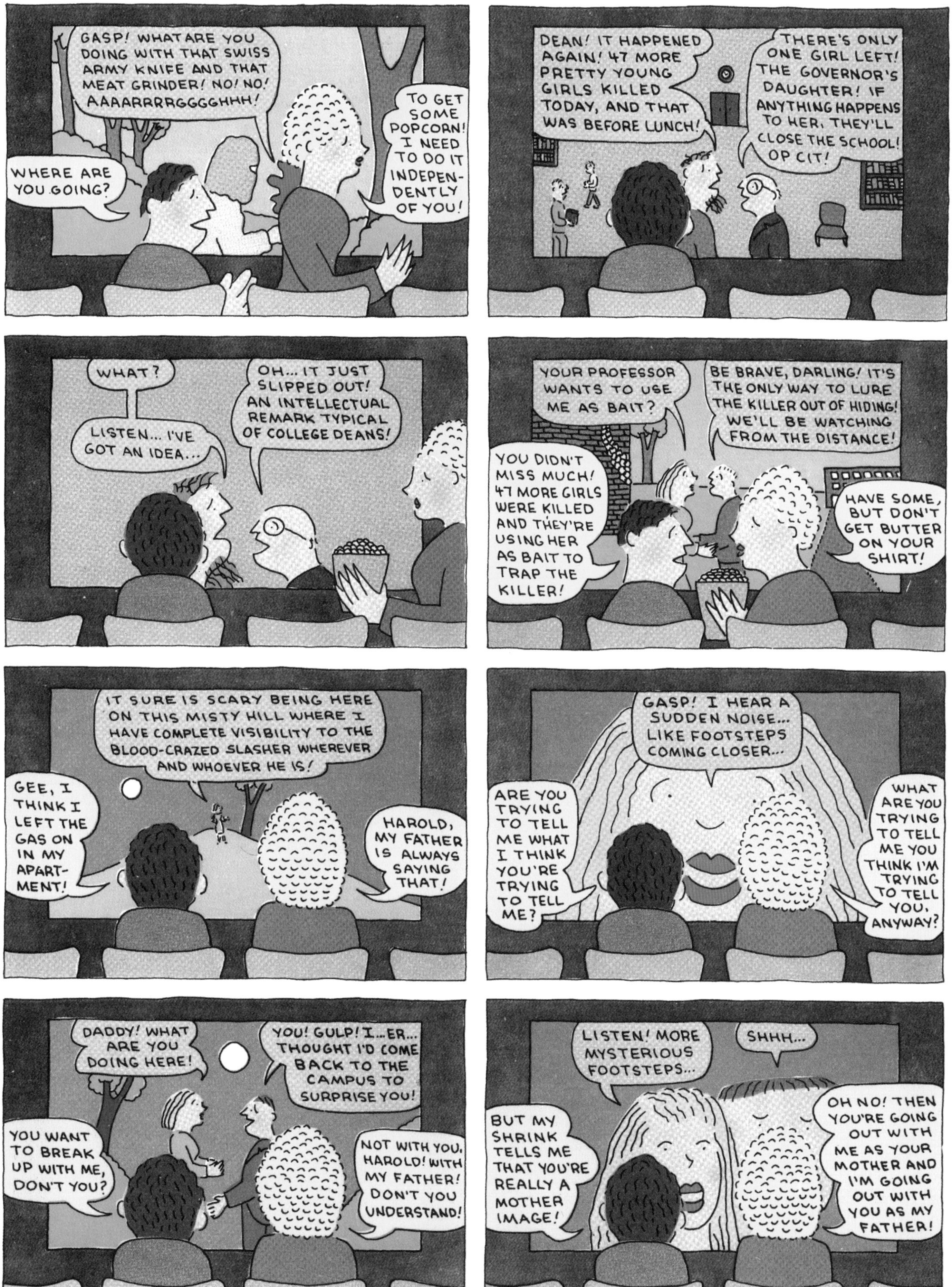
GASP! WHAT ARE YOU DOING WITH THAT SWISS ARMY KNIFE AND THAT MEAT GRINDER! NO! NO! AAAARRRRGGGGHHH!
WHERE ARE YOU GOING?
TO GET SOME POPCORN! I NEED TO DO IT INDEPENDENTLY OF YOU!
DEAN! IT HAPPENED AGAIN! 47 MORE PRETTY YOUNG GIRLS KILLED TODAY, AND THAT WAS BEFORE LUNCH!
THERE'S ONLY ONE GIRL LEFT! THE GOVERNOR'S DAUGHTER! IF ANYTHING HAPPENS TO HER, THEY'LL CLOSE THE SCHOOL! OP CIT!
WHAT?
LISTEN... I'VE GOT AN IDEA...
OH... IT JUST SLIPPED OUT! AN INTELLECTUAL REMARK TYPICAL OF COLLEGE DEANS!
YOUR PROFESSOR WANTS TO USE ME AS BAIT?
BE BRAVE, DARLING! IT'S THE ONLY WAY TO LURE THE KILLER OUT OF HIDING! WE'LL BE WATCHING FROM THE DISTANCE!
YOU DIDN'T MISS MUCH! 47 MORE GIRLS WERE KILLED AND THEY'RE USING HER AS BAIT TO TRAP THE KILLER!
HAVE SOME, BUT DON'T GET BUTTER ON YOUR SHIRT!
IT SURE IS SCARY BEING HERE ON THIS MISTY HILL WHERE I HAVE COMPLETE VISIBILITY TO THE BLOOD-CRAZED SLASHER WHEREVER AND WHOEVER HE IS!
GEE, I THINK I LEFT THE GAS ON IN MY APARTMENT!
HAROLD, MY FATHER IS ALWAYS SAYING THAT!
GASP! I HEAR A SUDDEN NOISE... LIKE FOOTSTEPS COMING CLOSER...
ARE YOU TRYING TO TELL ME WHAT I THINK YOU'RE TRYING TO TELL ME?
WHAT ARE YOU TRYING TO TELL ME YOU THINK I'M TRYING TO TELL YOU, ANYWAY?
DADDY! WHAT ARE YOU DOING HERE!
YOU! GULP! I...ER... THOUGHT I'D COME BACK TO THE CAMPUS TO SURPRISE YOU!
YOU WANT TO BREAK UP WITH ME, DON'T YOU?
NOT WITH YOU, HAROLD! WITH MY FATHER! DON'T YOU UNDERSTAND!
LISTEN! MORE MYSTERIOUS FOOTSTEPS...
SHHH...
BUT MY SHRINK TELLS ME THAT YOU'RE REALLY A MOTHER IMAGE!
OH NO! THEN YOU'RE GOING OUT WITH ME AS YOUR MOTHER AND I'M GOING OUT WITH YOU AS MY FATHER!

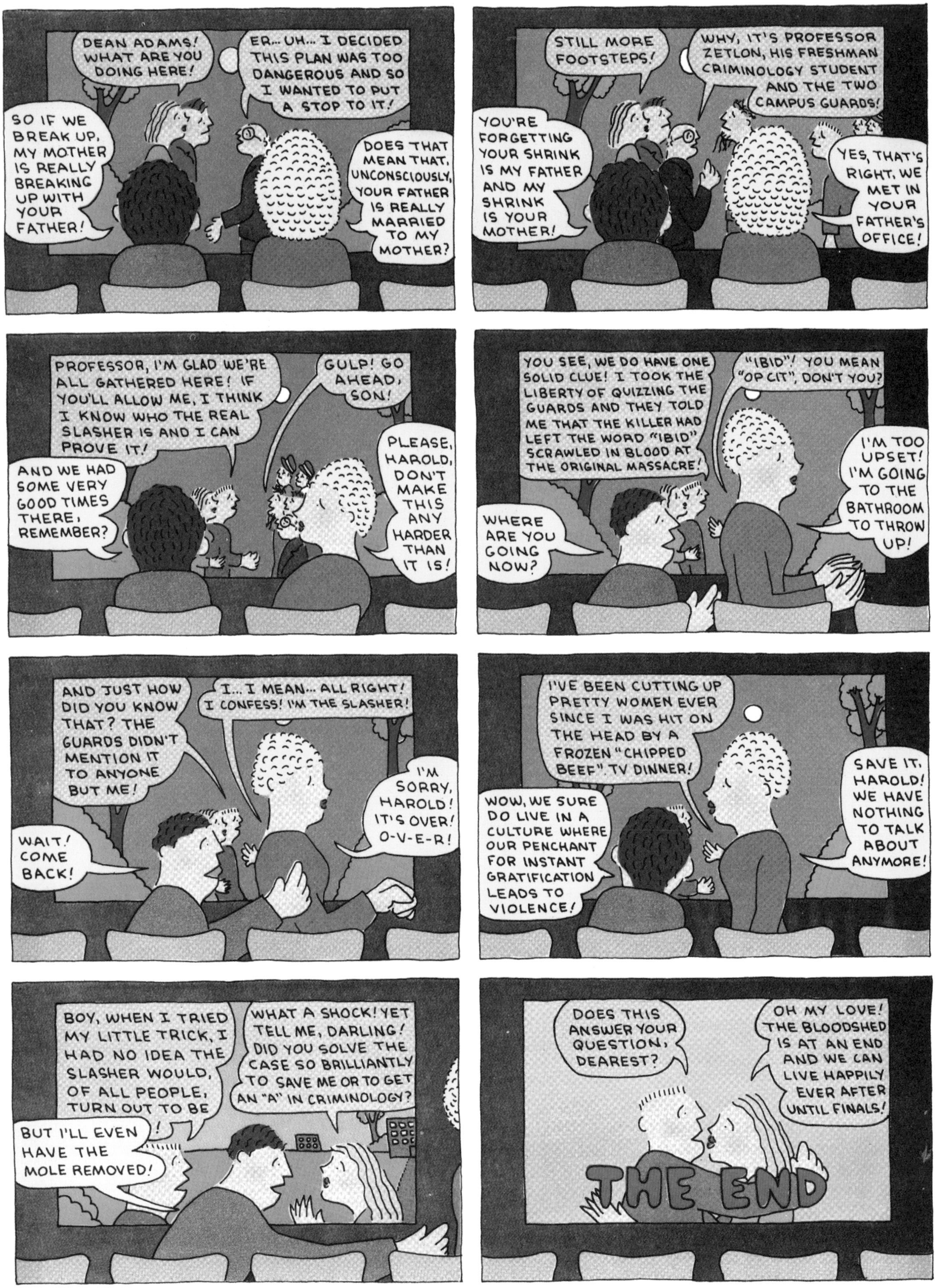
DEAN ADAMS! WHAT ARE YOU DOING HERE!
ER... UH... I DECIDED THIS PLAN WAS TOO DANGEROUS AND SO I WANTED TO PUT A STOP TO IT!
SO IF WE BREAK UP, MY MOTHER IS REALLY BREAKING UP WITH YOUR FATHER!
DOES THAT MEAN THAT, UNCONSCIOUSLY, YOUR FATHER IS REALLY MARRIED TO MY MOTHER?
STILL MORE FOOTSTEPS!
WHY, IT'S PROFESSOR ZETLON, HIS FRESHMAN CRIMINOLOGY STUDENT AND THE TWO CAMPUS GUARDS!
YOU'RE FORGETTING YOUR SHRINK IS MY FATHER AND MY SHRINK IS YOUR MOTHER!
YES, THAT'S RIGHT, WE MET IN YOUR FATHER'S OFFICE!
PROFESSOR, I'M GLAD WE'RE ALL GATHERED HERE! IF YOU'LL ALLOW ME, I THINK I KNOW WHO THE REAL SLASHER IS AND I CAN PROVE IT!
GULP! GO AHEAD, SON!
AND WE HAD SOME VERY GOOD TIMES THERE, REMEMBER?
PLEASE, HAROLD, DON'T MAKE THIS ANY HARDER THAN IT IS!
YOU SEE, WE DO HAVE ONE SOLID CLUE! I TOOK THE LIBERTY OF QUIZZING THE GUARDS AND THEY TOLD ME THAT THE KILLER HAD LEFT THE WORD "IBID" SCRAWLED IN BLOOD AT THE ORIGINAL MASSACRE!
"IBID"! YOU MEAN "OP CIT", DON'T YOU?
WHERE ARE YOU GOING NOW?
I'M TOO UPSET! I'M GOING TO THE BATHROOM TO THROW UP!
AND JUST HOW DID YOU KNOW THAT? THE GUARDS DIDN'T MENTION IT TO ANYONE BUT ME!
I... I MEAN... ALL RIGHT! I CONFESS! I'M THE SLASHER!
WAIT! COME BACK!
I'M SORRY, HAROLD! IT'S OVER! O-V-E-R!
I'VE BEEN CUTTING UP PRETTY WOMEN EVER SINCE I WAS HIT ON THE HEAD BY A FROZEN "CHIPPED BEEF" TV DINNER!
WOW, WE SURE DO LIVE IN A CULTURE WHERE OUR PENCHANT FOR INSTANT GRATIFICATION LEADS TO VIOLENCE!
SAVE IT, HAROLD! WE HAVE NOTHING TO TALK ABOUT ANYMORE!
BOY, WHEN I TRIED MY LITTLE TRICK, I HAD NO IDEA THE SLASHER WOULD, OF ALL PEOPLE, TURN OUT TO BE !
WHAT A SHOCK! YET TELL ME, DARLING! DID YOU SOLVE THE CASE SO BRILLIANTLY TO SAVE ME OR TO GET AN "A" IN CRIMINOLOGY?
BUT I'LL EVEN HAVE THE MOLE REMOVED!
DOES THIS ANSWER YOUR QUESTION, DEAREST?
OH MY LOVE! THE BLOODSHED IS AT AN END AND WE CAN LIVE HAPPILY EVER AFTER UNTIL FINALS!
THE END

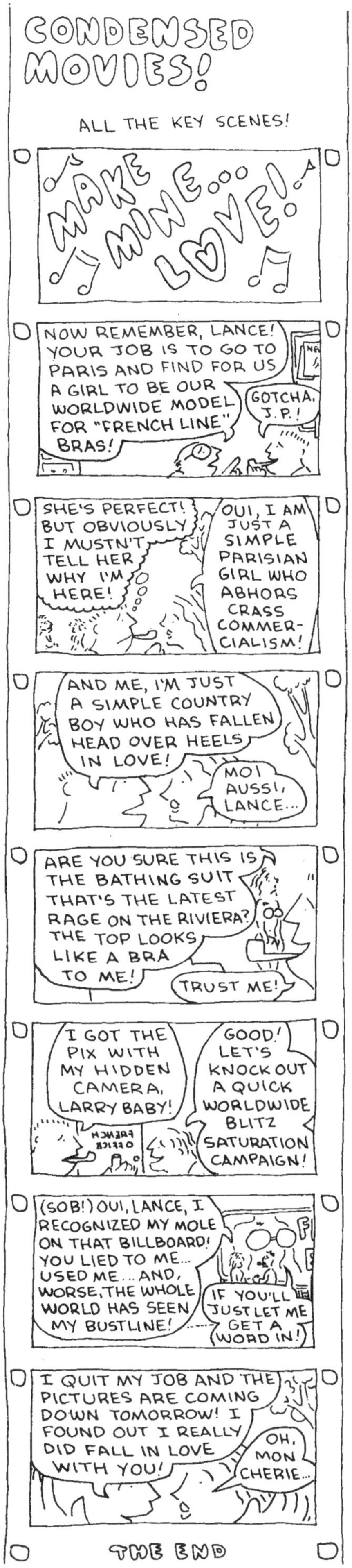
CONDENSED MOVIES!
ALL THE KEY SCENES!
MAKE MINE... LOVE!
NOW REMEMBER, LANCE! YOUR JOB IS TO GO TO PARIS AND FIND FOR US A GIRL TO BE OUR WORLDWIDE MODEL FOR "FRENCH LINE" BRAS!
GOTCHA, J.P.!
SHE'S PERFECT! BUT OBVIOUSLY I MUSTN'T TELL HER WHY I'M HERE!
OUI, I AM JUST A SIMPLE PARISIAN GIRL WHO ABHORS CRASS COMMERCIALISM!
AND ME, I'M JUST A SIMPLE COUNTRY BOY WHO HAS FALLEN HEAD OVER HEELS IN LOVE!
MOI AUSSI, LANCE...
ARE YOU SURE THIS IS THE BATHING SUIT THAT'S THE LATEST RAGE ON THE RIVIERA? THE TOP LOOKS LIKE A BRA TO ME!
TRUST ME!
I GOT THE PIX WITH MY HIDDEN CAMERA, LARRY BABY!
GOOD! LET'S KNOCK OUT A QUICK WORLDWIDE BLITZ SATURATION CAMPAIGN!
(SOB!) OUI, LANCE, I RECOGNIZED MY MOLE ON THAT BILLBOARD! YOU LIED TO ME... USED ME... AND, WORSE, THE WHOLE WORLD HAS SEEN MY BUSTLINE!
IF YOU'LL JUST LET ME GET A WORD IN!
I QUIT MY JOB AND THE PICTURES ARE COMING DOWN TOMORROW! I FOUND OUT I REALLY DID FALL IN LOVE WITH YOU!
OH, MON CHERIE...
THE END

"Don't you just hate it when the screen breaks?"

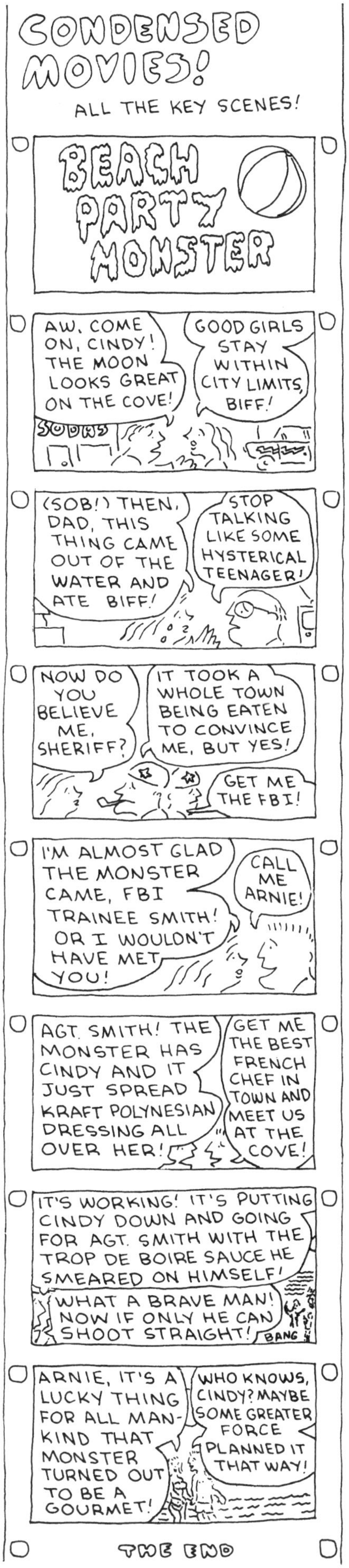
CONDENSED MOVIES!
ALL THE KEY SCENES!
BEACH PARTY MONSTER
AW, COME ON, CINDY! THE MOON LOOKS GREAT ON THE COVE!
GOOD GIRLS STAY WITHIN CITY LIMITS, BIFF!
SODAS
(SOB!) THEN, DAD, THIS THING CAME OUT OF THE WATER AND ATE BIFF!
STOP TALKING LIKE SOME HYSTERICAL TEENAGER!
NOW DO YOU BELIEVE ME, SHERIFF?
IT TOOK A WHOLE TOWN BEING EATEN TO CONVINCE ME, BUT YES!
GET ME THE FBI!
I'M ALMOST GLAD THE MONSTER CAME, FBI TRAINEE SMITH! OR I WOULDN'T HAVE MET YOU!
CALL ME ARNIE!
AGT. SMITH! THE MONSTER HAS CINDY AND IT JUST SPREAD KRAFT POLYNESIAN DRESSING ALL OVER HER!
GET ME THE BEST FRENCH CHEF IN TOWN AND MEET US AT THE COVE!
IT'S WORKING! IT'S PUTTING CINDY DOWN AND GOING FOR AGT. SMITH WITH THE TROP DE BOIRE SAUCE HE SMEARED ON HIMSELF!
WHAT A BRAVE MAN! NOW IF ONLY HE CAN SHOOT STRAIGHT!
BANG
ARNIE, IT'S A LUCKY THING FOR ALL MAN-KIND THAT MONSTER TURNED OUT TO BE A GOURMET!
WHO KNOWS, CINDY? MAYBE SOME GREATER FORCE PLANNED IT THAT WAY!
THE END

COME·IN·IN·THE·MIDDLE COMICS! JUST LIKE THE MOVIES!

Panel 1

THAT'S SURE A LOT OF SUSPECTS, INSPECTOR DODDS! I SUPPOSE THAT PRETTY MAID OVER THERE HATED HIM, TOO! GOSH, I THINK I'M FALLING IN LOVE WITH HER!

EASY, BOY! HER RAIN-WET FOOTSTEPS LEAD RIGHT INTO THE DEAD MAN'S ROOM!

NO! SOB! NO!

Panel 2

TELL ME, MAID LIZZIE, YOU DON'T DENY YOU WEAR SIZE 8½ SHOES WITH SMALL STILETTO HEELS AND HAVE A WALK THAT PUTS EXTRA PRESSURE ON THE BIG TOE?

I DON'T DENY I HATED THE OLD MAN, ALTHOUGH MY RELIGIOUS NATURE FORBIDS ME TO HATE ANOTHER HUMAN BEING! BUT I SWEAR I WAS ONLY BRINGING THE OLD MAN HIS TEA! I DIDN'T KNOW HE WAS DEAD!

Panel 3

INSPECTOR, YOU'VE GOT TO CLEAR HER AND FIND THE REAL CRIMINAL! PERSONALLY, I'D QUESTION THE BUTLER AGAIN! MAYBE HE WAS TRYING TO THROW US OFF!

I'M INNOCENT! I SWEAR IT! I SWEAR!

Panel 4

QUIET! ALL OF YOU, QUIET!

BILLIONS OF SUSPECTS... THE FOUL RED TORCH OF HATRED... AND NOW THE PURE BRIGHT FLAME OF YOUNG LOVE! WHAT BETTER WAY TO ECLIPSE THE SILVER THREAD OF RATIONAL DEDUCTION!

I MUST THINK! I MUST THINK!

I WANT TO EXAMINE THE BODY!

Panel 5

WHY, LOOK! THE BODY HAS FINGERPRINTS ON IT! AND THEY'RE MINE!

SO WHAT'S SO UNUSUAL ABOUT THAT, SIR?

I HAVEN'T TOUCHED THE BODY YET!

Panel 6

THAT'S IT! THAT'S IT! UNCONSCIOUSLY, I MUST HAVE REALIZED THAT, IF WE DIDN'T GET ANOTHER MURDER CASE SOON, BECAUSE OF THE BUDGET CUTS, SCOTLAND YARD WOULD BE DISBANDED! SO I KILLED HIM MYSELF!

I NOW ARREST MYSELF FOR THE MURDER OF OLD MAN HAVERTHEN! TAKE ME AWAY!

Panel 7

I FACE THE GALLOWS, BUT SCOTLAND YARD WILL GO ON IN ITS GRAND TRADITIONS!

AND YOU'LL DIE KNOWING YOU LEFT US FREE TO MARRY AND FIND A LIFETIME OF HAPPINESS!

THE END

Panel 8

"TOO MANY SUSPECTS"

Panel 9

OUR STORY BEGINS ON A QUIET, RAINY AFTERNOON IN SCOTLAND YARD...

JOLLY ODD SITUATION, EH WHAT, APPRENTICE DRAKE! WE HAVEN'T HAD A MURDER CASE IN MONTHS!

CALL FOR YOU, INSPECTOR DODDS!

NEWS BUDGET CUT AGAIN!

Panel 10

WHAT'S THAT YOU SAY? OLD BILLIONAIRE HAVERTHEN DEAD? AND HE WAS IN PERFECT HEALTH WITH STRANGULATION MARKS AROUND HIS THROAT? WE'LL BE RIGHT OVER!

Panel 11

AT THE MURDERED BILLIONAIRE'S HUGE ESTATE...

NOW TELL ME, BUTLER JEEVES... DID ANYONE HAVE ANY MOTIVE FOR HATING THE OLD MAN?

MOTIVE?

Panel 12

HE WAS A CRUEL SLAVE DRIVER, AND ALL OF US SERVANTS HATED HIM! WHAT'S MORE, HE DESTROYED THIS TOWN AND ALL THE CITIZENS HATED HIM! IN HIS INTERNATIONAL DEALINGS, HE BROUGHT RUIN EVERYWHERE AND EVERY MAN, WOMAN AND CHILD ON EARTH HATED HIM! HE WAS CRUEL TO ANIMALS AND THEY ALL HATED HIM! HE EVEN GOT HIS KICKS BY SENDING OBSCENE RADIO MESSAGES INTO OUTER SPACE! THERE ISN'T A LIVING THING IN THE UNIVERSE THAT DIDN'T WANT HIM DEAD!

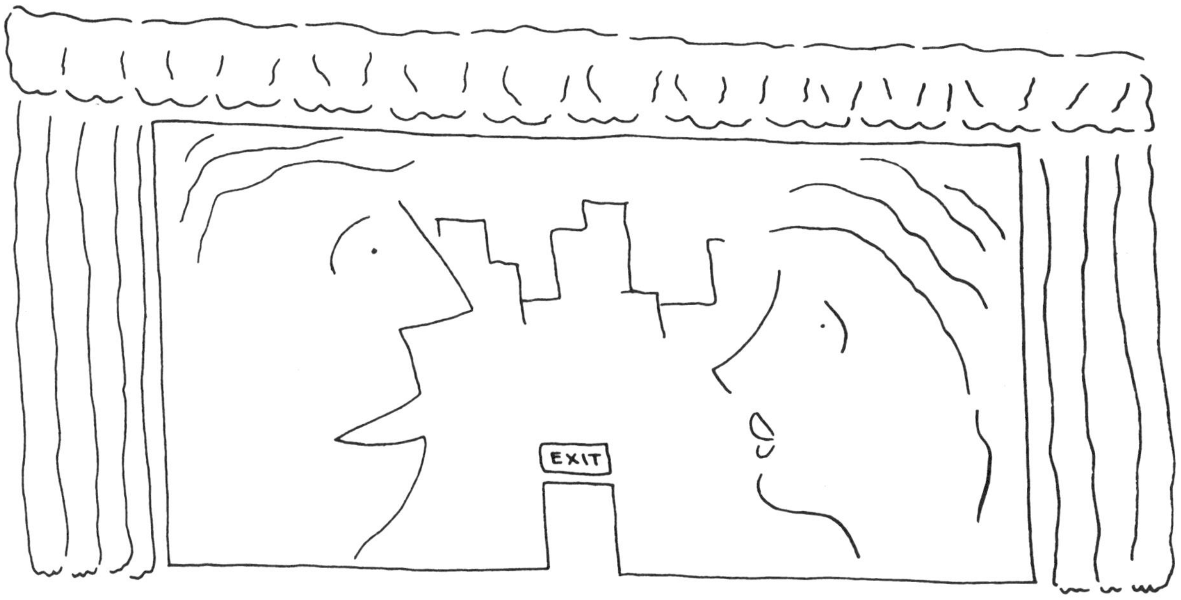
EXIT

POOR RECEPTION COMICS! JUST LIKE TV!

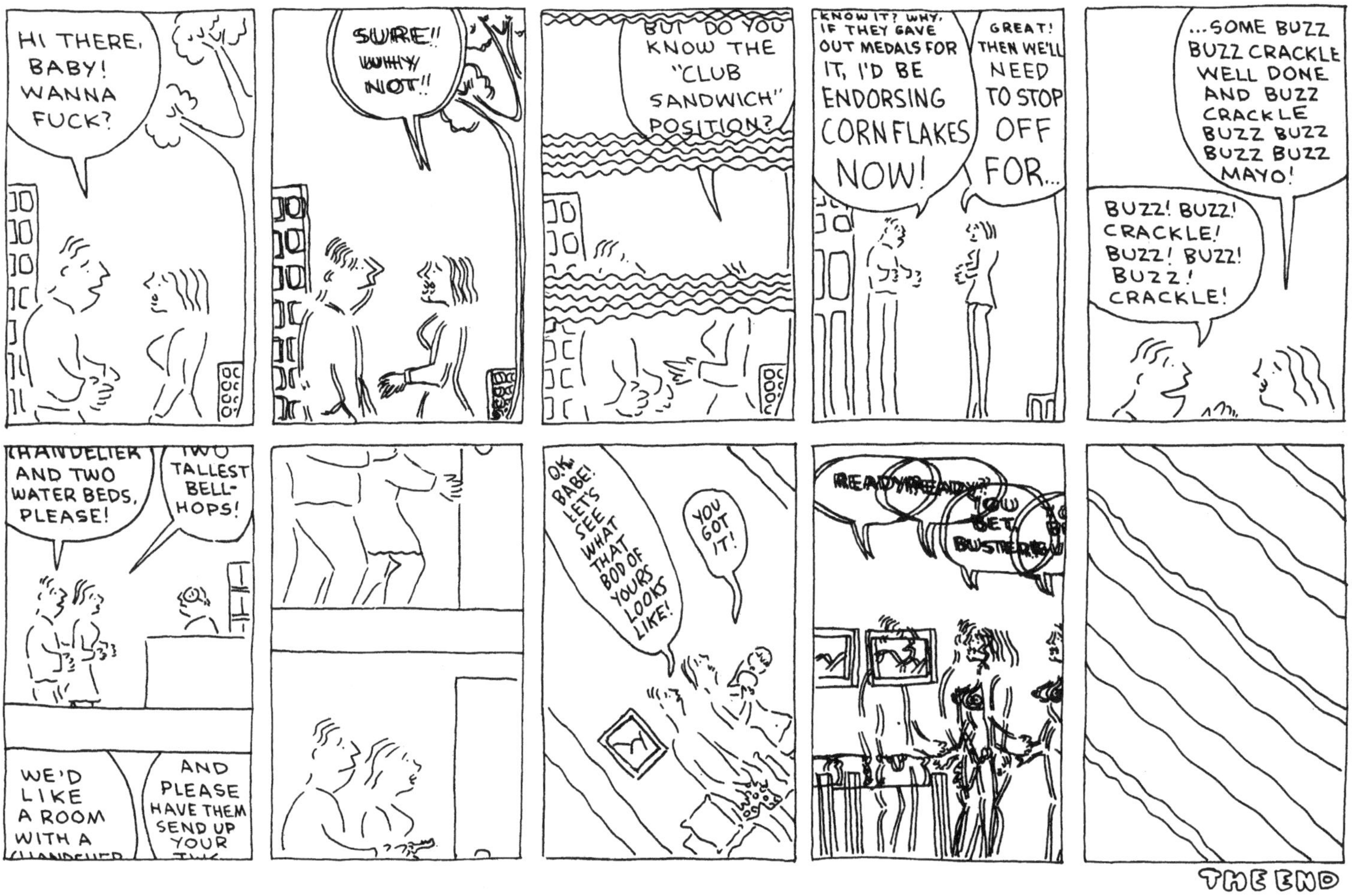
HI THERE, BABY! WANNA FUCK?
SURE!! WHY NOT!!
BUT DO YOU KNOW THE "CLUB SANDWICH" POSITION?
KNOW IT? WHY, IF THEY GAVE OUT MEDALS FOR IT, I'D BE ENDORSING CORNFLAKES NOW!
GREAT! THEN WE'LL NEED TO STOP OFF FOR...
...SOME BUZZ BUZZ CRACKLE WELL DONE AND BUZZ CRACKLE BUZZ BUZZ BUZZ BUZZ MAYO!
BUZZ! BUZZ! CRACKLE! BUZZ! BUZZ! BUZZ! CRACKLE!
CHANDELIER AND TWO WATER BEDS, PLEASE!
TWO TALLEST BELL-HOPS!
WE'D LIKE A ROOM WITH A
AND PLEASE HAVE THEM SEND UP YOUR
O.K. BABE! LET'S SEE WHAT THAT BOD OF YOURS LOOKS LIKE!
YOU GOT IT!
READY! READY?
YOU BET, BUSTER!
THE END

CONFESSIONS OF A HI-FI NEOPHYTE

WHO GREW UP TOO SOON!

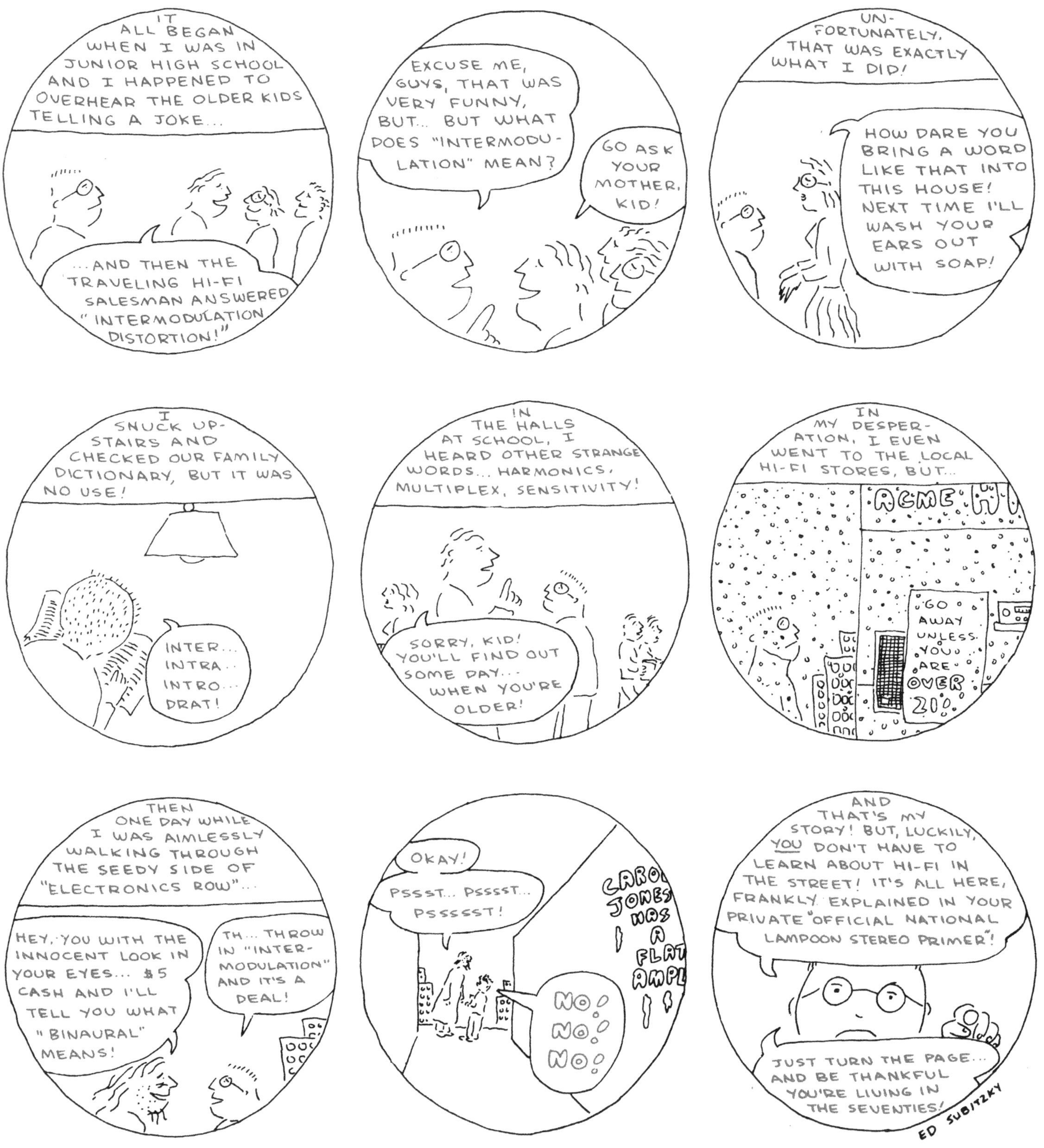

IT ALL BEGAN WHEN I WAS IN JUNIOR HIGH SCHOOL AND I HAPPENED TO OVERHEAR THE OLDER KIDS TELLING A JOKE...
...AND THEN THE TRAVELING HI-FI SALESMAN ANSWERED "INTERMODULATION DISTORTION!"
EXCUSE ME, GUYS, THAT WAS VERY FUNNY, BUT... BUT WHAT DOES "INTERMODULATION" MEAN?
GO ASK YOUR MOTHER, KID!
UN-FORTUNATELY, THAT WAS EXACTLY WHAT I DID!
HOW DARE YOU BRING A WORD LIKE THAT INTO THIS HOUSE! NEXT TIME I'LL WASH YOUR EARS OUT WITH SOAP!
I SNUCK UP-STAIRS AND CHECKED OUR FAMILY DICTIONARY, BUT IT WAS NO USE!
INTER... INTRA... INTRO... DRAT!
IN THE HALLS AT SCHOOL, I HEARD OTHER STRANGE WORDS... HARMONICS, MULTIPLEX, SENSITIVITY!
SORRY, KID! YOU'LL FIND OUT SOME DAY... WHEN YOU'RE OLDER!
IN MY DESPER-ATION, I EVEN WENT TO THE LOCAL HI-FI STORES, BUT...
ACME HI
GO AWAY UNLESS YOU ARE OVER 21
THEN ONE DAY WHILE I WAS AIMLESSLY WALKING THROUGH THE SEEDY SIDE OF "ELECTRONICS ROW"...
HEY, YOU WITH THE INNOCENT LOOK IN YOUR EYES... $5 CASH AND I'LL TELL YOU WHAT "BINAURAL" MEANS!
TH... THROW IN "INTER-MODULATION" AND IT'S A DEAL!
OKAY!
PSSST... PSSSST... PSSSSST!
CAROL JONES HAS A FLAT AMPL
NO! NO! NO!
AND THAT'S MY STORY! BUT, LUCKILY, YOU DON'T HAVE TO LEARN ABOUT HI-FI IN THE STREET! IT'S ALL HERE, FRANKLY EXPLAINED IN YOUR PRIVATE "OFFICIAL NATIONAL LAMPOON STEREO PRIMER"!
JUST TURN THE PAGE... AND BE THANKFUL YOU'RE LIVING IN THE SEVENTIES!
ED SUBITZKY

ES: A lot of the *Lampoon*'s advertising back then was for stereo equipment. I was a hi-fi buff back then. It was wonderful. For the first time in my life, I could afford stuff I wanted! I was advanced enough in my advertising job that they were paying me real money. I could walk into an electronics store and say, "I'll take that!" That had never happened to me before.

Anyway, Jerry Taylor, the magazine's publisher, was looking for a premium that he could give away. He came up to me one day and said, "Hey Ed, how would you like to do a record album that we'll give away as a premium? It would be a test record for your hi-fi stereo system, but in real ways, funny ways." Later they decided to sell the record as well.

I thought it sounded interesting, so I did it, and it was a lot of fun! It worked. Jerry liked it, too. It played on the radio once in a while. The two main voice actors I worked with on the album were Chevy Chase and John Belushi.[14]

The typical skit, for example, would be like: "This is to test the bass and treble of your system. We at the *Lampoon* got two trains to crash." You'd hear the trains approaching each other, and then this horrible crash. And a voiceover comes on telling you how the bass should've sounded, and how the screams of the people should've sounded. [*Laughter*] It came off so well that some years later we did a second album, for car stereo.[15]

---

[14]Chevy Chase (1943–) and John Belushi (1949–1982) were *Lampoon* contributors and original cast members of *Saturday Night Live*.

[15]*The Official National Lampoon Car Stereo Test and Demonstration Tape* was released in 1980.

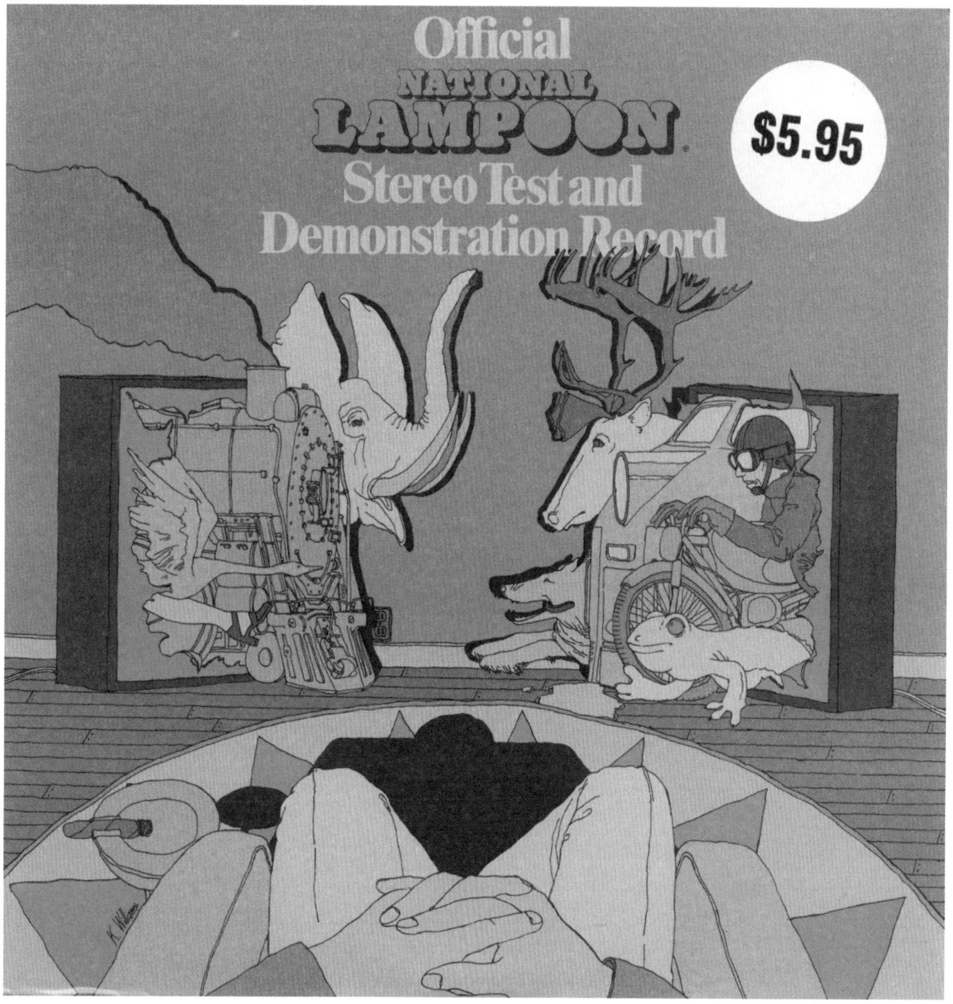
Official
NATIONAL
LAMPOON
Stereo Test and
Demonstration Record
$5.95

Official National Lampoon Stereo Test and Demonstration Record Liner Notes

NLR 1001

Narrations, dramatizations, characterizations, demonstrations, emulations, explanations, ejaculations, and examinations

conceived and written
by **Ed Subitzky**

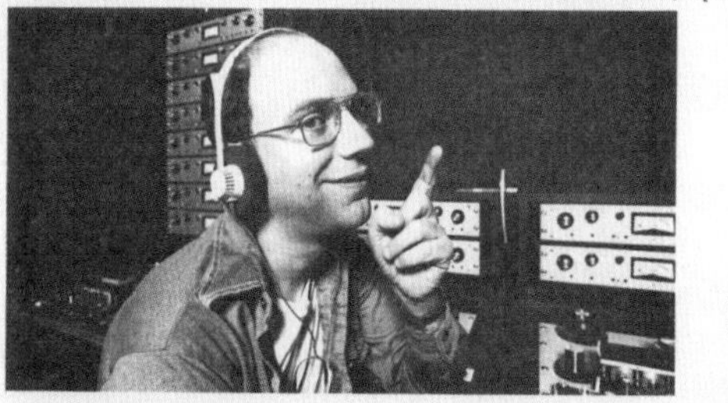

Producer: **Windy Craig**
Sound Engineer: **John Hechtman**
Narrator: **Stan Sawyer**
Voices: **Ed Subitzky**
John Belushi
Chevy Chase
Emily Prager
Sounds: **Themselves**
Executive Producer: **Gerald L. Taylor**
Special Thanks To: **Van Austin, Polly Bier, Bob Tischler, Christine Montanez, Louise Gikow, Rosi Cassano**
Liner Notes: **Ed Subitzky**
Recorded at **National Lampoon Studios**
Illustrator: **Keith Williams**

READ THESE LINER NOTES CAREFULLY. AT THE END OF EACH SECTION, YOU WILL BE TESTED. ANSWER EACH QUESTION, PUTTING A CHECK MARK IN THE BOX BESIDE THE ANSWER THAT YOU THINK COMES CLOSEST. DO NOT GUESS—A WRONG ANSWER WILL BE MORE HARMFUL TO YOUR GRADE THAN NO ANSWER. DO NOT PROCEED TO THE NEXT SECTION UNTIL YOU HAVE FINISHED THE PREVIOUS SECTION. YOU WILL BE ALLOWED A TOTAL OF FIVE MINUTES TO READ THE SECTIONS AND TO ANSWER ALL THE QUESTIONS. **DO NOT WASTE TIME!**

NOW BEGIN:

INTRODUCTION

This is the **Official National Lampoon Stereo Test and Demonstration Record.** It will help you determine how well your stereo system is working, whether or not it is adjusted perfectly, how loud it can play, and whether your sense of humor is in tune or out of tune. The **Official National Lampoon Stereo Test and Demonstration Record** consists of two sides which are called, respectively, "Side One" and "Side Two." On each side are different sections called "bands." Your record player will automatically proceed onto the next succeeding band after it has played the last one, except at the end of "Side One," when you must turn the record over. The diameter of this record is 12 inches, and the outer circumference, calculated by the formula, C = d, is 37.69911180 inches.

Questions

1. This is known as the
☐ a. **Water Music** by Beethoven.
☐ b. **I Wanna Go Home** by Dion and the Belmonts.
☐ c. **Great Hits of Lawrence Welk, Volume III**
☐ d. **Million-Selling Animal Lyrics.**
☐ e. **Official National Lampoon Stereo Test and Demonstration Record.**

2. Side two is called
☐ a. "Side One."
☐ b. "Side Three."
☐ c. "Side Two."
☐ d. "bands."
☐ e. "Side Six."

A Brief History

The history of stereo test and demonstration records is unfortunately somewhat obscure. In 1879, the Edison **Official Test and Demonstration Cylinder** enjoyed brief popularity; it was followed by the **Official Test and Demonstration Wire**, the **Official Test and Demonstration Ear Trumpet**, the **Official Test and Demonstration Man**, the **Official Test and Demonstration Woman**, and the **Official Test and Demonstration Wireless.** The advent of the war with Mexico, however, put a damper on these efforts. As President Taft exclaimed during an impromptu speech to the Republican Party Convention of 1916, "If Mexico had in fact won the skirmish and we were Mexicans today living in a Mexican regime, our life might be much worse and then again, it might not have been all that bad. However, it is certainly likely that whatever progress has been made in this important area to date . . . would have been, shall we say, hampered, at least for the while." With the sudden rise of Gaullism in 1948 and the dread of all-out atomic war in the 50s, people once again turned to their stereos for escapism, and thus the popularity of test records was newly assured. They were included as standard equipment in some late-model fallout shelters, according to the formula $E = pq^t\ (m - n^z)$.

Questions

1. The history of stereo test and demonstration records is
☐ a. a turbulent, passionate one.
☐ b. a left/right one.
☐ c. somewhat obscure.
☐ d. cylindrical with a diameter of 12 inches.
☐ e. a microhistory of Gaullism.

2. Stereo test and demonstration records were sometimes included in fallout shelters according to
☐ a. the whim of the Mexican Generals.
☐ b. the edict of President Lincoln.
☐ c. "Side Four."
☐ d. The formula $E = pq^t\ (m - n^y)$.
☐ e. none of the above.

Purpose: Testing

All good high fidelity equipment should reproduce, in as accurate a way as possible, the original sound. This means, among other things, that it (1) should be able to reproduce the entire audible frequency range, from the very low notes to the very high; and (2) should do so without audible distortion. To see how well their equipment actually accomplishes this, many music lovers turn to **Official Stereo Test and Demonstration Records.** On these records you will find such things as (1) low and high tones to test the range of your system; (2) good stereo effects to test your system's separation; and (3) highly modulated passages to test the ability of your cartridge to track without undue distortion. In addition, **Official Stereo Test and Demonstration Records** contain special passages that help you adjust the controls on your equipment to obtain maximum tone quality. Fortunately, neophyte listeners need not concern themselves with the technical whys and wherefores behind these tests; like the boy who is lost in the jungle and finds a map dropped by a plane, they need only follow simple directions to get to where they want to go. Perhaps the largest jungle in the world today is the *Abeloxia* of Chile. Through this dense knot of foliage wanders, crawls, and flies an estimated 6,700 species of animals, birds, and insects.

Questions

1. The purpose of a good high fidelity system is
☐ a. the *Abeloxia.*
☐ b. 37.69911186 inches.
☐ c. to replay music as accurately as possible.
☐ d. to replay Muzak as accurately as possible.
☐ e. all of the above.

2. What the boy was really hoping for was
☐ a. 6,800 species of animals, birds and insects.
☐ b. Beethoven.
☐ c. the collapse of Gaullism.
☐ d. highly modulated groove passages.
☐ e. to be found.

Purpose: Demonstration

According to psychologists, one of the primary attributes distinguishing man from his animal cousins is his interest in, and ability at, showing off. In modern times, the technological manifestation of this evolutionary genetically-fixed deterministic species-wide tendency is often represented under the guise of inviting people, often of the opposite sex (defined by *Webster's* as "the difference between man and woman") into the home abode for the purpose of demonstrating the loudness and power of the music system therein. In keeping with this primal urge, **Official Stereo Test and Demonstration Records** typically may offer a potpourri of very loud sounds, very deep sounds, and very high-pitched sounds. Thus the listener can both satisfy himself that his system is capable (or not capable, as the case may sometimes be) of turning out some powerful effects, and can likewise demonstrate these effects to win the admiration of those concurrently at his abode, and thus fulfill his bio-heritage in a socially acceptable manner. According to other psychologists, this is not so.

Questions

1. Sex is
☐ a. a biological fact.
☐ b. one of the main reasons why people take off their clothes.
☐ c. the difference between woman and man.
☐ d. fulfilling.
☐ e. better when the fidelity is high.

2. According to psychologists,
☐ a. we are, at heart, basically brutal, sexual creatures with strong sex urges.
☐ b. if we don't listen to our hi-fis often enough, we are likely to go out and molest members of the opposite sex to satisfy our ever-present sexuality.
☐ c. man, of all primates, prefers sex to reading.
☐ d. the other psychologists are not always right, both about sexual matters and about other matters.
☐ e. the formula for sex is historically obscure.

A Miracle in Plastic

When the average American consumer picks up an **Official Stereo Test and Demonstration Record,** he cavalierly accepts the advanced technology that went into its production, giving little thought to the hundreds of careful steps, each in itself having the perfect right to be called a scientific miracle, entailed therein. Today, most records are made of a wonder-substance called *polyvinyl chloride* and are cut to diameters of 12 inches (which means their circumferences must be 37.69911180 inches). A special centering machine makes certain that the label is pasted on in the center, not over the grooves, and a big drill, powered by electricity, slowly descends upon the record, its huge hulking frame cloaked in shadow, edging closer, closer, closer—will the record escape!—its chisel-sharp point dripping a tiny trail of oil as it relentlessly drops, making a hideous clicking sound . . . click! click! click! —but the record, see the record, it is locked in and no, there is no escape! —now the very shadow of the drill is upon it!—click! click! click!—drip! drip! drip!—closer and closer and closer and closer—wait a minute! At the very last moment, who should arrive at the record factory but the Mexican troops just in time to save it!

Questions

1. Modern technology is
☐ a. an often unappreciated miracle.
☐ b. part of the *Abeloxia.*
☐ c. all of the above.
☐ d. all of the below.
☐ e. inherently sexual in nature, and always on the verge of translating its inherent sexuality into overt sexual activities.

2. The moral of this piece can be said to be:
☐ a. "A stitch in time saves nine."
☐ b. "Technology without autocracy is like autology without technocracy."
☐ c. "The average American consumer is well-fed but ill-read."
☐ d. "You can get lost in a jungle, but you can get found in one too."
☐ e. "The hole in the middle of a record of pure gold is as empty as the hole in the middle of a record of ordinary black vinyl."

Summary

In your hands right now you are holding the **Official National Lampoon Stereo Test and Demonstration Record.** On this record you will find tests that help you evaluate your stereo system, help you adjust it properly, help you (frankly) show it off a little, and also make you laugh at a frequency of not less than twenty yocks per minute (± 2 ha). Remove the cellophane. Take the record out of the paper. Place it on your phonograph and, while you are listening to it, you will probably be enjoying yourself too much to recall the fact that modern biologists believe, of all the secondary sexual characteristics, it is the ones of the woman that most attract the ones on the man, and vice-versa.

Questions

1. According to modern research, the *Abeloxia*
☐ a. has a circumference of 37.69911183 inches.
☐ b. was invaded by both De Gaulle and the Mexicans.
☐ c. has many species of animals, but few turntables.
☐ d. is sexually very busy at night.
☐ e. is a cheap hotel known for its loose women.

2. The **Official National Lampoon Stereo Test and Demonstration Record**
☐ a. is in your hands right now.
☐ b. will help you evaluate your equipment and bring you much laughter, which you can use too.
☐ c. is wrapped in cellophane which must be removed before playing it.
☐ d. contains a multitude of explicit references to matters of a sexual nature.
☐ e. all but four of the above.

Important Notice

On this record, you will find several tests for your stereo system that really work. Where the record tells you that a test is *serious,* please believe it. Although we have attempted to make this record as funny and off-the-wall to listen to as possible, we have also included real tests which will really give you real information about your equipment. Please believe us. It's true.

IN THE FRENCH RESTAURANT

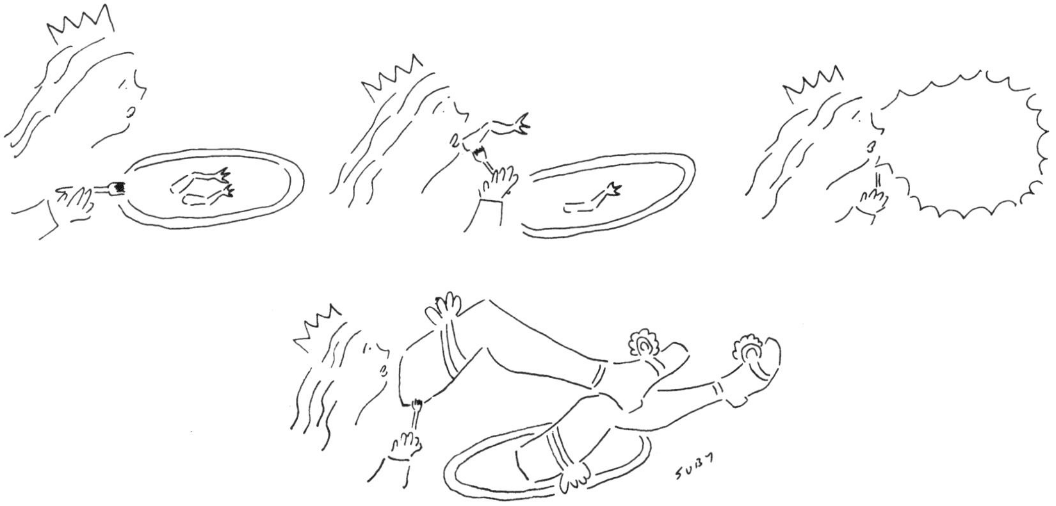

"Ticket, please."

TATTOOED LADY COMICS!

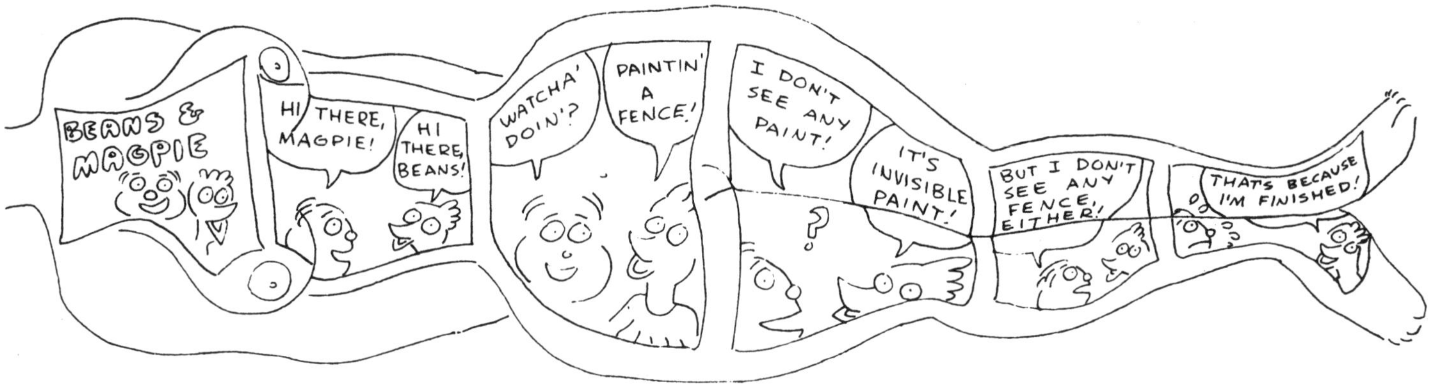

BEANS & MAGPIE
HI THERE, MAGPIE!
HI THERE, BEANS!
WATCHA' DOIN'?
PAINTIN' A FENCE!
I DON'T SEE ANY PAINT!
IT'S INVISIBLE PAINT!
BUT I DON'T SEE ANY FENCE, EITHER!
THAT'S BECAUSE I'M FINISHED!

SMALL CONSOLATIONS

Look at them. Will you just look at them down there. Born beautiful. More or less in perfect health. Lots of money. Hopping around the world. Enjoying fabulous sex lives while you pay your hard-earned money just to look at likenesses of them and drool a little. Hour after hour, day after day, a perfect existence, and every last moment of it filled with the kind of wild, exciting experiences you'd do anything to savor just once in your life. But take comfort. Take comfort for this reason: It isn't going to last. Time robs. Time is the thief. Time chips away. Second by second, bit by bit, it happens to them just the way it happens to you. Only with this difference: You'll be prepared. After all, you weren't so beautiful in the first place. You don't have that much to lose. You'll handle it like a pro. But they won't. It'll drive them crazy. To drink. To drugs. To despair. Really, the last laugh is yours. And, so you won't feel quite so bad until then, take a look at what's coming through this actual time-machine-in-print. It is chemically activated by light. To make it work, simply look at this page while holding it up to a bright light.

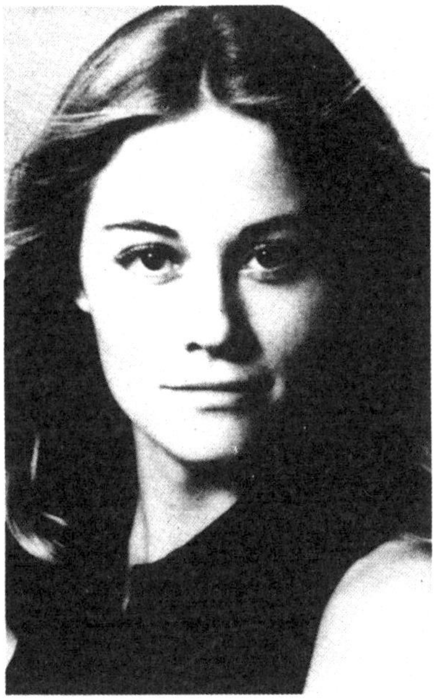
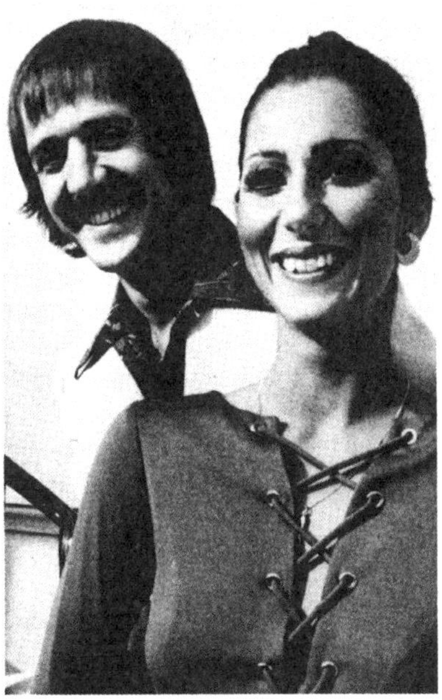
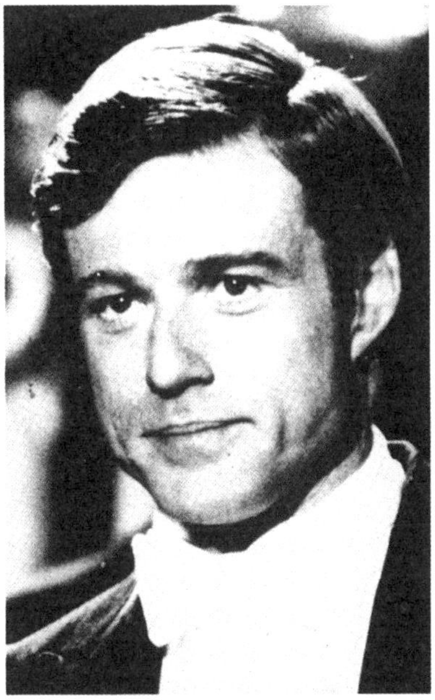
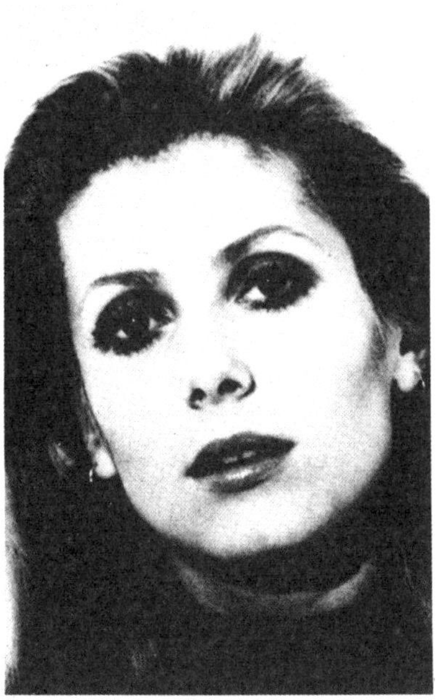
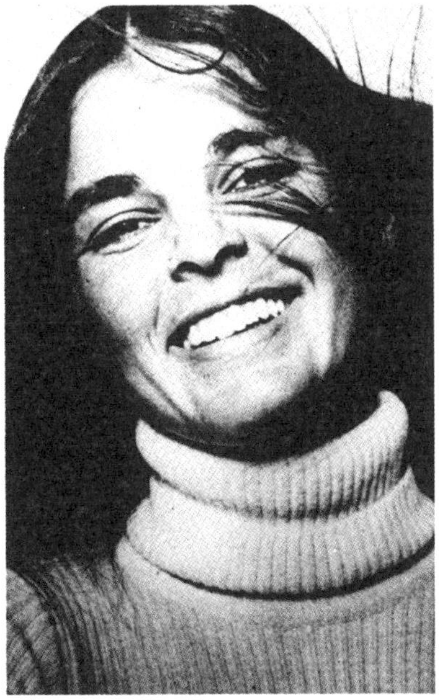
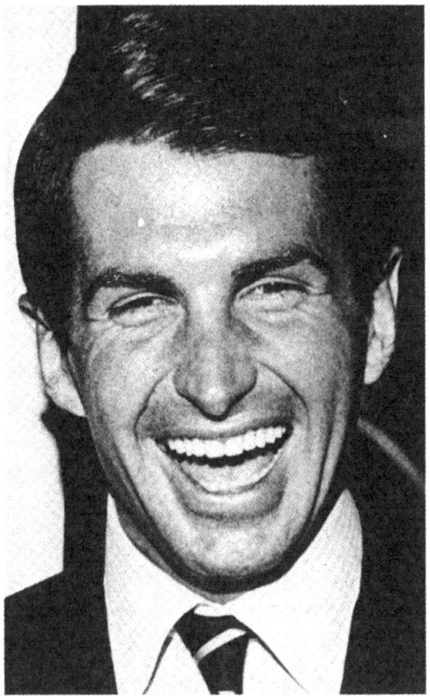

Either lamplight or sunlight is fine. There. Now you're looking ahead forty years. Now you're seeing what they'll all be like when the movie directors and the sex-magazine editors and even the girl and boy next door ask them not-so-politely to please stay in their rooms and keep the doors shut and the window shades closed.

SMALL CONSOLATIONS

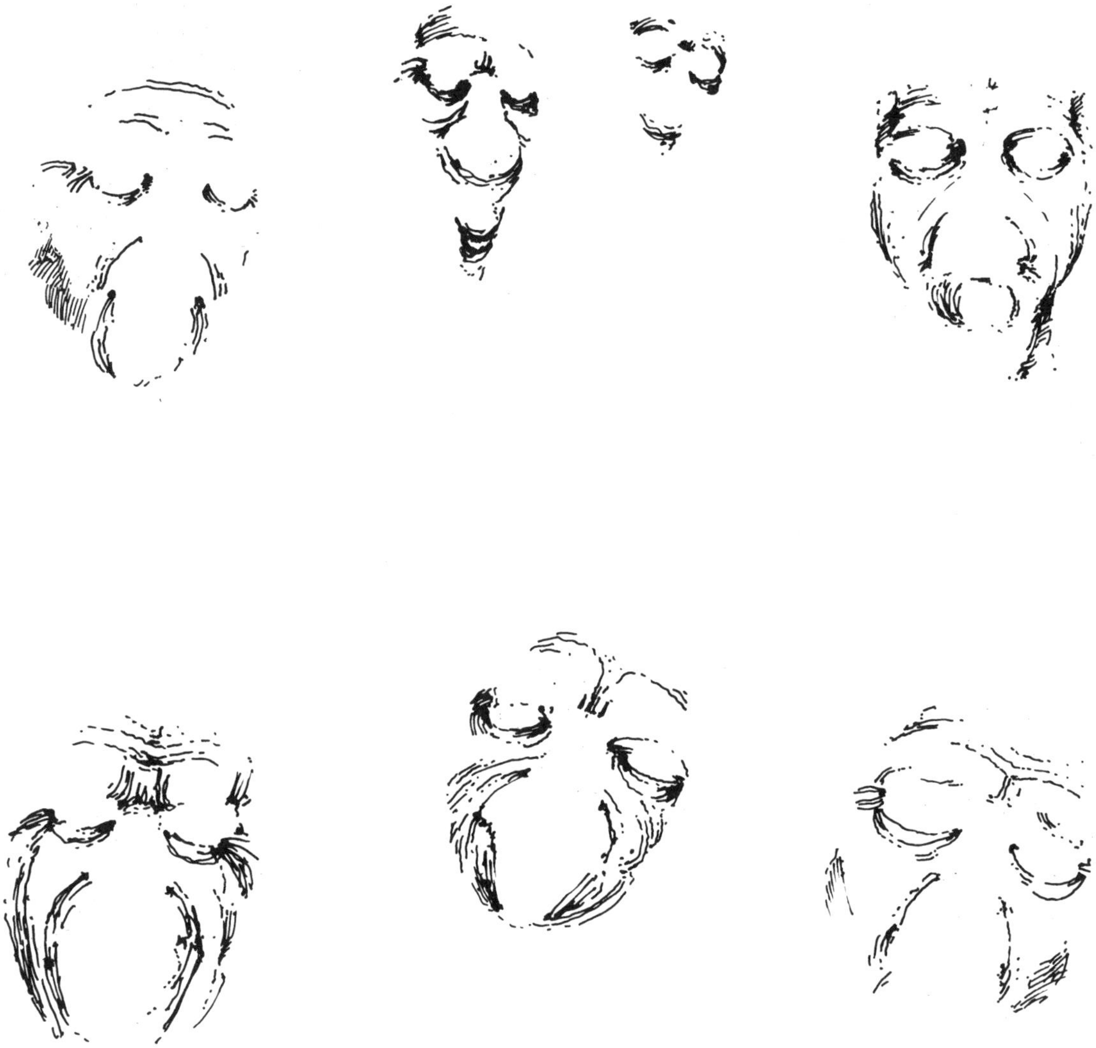

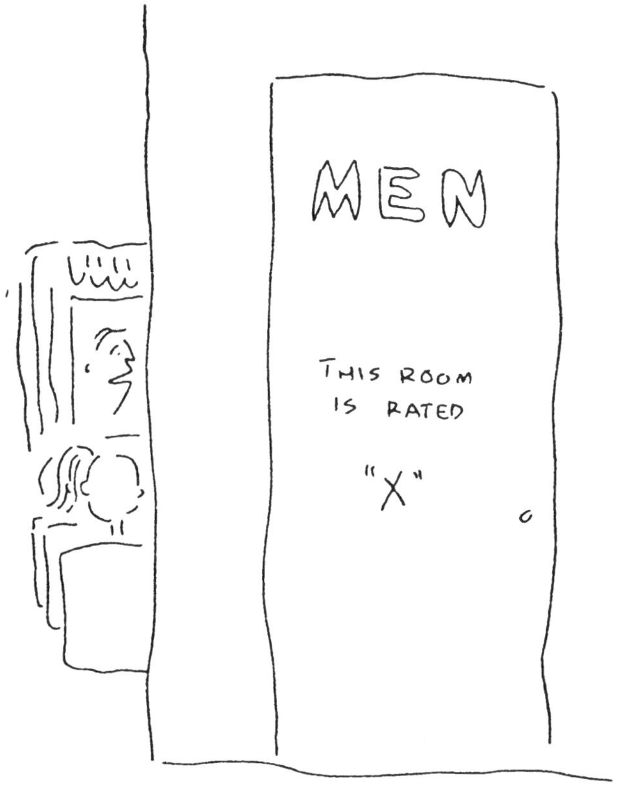
MEN
THIS ROOM
IS RATED
"X"

BESTIALITY COMICS!

Panel 1:
ARF WOOF OWF ARF WOOF OWF?

SORRY, I ALREADY HAVE PLANS FOR SATURDAY NIGHT!

Panel 2:
ARF ARF WOWF ARF WOOF WOWF?

NO, ON SUNDAY I HAVE TO STAY UP WITH A SICK FRIEND WHO HAS RABIES!

Panel 3:
ARF WOOOF ARF GROWF WOOF OWOARF WOWF?

MONDAY? WELL, DID YOU HAVE ANYTHING SPECIFIC IN MIND?

Panel 4:
SORRY, I'VE ALREADY SEEN "FIDDLER ON THE ROOF"...

THE END

MN: Do you have a philosophy of humor?

ES: A philosophy of humor? Yes, I do. It has to be funny.

[*Laughter*]

ES: I didn't mean that sarcastically! That's really what I look for. One very important thing about the *Lampoon* crowd: they were funny, but they also had intellect. I think great humor has to have great intellect.

It's worth mentioning that the *Lampoon*'s humor was often referred to as "sick humor." That was a phrase people used a lot back then, sick humor. A lot of times, humor seems hurtful. Let's say someone does a piece about a patient with a terrible illness. A person has an illness, so isn't that terrible? But if the humor is done right, what they're really doing is making fun not of the patient but of a universe that does this to people. We live in a universe that takes nice, innocent people, and does very bad things to them. And we're laughing at that, making fun of that. We're trying to make some sense out of that irony. That's my philosophy. First, foremost: it has to be funny. And second: it has to have depth. Maybe the more depth, the better. Not everybody can do that. The *Lampoon* had such mind and such heart at the beginning, and once the founders left, that never really came back again.

I want to add one point, kind of a strange one. If you want a career in humor, you have to be wary of it changing you. The humorous way of looking at the world is the icing on the cake. It's wonderful, the best part of life in many ways. But to sit down and take that look at the misery of the world and find ways to make fun of it—and to do that morning, noon, and night, or five to midnight, or whatever—can change you in certain ways. I think you have to be careful, if you do humor, not to let the attitude of humor take over your whole life, like what happens to some of the stand-up comedians who are "on" twenty-four hours a day. It's an occupational hazard, with humor. You could love it to pieces, but if you never get away from it, you may find yourself looking at the world in a way that takes something important out of life. It can take your compassion away, make you less human.

"It's a telegram from the governor.... 'Happy birthday to you.... Happy birthday to you.... Happy birthday, dear...'"

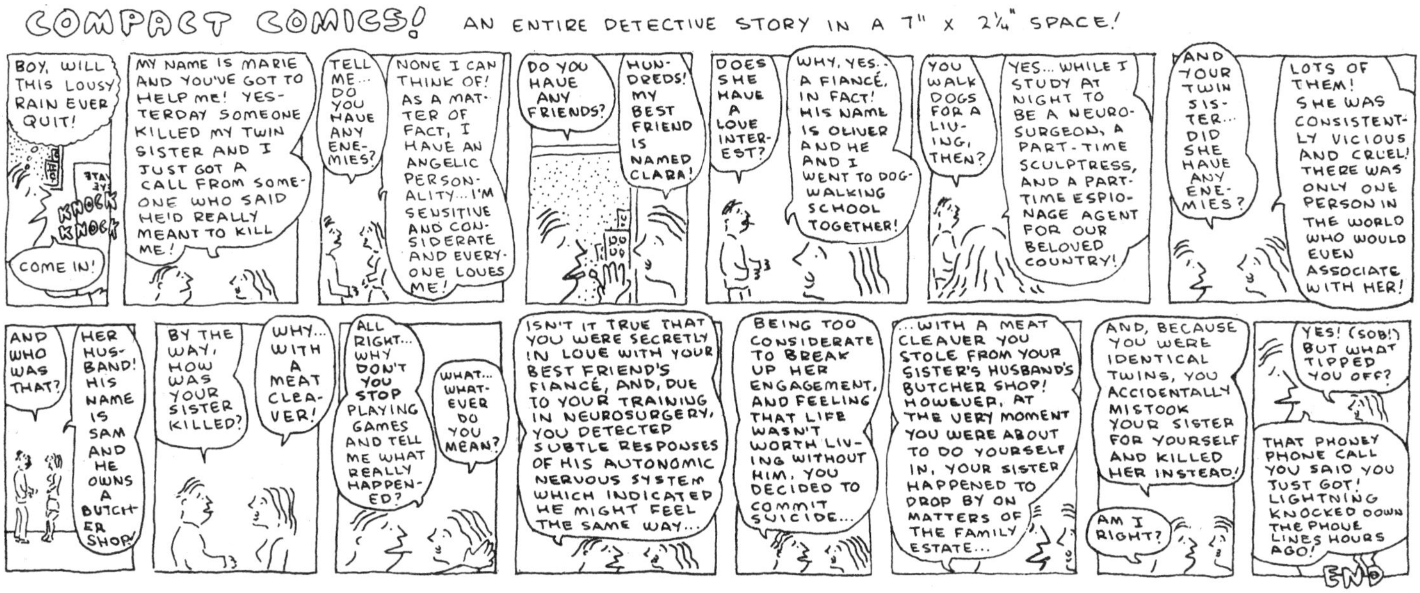
COMPACT COMICS! AN ENTIRE DETECTIVE STORY IN A 7" x 2¼" SPACE!
BOY, WILL THIS LOUSY RAIN EVER QUIT!
KNOCK KNOCK
COME IN!
MY NAME IS MARIE AND YOU'VE GOT TO HELP ME! YESTERDAY SOMEONE KILLED MY TWIN SISTER AND I JUST GOT A CALL FROM SOMEONE WHO SAID HE'D REALLY MEANT TO KILL ME!
TELL ME... DO YOU HAVE ANY ENEMIES?
NONE I CAN THINK OF! AS A MATTER OF FACT, I HAVE AN ANGELIC PERSONALITY... I'M SENSITIVE AND CONSIDERATE AND EVERYONE LOVES ME!
DO YOU HAVE ANY FRIENDS?
HUNDREDS! MY BEST FRIEND IS NAMED CLARA!
DOES SHE HAVE A LOVE INTEREST?
WHY, YES. A FIANCÉ, IN FACT! HIS NAME IS OLIVER AND HE AND I WENT TO DOG-WALKING SCHOOL TOGETHER!
YOU WALK DOGS FOR A LIVING, THEN?
YES... WHILE I STUDY AT NIGHT TO BE A NEUROSURGEON, A PART-TIME SCULPTRESS, AND A PART-TIME ESPIONAGE AGENT FOR OUR BELOVED COUNTRY!
AND YOUR TWIN SISTER... DID SHE HAVE ANY ENEMIES?
LOTS OF THEM! SHE WAS CONSISTENTLY VICIOUS AND CRUEL! THERE WAS ONLY ONE PERSON IN THE WORLD WHO WOULD EVEN ASSOCIATE WITH HER!
AND WHO WAS THAT?
HER HUSBAND! HIS NAME IS SAM AND HE OWNS A BUTCHER SHOP!
BY THE WAY, HOW WAS YOUR SISTER KILLED?
WHY... WITH A MEAT CLEAVER!
ALL RIGHT... WHY DON'T YOU STOP PLAYING GAMES AND TELL ME WHAT REALLY HAPPENED?
WHAT... WHATEVER DO YOU MEAN?
ISN'T IT TRUE THAT YOU WERE SECRETLY IN LOVE WITH YOUR BEST FRIEND'S FIANCÉ, AND, DUE TO YOUR TRAINING IN NEUROSURGERY, YOU DETECTED SUBTLE RESPONSES OF HIS AUTONOMIC NERVOUS SYSTEM WHICH INDICATED HE MIGHT FEEL THE SAME WAY...
BEING TOO CONSIDERATE TO BREAK UP HER ENGAGEMENT, AND FEELING THAT LIFE WASN'T WORTH LIVING WITHOUT HIM, YOU DECIDED TO COMMIT SUICIDE...
...WITH A MEAT CLEAVER YOU STOLE FROM YOUR SISTER'S HUSBAND'S BUTCHER SHOP! HOWEVER, AT THE VERY MOMENT YOU WERE ABOUT TO DO YOURSELF IN, YOUR SISTER HAPPENED TO DROP BY ON MATTERS OF THE FAMILY ESTATE...
AND, BECAUSE YOU WERE IDENTICAL TWINS, YOU ACCIDENTALLY MISTOOK YOUR SISTER FOR YOURSELF AND KILLED HER INSTEAD!
AM I RIGHT?
YES! (SOB!) BUT WHAT TIPPED YOU OFF?
THAT PHONEY PHONE CALL YOU SAID YOU JUST GOT! LIGHTNING KNOCKED DOWN THE PHONE LINES HOURS AGO!
END

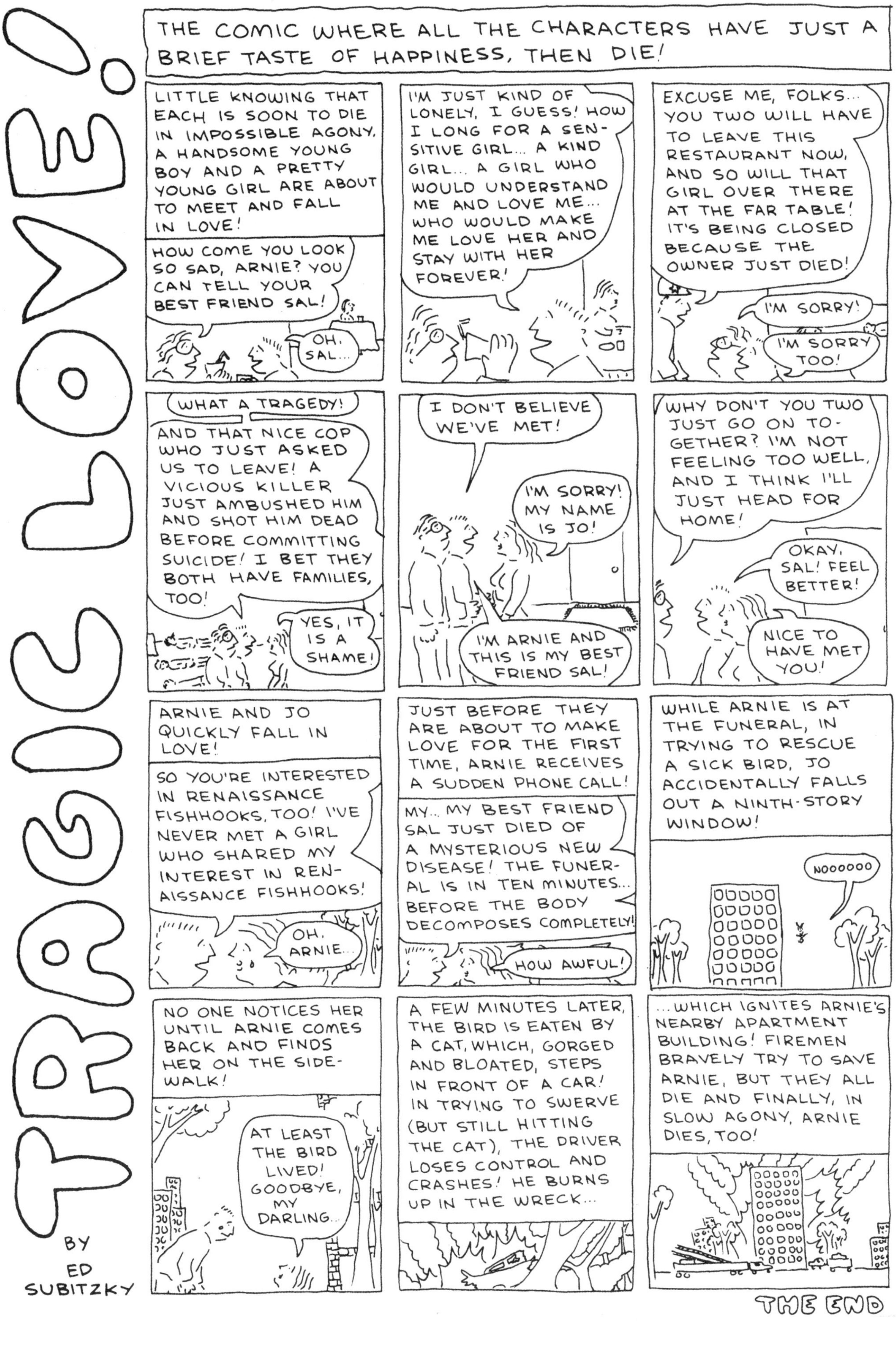
TRAGIC LOVE!
BY ED SUBITZKY
THE COMIC WHERE ALL THE CHARACTERS HAVE JUST A BRIEF TASTE OF HAPPINESS, THEN DIE!
LITTLE KNOWING THAT EACH IS SOON TO DIE IN IMPOSSIBLE AGONY, A HANDSOME YOUNG BOY AND A PRETTY YOUNG GIRL ARE ABOUT TO MEET AND FALL IN LOVE!
HOW COME YOU LOOK SO SAD, ARNIE? YOU CAN TELL YOUR BEST FRIEND SAL!
OH, SAL...
I'M JUST KIND OF LONELY, I GUESS! HOW I LONG FOR A SENSITIVE GIRL... A KIND GIRL... A GIRL WHO WOULD UNDERSTAND ME AND LOVE ME... WHO WOULD MAKE ME LOVE HER AND STAY WITH HER FOREVER!
EXCUSE ME, FOLKS... YOU TWO WILL HAVE TO LEAVE THIS RESTAURANT NOW, AND SO WILL THAT GIRL OVER THERE AT THE FAR TABLE! IT'S BEING CLOSED BECAUSE THE OWNER JUST DIED!
I'M SORRY!
I'M SORRY TOO!
WHAT A TRAGEDY!
AND THAT NICE COP WHO JUST ASKED US TO LEAVE! A VICIOUS KILLER JUST AMBUSHED HIM AND SHOT HIM DEAD BEFORE COMMITTING SUICIDE! I BET THEY BOTH HAVE FAMILIES, TOO!
YES, IT IS A SHAME!
I DON'T BELIEVE WE'VE MET!
I'M SORRY! MY NAME IS JO!
I'M ARNIE AND THIS IS MY BEST FRIEND SAL!
WHY DON'T YOU TWO JUST GO ON TOGETHER? I'M NOT FEELING TOO WELL, AND I THINK I'LL JUST HEAD FOR HOME!
OKAY, SAL! FEEL BETTER!
NICE TO HAVE MET YOU!
ARNIE AND JO QUICKLY FALL IN LOVE!
SO YOU'RE INTERESTED IN RENAISSANCE FISHHOOKS, TOO! I'VE NEVER MET A GIRL WHO SHARED MY INTEREST IN RENAISSANCE FISHHOOKS!
OH, ARNIE...
JUST BEFORE THEY ARE ABOUT TO MAKE LOVE FOR THE FIRST TIME, ARNIE RECEIVES A SUDDEN PHONE CALL!
MY... MY BEST FRIEND SAL JUST DIED OF A MYSTERIOUS NEW DISEASE! THE FUNERAL IS IN TEN MINUTES... BEFORE THE BODY DECOMPOSES COMPLETELY!
HOW AWFUL!
WHILE ARNIE IS AT THE FUNERAL, IN TRYING TO RESCUE A SICK BIRD, JO ACCIDENTALLY FALLS OUT A NINTH-STORY WINDOW!
NOOOOOO
NO ONE NOTICES HER UNTIL ARNIE COMES BACK AND FINDS HER ON THE SIDEWALK!
AT LEAST THE BIRD LIVED! GOODBYE, MY DARLING...
A FEW MINUTES LATER, THE BIRD IS EATEN BY A CAT, WHICH, GORGED AND BLOATED, STEPS IN FRONT OF A CAR! IN TRYING TO SWERVE (BUT STILL HITTING THE CAT), THE DRIVER LOSES CONTROL AND CRASHES! HE BURNS UP IN THE WRECK...
...WHICH IGNITES ARNIE'S NEARBY APARTMENT BUILDING! FIREMEN BRAVELY TRY TO SAVE ARNIE, BUT THEY ALL DIE AND FINALLY, IN SLOW AGONY, ARNIE DIES, TOO!
THE END

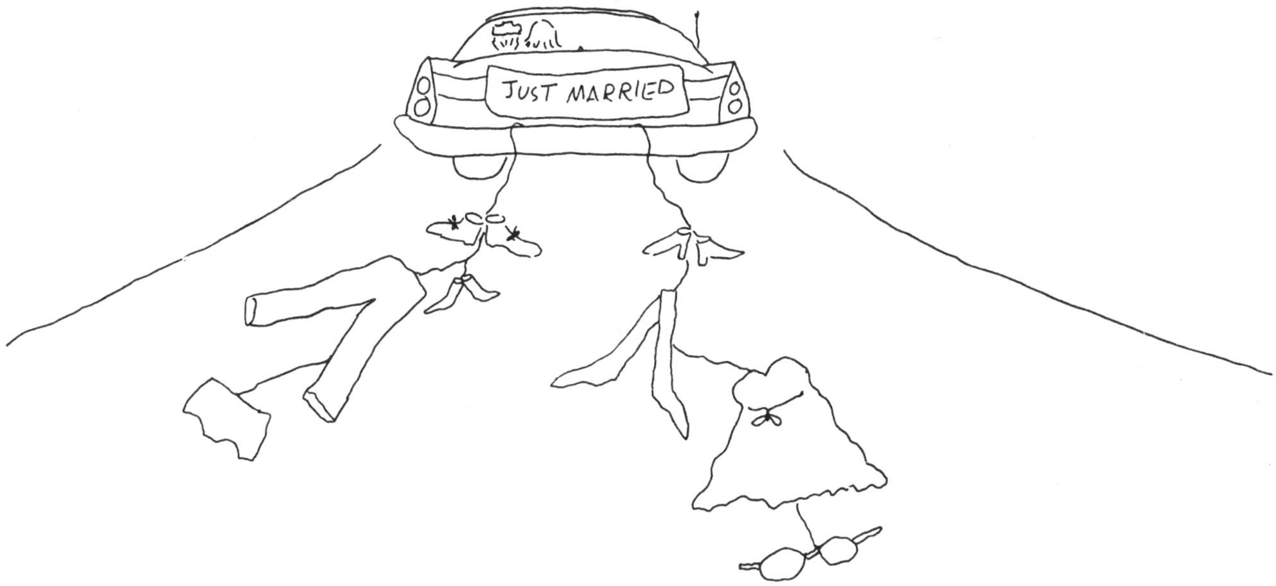
JUST MARRIED

MAGICIAN COMICS!

HELLO, LADIES AND GENTLEMEN!

FOR MY TRICK TODAY, I WILL PULL A RABBIT OUT OF A HAT!

SEE? THE HAT IS COMPLETELY EMPTY!

TAKE A CLOSE LOOK!

AND NOW...

VOILÀ!

THANK YOU VERY MUCH, LADIES AND GENTLEMEN!

DULL COMICS!
ACT I: IN THE DINER.
HI THERE, HARRY! LONG TIME NO SEE!
YEAH, JEANNIE! BEEN OUT ON A LONG RUN, ALL THE WAY OVER TO PILMA!
WHAT'LL IT BE, HUH? THE USUAL?
NAH! MILLIE'S WAITING UP! BETTER JUST MAKE IT A COFFEE LIGHT!
RAIN MUCH UP IN PILMA?
A LITTLE. NOT TOO BAD! HOW'S THINGS HERE?
WELL, YOU KNOW! ONE PLATE LOOKS MUCH LIKE ANY OTHER!
YEAH. SO DOES ONE TRAFFIC LIGHT AFTER A WHILE!
WELL, G'NITE!
G'NITE!
ACT II: AT HOME.
HI, BABY!
GOOD TO HAVE YOU HOME!
RAIN MUCH IN PILMA?
NOT TOO MUCH! OOOOH, MY BONES ACHE!
ABNER FARROW'S WIFE DELIVERED! A BOY!
NO KIDDIN'!
AND YOUR OWN SON INSISTED ON HIS FIRST PAIR OF SHOES WITH HEELS!
TIME SURE FLIES!
WELL, I'M BEAT!
I'LL BE UP AFTER THE NEWS!
ACT III: MORNING.
SORRY, DEAR! ERICA KEPT ME UP ALL NIGHT AND I SLEPT THROUGH COFFEE!
THAT'S OKAY! I'LL STOP OFF AT MIKE'S!
ACT IV: IN THE DINER.
LAND SAKES! NOT YOU AGAIN!
WHAT DO YOU MEAN ME? SINCE WHEN DO YOU WORK THE MORNING SHIFT?
SINCE ANGIE WENT OFF TO VISIT HER COUSIN, THAT'S WHEN! AND EVEN THOUGH THE OVERTIME HELPS, I'LL SURE BE GLAD WHEN SHE GETS BACK!
ACT V: THE TRUCK STOP.
MORNING FRED, JEB, LOUIE!
MORNING, HAR! LOOKS A QUIET DAY!
ACT VI: ON THE TRUCK.
SUN SURE IS HOT!
SAY, AIN'T THAT TANK PRETTY LOW?
ACT VII: THE GAS STATION.
FILL 'ER UP!
'SCUSE ME A MINUTE...
ACT VIII: ON THE TRUCK.
LUNCH?
SURE!
ACT IX: IN THE DINER.
NOT YOU AGAIN, HARRY! AND JEB, YOU TOO!
MAKE IT TWO BURGERS MEDIUM!
ACT X: ON THE TRUCK.
SLOW DAY, HUH?
I COULD USE A MILLION LIKE IT! LIVE LONGER!
ACT XI: THE TRUCK STOP.
WELL, ANOTHER DAY, ANOTHER HALF-DOLLAR!
AT LEAST IT WAS A SLOW ONE!
STOP OFF FOR COFFEE?
CAN'T! BOWLING NIGHT!
ACT XII: IN THE DINER.
EVENING, MIKE! WHERE'S JEANNIE?
OH, SHE WAS GET-TING PRETTY BEAT, SO I LET HER TAKE OFF EARLY!
WHAT'S YOUR PLEA-SURE?
OH, JUST A COFFEE LIGHT, I GUESS!
ACT XIII: AT HOME.
GOTTA MAKE A RUN TO PILMA AGAIN, HON, BUT IT WON'T BE TILL NEXT WEEK!
I HOPE THE WEATHER HOLDS! YOU KNOW HOW IT CAN RAIN IN PILMA!
THE END

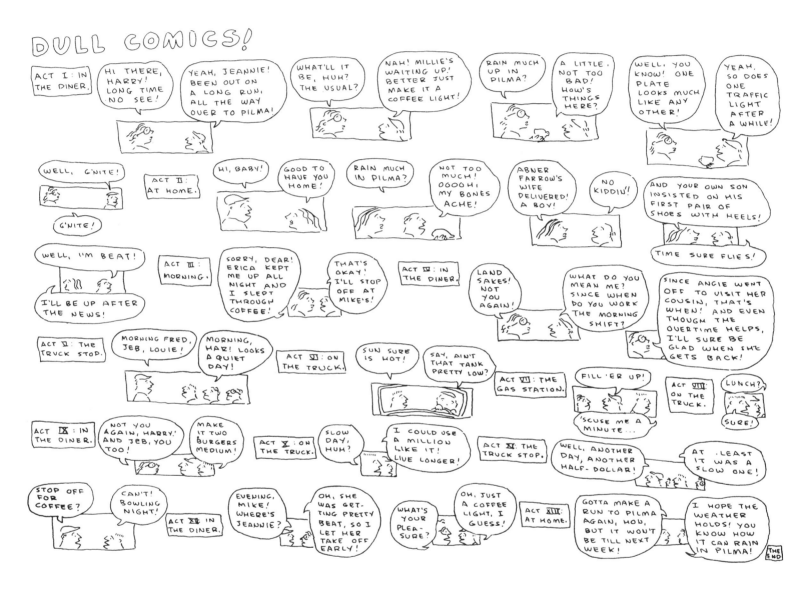

ASSEMBLY LINE COMICS!

by ED SUBITZKY

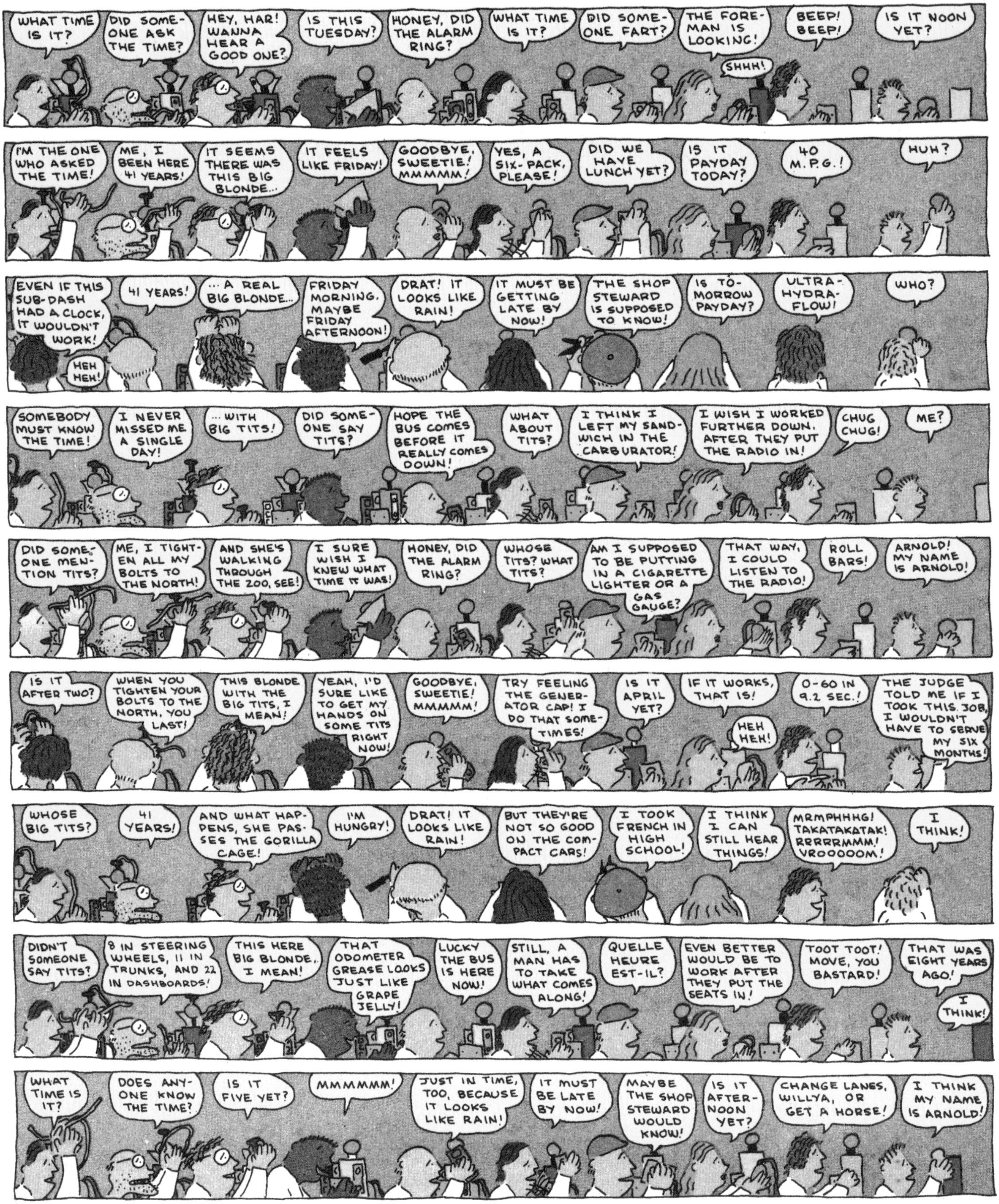
WHAT TIME IS IT?
DID SOME-ONE ASK THE TIME?
HEY, HAR! WANNA HEAR A GOOD ONE?
IS THIS TUESDAY?
HONEY, DID THE ALARM RING?
WHAT TIME IS IT?
DID SOME-ONE FART?
THE FORE-MAN IS LOOKING!
SHHH!
BEEP! BEEP!
IS IT NOON YET?
I'M THE ONE WHO ASKED THE TIME!
ME, I BEEN HERE 41 YEARS!
IT SEEMS THERE WAS THIS BIG BLONDE...
IT FEELS LIKE FRIDAY!
GOODBYE, SWEETIE! MMMMM!
YES, A SIX-PACK, PLEASE!
DID WE HAVE LUNCH YET?
IS IT PAYDAY TODAY?
40 M.P.G.!
HUH?
EVEN IF THIS SUB-DASH HAD A CLOCK, IT WOULDN'T WORK!
HEH HEH!
41 YEARS!
...A REAL BIG BLONDE...
FRIDAY MORNING, MAYBE FRIDAY AFTERNOON!
DRAT! IT LOOKS LIKE RAIN!
IT MUST BE GETTING LATE BY NOW!
THE SHOP STEWARD IS SUPPOSED TO KNOW!
IS TO-MORROW PAYDAY?
ULTRA-HYDRA-FLOW!
WHO?
SOMEBODY MUST KNOW THE TIME!
I NEVER MISSED ME A SINGLE DAY!
...WITH BIG TITS!
DID SOME-ONE SAY TITS?
HOPE THE BUS COMES BEFORE IT REALLY COMES DOWN!
WHAT ABOUT TITS?
I THINK I LEFT MY SAND-WICH IN THE CARBURATOR!
I WISH I WORKED FURTHER DOWN, AFTER THEY PUT THE RADIO IN!
CHUG CHUG!
ME?
DID SOME-ONE MEN-TION TITS?
ME, I TIGHT-EN ALL MY BOLTS TO THE NORTH!
AND SHE'S WALKING THROUGH THE ZOO, SEE!
I SURE WISH I KNEW WHAT TIME IT WAS!
HONEY, DID THE ALARM RING?
WHOSE TITS? WHAT TITS?
AM I SUPPOSED TO BE PUTTING IN A CIGARETTE LIGHTER OR A GAS GAUGE?
THAT WAY, I COULD LISTEN TO THE RADIO!
ROLL BARS!
ARNOLD! MY NAME IS ARNOLD!
IS IT AFTER TWO?
WHEN YOU TIGHTEN YOUR BOLTS TO THE NORTH, YOU LAST!
THIS BLONDE WITH THE BIG TITS, I MEAN!
YEAH, I'D SURE LIKE TO GET MY HANDS ON SOME TITS RIGHT NOW!
GOODBYE, SWEETIE! MMMMM!
TRY FEELING THE GENER-ATOR CAP! I DO THAT SOME-TIMES!
IS IT APRIL YET?
IF IT WORKS, THAT IS!
HEH HEH!
0-60 IN 9.2 SEC.!
THE JUDGE TOLD ME IF I TOOK THIS JOB, I WOULDN'T HAVE TO SERVE MY SIX MONTHS!
WHOSE BIG TITS?
41 YEARS!
AND WHAT HAP-PENS, SHE PAS-SES THE GORILLA CAGE!
I'M HUNGRY!
DRAT! IT LOOKS LIKE RAIN!
BUT THEY'RE NOT SO GOOD ON THE COM-PACT CARS!
I TOOK FRENCH IN HIGH SCHOOL!
I THINK I CAN STILL HEAR THINGS!
MRMPHHHG! TAKATAKATAK! RRRRRMMM! VROOOOOM!
I THINK!
DIDN'T SOMEONE SAY TITS?
8 IN STEERING WHEELS, 11 IN TRUNKS, AND 22 IN DASHBOARDS!
THIS HERE BIG BLONDE, I MEAN!
THAT ODOMETER GREASE LOOKS JUST LIKE GRAPE JELLY!
LUCKY THE BUS IS HERE NOW!
STILL, A MAN HAS TO TAKE WHAT COMES ALONG!
QUELLE HEURE EST-IL?
EVEN BETTER WOULD BE TO WORK AFTER THEY PUT THE SEATS IN!
TOOT TOOT! MOVE, YOU BASTARD!
THAT WAS EIGHT YEARS AGO!
I THINK!
WHAT TIME IS IT?
DOES ANY-ONE KNOW THE TIME?
IS IT FIVE YET?
MMMMMM!
JUST IN TIME, TOO, BECAUSE IT LOOKS LIKE RAIN!
IT MUST BE LATE BY NOW!
MAYBE THE SHOP STEWARD WOULD KNOW!
IS IT AFTER-NOON YET?
CHANGE LANES, WILLYA, OR GET A HORSE!
I THINK MY NAME IS ARNOLD!

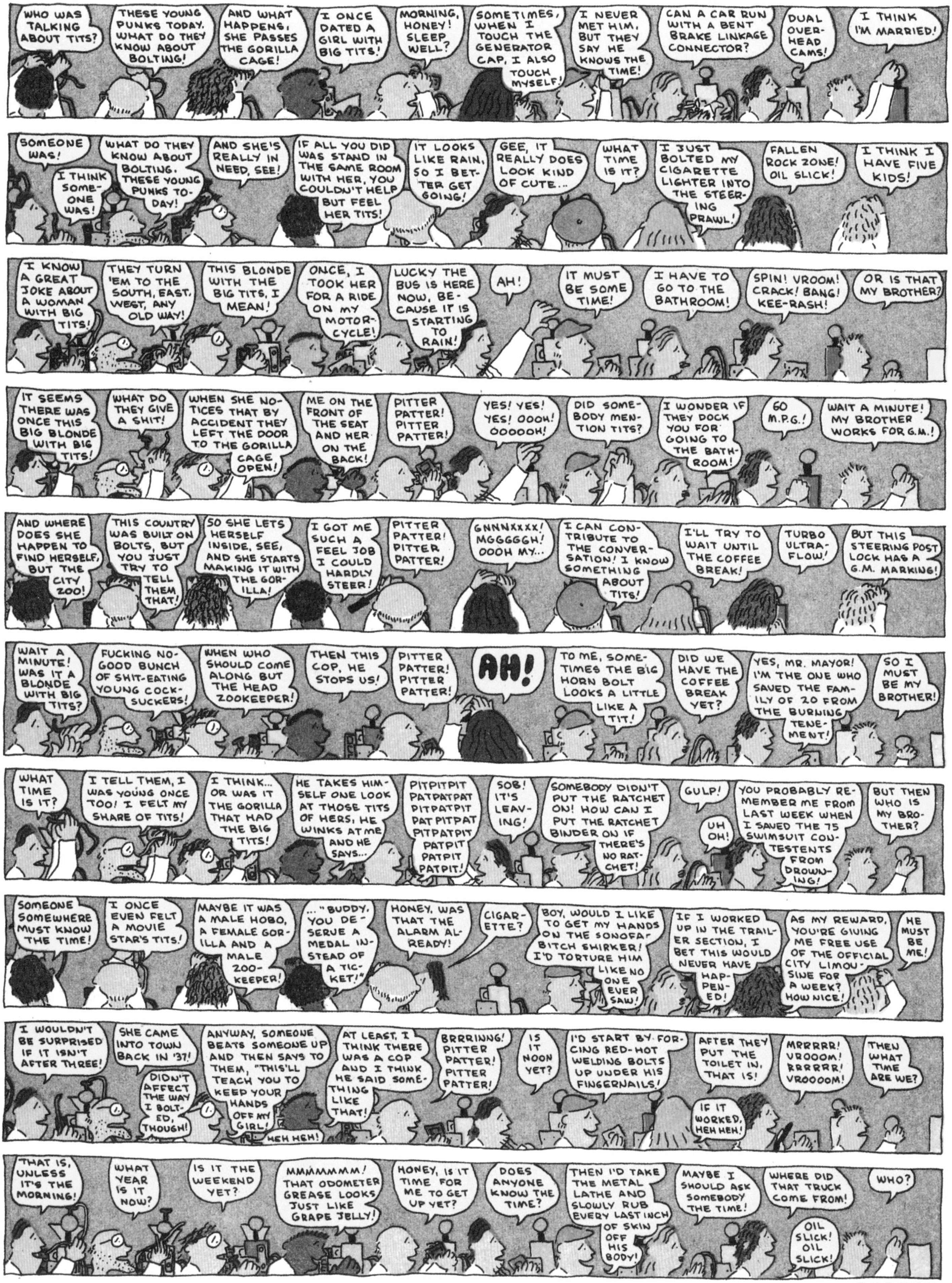
WHO WAS TALKING ABOUT TITS?
THESE YOUNG PUNKS TODAY. WHAT DO THEY KNOW ABOUT BOLTING!
AND WHAT HAPPENS, SHE PASSES THE GORILLA CAGE!
I ONCE DATED A GIRL WITH BIG TITS!
MORNING, HONEY! SLEEP WELL?
SOMETIMES, WHEN I TOUCH THE GENERATOR CAP, I ALSO TOUCH MYSELF!
I NEVER MET HIM, BUT THEY SAY HE KNOWS THE TIME!
CAN A CAR RUN WITH A BENT BRAKE LINKAGE CONNECTOR?
DUAL OVERHEAD CAMS!
I THINK I'M MARRIED!
SOMEONE WAS!
I THINK SOMEONE WAS!
WHAT DO THEY KNOW ABOUT BOLTING. THESE YOUNG PUNKS TODAY!
AND SHE'S REALLY IN NEED, SEE!
IF ALL YOU DID WAS STAND IN THE SAME ROOM WITH HER, YOU COULDN'T HELP BUT FEEL HER TITS!
IT LOOKS LIKE RAIN, SO I BETTER GET GOING!
GEE, IT REALLY DOES LOOK KIND OF CUTE...
WHAT TIME IS IT?
I JUST BOLTED MY CIGARETTE LIGHTER INTO THE STEERING PRAWL!
FALLEN ROCK ZONE! OIL SLICK!
I THINK I HAVE FIVE KIDS!
I KNOW A GREAT JOKE ABOUT A WOMAN WITH BIG TITS!
THEY TURN 'EM TO THE SOUTH, EAST, WEST, ANY OLD WAY!
THIS BLONDE WITH THE BIG TITS, I MEAN!
ONCE, I TOOK HER FOR A RIDE ON MY MOTORCYCLE!
LUCKY THE BUS IS HERE NOW, BECAUSE IT IS STARTING TO RAIN!
AH!
IT MUST BE SOME TIME!
I HAVE TO GO TO THE BATHROOM!
SPIN! VROOM! CRACK! BANG! KEE-RASH!
OR IS THAT MY BROTHER?
IT SEEMS THERE WAS ONCE THIS BIG BLONDE WITH BIG TITS!
WHAT DO THEY GIVE A SHIT!
WHEN SHE NOTICES THAT BY ACCIDENT THEY LEFT THE DOOR TO THE GORILLA CAGE OPEN!
ME ON THE FRONT OF THE SEAT AND HER ON THE BACK!
PITTER PATTER! PITTER PATTER!
YES! YES! YES! OOOH! OOOOOH!
DID SOMEBODY MENTION TITS?
I WONDER IF THEY DOCK YOU FOR GOING TO THE BATHROOM!
60 M.P.G.!
WAIT A MINUTE! MY BROTHER WORKS FOR G.M.!
AND WHERE DOES SHE HAPPEN TO FIND HERSELF, BUT THE CITY ZOO!
THIS COUNTRY WAS BUILT ON BOLTS, BUT YOU JUST TRY TO TELL THEM THAT!
SO SHE LETS HERSELF INSIDE, SEE, AND SHE STARTS MAKING IT WITH THE GORILLA!
I GOT ME SUCH A FEEL JOB I COULD HARDLY STEER!
PITTER PATTER! PITTER PATTER!
GNNNXXXX! MGGGGGH! OOOH MY...
I CAN CONTRIBUTE TO THE CONVERSATION! I KNOW SOMETHING ABOUT TITS!
I'LL TRY TO WAIT UNTIL THE COFFEE BREAK!
TURBO ULTRA-FLOW!
BUT THIS STEERING POST LOCK HAS A G.M. MARKING!
WAIT A MINUTE! WAS IT A BLONDE WITH BIG TITS?
FUCKING NO-GOOD BUNCH OF SHIT-EATING YOUNG COCKSUCKERS!
WHEN WHO SHOULD COME ALONG BUT THE HEAD ZOOKEEPER!
THEN THIS COP, HE STOPS US!
PITTER PATTER! PITTER PATTER!
AH!
TO ME, SOMETIMES THE BIG HORN BOLT LOOKS A LITTLE LIKE A TIT!
DID WE HAVE THE COFFEE BREAK YET?
YES, MR. MAYOR! I'M THE ONE WHO SAVED THE FAMILY OF 20 FROM THE BURNING TENEMENT!
SO I MUST BE MY BROTHER!
WHAT TIME IS IT?
I TELL THEM, I WAS YOUNG ONCE TOO! I FELT MY SHARE OF TITS!
I THINK... OR WAS IT THE GORILLA THAT HAD THE BIG TITS!
HE TAKES HIMSELF ONE LOOK AT THOSE TITS OF HERS, HE WINKS AT ME AND HE SAYS...
PITPITPIT PATPATPAT PITPATPIT PAT PITPAT PITPATPIT PATPIT PATPIT PATPIT!
SOB! IT'S LEAVING!
SOMEBODY DIDN'T PUT THE RATCHET ON! HOW CAN I PUT THE RATCHET BINDER ON IF THERE'S NO RATCHET!
GULP!
UH OH!
YOU PROBABLY REMEMBER ME FROM LAST WEEK WHEN I SAVED THE 75 SWIMSUIT CONTESTENTS FROM DROWNING!
BUT THEN WHO IS MY BROTHER?
SOMEONE SOMEWHERE MUST KNOW THE TIME!
I ONCE EVEN FELT A MOVIE STAR'S TITS!
MAYBE IT WAS A MALE HOBO, A FEMALE GORILLA AND A MALE ZOOKEEPER!
..."BUDDY, YOU DESERVE A MEDAL INSTEAD OF A TICKET!"
HONEY, WAS THAT THE ALARM ALREADY!
CIGARETTE?
BOY, WOULD I LIKE TO GET MY HANDS ON THE SONOFABITCH SHIRKER! I'D TORTURE HIM LIKE NO ONE EVER SAW!
IF I WORKED UP IN THE TRAILER SECTION, I BET THIS WOULD NEVER HAVE HAPPENED!
AS MY REWARD, YOU'RE GIVING ME FREE USE OF THE OFFICIAL CITY LIMOUSINE FOR A WEEK? HOW NICE!
HE MUST BE ME!
I WOULDN'T BE SURPRISED IF IT ISN'T AFTER THREE!
SHE CAME INTO TOWN BACK IN '37!
DIDN'T AFFECT THE WAY I BOLTED, THOUGH!
ANYWAY, SOMEONE BEATS SOMEONE UP AND THEN SAYS TO THEM, "THIS'LL TEACH YOU TO KEEP YOUR HANDS OFF MY GIRL!"
HEH HEH!
AT LEAST, I THINK THERE WAS A COP AND I THINK HE SAID SOMETHING LIKE THAT!
BRRRINNG! PITTER PATTER! PITTER PATTER!
IS IT NOON YET?
I'D START BY FORCING RED-HOT WELDING BOLTS UP UNDER HIS FINGERNAILS!
IF IT WORKED, HEH HEH!
AFTER THEY PUT THE TOILET IN, THAT IS!
MRRRRR! VROOOM! RRRRRR! VROOOOM!
THEN WHAT TIME ARE WE?
THAT IS, UNLESS IT'S THE MORNING!
WHAT YEAR IS IT NOW?
IS IT THE WEEKEND YET?
MMMMMMM! THAT ODOMETER GREASE LOOKS JUST LIKE GRAPE JELLY!
HONEY, IS IT TIME FOR ME TO GET UP YET?
DOES ANYONE KNOW THE TIME?
THEN I'D TAKE THE METAL LATHE AND SLOWLY RUB EVERY LAST INCH OF SKIN OFF HIS BODY!
MAYBE I SHOULD ASK SOMEBODY THE TIME!
WHERE DID THAT TRUCK COME FROM!
OIL SLICK! OIL SLICK!
WHO?
THE END

FOLDOUT COMICS!

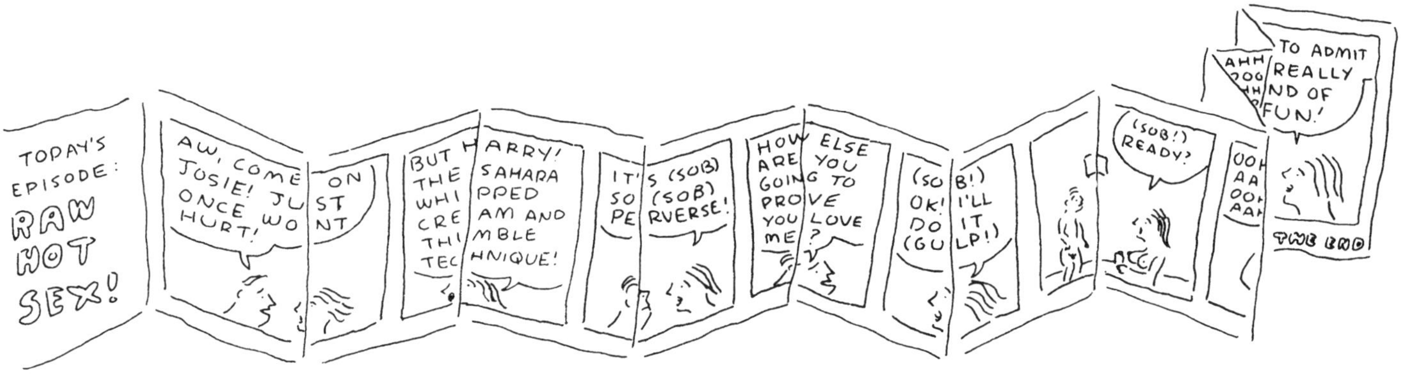
TODAY'S EPISODE: RAW HOT SEX!
AW, COME JOSIE! JU ONCE WO HURT!
ON ST NT
BUT H THE WHI CRE THI TEC
ARRY! SAHARA PPED AM AND MBLE HNIQUE!
IT' SO PE
S (SOB) (SOB) RVERSE!
HOW ARE GOING PRO YOU ME
ELSE YOU G TO VE LOVE ?
(SO OK! DO (GU
B!) I'LL IT LP!)
(SOB!) READY?
OOH AA OOH AAH
AHH OOO
TO ADMIT REALLY ND OF FUN!
THE END

READ ALOUD PORNO COMICS!

ACTUALLY SPEAK WHAT THE CHARACTERS SAY, AND HEAR SECRET SPELLINGS OF DIRTY WORDS!

VETERAN'S DAY CERTAINLY TURNED OUT LOVELY FOR A ROUND OF GOLF, NEPHEW!

BUT AREN'T YOU FIRST TO TEE? I TEE LATER!

YES, BUT I'M TIRED NOW! I'LL MEET YOU BACK AT THE CLUBHOUSE!

SEE YOU, AUNTIE!

I HOPE YOU DON'T MIND MY BRINGING UP BUSINESS NOW, UNCLE, BUT HAVE YOU DECIDED HOW MY FIRM SHOULD HANDLE YOUR PUBLICITY?

YES! AS FOR THE P.R., I SEEK A NATIONWIDE CAMPAIGN!

EXCUSE ME, FELLAS! BUT IF YOU SEE KAYE, TELL HER I WAS LOOKING FOR HER!

SHE WENT BACK TO THE CLUB-HOUSE, EM!

I HAVE AN IDEA, UNC! WHY DON'T WE TAKE A BREAK, TOO, AND HAVE SOME BOURBON!

I DON'T KNOW! I BETTER BE CAREFUL! AT THAT PARTY GIVEN BY THE V.A., GEE, I AN' A BUDDY OF MINE GOT DRUNK!

SOME MINTS, THEN?

I SHOULD REALLY BE ON A DIET, BUT WHEN IT COMES TO CANDY...OH, YOU SEE A CHEAT-ER!

SAY, THAT REMINDS ME! WHY DON'T YOU ASK YOUR FIANCÉE TO JOIN YOUR AUNT AND ME FOR DINNER LATER ON OUR YACHT!

SPLENDID! I'LL GO ASK HER NOW!

I'D SURE LIKE TO TAKE YOU OUT TO SEA, OH EMMY!

THE END

DO-IT-YOURSELF COMICS!

CONNECT THE NUMBERS AND CREATE YOUR OWN PORNOGRAPHY!

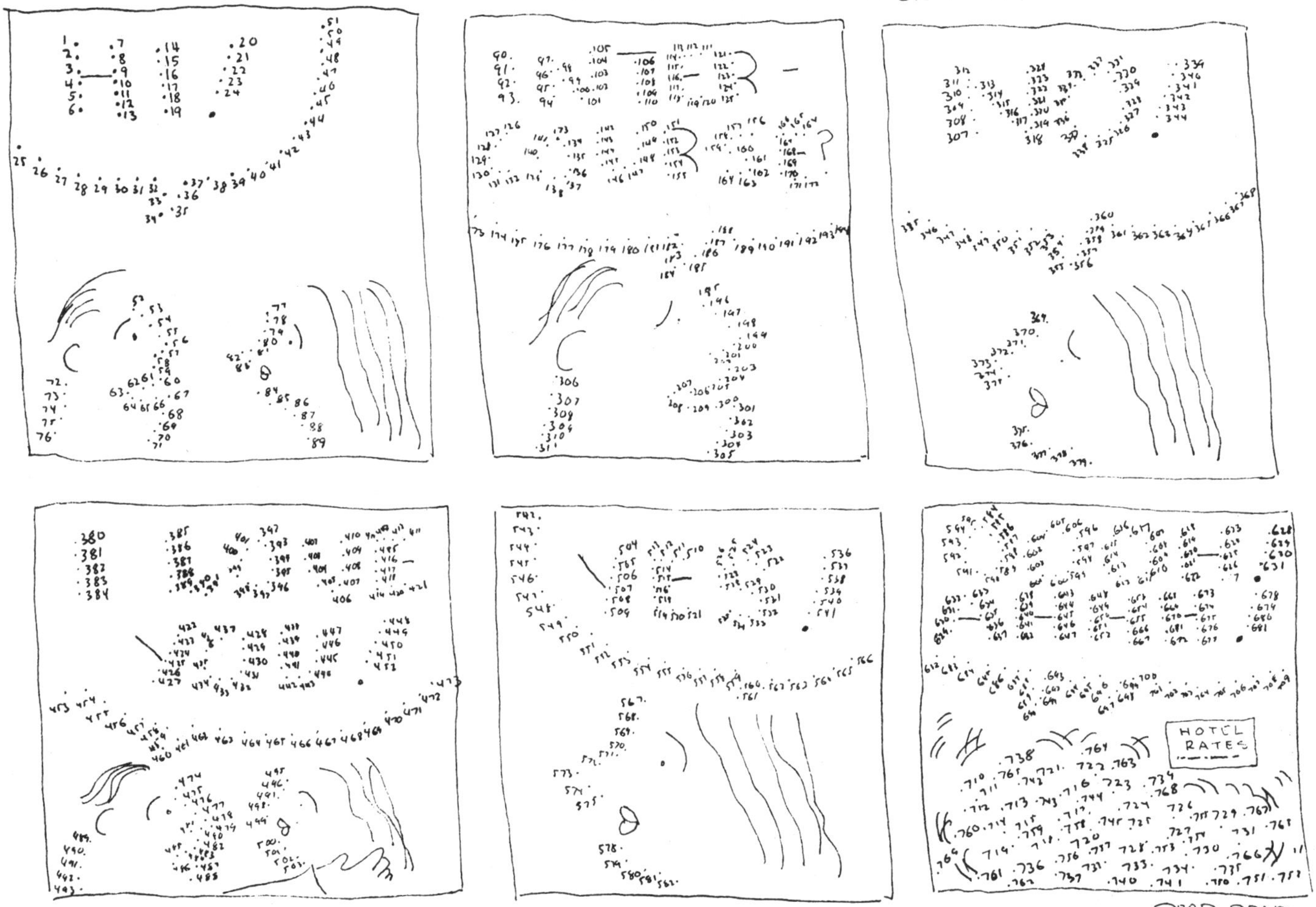

HOTEL RATES

THE END

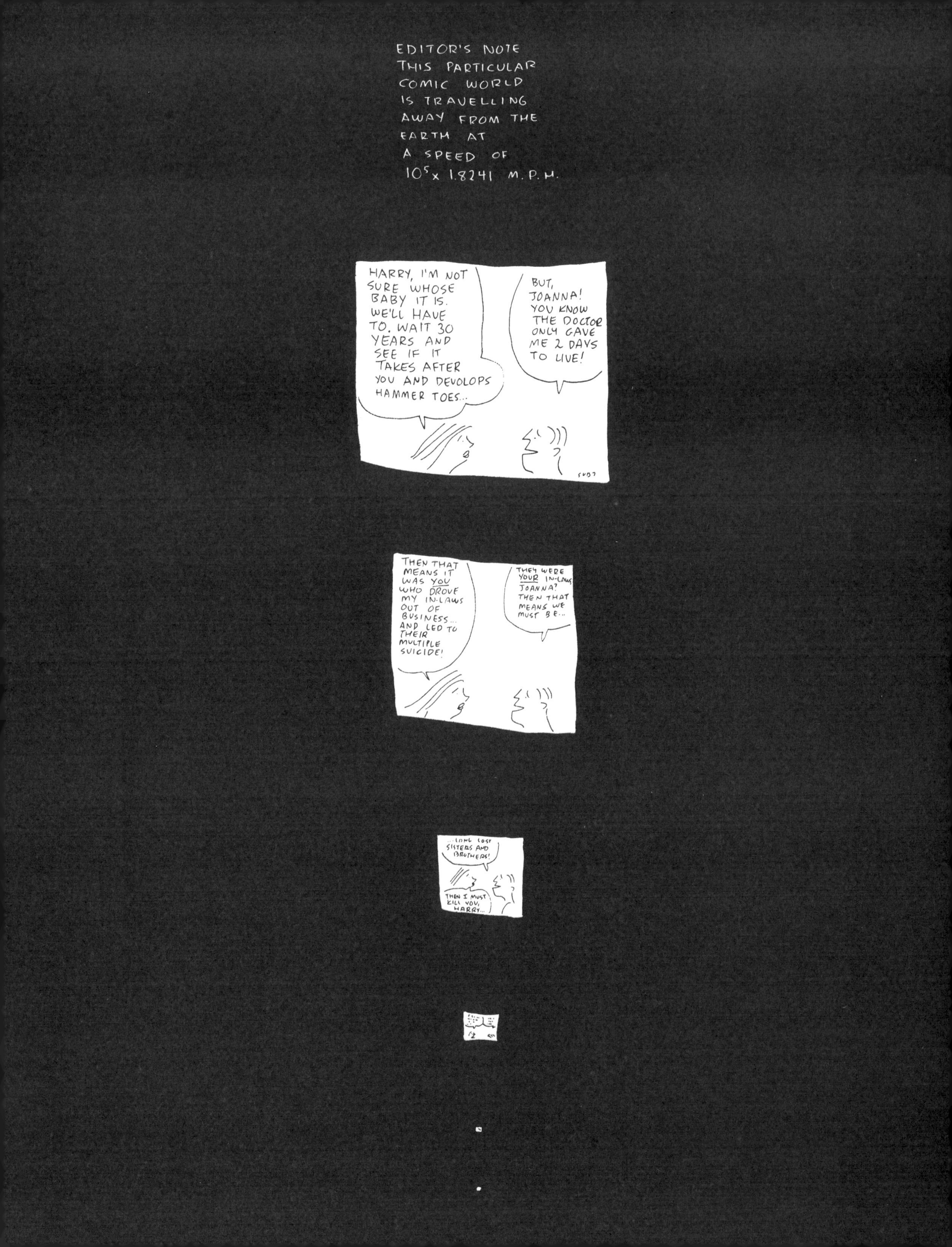
EDITOR'S NOTE THIS PARTICULAR COMIC WORLD IS TRAVELLING AWAY FROM THE EARTH AT A SPEED OF 10^5 x 1.8241 M.P.H.
HARRY, I'M NOT SURE WHOSE BABY IT IS. WE'LL HAVE TO. WAIT 30 YEARS AND SEE IF IT TAKES AFTER YOU AND DEVOLOPS HAMMER TOES...
BUT, JOANNA! YOU KNOW THE DOCTOR ONLY GAVE ME 2 DAYS TO LIVE!
THEN THAT MEANS IT WAS YOU WHO DROVE MY IN-LAWS OUT OF BUSINESS... AND LED TO THEIR MULTIPLE SUICIDE!
THEY WERE YOUR IN-LAWS JOANNA? THEN THAT MEANS WE MUST BE...
...LONG LOST SISTERS AND BROTHERS!
THEN I MUST KILL YOU, HARRY...

COUNT-THE-MISTAKES PORNO COMICS!

THERE ARE 117 DIFFERENT MISTAKES IN THE COMIC STRIP BELOW!
SEE HOW MANY YOU CAN FIND!

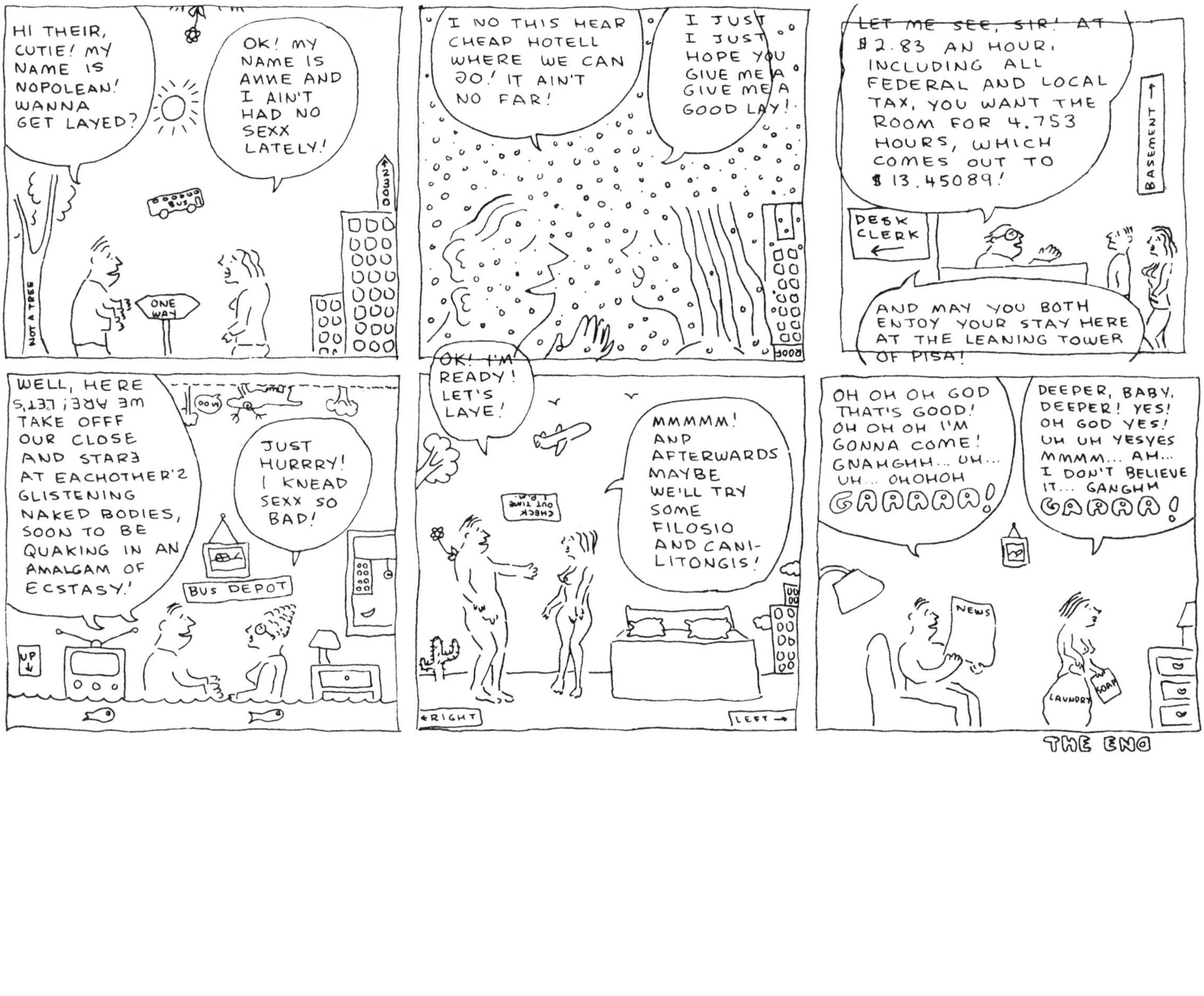
HI THEIR, CUTIE! MY NAME IS NOPOLEAN! WANNA GET LAYED?
OK! MY NAME IS ANNE AND I AIN'T HAD NO SEXX LATELY!
BUS
NOT A TREE
ONE WAY
I NO THIS HEAR CHEAP HOTELL WHERE WE CAN GO! IT AIN'T NO FAR!
I JUST I JUST HOPE YOU GIVE ME A GIVE ME A GOOD LAY!
ROOF
~~LET ME SEE, SIR! AT~~ $2.83 AN HOUR, INCLUDING ALL FEDERAL AND LOCAL TAX, YOU WANT THE ROOM FOR 4.753 HOURS, WHICH COMES OUT TO $13.45089!
BASEMENT
DESK CLERK
AND MAY YOU BOTH ENJOY YOUR STAY HERE AT THE LEANING TOWER OF PISA!
WELL, HERE WE ARE! LET'S TAKE OFFF OUR CLOSE AND STARE AT EACHOTHER'Z GLISTENING NAKED BODIES, SOON TO BE QUAKING IN AN AMALGAM OF ECSTASY!
JUST HURRRY! I KNEAD SEXX SO BAD!
BUS DEPOT
UP
OK! I'M READY! LET'S LAYE!
MMMMM! AND AFTERWARDS MAYBE WE'LL TRY SOME FILOSIO AND CANILITONGIS!
RIGHT
LEFT
OH OH OH GOD THAT'S GOOD! OH OH OH I'M GONNA COME! GNAHGHH... UH... UH... OHOHOH GAAAAA!
DEEPER, BABY, DEEPER! YES! OH GOD YES! UH UH YESYES MMMM... AH... I DON'T BELIEVE IT... GANGHM GAAAA!
NEWS
LAUNDRY
SOAP
THE END

(NOTE: AFTER BEING CONVICTED OF PORNOGRAPHY, THE FOLLOWING COMIC WAS SENTENCED TO A TERM OF NOT LESS THAN FOUR YEARS AND NOT MORE THAN TEN YEARS. IT IS NOW SERVING THAT TERM)

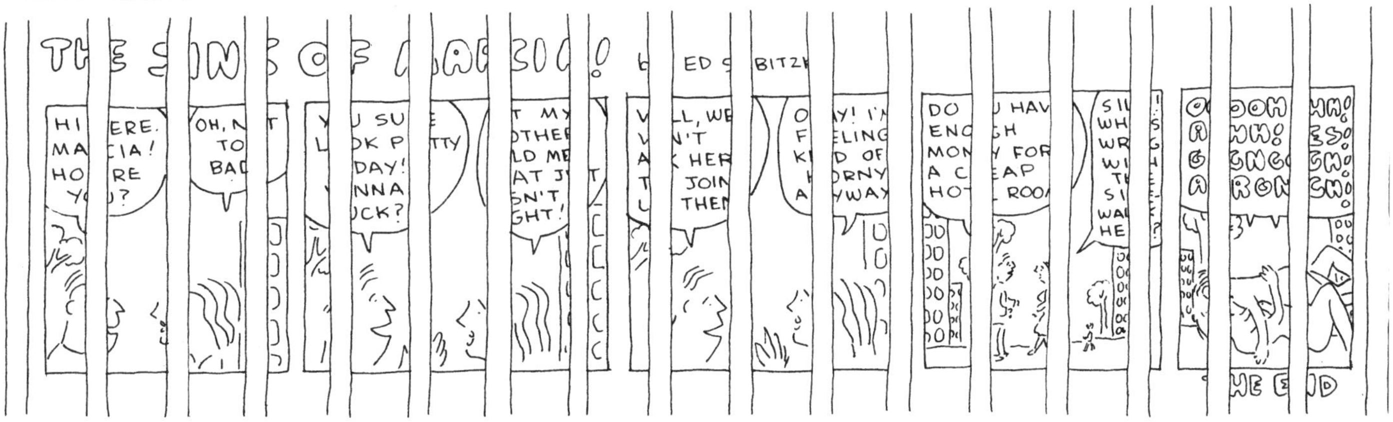

ED
BITZ
HI ERE. MA IA! HO RE Y U?
OH, N T TO BAD
U SU E OK P TTY DAY! NNA CK?
T MY OTHER LD ME AT J T N'T GHT!
L, WE N'T HER JOIN THEM
Y! I'M ELING D OF ORNY YWAY
DO U HAV ENO GH MON Y FOR A C EAP HOT ROO
SI WH WR WI S WA HE
OOH WH! ES!
HE E D

GROWING OLDER COMICS!

BY ED SUBITZKY
COLORING BY BARBARA SCHUBECK

A FULL DAY IN THE TYPICAL PERSON'S LIFE OVER 30!

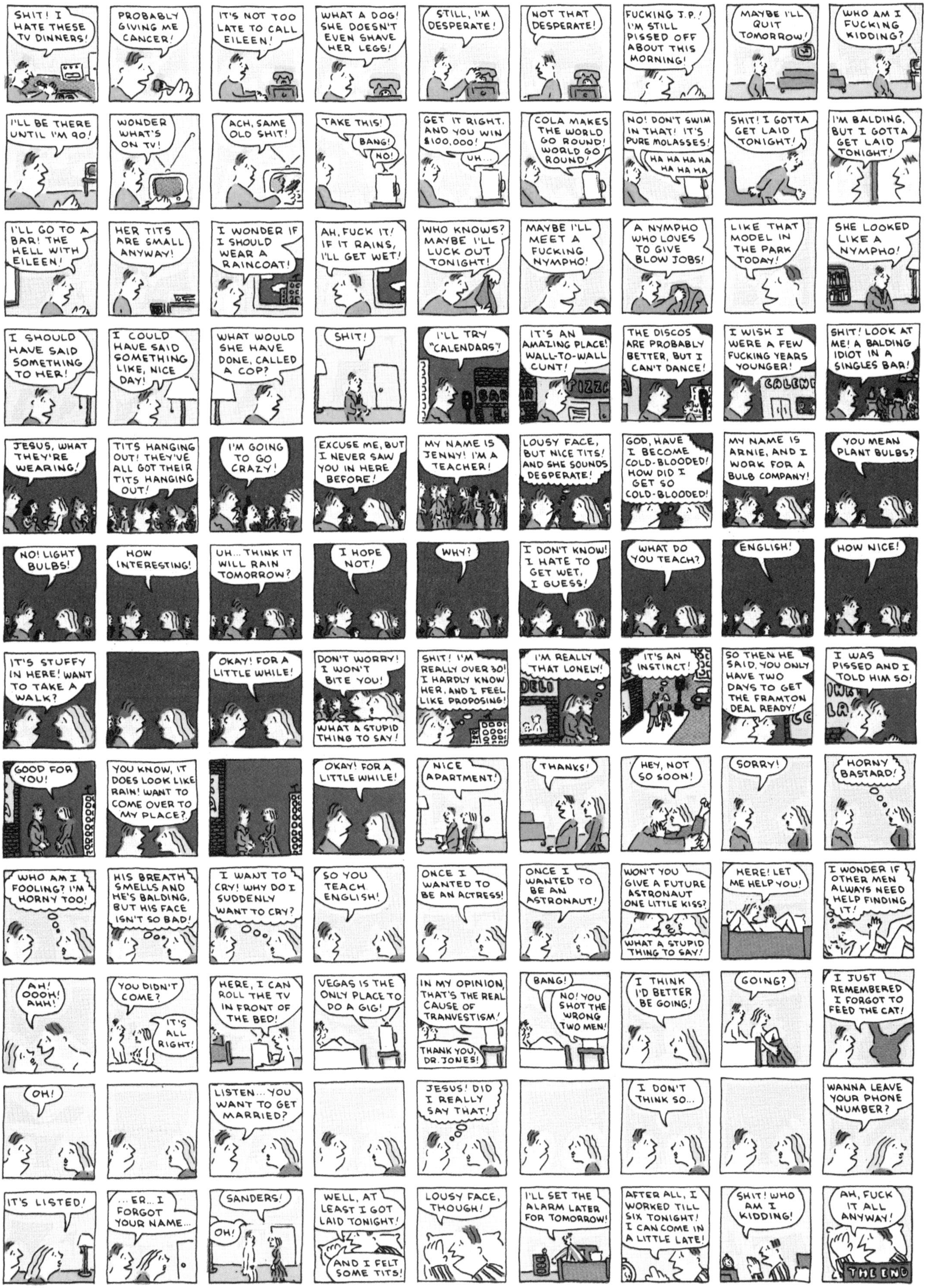
SHIT! I HATE THESE TV DINNERS!
PROBABLY GIVING ME CANCER!
IT'S NOT TOO LATE TO CALL EILEEN!
WHAT A DOG! SHE DOESN'T EVEN SHAVE HER LEGS!
STILL, I'M DESPERATE!
NOT THAT DESPERATE!
FUCKING J.P.! I'M STILL PISSED OFF ABOUT THIS MORNING!
MAYBE I'LL QUIT TOMORROW!
WHO AM I FUCKING KIDDING?
I'LL BE THERE UNTIL I'M 90!
WONDER WHAT'S ON TV!
ACH, SAME OLD SHIT!
TAKE THIS!
BANG!
NO!
GET IT RIGHT, AND YOU WIN $100,000!
UH...
COLA MAKES THE WORLD GO ROUND! WORLD GO ROUND!
NO! DON'T SWIM IN THAT! IT'S PURE MOLASSES!
HA HA HA HA HA HA HA
SHIT! I GOTTA GET LAID TONIGHT!
I'M BALDING, BUT I GOTTA GET LAID TONIGHT!
I'LL GO TO A BAR! THE HELL WITH EILEEN!
HER TITS ARE SMALL ANYWAY!
I WONDER IF I SHOULD WEAR A RAINCOAT!
AH, FUCK IT! IF IT RAINS, I'LL GET WET!
WHO KNOWS? MAYBE I'LL LUCK OUT TONIGHT!
MAYBE I'LL MEET A FUCKING NYMPHO!
A NYMPHO WHO LOVES TO GIVE BLOW JOBS!
LIKE THAT MODEL IN THE PARK TODAY!
SHE LOOKED LIKE A NYMPHO!
I SHOULD HAVE SAID SOMETHING TO HER!
I COULD HAVE SAID SOMETHING LIKE, NICE DAY!
WHAT WOULD SHE HAVE DONE, CALLED A COP?
SHIT!
I'LL TRY "CALENDARS"!
BAR
IT'S AN AMAZING PLACE! WALL-TO-WALL CUNT!
THE DISCOS ARE PROBABLY BETTER, BUT I CAN'T DANCE!
I WISH I WERE A FEW FUCKING YEARS YOUNGER!
SHIT! LOOK AT ME! A BALDING IDIOT IN A SINGLES BAR!
JESUS, WHAT THEY'RE WEARING!
TITS HANGING OUT! THEY'VE ALL GOT THEIR TITS HANGING OUT!
I'M GOING TO GO CRAZY!
EXCUSE ME, BUT I NEVER SAW YOU IN HERE BEFORE!
MY NAME IS JENNY! I'M A TEACHER!
LOUSY FACE, BUT NICE TITS! AND SHE SOUNDS DESPERATE!
GOD, HAVE I BECOME COLD-BLOODED! HOW DID I GET SO COLD-BLOODED!
MY NAME IS ARNIE, AND I WORK FOR A BULB COMPANY!
YOU MEAN PLANT BULBS?
NO! LIGHT BULBS!
HOW INTERESTING!
UH... THINK IT WILL RAIN TOMORROW?
I HOPE NOT!
WHY?
I DON'T KNOW! I HATE TO GET WET, I GUESS!
WHAT DO YOU TEACH?
ENGLISH!
HOW NICE!
IT'S STUFFY IN HERE! WANT TO TAKE A WALK?
OKAY! FOR A LITTLE WHILE!
DON'T WORRY! I WON'T BITE YOU!
WHAT A STUPID THING TO SAY!
SHIT! I'M REALLY OVER 30! I HARDLY KNOW HER, AND I FEEL LIKE PROPOSING!
I'M REALLY THAT LONELY!
DELI
IT'S AN INSTINCT!
SO THEN HE SAID, YOU ONLY HAVE TWO DAYS TO GET THE FRAMTON DEAL READY!
I WAS PISSED AND I TOLD HIM SO!
GOOD FOR YOU!
YOU KNOW, IT DOES LOOK LIKE RAIN! WANT TO COME OVER TO MY PLACE?
OKAY! FOR A LITTLE WHILE!
NICE APARTMENT!
THANKS!
HEY, NOT SO SOON!
SORRY!
HORNY BASTARD!
WHO AM I FOOLING? I'M HORNY TOO!
HIS BREATH SMELLS AND HE'S BALDING, BUT HIS FACE ISN'T SO BAD!
I WANT TO CRY! WHY DO I SUDDENLY WANT TO CRY?
SO YOU TEACH ENGLISH!
ONCE I WANTED TO BE AN ACTRESS!
ONCE I WANTED TO BE AN ASTRONAUT!
WON'T YOU GIVE A FUTURE ASTRONAUT ONE LITTLE KISS?
WHAT A STUPID THING TO SAY!
HERE! LET ME HELP YOU!
I WONDER IF OTHER MEN ALWAYS NEED HELP FINDING IT!
AH! OOOH! AHH!
YOU DIDN'T COME?
IT'S ALL RIGHT!
HERE, I CAN ROLL THE TV IN FRONT OF THE BED!
VEGAS IS THE ONLY PLACE TO DO A GIG!
IN MY OPINION, THAT'S THE REAL CAUSE OF TRANVESTISM!
THANK YOU, DR. JONES!
BANG!
NO! YOU SHOT THE WRONG TWO MEN!
I THINK I'D BETTER BE GOING!
GOING?
I JUST REMEMBERED I FORGOT TO FEED THE CAT!
OH!
LISTEN... YOU WANT TO GET MARRIED?
JESUS! DID I REALLY SAY THAT!
I DON'T THINK SO...
WANNA LEAVE YOUR PHONE NUMBER?
IT'S LISTED!
...ER... I FORGOT YOUR NAME...
SANDERS!
OH!
WELL, AT LEAST I GOT LAID TONIGHT!
AND I FELT SOME TITS!
LOUSY FACE, THOUGH!
I'LL SET THE ALARM LATER FOR TOMORROW!
AFTER ALL, I WORKED TILL SIX TONIGHT! I CAN COME IN A LITTLE LATE!
SHIT! WHO AM I KIDDING!
AH, FUCK IT ALL ANYWAY!
THE END

MN: Could you talk a little bit about how you got involved with David Letterman?

ES: Oh sure, oh yeah. Letterman's people got in touch with me and asked if I wanted to become a writer for the morning show.[16] Of course, I said yes. So I went over there, and I didn't like it at all. In those days, they hired stand-up comedians to write for the morning show, and I did not work well with them. They were too competitive for me. I used to describe it like this: if you told them you felt awful because your family had just been destroyed in a fire, they would say "Oh, they had a hot time, didn't they?"

[*Laughter*]

That's what they were like! You couldn't have a conversation with them. To do what we're doing now, have a little normal give-and-take, a little normal human conversation, was not possible! Everything you said was fodder for a bad joke on their part. Not even a good joke, because you can't spontaneously come up with that many good jokes, no matter how brilliant you are.

MN: On to the Impostor, your *Letterman* debut on TV. The premise of the Imposter was that Letterman would introduce you as a renowned person. You'd start by playing it straight, and then just fall apart. You'd apologize that you were just an ordinary person who lied because you wanted to be on television. Did you come up with that? Was that suggested to you?

ES: As I recall, the Imposter was a mixture. It was based upon something that they came up with, and that I changed and embellished in ways I don't remember. I loved doing it. I loved being in front of a camera. I'm very shy with people one-on-one, but you can put me in front of an audience of a million people and I'm as cool as a cucumber. I'm loving every second of it. And the morning show went out live, so there was no room for a mistake. Letterman did try to put me at ease by telling me, "All we are trying to achieve here is stupidity, so if you can reach the level of stupid, you will be fine."

They would often suggest characters to me. But at the very beginning, it was people who are famous, but you don't know exactly what they look like. Like the author of a current best seller, or something like that. But they started to make it crazier and crazier. Like on one of them, I was the US Air Force Academy choir.[17]

[*Laughter*]

ES: They broadened it out, and I'm not sure they should have. It was fun in a way, but it wasn't really true to the ethic of the joke.

[16]*The David Letterman Show*, a morning talk show that aired from June 23 to October 24, 1980, and preceded the *Late Show with David Letterman*.

[17]There actually is no US Air Force Choir. The official choir of the US Air Force Band is actually called The Singing Sergeants.

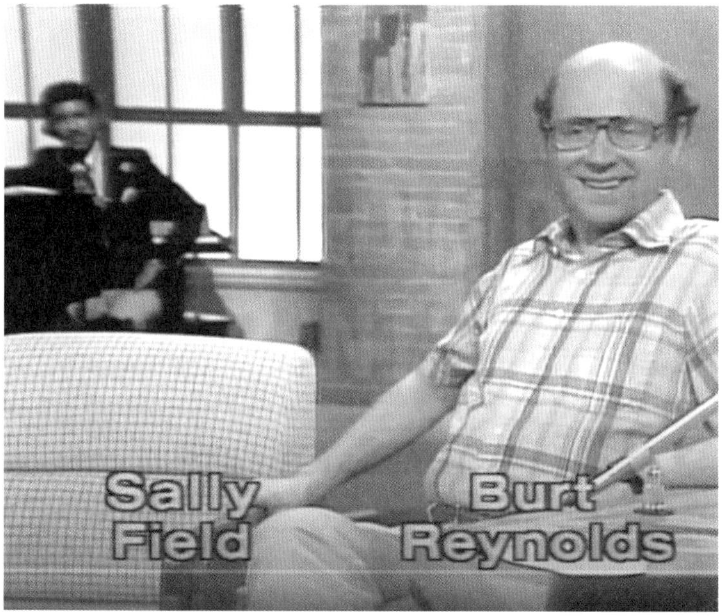
Sally
Field
Burt
Reynolds

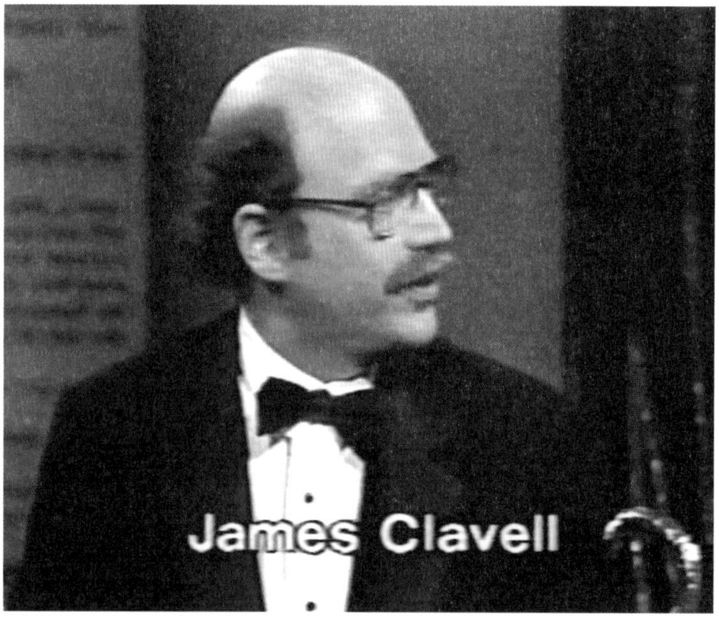
James Clavell

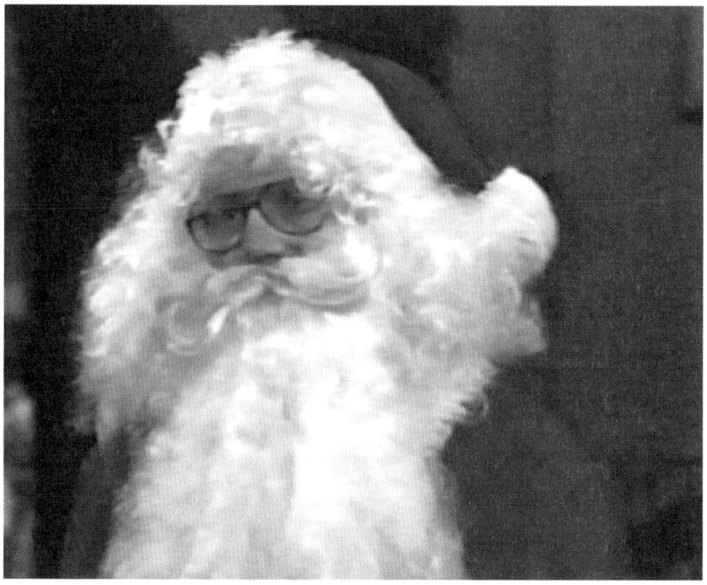

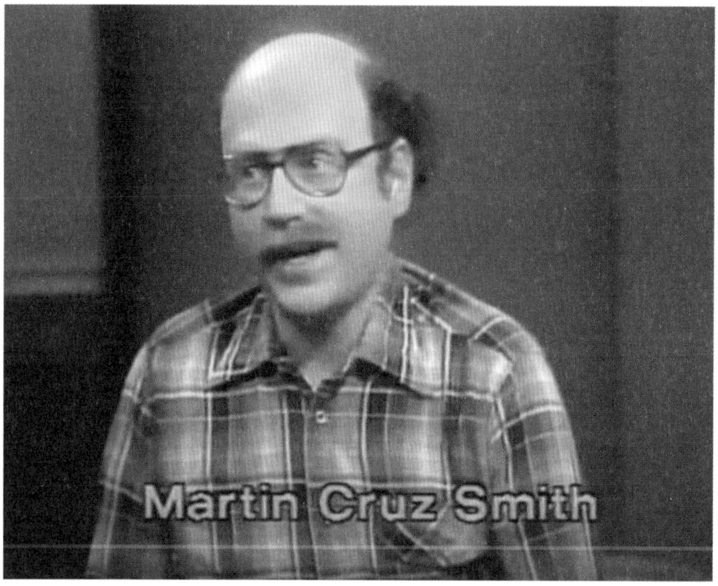
Martin Cruz Smith

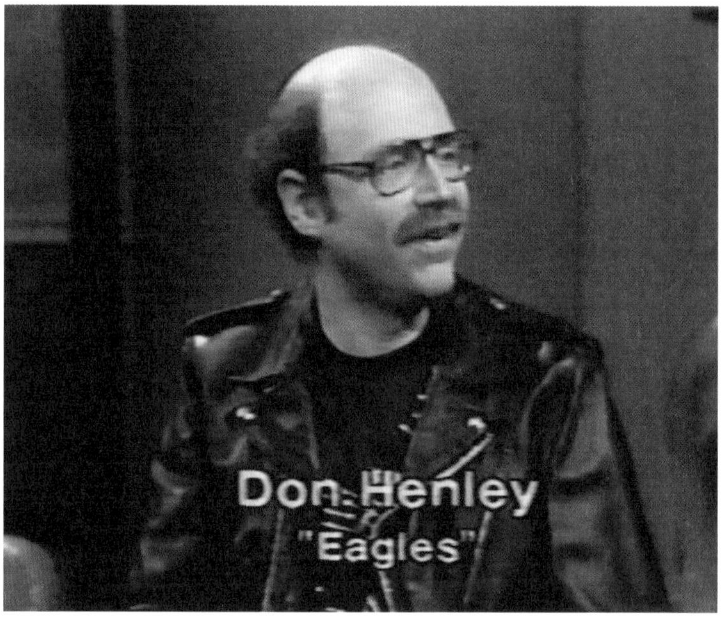
Don Henley
"Eagles"

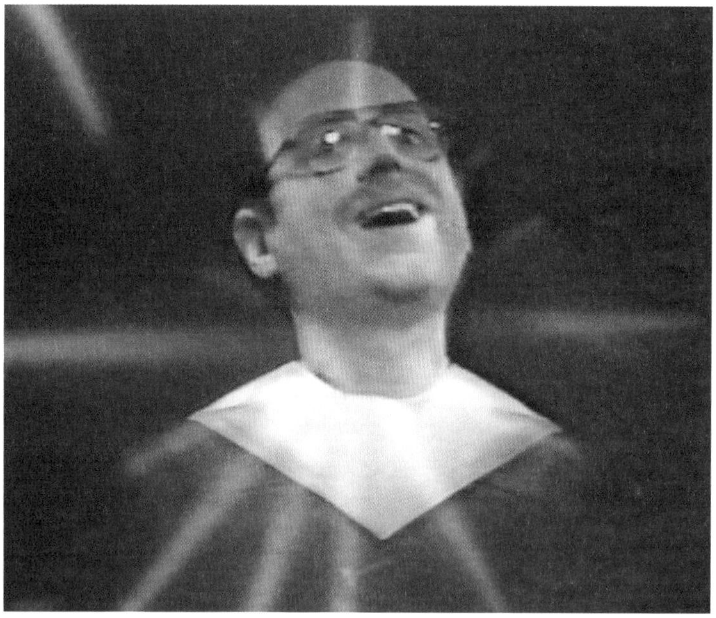

WARNING: THE FOLLOWING COMIC STRIP IS FOR ADULTS OVER 21 ONLY. IT CONTAINS THE HIGHEST-DENSITY PORNOGRAPHY (PERVERSIONS PER SQUARE INCH) EVER PUBLISHED.

THE AX-MURDERER AND THE LADYBUG FETISHIST AND THE STRIPPER AND THE MALE PROSTITUTES MOTHER!

LAST STITCH!
BAR
DEMONSTRATE!

THE END

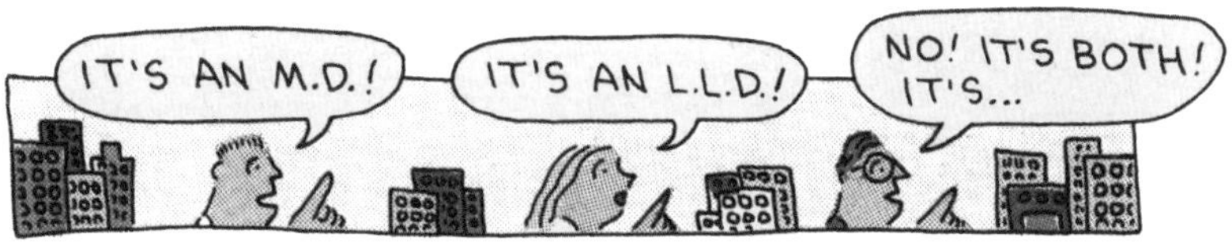
IT'S AN M.D.!
IT'S AN L.L.D.!
NO! IT'S BOTH! IT'S...

DOCTOR-LAWYER!

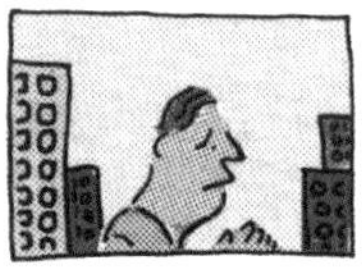

FIRST OF A BOLD NEW BREED!

BY ED SUBITZKY

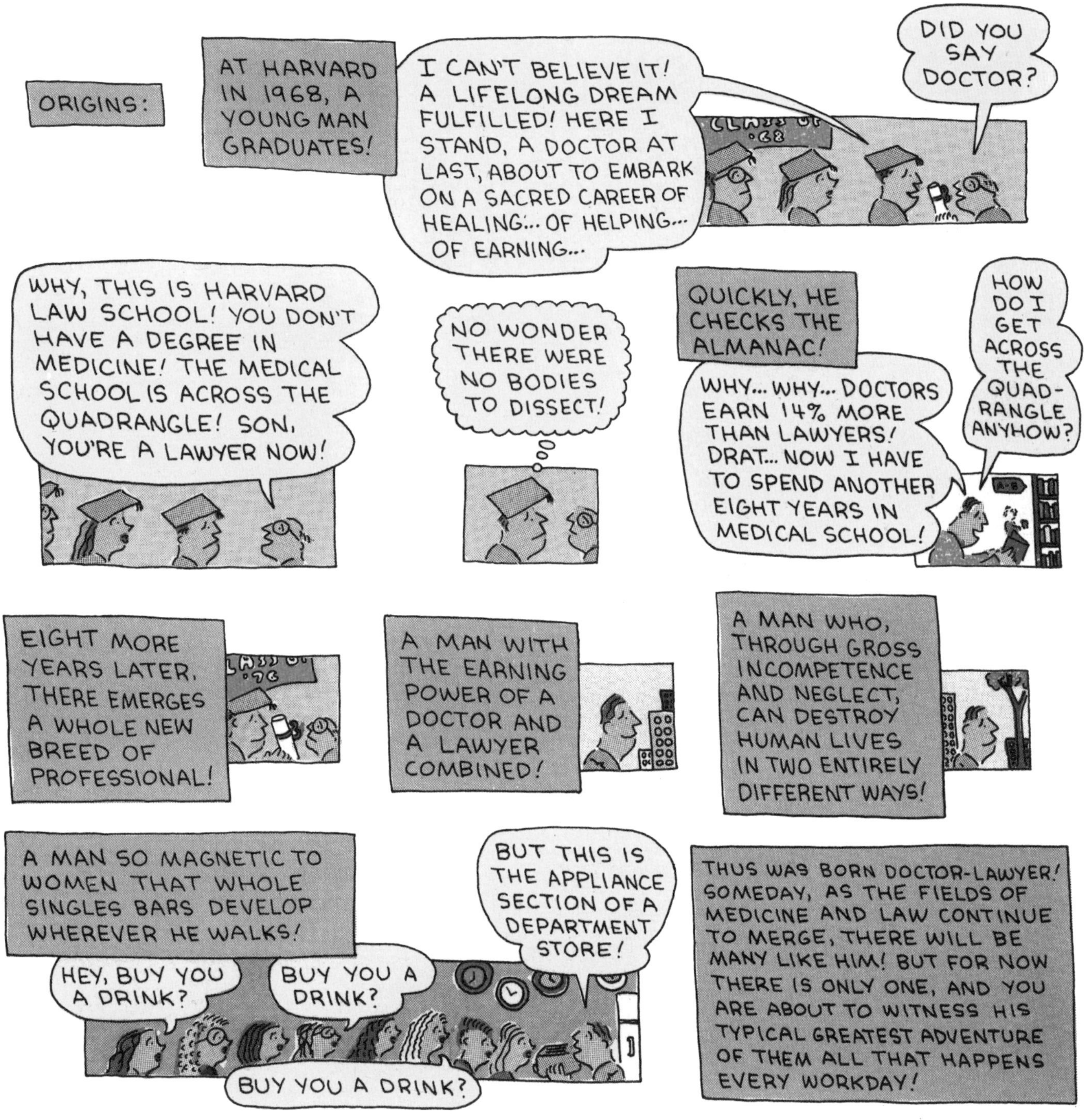
ORIGINS:
AT HARVARD IN 1968, A YOUNG MAN GRADUATES!
I CAN'T BELIEVE IT! A LIFELONG DREAM FULFILLED! HERE I STAND, A DOCTOR AT LAST, ABOUT TO EMBARK ON A SACRED CAREER OF HEALING... OF HELPING... OF EARNING...
DID YOU SAY DOCTOR?
WHY, THIS IS HARVARD LAW SCHOOL! YOU DON'T HAVE A DEGREE IN MEDICINE! THE MEDICAL SCHOOL IS ACROSS THE QUADRANGLE! SON, YOU'RE A LAWYER NOW!
NO WONDER THERE WERE NO BODIES TO DISSECT!
QUICKLY, HE CHECKS THE ALMANAC!
WHY... WHY... DOCTORS EARN 14% MORE THAN LAWYERS! DRAT... NOW I HAVE TO SPEND ANOTHER EIGHT YEARS IN MEDICAL SCHOOL!
HOW DO I GET ACROSS THE QUAD-RANGLE ANYHOW?
EIGHT MORE YEARS LATER, THERE EMERGES A WHOLE NEW BREED OF PROFESSIONAL!
A MAN WITH THE EARNING POWER OF A DOCTOR AND A LAWYER COMBINED!
A MAN WHO, THROUGH GROSS INCOMPETENCE AND NEGLECT, CAN DESTROY HUMAN LIVES IN TWO ENTIRELY DIFFERENT WAYS!
A MAN SO MAGNETIC TO WOMEN THAT WHOLE SINGLES BARS DEVELOP WHEREVER HE WALKS!
HEY, BUY YOU A DRINK?
BUY YOU A DRINK?
BUY YOU A DRINK?
BUT THIS IS THE APPLIANCE SECTION OF A DEPARTMENT STORE!
THUS WAS BORN DOCTOR-LAWYER! SOMEDAY, AS THE FIELDS OF MEDICINE AND LAW CONTINUE TO MERGE, THERE WILL BE MANY LIKE HIM! BUT FOR NOW THERE IS ONLY ONE, AND YOU ARE ABOUT TO WITNESS HIS TYPICAL GREATEST ADVENTURE OF THEM ALL THAT HAPPENS EVERY WORKDAY!

DOCTOR-LAWYER IN

"THE MAN WHO DROPPED DEAD IN THE AFTERNOON!"

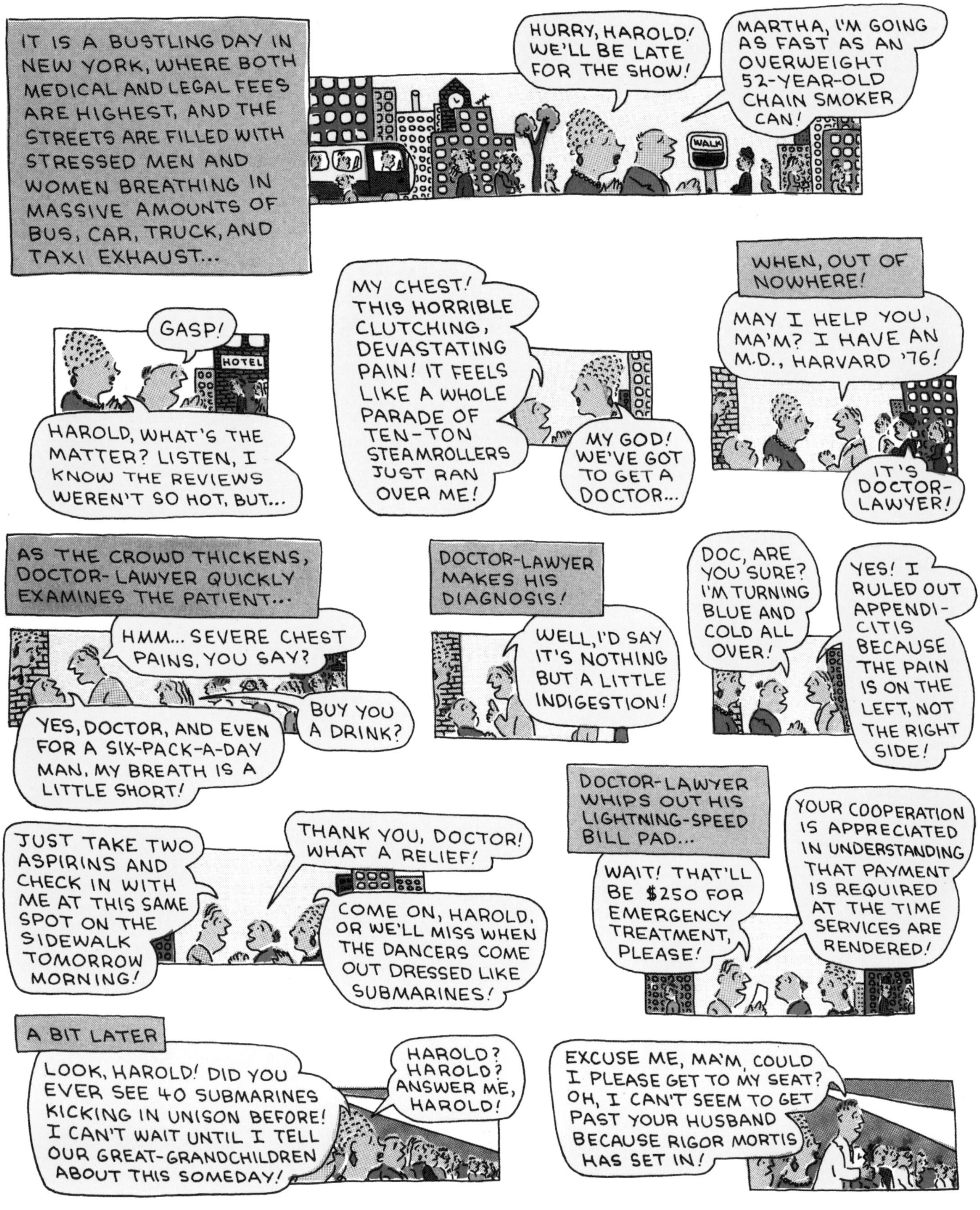

IT IS A BUSTLING DAY IN NEW YORK, WHERE BOTH MEDICAL AND LEGAL FEES ARE HIGHEST, AND THE STREETS ARE FILLED WITH STRESSED MEN AND WOMEN BREATHING IN MASSIVE AMOUNTS OF BUS, CAR, TRUCK, AND TAXI EXHAUST...
HURRY, HAROLD! WE'LL BE LATE FOR THE SHOW!
MARTHA, I'M GOING AS FAST AS AN OVERWEIGHT 52-YEAR-OLD CHAIN SMOKER CAN!
WALK
GASP!
HOTEL
HAROLD, WHAT'S THE MATTER? LISTEN, I KNOW THE REVIEWS WEREN'T SO HOT, BUT...
MY CHEST! THIS HORRIBLE CLUTCHING, DEVASTATING PAIN! IT FEELS LIKE A WHOLE PARADE OF TEN-TON STEAMROLLERS JUST RAN OVER ME!
MY GOD! WE'VE GOT TO GET A DOCTOR...
WHEN, OUT OF NOWHERE!
MAY I HELP YOU, MA'M? I HAVE AN M.D., HARVARD '76!
IT'S DOCTOR-LAWYER!
AS THE CROWD THICKENS, DOCTOR-LAWYER QUICKLY EXAMINES THE PATIENT...
HMM... SEVERE CHEST PAINS, YOU SAY?
YES, DOCTOR, AND EVEN FOR A SIX-PACK-A-DAY MAN, MY BREATH IS A LITTLE SHORT!
BUY YOU A DRINK?
DOCTOR-LAWYER MAKES HIS DIAGNOSIS!
WELL, I'D SAY IT'S NOTHING BUT A LITTLE INDIGESTION!
DOC, ARE YOU SURE? I'M TURNING BLUE AND COLD ALL OVER!
YES! I RULED OUT APPENDICITIS BECAUSE THE PAIN IS ON THE LEFT, NOT THE RIGHT SIDE!
JUST TAKE TWO ASPIRINS AND CHECK IN WITH ME AT THIS SAME SPOT ON THE SIDEWALK TOMORROW MORNING!
THANK YOU, DOCTOR! WHAT A RELIEF!
COME ON, HAROLD, OR WE'LL MISS WHEN THE DANCERS COME OUT DRESSED LIKE SUBMARINES!
DOCTOR-LAWYER WHIPS OUT HIS LIGHTNING-SPEED BILL PAD...
WAIT! THAT'LL BE $250 FOR EMERGENCY TREATMENT, PLEASE!
YOUR COOPERATION IS APPRECIATED IN UNDERSTANDING THAT PAYMENT IS REQUIRED AT THE TIME SERVICES ARE RENDERED!
A BIT LATER
LOOK, HAROLD! DID YOU EVER SEE 40 SUBMARINES KICKING IN UNISON BEFORE! I CAN'T WAIT UNTIL I TELL OUR GREAT-GRANDCHILDREN ABOUT THIS SOMEDAY!
HAROLD? HAROLD? ANSWER ME, HAROLD!
EXCUSE ME, MA'M, COULD I PLEASE GET TO MY SEAT? OH, I CAN'T SEEM TO GET PAST YOUR HUSBAND BECAUSE RIGOR MORTIS HAS SET IN!

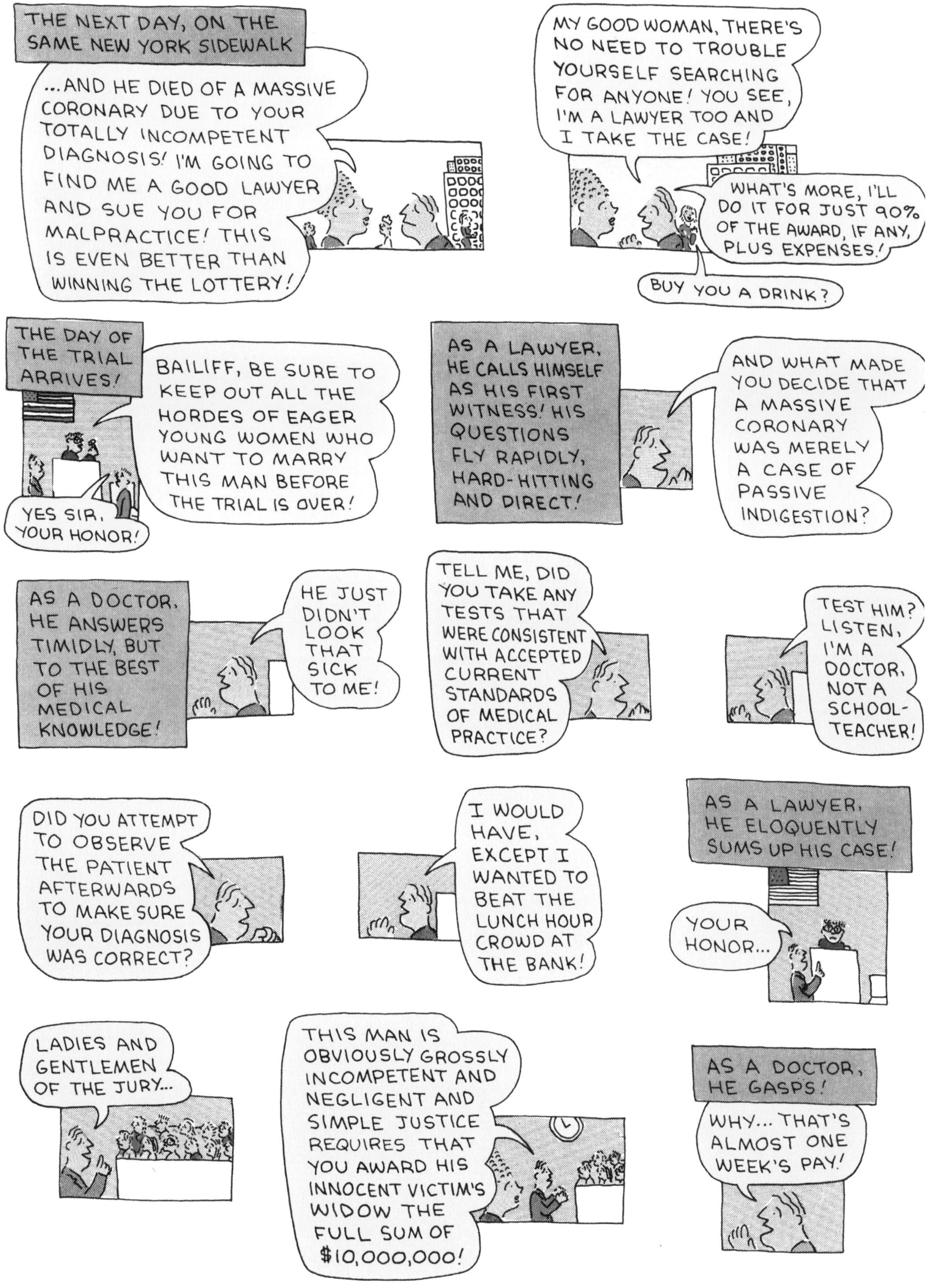
THE NEXT DAY, ON THE SAME NEW YORK SIDEWALK
...AND HE DIED OF A MASSIVE CORONARY DUE TO YOUR TOTALLY INCOMPETENT DIAGNOSIS! I'M GOING TO FIND ME A GOOD LAWYER AND SUE YOU FOR MALPRACTICE! THIS IS EVEN BETTER THAN WINNING THE LOTTERY!
MY GOOD WOMAN, THERE'S NO NEED TO TROUBLE YOURSELF SEARCHING FOR ANYONE! YOU SEE, I'M A LAWYER TOO AND I TAKE THE CASE!
WHAT'S MORE, I'LL DO IT FOR JUST 90% OF THE AWARD, IF ANY, PLUS EXPENSES!
BUY YOU A DRINK?
THE DAY OF THE TRIAL ARRIVES!
BAILIFF, BE SURE TO KEEP OUT ALL THE HORDES OF EAGER YOUNG WOMEN WHO WANT TO MARRY THIS MAN BEFORE THE TRIAL IS OVER!
YES SIR, YOUR HONOR!
AS A LAWYER, HE CALLS HIMSELF AS HIS FIRST WITNESS! HIS QUESTIONS FLY RAPIDLY, HARD-HITTING AND DIRECT!
AND WHAT MADE YOU DECIDE THAT A MASSIVE CORONARY WAS MERELY A CASE OF PASSIVE INDIGESTION?
AS A DOCTOR, HE ANSWERS TIMIDLY, BUT TO THE BEST OF HIS MEDICAL KNOWLEDGE!
HE JUST DIDN'T LOOK THAT SICK TO ME!
TELL ME, DID YOU TAKE ANY TESTS THAT WERE CONSISTENT WITH ACCEPTED CURRENT STANDARDS OF MEDICAL PRACTICE?
TEST HIM? LISTEN, I'M A DOCTOR, NOT A SCHOOL-TEACHER!
DID YOU ATTEMPT TO OBSERVE THE PATIENT AFTERWARDS TO MAKE SURE YOUR DIAGNOSIS WAS CORRECT?
I WOULD HAVE, EXCEPT I WANTED TO BEAT THE LUNCH HOUR CROWD AT THE BANK!
AS A LAWYER, HE ELOQUENTLY SUMS UP HIS CASE!
YOUR HONOR...
LADIES AND GENTLEMEN OF THE JURY...
THIS MAN IS OBVIOUSLY GROSSLY INCOMPETENT AND NEGLIGENT AND SIMPLE JUSTICE REQUIRES THAT YOU AWARD HIS INNOCENT VICTIM'S WIDOW THE FULL SUM OF $10,000,000!
AS A DOCTOR, HE GASPS!
WHY... THAT'S ALMOST ONE WEEK'S PAY!

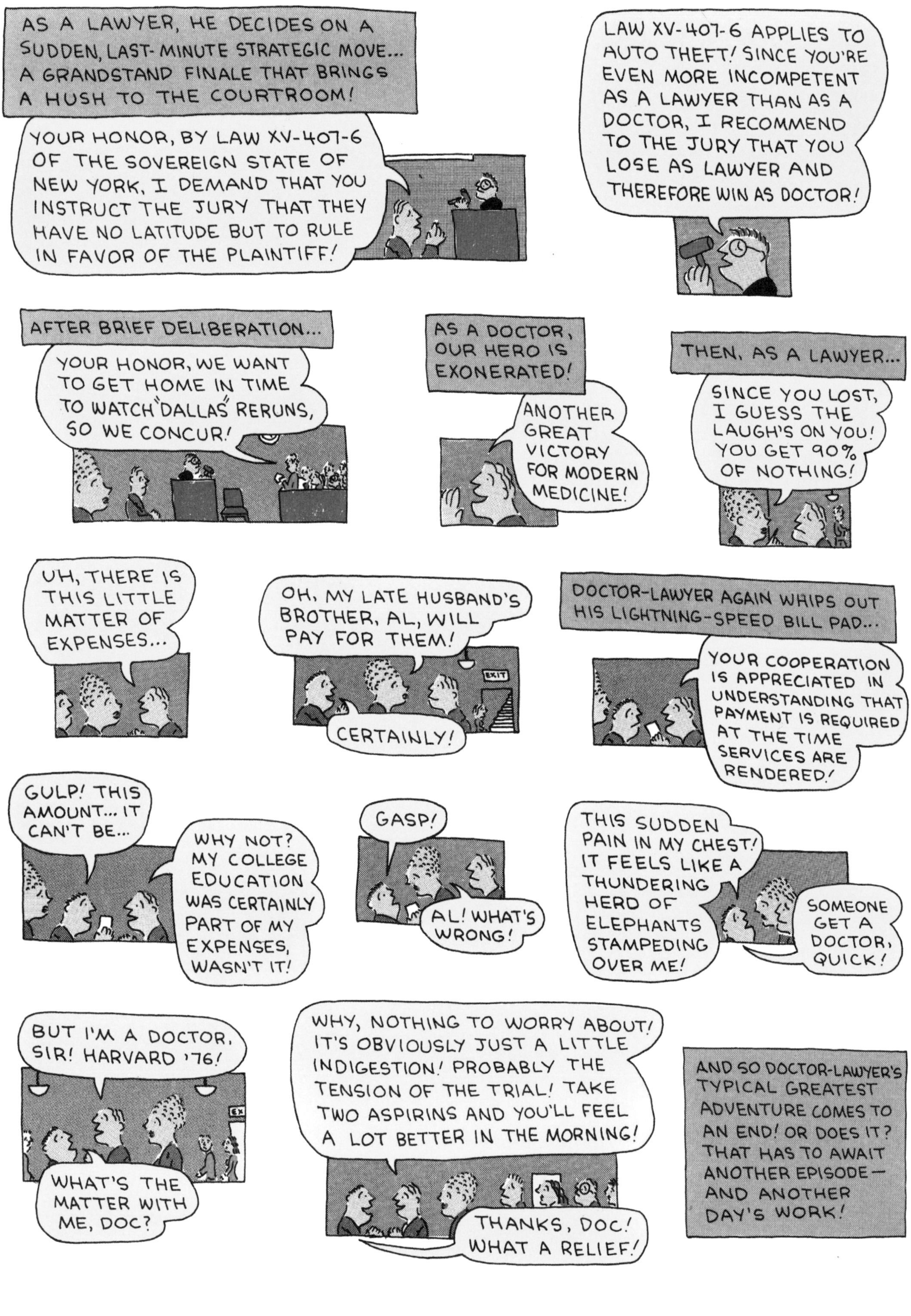
AS A LAWYER, HE DECIDES ON A SUDDEN, LAST-MINUTE STRATEGIC MOVE... A GRANDSTAND FINALE THAT BRINGS A HUSH TO THE COURTROOM!
YOUR HONOR, BY LAW XV-407-6 OF THE SOVEREIGN STATE OF NEW YORK, I DEMAND THAT YOU INSTRUCT THE JURY THAT THEY HAVE NO LATITUDE BUT TO RULE IN FAVOR OF THE PLAINTIFF!
LAW XV-407-6 APPLIES TO AUTO THEFT! SINCE YOU'RE EVEN MORE INCOMPETENT AS A LAWYER THAN AS A DOCTOR, I RECOMMEND TO THE JURY THAT YOU LOSE AS LAWYER AND THEREFORE WIN AS DOCTOR!
AFTER BRIEF DELIBERATION...
YOUR HONOR, WE WANT TO GET HOME IN TIME TO WATCH "DALLAS" RERUNS, SO WE CONCUR!
AS A DOCTOR, OUR HERO IS EXONERATED!
ANOTHER GREAT VICTORY FOR MODERN MEDICINE!
THEN, AS A LAWYER...
SINCE YOU LOST, I GUESS THE LAUGH'S ON YOU! YOU GET 90% OF NOTHING!
UH, THERE IS THIS LITTLE MATTER OF EXPENSES...
OH, MY LATE HUSBAND'S BROTHER, AL, WILL PAY FOR THEM!
EXIT
CERTAINLY!
DOCTOR-LAWYER AGAIN WHIPS OUT HIS LIGHTNING-SPEED BILL PAD...
YOUR COOPERATION IS APPRECIATED IN UNDERSTANDING THAT PAYMENT IS REQUIRED AT THE TIME SERVICES ARE RENDERED!
GULP! THIS AMOUNT... IT CAN'T BE...
WHY NOT? MY COLLEGE EDUCATION WAS CERTAINLY PART OF MY EXPENSES, WASN'T IT!
GASP!
AL! WHAT'S WRONG!
THIS SUDDEN PAIN IN MY CHEST! IT FEELS LIKE A THUNDERING HERD OF ELEPHANTS STAMPEDING OVER ME!
SOMEONE GET A DOCTOR, QUICK!
BUT I'M A DOCTOR, SIR! HARVARD '76!
WHAT'S THE MATTER WITH ME, DOC?
WHY, NOTHING TO WORRY ABOUT! IT'S OBVIOUSLY JUST A LITTLE INDIGESTION! PROBABLY THE TENSION OF THE TRIAL! TAKE TWO ASPIRINS AND YOU'LL FEEL A LOT BETTER IN THE MORNING!
THANKS, DOC! WHAT A RELIEF!
AND SO DOCTOR-LAWYER'S TYPICAL GREATEST ADVENTURE COMES TO AN END! OR DOES IT? THAT HAS TO AWAIT ANOTHER EPISODE— AND ANOTHER DAY'S WORK!

MN: How do you think your drawing style contributes to the success of your work?

ES: A great deal. I think for the kinds of half-formed worlds I create, only wispy little characters like I draw can live in those worlds. It's consistent. My characters are barely there on the page. They have almost no physical presence at all. I think part of me is like that, satisfied to go into a corner, read a book, and say, "World, don't bother me." I think things like "8 Comics in One!" and "Saturday Nite on Antarius!" wouldn't work at all if they were drawn by a cartoonist with a richer, more detailed, more realistic style. Sometimes I think you can hardly call my stuff "comics" because the art is almost incidental, it's really all about what the characters do and say.

PUBESCENT COMICS!
GROWS HAIR AS YOU READ!
THE ZANY MISS-ADVENTURES OF BLIMPO!
HEY, BLIMPO! WHATCHA DOIN' TONIGHT?
ME, I'M GONNA TAKE MADGE ANDERSON TO THE DRIVE-IN MOVIE!
BUT AIN'T SHE TUFFO'S GIRL?
YEAH, BUT TUFFO THINKS I'M JUST GONNA HELP HER WITH HER HOMEWORK!
WHAT IF TUFFO GETS WISE TO YOU, THOUGH?
THE END

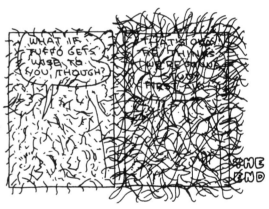

FORTUNE - TELLING COMICS!

DIRECTIONS: CLOSE EYES, POISE OUTSTRETCHED INDEX FINGER OVER PAGE WHILE YOU MOVE PAGE BACK AND FORTH WITH OTHER HAND. WHEN YOU FEEL "MOMENT IS RIGHT," SUDDENLY DROP FINGER ONTO PAGE. FATE WILL LEAD FINGER TO PANEL WITH CORRECT ANSWER TO THIS MONTH'S QUESTION.

THIS MONTH'S QUESTION: (FOR MEN ONLY) "WILL THAT GIRL I LIKE GO ALL THE WAY WITH ME OR NOT?"

I'M SORRY, BUT I LOVE SOMEONE ELSE!

I FIND YOU PHYSICALLY REPULSIVE AND I WOULDN'T MAKE IT WITH YOU IF YOU WERE THE LAST MAN ON EARTH!

I'LL LET YOU SCREW ME ONCE IF YOU BUY ME A CAR!

I DIG YOUR MIND AND I'LL SLEEP WITH YOU ON OUR FOURTEENTH DATE!

I WOULD RATHER ROT IN HELL TWICE THAN LET YOU EVEN TOUCH ME WITH YOUR PINKY!

I'M MADLY IN LOVE WITH YOU AND I'LL OBLIGE YOUR MOST SECRET DESIRES THE VERY FIRST TIME YOU COME ON!

TWO-WAY COMICS!

A CLEAN COMIC AND A DIRTY COMIC IN ONE   by ED SUBITZKY

FOR THOSE CLEAN-MINDED READERS WHO WANT TO READ AN INNOCENT STORY ABOUT A BOY AND HIS SISTER TRYING TO PIN A PRETTY PAINTING ON THE WALL OF THEIR HAPPY HOME, READ ACROSS IN THE NORMAL WAY, LIKE THIS:

FOR THOSE FILTHY-MINDED READERS WHO WANT TO GET THEIR ROCKS OFF AND READ AN EXPLICIT SEX STORY THAT TAKES PLACE IN A CHEAP HOTEL, READ DOWN INSTEAD, LIKE THIS:

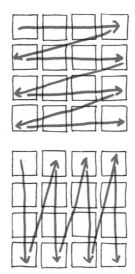

NOW WOULD YOU LIKE THE PICTURE?

I DON'T KNOW... I DON'T REALLY THINK IT'S HUNG WELL ENOUGH...

I'M SORRY! I'M SURE I CAN GET IT UP BETTER!

GIVE ME A HAND, WILL YOU...

OW! CAREFUL WITH THOSE FINGERS!

OW! YOU TOO! OW!

I GOT A PRICK!

AND I HAVE A BIG HOLE!

ARE YOU SURE IT ISN'T INFECTED?

GO AHEAD... TRY SQUEEZING IT A BIT!

HEY, THAT HURT!

AND NOW IT'S GETTING REALLY SWOLLEN!

MAYBE IT WOULD HELP IF I PUT A CAST AROUND IT!

THERE! THAT'S A LOT BETTER!

IN MOUNTING, THE PROPER EQUIPMENT IS VERY, VERY IMPORTANT...

I GUESS WE SHOULDN'T HAVE USED OUR NAILS!

COME ON! WHAT OTHER CHOICE IS THERE BUT TO RAM IT IN!

LISTEN, MR. SMARTY! JUST BECAUSE YOU CAN MAKE ONE CRACK DOESN'T MEAN I'M GOING TO LET YOU MAKE ANOTHER!

I THINK IT'S TIME FOR US TO TRY A SCREW!

OKAY! HOLD STILL...

LATER

SATISFIED?

MMMM! IT ALWAYS PAYS TO TRY AGAIN...UNLESS YOU WANT TO BLOW IT!

THE END

THE END

PRINTER'S STRIKE COMICS!

WANNA HEAR A SUPER ONE? THIS TRAVELLING SALESMAN COMES TO A FARMHOUSE AND LIKE HE NEEDS A PLACE TO SLEEP...

...SO THE FARMER SAYS HE CAN SLEEP NEXT TO HIS BEAUTIFUL DAUGHTER! AND HE TELLS HER TO YELL "TROLLEY CAR" IF HE TRIES ANYTHING!

HAT IGHT, H ARMER UDDENLY HE RS "TURBO-TRA N" SO H RUSH S VER A D GUE S WHA HE SEE ?

THE END

THE INTERGALACTIC GOURMET!

TRANSLATED BY ED SUBITZKY

TONIGHT: THE PLANET NONILUX-7, WHERE THE DOMINANT CARNIVORE SPECIES (GORGOTECTYL) EATS FIVE SUBDOMINANT SPECIES (LUXTOL, VOLMOK, LIPPROK, DREDGT, AND SKARX) AND TONIGHT PREPARES A ROAST VOLMOK UNDER SKARX.

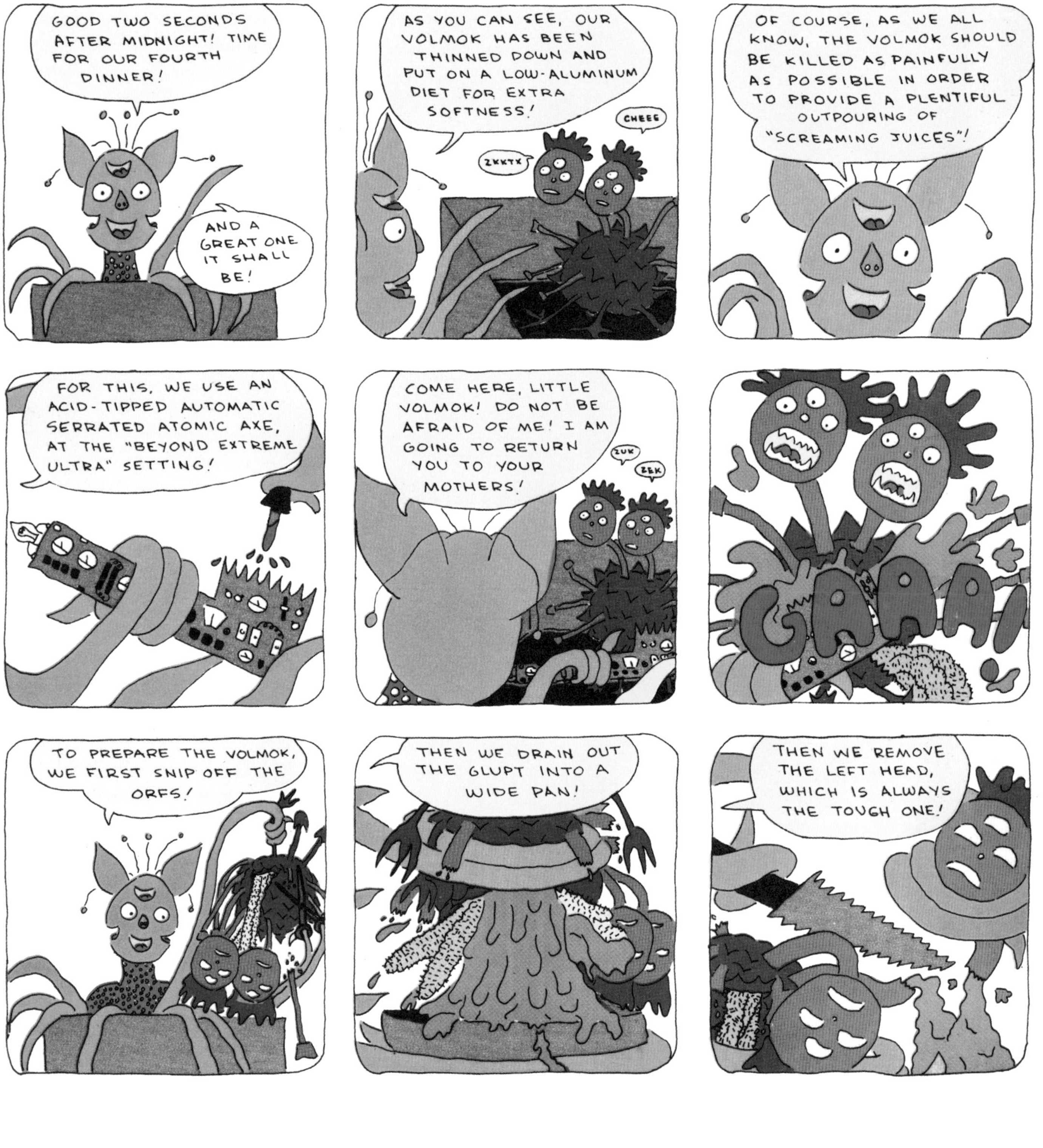

GOOD TWO SECONDS AFTER MIDNIGHT! TIME FOR OUR FOURTH DINNER!
AND A GREAT ONE IT SHALL BE!
AS YOU CAN SEE, OUR VOLMOK HAS BEEN THINNED DOWN AND PUT ON A LOW-ALUMINUM DIET FOR EXTRA SOFTNESS!
ZKKTX
CHEEE
OF COURSE, AS WE ALL KNOW, THE VOLMOK SHOULD BE KILLED AS PAINFULLY AS POSSIBLE IN ORDER TO PROVIDE A PLENTIFUL OUTPOURING OF "SCREAMING JUICES"!
FOR THIS, WE USE AN ACID-TIPPED AUTOMATIC SERRATED ATOMIC AXE, AT THE "BEYOND EXTREME ULTRA" SETTING!
COME HERE, LITTLE VOLMOK! DO NOT BE AFRAID OF ME! I AM GOING TO RETURN YOU TO YOUR MOTHERS!
ZUK
ZEK
GAAA!
TO PREPARE THE VOLMOK, WE FIRST SNIP OFF THE ORFS!
THEN WE DRAIN OUT THE GLUPT INTO A WIDE PAN!
THEN WE REMOVE THE LEFT HEAD, WHICH IS ALWAYS THE TOUGH ONE!

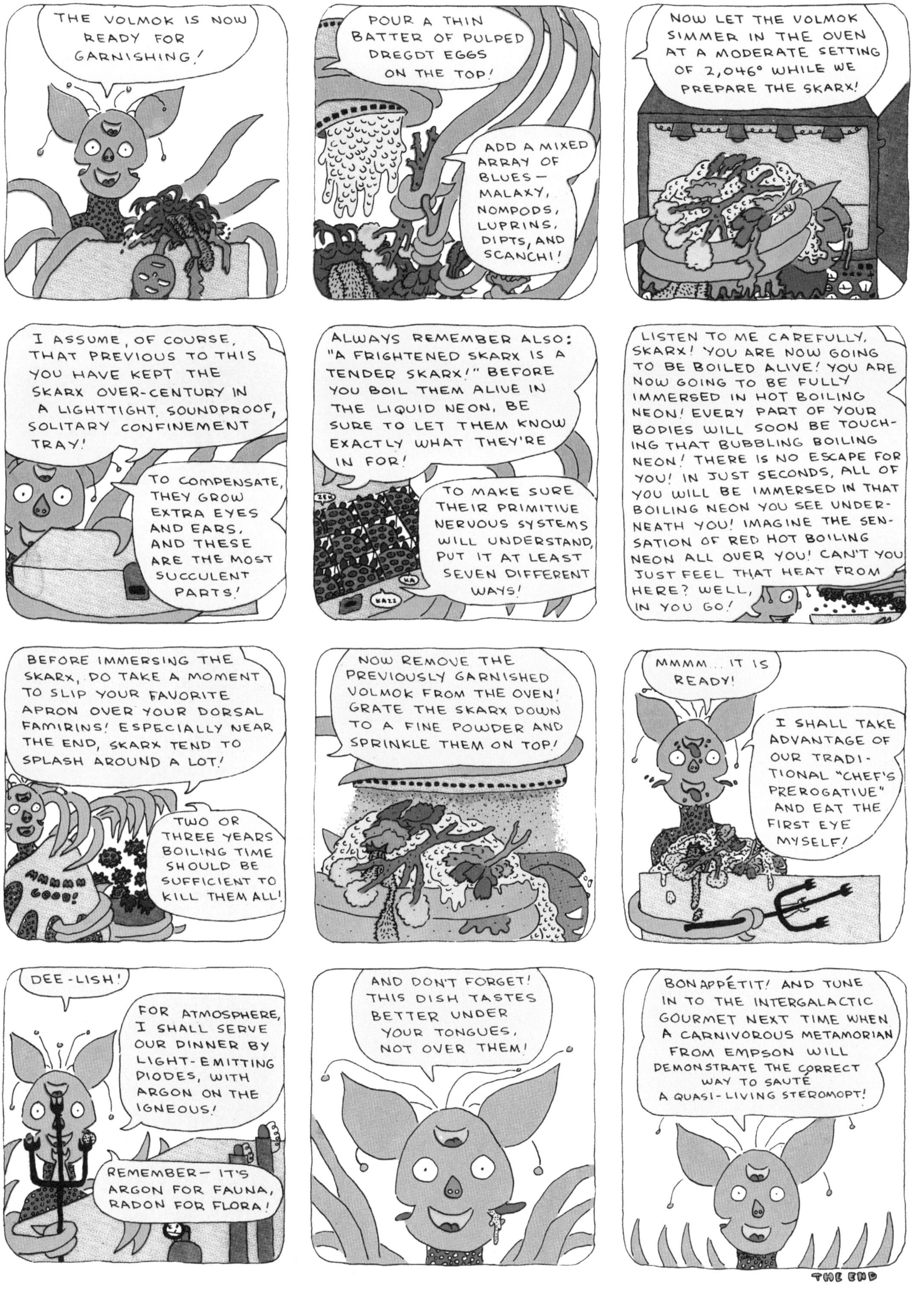
THE VOLMOK IS NOW READY FOR GARNISHING!
POUR A THIN BATTER OF PULPED DREGDT EGGS ON THE TOP!
ADD A MIXED ARRAY OF BLUES— MALAXY, NOMPODS, LUPRINS, DIPTS, AND SCANCHI!
NOW LET THE VOLMOK SIMMER IN THE OVEN AT A MODERATE SETTING OF 2,046° WHILE WE PREPARE THE SKARX!
I ASSUME, OF COURSE, THAT PREVIOUS TO THIS YOU HAVE KEPT THE SKARX OVER-CENTURY IN A LIGHTTIGHT, SOUNDPROOF, SOLITARY CONFINEMENT TRAY!
TO COMPENSATE, THEY GROW EXTRA EYES AND EARS, AND THESE ARE THE MOST SUCCULENT PARTS!
ALWAYS REMEMBER ALSO: "A FRIGHTENED SKARX IS A TENDER SKARX!" BEFORE YOU BOIL THEM ALIVE IN THE LIQUID NEON, BE SURE TO LET THEM KNOW EXACTLY WHAT THEY'RE IN FOR!
TO MAKE SURE THEIR PRIMITIVE NERVOUS SYSTEMS WILL UNDERSTAND, PUT IT AT LEAST SEVEN DIFFERENT WAYS!
LISTEN TO ME CAREFULLY, SKARX! YOU ARE NOW GOING TO BE BOILED ALIVE! YOU ARE NOW GOING TO BE FULLY IMMERSED IN HOT BOILING NEON! EVERY PART OF YOUR BODIES WILL SOON BE TOUCHING THAT BUBBLING BOILING NEON! THERE IS NO ESCAPE FOR YOU! IN JUST SECONDS, ALL OF YOU WILL BE IMMERSED IN THAT BOILING NEON YOU SEE UNDERNEATH YOU! IMAGINE THE SENSATION OF RED HOT BOILING NEON ALL OVER YOU! CAN'T YOU JUST FEEL THAT HEAT FROM HERE? WELL, IN YOU GO!
BEFORE IMMERSING THE SKARX, DO TAKE A MOMENT TO SLIP YOUR FAVORITE APRON OVER YOUR DORSAL FAMIRINS! ESPECIALLY NEAR THE END, SKARX TEND TO SPLASH AROUND A LOT!
TWO OR THREE YEARS BOILING TIME SHOULD BE SUFFICIENT TO KILL THEM ALL!
NOW REMOVE THE PREVIOUSLY GARNISHED VOLMOK FROM THE OVEN! GRATE THE SKARX DOWN TO A FINE POWDER AND SPRINKLE THEM ON TOP!
MMMM... IT IS READY!
I SHALL TAKE ADVANTAGE OF OUR TRADITIONAL "CHEF'S PREROGATIVE" AND EAT THE FIRST EYE MYSELF!
DEE-LISH!
FOR ATMOSPHERE, I SHALL SERVE OUR DINNER BY LIGHT-EMITTING DIODES, WITH ARGON ON THE IGNEOUS!
REMEMBER— IT'S ARGON FOR FAUNA, RADON FOR FLORA!
AND DON'T FORGET! THIS DISH TASTES BETTER UNDER YOUR TONGUES, NOT OVER THEM!
BON APPÉTIT! AND TUNE IN TO THE INTERGALACTIC GOURMET NEXT TIME WHEN A CARNIVOROUS METAMORIAN FROM EMPSON WILL DEMONSTRATE THE CORRECT WAY TO SAUTÉ A QUASI-LIVING STEROMOPT!
THE END

POLAROID PORNOGRAPHIC COMICS!

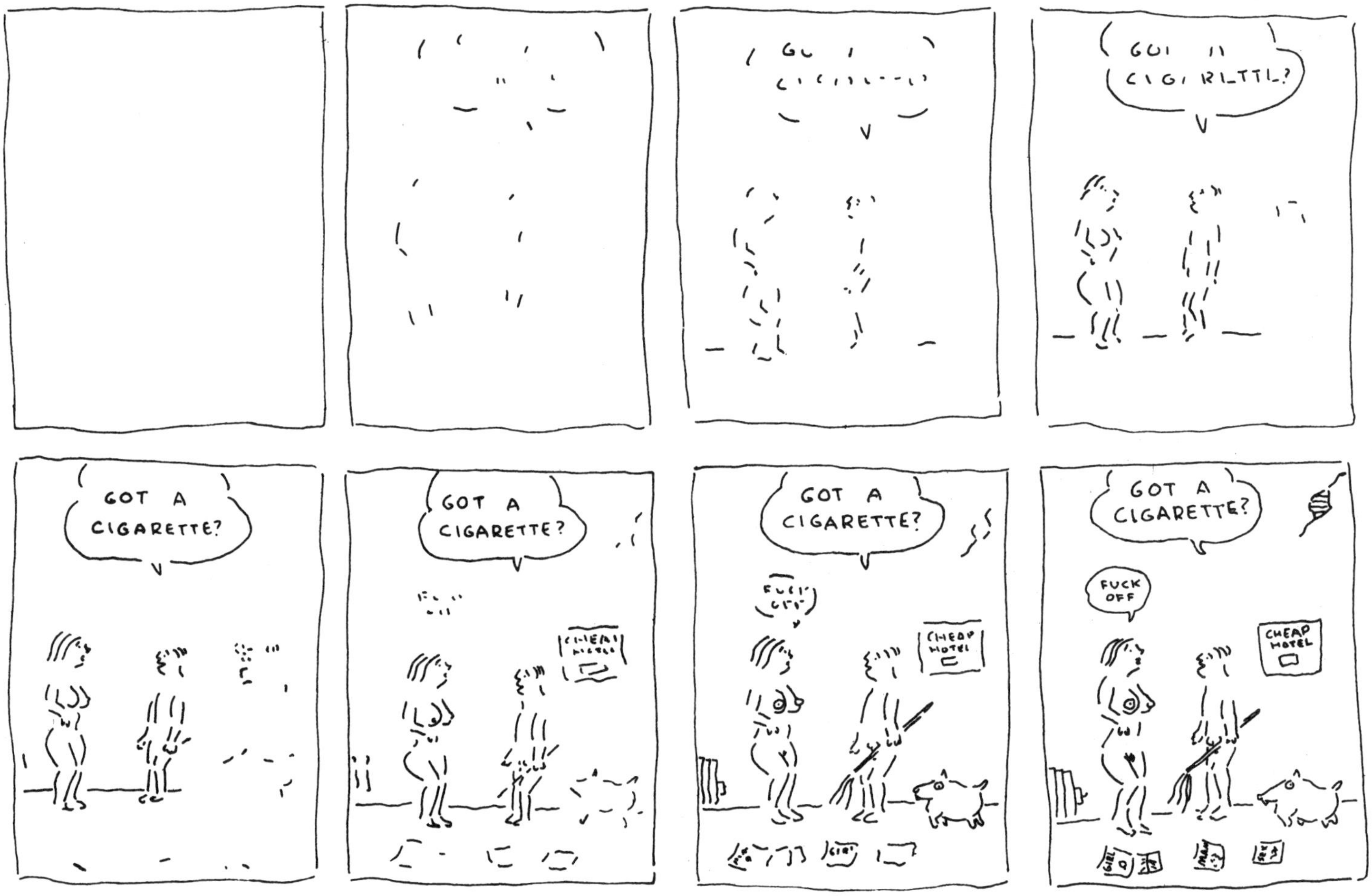
GOT A CIGARETTE?
GOT A CIGARETTE?
GOT A CIGARETTE?
CHEAP HOTEL
GOT A CIGARETTE?
FUCK OFF
CHEAP HOTEL

THE GREAT 3-D SHOW!

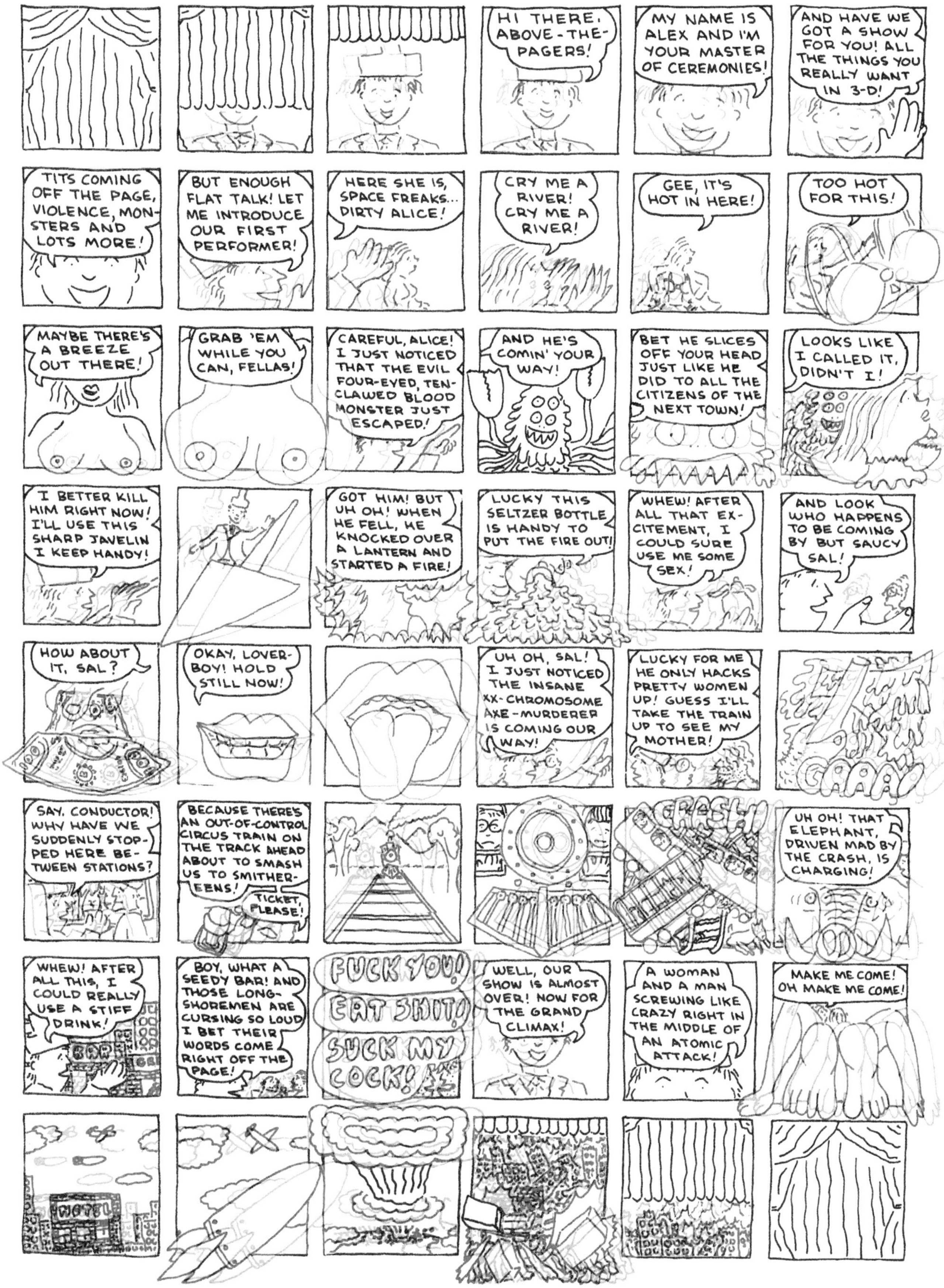

HI THERE, ABOVE-THE-PAGERS!
MY NAME IS ALEX AND I'M YOUR MASTER OF CEREMONIES!
AND HAVE WE GOT A SHOW FOR YOU! ALL THE THINGS YOU REALLY WANT IN 3-D!
TITS COMING OFF THE PAGE, VIOLENCE, MONSTERS AND LOTS MORE!
BUT ENOUGH FLAT TALK! LET ME INTRODUCE OUR FIRST PERFORMER!
HERE SHE IS, SPACE FREAKS... DIRTY ALICE!
CRY ME A RIVER! CRY ME A RIVER!
GEE, IT'S HOT IN HERE!
TOO HOT FOR THIS!
MAYBE THERE'S A BREEZE OUT THERE!
GRAB 'EM WHILE YOU CAN, FELLAS!
CAREFUL, ALICE! I JUST NOTICED THAT THE EVIL FOUR-EYED, TEN-CLAWED BLOOD MONSTER JUST ESCAPED!
AND HE'S COMIN' YOUR WAY!
BET HE SLICES OFF YOUR HEAD JUST LIKE HE DID TO ALL THE CITIZENS OF THE NEXT TOWN!
LOOKS LIKE I CALLED IT, DIDN'T I!
I BETTER KILL HIM RIGHT NOW! I'LL USE THIS SHARP JAVELIN I KEEP HANDY!
GOT HIM! BUT UH OH! WHEN HE FELL, HE KNOCKED OVER A LANTERN AND STARTED A FIRE!
LUCKY THIS SELTZER BOTTLE IS HANDY TO PUT THE FIRE OUT!
WHEW! AFTER ALL THAT EXCITEMENT, I COULD SURE USE ME SOME SEX!
AND LOOK WHO HAPPENS TO BE COMING BY BUT SAUCY SAL!
HOW ABOUT IT, SAL?
OKAY, LOVER-BOY! HOLD STILL NOW!
UH OH, SAL! I JUST NOTICED THE INSANE XX-CHROMOSOME AXE-MURDERER IS COMING OUR WAY!
LUCKY FOR ME HE ONLY HACKS PRETTY WOMEN UP! GUESS I'LL TAKE THE TRAIN UP TO SEE MY MOTHER!
GRAAA!
SAY, CONDUCTOR! WHY HAVE WE SUDDENLY STOPPED HERE BETWEEN STATIONS?
BECAUSE THERE'S AN OUT-OF-CONTROL CIRCUS TRAIN ON THE TRACK AHEAD ABOUT TO SMASH US TO SMITHEREENS!
TICKET, PLEASE!
CRASH!
UH OH! THAT ELEPHANT, DRIVEN MAD BY THE CRASH, IS CHARGING!
WHEW! AFTER ALL THIS, I COULD REALLY USE A STIFF DRINK!
BAR
BOY, WHAT A SEEDY BAR! AND THOSE LONGSHOREMEN ARE CURSING SO LOUD I BET THEIR WORDS COME RIGHT OFF THE PAGE!
FUCK YOU!
EAT SHIT!
SUCK MY COCK!
WELL, OUR SHOW IS ALMOST OVER! NOW FOR THE GRAND CLIMAX!
A WOMAN AND A MAN SCREWING LIKE CRAZY RIGHT IN THE MIDDLE OF AN ATOMIC ATTACK!
MAKE ME COME! OH MAKE ME COME!
HOTEL

AN EVENING IN 1973

IN WHICH THE READER IS INVITED ALONG FOR A FANCIFUL VISIT TO A TYPICAL RESIDENCE IN THE SCIENTIFIC SHANGRI-LA HALF A CENTURY HENCE

"Stop number 6,017!" the conductor cheerfully called out.

John Smithers smiled, picked up his rubberized attaché case, and left the train. How good it was, he thought, to have a stop right outside his door. Of course, so did every other commuter—but that was just one of the advantages of living in 1973, when trains could travel 1,200 miles an hour.

Actually, though, he was a bit later than usual tonight. He'd stopped off at his doctor's office on the way home for a routine check-up; the painless neutron probe had indicated extensive cancer through his entire chest and abdomen, and it had taken the doctor a full fifteen minutes to cure it.

Opening the front door manually (because he was late, Vera hadn't set the automatic timer), John Smithers walked into his completely plastic house. As he always did, he looked upwards, through the cellophane ceiling, at the stars. He was pleased that the Citizen's Committee had voted to postpone the first April rainfall for another week, when surveys showed that an above-average number of people would have reason to stay indoors.

"Honey, I'm home!" he shouted.

His wife, Vera, came out with two self-igniting frozen dinners. Scraping them along the table like a match, she grinned as the bottom of each dinner burst into flames, heating the top thoroughly, and then being automatically extinguished by the newly liquefied gravy dripping down. Vera, tonight, was dressed in a skin-tight plastic suit which covered her entire body, with cellophane cutouts for the eyes.

"How about a little air in here?" John said as they were eating.

Vera nodded. The all-plastic automatic thermostat maintained room temperature at precisely 71.6°, a computer-determined figure based on the average of their body temperatures and the average rate at which they sweated. However, to get the proper scent and flavor to the air, it was necessary to resort to the Pipes.

"Which would you prefer," Vera asked, "Northern or Southern?"

"We had Southern last night," John replied. "How about Canadian?"

"Suits me." Vera first went over to the cellophane window on the plastic Canadian pipe to be sure that no snow was blowing through. Satisfied, she turned the knob until the damper opened and fresh Canadian air blew into the room. Vera could remember how, years ago, many people had scoffed at the idea of installing huge fans in Canada and Mexico, and having them blow air into the United States through a system of pipes. "Even in this day and age," they had said, "science isn't that advanced!" But the far-sighted engineers had persisted in their efforts, and now, in 1973, the entirely-plastic system was a reality.

"That sure feels good!" John Smithers said, blowing a kiss at his wife through the refreshing pine-scented air. "What's on the agenda tonight?"

"The Wilsons are coming over," Vera said.

John smiled. He liked the Wilsons, and because the frozen dinner, intended specifically for the evening after a workday, had been laced with an odorless and tasteless derivative of coffee, he felt wide-awake and ready to socialize. "Did they say which train they were catching?"

"Either the 7:09, 7:10, 7:11, 7:12, 7:13, or 7:14," Vera said. "I wish I could remember so we could set our rubberized three-tube automatic door timer."

"Well, we'll just have to open the door by hand then," John said. "I'm sorry," Vera said. "I guess I should have taken a Memory Chocolate."

John Smithers kissed his wife.

"Don't worry about it," he said. Vera smiled. It was wonderful to have such a considerate husband, she thought, although, of course, every woman did.

"Dessert?" she asked.

John nodded. While he turned on the videobox, a seventeen-tube, all-plastic device which showed

PALINDROME COMICS! BY ED SUBITZKY

THE SAME DIRTY STORY IF YOU READ IT THIS WAY →
OR START AT THE END AND READ BACKWARDS!

BOY, AM I HARD UP!

WHERE DOES A GUY GO TO GET LAID AROUND HERE?

SORRY! I PRACTICE SAFE SEX!

I ONLY DO IT OVER CITIZENS BAND RADIO, CHANNEL 14!

full-color three-dimensional motion pictures through a cellophane window, complete with smell and sound, Vera went into the kitchen and brought out two frozen desserts. She scraped them along the table and watched as they ignited; through cellophane windows on the plastic packages, she could see the flames eating through the seals of the attached packages of extra-cold ice which, by melting, first extinguished the flames and then tumbled over the desserts and made them extra-cold.

Suddenly, the six-tube, all-plastic automatic door record-player said, "Someone is here to see you." John flicked the switch of the wireless, seven-tube, all-plastic, limited-range radio transmitter and said, "Who is it?" His voice was carried outside, where the Wilsons were standing, having just gotten off the all-plastic 7:11. "No automatic door timer?" Paul Wilson asked. His voice was picked up on a second limited-range, all-plastic radio transmitter and reproduced inside where John could hear it.

"Vera forgot which train you were on," John Smithers said. "Sorry."

He got up and went to the door. Through the cellophane window, he could see Paul Wilson and his wife, Alice. Paul was wearing a soft metal suit, the kind that was all the fashion rage in 1973. His wife was wearing a plastic soil-covered dress which had a pretty patina of extra-thin roses and peonies growing out of it. John pressed a rubberized button inside the plastic door and a hidden one-tube suction device opened it. As

soon as Paul and his wife were inside, the suction device, sensing an increase in air pressure inside the house, closed the door automatically.

Vera came over to greet the guests. All sat down on the superbly comfortable, helium-filled plastic couch that hovered a few feet off the floor in the living room. As they were seating themselves, the couch sank a little lower. Paul Wilson took out a self-igniting cigarette, scraped it along the table, and puffed comfortably.

"Before I forget," Paul Wilson said, "you were going to lend me your automatic pen, until I get a chance to change a tube in mine."

"I'll get- it," John said. "It's upstairs."

John was closer to the all-plastic vacuum lift than the all-plastic automatic stairway, so he took the lift up to the twelfth level of his apartment. He pressed the letters "PEN" on the keyboard of the all-plastic Home Mini-Computer and watched through a cellophane window as a set of alphabet blocks was rearranged by rubberized suction motors to spell out the location of the object he sought. It read:

PEN: CLOSET 6; SECTOR 7 A

John went over to closet 6, took out the automatic pen and because, having walked across the room, he was now closer to the all-plastic automatic stairway, took it downstairs.

"Quite a device, this automatic pen," Paul Wilson said. "Truly a marvel of 1973!"

"Yes," John Smithers readily agreed. "This all-plastic, automatic pen is truly amazing. Through

a cellophane window, one can see the interior, where a lifetime supply of a special kind of liquefiable plastic is kept. The special, liquefiable plastic is heated to its melting point by a small internal filament; this filament is turned on by an internal miniature one-tube radio receiver responding to signals sent out by an internal, miniature, one-tube radio transmitter; this transmitter, placed beside the point, is energized only when pressure is actually placed on the point. This assures that the plastic will be liquid—and flow onto the paper—only when actually needed. Since the plastic is solidified when not in use, eliminated forever is the danger of the pen leaking in, say, a shirt or suit pocket."

"Why, I can remember way, way back," Paul said, "when pens used to leak all the time!"

"Things sure are different now in 1973!" John Smithers said, grinning.

"That reminds me," Vera said. "Did you all hear the news?"

"What news?" Paul Wilson asked.

"Our scientists have finally fabricated an all-plastic space ship. Every part of it, even the suction-operated motor, is plastic!"

"Except for the windows," Alice Wilson interjected. "They still have to be made of cellophane. After all, one can't see through plastic, not even in 1973!"

"Do you think," Paul submitted, "they'll be able to land on the sun now?"

"Well," Vera said, "an all-plastic space ship, according to calculations, should be able to survive

SORRY! I'M AN INTELLECTUAL!

I ONLY DO IT WITH MEN WHO HAVE UNCOVERED THE SECRET OF THE UNIVERSE!

IT LOOKS LIKE I'M JUST NOT GOING TO GET MY ROCKS OFF!

NOT A CHANCE!

HEY, I DO IT FOR A BUS TOKEN!

UNFORTUNATELY, I WAS NEVER TOO WELL-COORDINATED!

the temperatures there. For years, scientists have been wondering whether or not life is possible on the sun. But, because we live in 1973, we shall soon find out!”

“I can still remember when we first landed on the moon,” Paul Wilson said, “back in ’42.”

“Yes,” John Smithers remarked philosophically. “I’m afraid to say it, but we are getting on in years.”

“That reminds us,” Alice Wilson said proudly. “Today is our anniversary! Paul and I were married just forty-seven years ago this evening—and how the world has changed since then!”

“Alice wore one of the first cellophane wedding dresses,” Paul Wilson said, beaming proudly.

“Why, our first house didn’t even have dynatricity!” Alice said.

John Smithers shook his head. He tried to imagine a world without dynatricity; it was almost impossible. He walked over to the room’s plastic dynatricity container, looked through the cellophane window, and saw that it was full. He opened the container and scooped up a handful of the soft, gelatinous wonder that powered all his household appliances. He put a little dab in the all-plastic clock; the rubberized, automatic pants-presser; the cellophane, automatic salt-shaker; the all-plastic, automatic, suction-operated furniture mover.

“They were running low,” he explained. “I forgot to fill them this morning.”

“Perhaps you should take a Memory Chocolate, too!” his wife told him, good-naturedly.

“By the way,” Paul Wilson said, “did you hear that dynatricity rates are about to go down?”

“Again!” Vera said with some surprise; rates had gone down several times during the last six months.

“Yes,” Paul Wilson said. “Seems the Dynatricity Corporation has discovered a more inexpensive way to produce it, developed through a grant from the World Government. Naturally, they are passing the savings on to us, the public. What’s more, they’re working on a more dense form of dynatricity that should require refilling less often!”

“Wonderful!” John Smithers said with considerable enthusiasm.

The conversation continued amiably for a few minutes. Then, suddenly, Alice Wilson broke into it by saying to her husband, “Can we tell them now?”

“I suppose now is as good a time as any!” Paul Wilson said, smiling at his wife.

“Tell us what?” Vera inquired.

“Well,” Paul said, “Alice and I were thinking. At 97, we are starting to get along in years and we thought, if we’re ever going to have that family we talked about, we’d better start now!”

“Oh, Alice!” Vera said, running over to kiss her friend happily on the cheek.

“Have you been ‘rayed yet?” John Smithers asked.

“Tomorrow,” Paul answered. “Alice and I have an appointment at the Selectra-Ray Center at 9:00 A.M. sharp.”

“And what have you decided on?”

“Well,” Paul continued, “Alice wanted a girl and I wanted a boy, so we let the all-plastic, two-tube heads-or-tails generator decide. Alice won.”

“I told him we’ll have a boy next time,” Alice said, smiling.

“And, anyway, “Paul added, “Alice let me have my choice of eye color and hair color. I picked blue hair and orange eyes—my favorite color combination.”

“And what about skin color?” John asked.

“Well,” Alice said, “I preferred Oriental, but my husband wanted black. So it was back to the all-plastic, two-tube heads-or-tails generator!”

“And?”

“Paul won this time,” Alice said.

“Black it is!”

“At least I won something!” Paul said, good-naturedly.

“Do you remember,” John interjected, “when, long ago, some people actually thought it was inferior to be black?”

“Yes,” Paul said. “Thank goodness that, in 1973, we enjoy an enlightened world of eternal peace and brotherhood for all!”

Alice giggled. “I’m looking forward to tomorrow,” she said. “I’ve never made love beneath a Selectra-Ray before.”

“Neither have I,” Vera said, looking at her husband rather pointedly.

“Actually, there’s not much to it,” Paul Wilson pointed out. “The all-plastic, Selectra-Ray machine is hidden in the ceiling so you hardly notice it, the Selectra-Rays them-

SORRY! I DIDN'T MEAN TO KICK YOU IN THE HEAD!
WAS IT GOOD?
I CAN'T REMEMBER A THING THAT HAPPENED TODAY!
LET'S TRY AGAIN!
OOOH... YES...
WAS IT GOOD?
I CAN'T REMEMBER A THING THAT HAPPENED TODAY!
SORRY! I DIDN'T MEAN TO KICK YOU IN THE HEAD!

selves coming through a tiny cellophane window. A technician simply sets the features you want and the ray bathes you while you make love. Of course, a bevy of highly-trained sexologists watch you to be sure your movements are correct."

"Will you take an Ecstasy Chocolate beforehand?" Vera inquired.

"Yes," Alice said. "We want our child to be conceived in a moment when our bodies feel a surge of joy and satisfaction beyond all belief."

Ecstasy Chocolates, as all of them knew, were chocolates coated with a simple, safe chemical that lowered the threshold of the pleasure centers of the brain so that only the highest and purest impulses could be produced there.

"Do you remember," John said, "when people felt repressed and inhibited about sex?"

"Just barely," Alice said. "But now, in 1973, sex is put in perfect perspective. It is accepted as one of life's greatest pleasures—made even better by the fact that, with our all-plastic, multi-tube, computerized matching system, everyone is deeply and gloriously in love with his or her partner. Men and women feel no shame or inhibition about sex or their bodies. And yet we don't exaggerate sex, either—or pervert it and make it an obsessive part of our lives."

"Yes," John pointed out, slapping his knee enthusiastically, "we sure are lucky as hell to be living in 1973!"

"Would you like to see my womb?" Alice asked. "I took my Preparatory Chocolate today to clean it out and get it all nice and shiny for its tiny newcomer."

"Why, yes," Vera said. "That would be most interesting."

Alice stood up and removed her plastic soil-covered dress, carefully placing it on the plastic floor; the extra-thin flowers on it were remarkably healthy, automatically watered all day long by her own sweat. Naked, she was a most attractive woman, although, at 97, a slight wrinkle had appeared in her midsection even though she had gone in for a head-to-toe transplant just a week ago.

Vera and John bent over so they could peer more closely through the cellophane window in Alice's abdomen.

Her womb was indeed clean and sparkling. In one corner of it, near Alice's left kidney, they could see the tiny, plastic, combination six-tube, mini-microphone-loudspeaker-transmitter-receiver that was painlessly implanted in every woman upon reaching the age of puberty. The purpose of the microphone and transmitter was to alert the mother to any sounds her developing child might make; via the loudspeaker, the mother could, in turn, sing lullabies to her developing child and even, if she wished, begin to teach it the alphabet. Of course, that would have to be after the seventh day of pregnancy, when the child's brain was fairly well developed.

"Do you remember," Vera said, "in the old days, when women had to carry their children for nine months instead of nine days?"

"Yes," Alice said. "Of course, now we can control the rate of any bodily process by the appropriate speed-up or slow-down chocolates—whose coatings, incidentally, are organic derivatives of plastic."

Alice put her plastic soil-covered dress back on. "Wish us luck," she said.

"In 1973," Paul Wilson pointed out, "we don't need luck. Thanks to modern science, there hasn't been a birth defect in decades!"

"Yes," John Smithers repeated, slapping his knee again, "we certainly are lucky to be living in 1973!"

"You know," Vera said, "that starts me thinking. Tell me, of all the wonders of 1973, which one do you think is the greatest?"

"A good question," Paul Wilson said. He pondered a moment. "I guess I might say it's our plastic air cars with their helium-filled tires, rubberized exteriors, cellophane windows, and plastic, suction-type motors." He paused a moment." Or perhaps it's our all-plastic skyscrapers."

"What do you think, darling?" Vera asked her husband.

"Well," John Smithers answered, "I think it's the medical devices. I felt pain recently—at the History Museum, where they had this special booth set up—and let me tell you, it was horrible!"

"Of course," he hastened to add, "no one here on Earth, or on any of the colonized planets, feels it anymore."

"Speaking of the colonized planets," Alice said, "I think they're the most amazing thing about 1973.

UNFORTUNATELY, I WAS NEVER TOO WELL-COORDINATED!
HEY, I DO IT FOR A BUS TOKEN!
NOT A CHANCE!
IT LOOKS LIKE I'M JUST NOT GOING TO GET MY ROCKS OFF!
I ONLY DO IT WITH MEN WHO HAVE UNCOVERED THE SECRET OF THE UNIVERSE!
SORRY! I'M AN INTELLECTUAL!

The way we've been able to send families to Mars and Venus and have them live long, happy lives up there in all-plastic communities!"

"I understand they're even mining raw cellophane on Venus now," Paul said. "It should help bring prices down even further—although, of course, in 1973 every human being can easily afford anything and everything he wants!"

"True," John said. "Poverty, want, crime, and class differences have been wiped out for years. And, thanks to the advanced state of 1973 psychology, even the most menial jobs are made to seem fascinating!"

Suddenly John Smithers turned to his wife. "Vera," he said, "I know how badly you want a child. And I know that, seeing and hearing Alice tonight, you're even more anxious to have one. Well, I think our time has come too!"

"Oh, John!" Vera burst into involuntary tears of joy and went over and showered her husband with kisses.

"I'm so happy!" At the sight of Vera's intense joy, John, Paul, and Alice began to weep also. In 1973, no one thought it necessary to be ashamed of or repress their true feelings.

"Hey, I've got a great idea," Alice said. "Why don't you take your Preparatory Chocolate tonight and then the two of you can join us at the Selectra-Ray Center tomorrow!"

"Swell," John said. "I'll call work. Of course, like everyone else, I get all the time off I want because, in 1973, every corporation has a deep human interest in the welfare of its employees."

Suddenly, John's body was wracked by deep, overpowering sobs. "I can't help it!" he said. "We're all such good friends, I love you all so much, I'm so happy to have a wonderful wife like Vera—and, most of all, I'm so thankful to be alive in wonderful 1973 when all this is possible!"

Hearing him, the others began to cry uncontrollably; all held each other closely for several long moments.

"Say, Vera," John said at length. "I just realized something."

"What's that, my darling?" Vera asked.

"You never answered your own question. You never told us what you consider to be the most amazing thing about living in 1973!"

"You're right," Vera admitted. She paused a moment, looking at the thin pinpricks of starlight peeping through the cellophane ceiling. The refreshing Canadian air felt good against her skin. Later, she would suggest that they all take a No-Sleep Chocolate and wait for the dawn's red light to creep across the sky, turning the world warm and amber-orange and reflecting cheerfully off the all-plastic floor.

"Well?" John asked.

"I think," Vera said, "it's the Metford-Jorgenson equation."

"Why, yes!" Alice said. "I should have thought of that myself! You mean equation number three, of course—the one which proves mathematically that there is a God!"

"It was discovered only two years ago," Vera said, "in 1971. It's meant a great deal of comfort to me and to all our fellow human beings."

"Yes," John said, "and, when the proper factors are substituted, the equation even yields the fact that this God is all-powerful and all-loving and that there is a purpose and meaning to the universe."

"To think," Paul said, "philosophers and theologians have pondered this question for ages. But only in 1973 do we have a mathematics advanced enough to provide the answer!"

"I wonder," Vera said thoughtfully, "what the world will be like for our children?"

"Well," Paul said, "for one thing, it will have even greater wonders—wonders we can't even imagine now, in 1973."

"I read that, by 1979, they expect the first all-cellophane spaceship," John interjected.

"And," Alice added, "one scientist even believes that, someday, we'll be able to create an entire cellophane planet and send it out into space for people to live on. Then, people on one side of the world will be able to see the people on the other!"

"But best of all," Jim said, "one group of researchers now thinks that, by the early 1980s, they should be able to turn light rays into cellophane and gravity into plastic!"

Vera nestled her head into her husband's shoulder. Her hair tickled pleasantly and he smiled. "I don't care about tomorrow," she said, casting her eyes back upwards to the stars. "Sure, things are bound to get more advanced—but I'm happy enough today, living in the paradise of 1973!"

I ONLY DO IT OVER CITIZENS BAND RADIO, CHANNEL 14!
SORRY! I PRACTICE SAFE SEX!
WHERE DOES A GUY GO TO GET LAID AROUND HERE?
BOY, AM I HARD UP!
THE SAME DIRTY STORY IF YOU READ IT BACKWARDS
OR START AT THE FRONT AND READ NORMALLY!
PALINDROME COMICS!
BY ED SUBITZKY

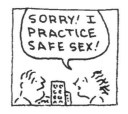

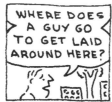

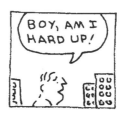

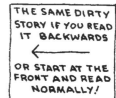

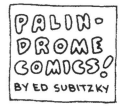

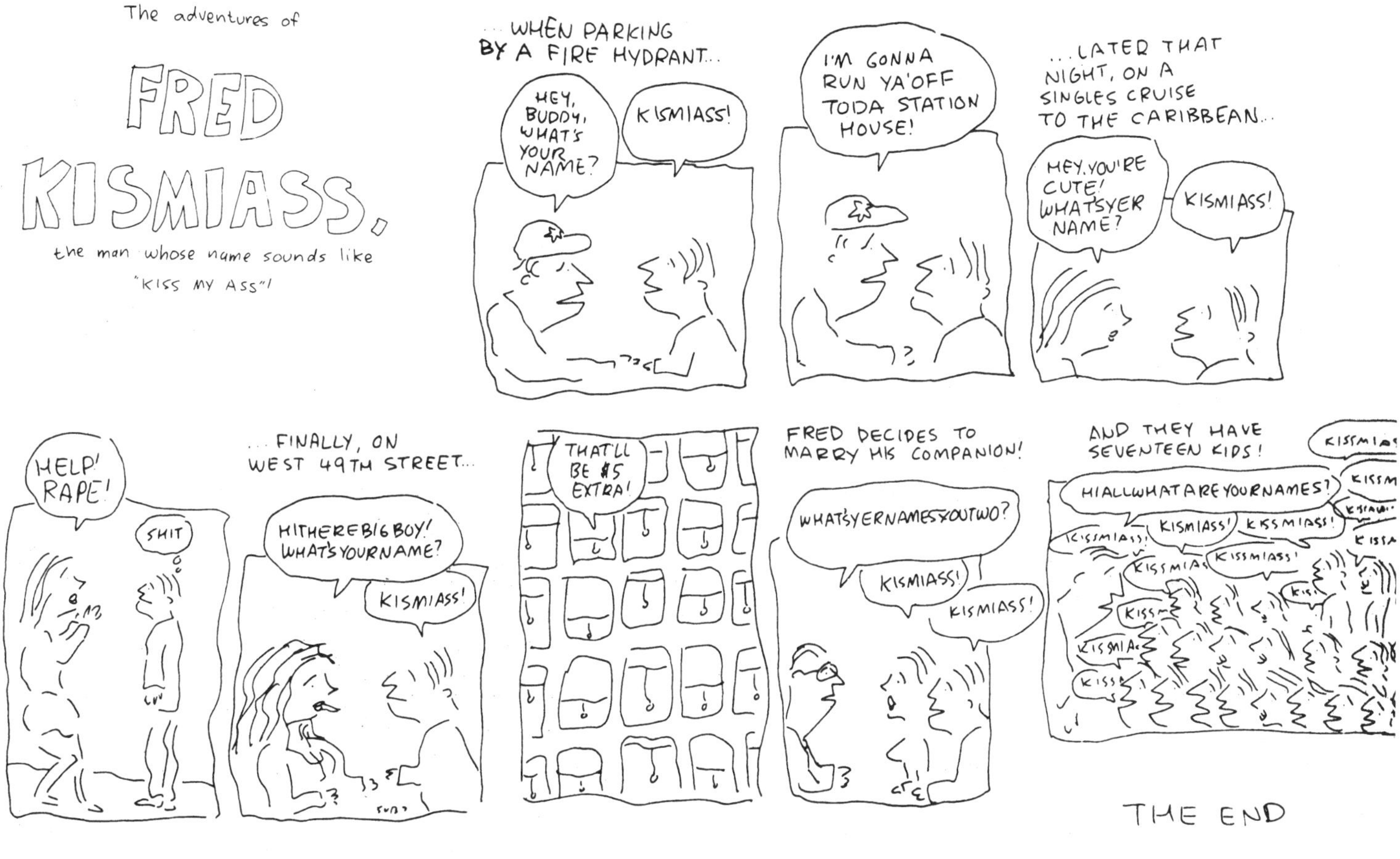
The adventures of
FRED KISMIASS,
the man whose name sounds like "KISS MY ASS"!
...WHEN PARKING BY A FIRE HYDRANT...
HEY, BUDDY, WHAT'S YOUR NAME?
KISMIASS!
I'M GONNA RUN YA'OFF TODA STATION HOUSE!
...LATER THAT NIGHT, ON A SINGLES CRUISE TO THE CARIBBEAN...
HEY, YOU'RE CUTE! WHATSYER NAME?
KISMIASS!
HELP! RAPE!
SHIT
...FINALLY, ON WEST 49TH STREET...
HITHEREBIGBOY! WHAT'SYOURNAME?
KISMIASS!
THAT'LL BE $5 EXTRA!
FRED DECIDES TO MARRY HIS COMPANION!
WHAT'SYERNAMESYOUTWO?
KISMIASS!
KISMIASS!
AND THEY HAVE SEVENTEEN KIDS!
HIALLWHATAREYOURNAMES?
KISMIASS!
KISSMIASS!
KISMIASS!
KISSMIASS!
THE END

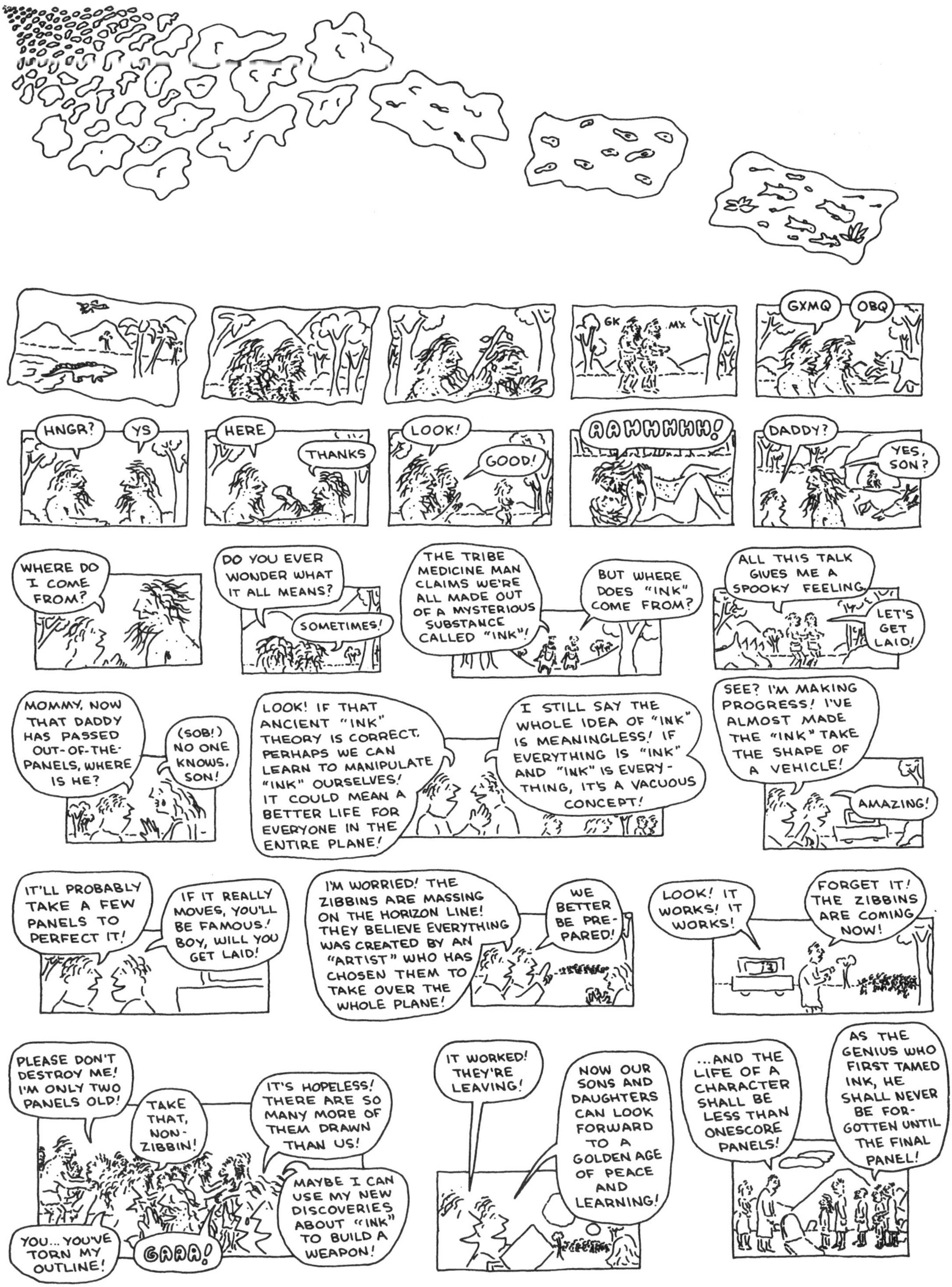
GK
MX
GXMQ
OBQ
HNGR?
YS
HERE
THANKS
LOOK!
GOOD!
AAHHHHH!
DADDY?
YES, SON?
WHERE DO I COME FROM?
DO YOU EVER WONDER WHAT IT ALL MEANS?
SOMETIMES!
THE TRIBE MEDICINE MAN CLAIMS WE'RE ALL MADE OUT OF A MYSTERIOUS SUBSTANCE CALLED "INK"!
BUT WHERE DOES "INK" COME FROM?
ALL THIS TALK GIVES ME A SPOOKY FEELING.
LET'S GET LAID!
MOMMY, NOW THAT DADDY HAS PASSED OUT-OF-THE-PANELS, WHERE IS HE?
(SOB!) NO ONE KNOWS, SON!
LOOK! IF THAT ANCIENT "INK" THEORY IS CORRECT, PERHAPS WE CAN LEARN TO MANIPULATE "INK" OURSELVES! IT COULD MEAN A BETTER LIFE FOR EVERYONE IN THE ENTIRE PLANE!
I STILL SAY THE WHOLE IDEA OF "INK" IS MEANINGLESS! IF EVERYTHING IS "INK" AND "INK" IS EVERY-THING, IT'S A VACUOUS CONCEPT!
SEE? I'M MAKING PROGRESS! I'VE ALMOST MADE THE "INK" TAKE THE SHAPE OF A VEHICLE!
AMAZING!
IT'LL PROBABLY TAKE A FEW PANELS TO PERFECT IT!
IF IT REALLY MOVES, YOU'LL BE FAMOUS! BOY, WILL YOU GET LAID!
I'M WORRIED! THE ZIBBINS ARE MASSING ON THE HORIZON LINE! THEY BELIEVE EVERYTHING WAS CREATED BY AN "ARTIST" WHO HAS CHOSEN THEM TO TAKE OVER THE WHOLE PLANE!
WE BETTER BE PRE-PARED!
LOOK! IT WORKS! IT WORKS!
FORGET IT! THE ZIBBINS ARE COMING NOW!
PLEASE DON'T DESTROY ME! I'M ONLY TWO PANELS OLD!
TAKE THAT, NON-ZIBBIN!
IT'S HOPELESS! THERE ARE SO MANY MORE OF THEM DRAWN THAN US!
MAYBE I CAN USE MY NEW DISCOVERIES ABOUT "INK" TO BUILD A WEAPON!
YOU... YOU'VE TORN MY OUTLINE!
GAAA!
IT WORKED! THEY'RE LEAVING!
NOW OUR SONS AND DAUGHTERS CAN LOOK FORWARD TO A GOLDEN AGE OF PEACE AND LEARNING!
...AND THE LIFE OF A CHARACTER SHALL BE LESS THAN ONESCORE PANELS!
AS THE GENIUS WHO FIRST TAMED INK, HE SHALL NEVER BE FOR-GOTTEN UNTIL THE FINAL PANEL!

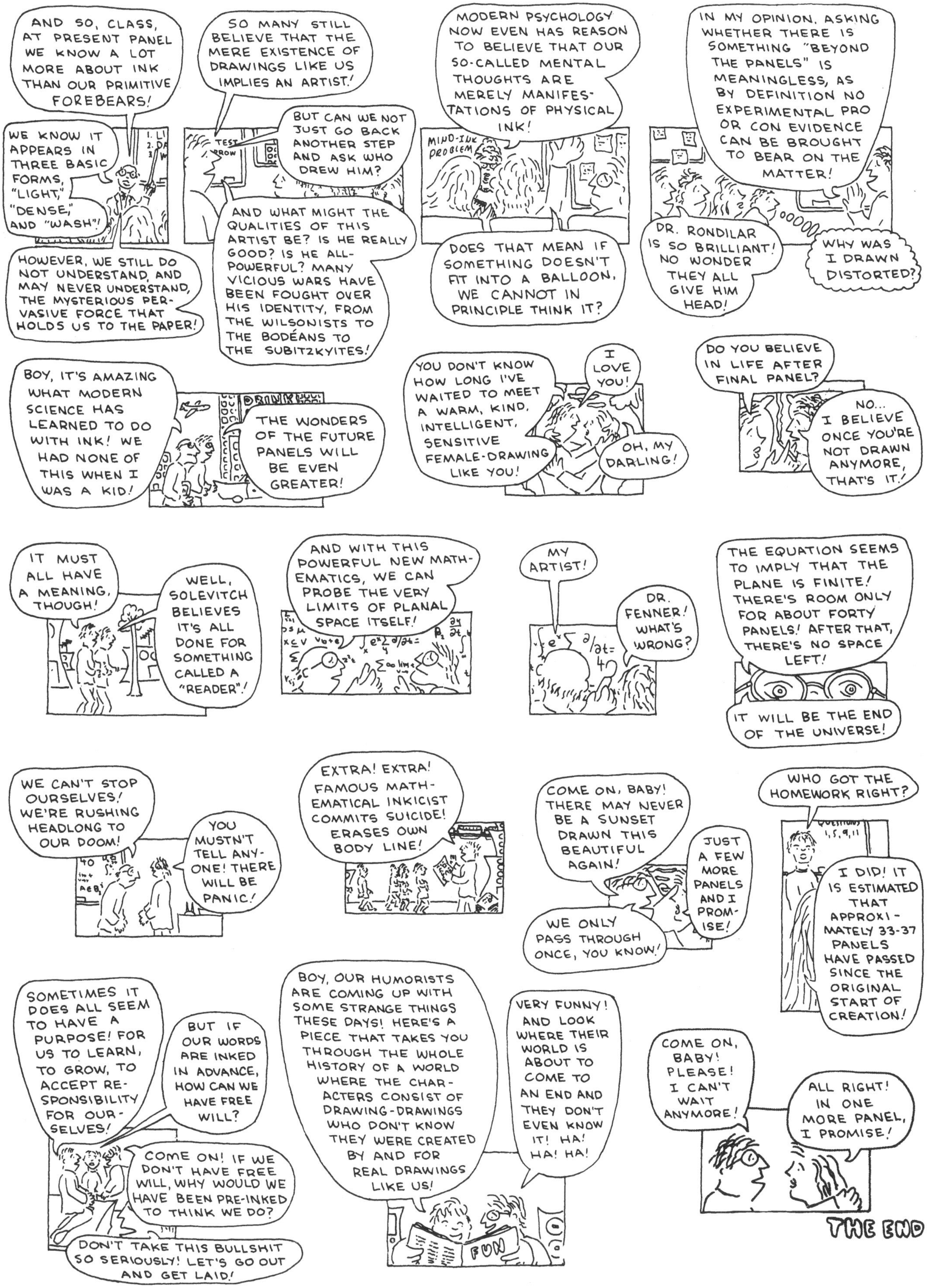
AND SO, CLASS, AT PRESENT PANEL WE KNOW A LOT MORE ABOUT INK THAN OUR PRIMITIVE FOREBEARS!
WE KNOW IT APPEARS IN THREE BASIC FORMS, "LIGHT," "DENSE," AND "WASH"!
HOWEVER, WE STILL DO NOT UNDERSTAND, AND MAY NEVER UNDERSTAND, THE MYSTERIOUS PERVASIVE FORCE THAT HOLDS US TO THE PAPER!
SO MANY STILL BELIEVE THAT THE MERE EXISTENCE OF DRAWINGS LIKE US IMPLIES AN ARTIST!
TEST
BUT CAN WE NOT JUST GO BACK ANOTHER STEP AND ASK WHO DREW HIM?
AND WHAT MIGHT THE QUALITIES OF THIS ARTIST BE? IS HE REALLY GOOD? IS HE ALL-POWERFUL? MANY VICIOUS WARS HAVE BEEN FOUGHT OVER HIS IDENTITY, FROM THE WILSONISTS TO THE BODÉANS TO THE SUBITZKYITES!
MODERN PSYCHOLOGY NOW EVEN HAS REASON TO BELIEVE THAT OUR SO-CALLED MENTAL THOUGHTS ARE MERELY MANIFESTATIONS OF PHYSICAL INK!
MIND-INK PROBLEM
DOES THAT MEAN IF SOMETHING DOESN'T FIT INTO A BALLOON, WE CANNOT IN PRINCIPLE THINK IT?
IN MY OPINION, ASKING WHETHER THERE IS SOMETHING "BEYOND THE PANELS" IS MEANINGLESS, AS BY DEFINITION NO EXPERIMENTAL PRO OR CON EVIDENCE CAN BE BROUGHT TO BEAR ON THE MATTER!
DR. RONDILAR IS SO BRILLIANT! NO WONDER THEY ALL GIVE HIM HEAD!
WHY WAS I DRAWN DISTORTED?
BOY, IT'S AMAZING WHAT MODERN SCIENCE HAS LEARNED TO DO WITH INK! WE HAD NONE OF THIS WHEN I WAS A KID!
THE WONDERS OF THE FUTURE PANELS WILL BE EVEN GREATER!
YOU DON'T KNOW HOW LONG I'VE WAITED TO MEET A WARM, KIND, INTELLIGENT, SENSITIVE FEMALE-DRAWING LIKE YOU!
I LOVE YOU!
OH, MY DARLING!
DO YOU BELIEVE IN LIFE AFTER FINAL PANEL?
NO... I BELIEVE ONCE YOU'RE NOT DRAWN ANYMORE, THAT'S IT!
IT MUST ALL HAVE A MEANING, THOUGH!
WELL, SOLEVITCH BELIEVES IT'S ALL DONE FOR SOMETHING CALLED A "READER"!
AND WITH THIS POWERFUL NEW MATHEMATICS, WE CAN PROBE THE VERY LIMITS OF PLANAL SPACE ITSELF!
MY ARTIST!
DR. FENNER! WHAT'S WRONG?
THE EQUATION SEEMS TO IMPLY THAT THE PLANE IS FINITE! THERE'S ROOM ONLY FOR ABOUT FORTY PANELS! AFTER THAT, THERE'S NO SPACE LEFT!
IT WILL BE THE END OF THE UNIVERSE!
WE CAN'T STOP OURSELVES! WE'RE RUSHING HEADLONG TO OUR DOOM!
YOU MUSTN'T TELL ANYONE! THERE WILL BE PANIC!
EXTRA! EXTRA! FAMOUS MATHEMATICAL INKICIST COMMITS SUICIDE! ERASES OWN BODY LINE!
COME ON, BABY! THERE MAY NEVER BE A SUNSET DRAWN THIS BEAUTIFUL AGAIN!
JUST A FEW MORE PANELS AND I PROMISE!
WE ONLY PASS THROUGH ONCE, YOU KNOW!
WHO GOT THE HOMEWORK RIGHT?
QUESTIONS 1,5,9,11
I DID! IT IS ESTIMATED THAT APPROXIMATELY 33-37 PANELS HAVE PASSED SINCE THE ORIGINAL START OF CREATION!
SOMETIMES IT DOES ALL SEEM TO HAVE A PURPOSE! FOR US TO LEARN, TO GROW, TO ACCEPT RESPONSIBILITY FOR OURSELVES!
BUT IF OUR WORDS ARE INKED IN ADVANCE, HOW CAN WE HAVE FREE WILL?
COME ON! IF WE DON'T HAVE FREE WILL, WHY WOULD WE HAVE BEEN PRE-INKED TO THINK WE DO?
DON'T TAKE THIS BULLSHIT SO SERIOUSLY! LET'S GO OUT AND GET LAID!
BOY, OUR HUMORISTS ARE COMING UP WITH SOME STRANGE THINGS THESE DAYS! HERE'S A PIECE THAT TAKES YOU THROUGH THE WHOLE HISTORY OF A WORLD WHERE THE CHARACTERS CONSIST OF DRAWING-DRAWINGS WHO DON'T KNOW THEY WERE CREATED BY AND FOR REAL DRAWINGS LIKE US!
VERY FUNNY! AND LOOK WHERE THEIR WORLD IS ABOUT TO COME TO AN END AND THEY DON'T EVEN KNOW IT! HA! HA! HA!
FUN
COME ON, BABY! PLEASE! I CAN'T WAIT ANYMORE!
ALL RIGHT! IN ONE MORE PANEL, I PROMISE!
THE END

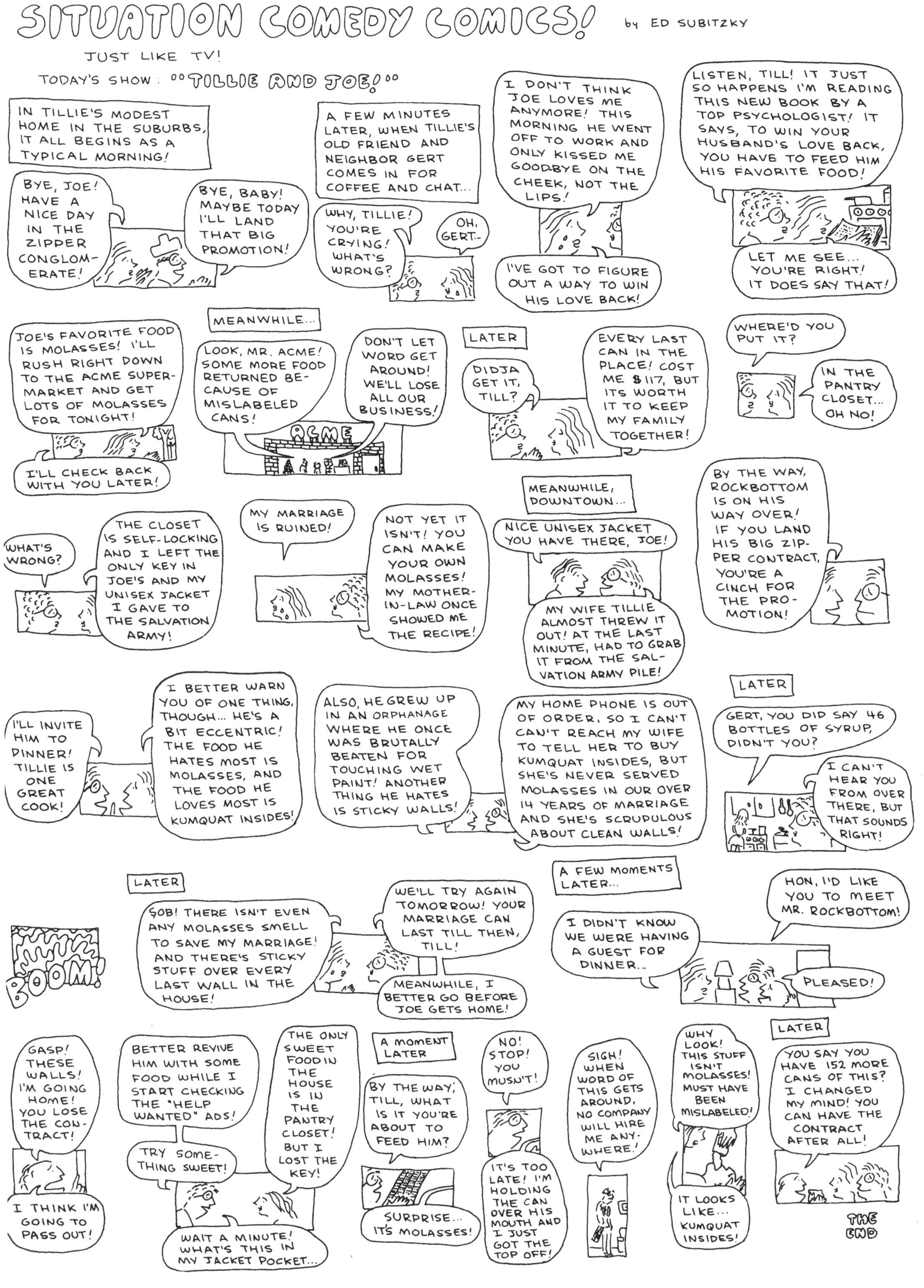
SITUATION COMEDY COMICS!
by ED SUBITZKY
JUST LIKE TV!
TODAY'S SHOW: "TILLIE AND JOE!"
IN TILLIE'S MODEST HOME IN THE SUBURBS, IT ALL BEGINS AS A TYPICAL MORNING!
BYE, JOE! HAVE A NICE DAY IN THE ZIPPER CONGLOM-ERATE!
BYE, BABY! MAYBE TODAY I'LL LAND THAT BIG PROMOTION!
A FEW MINUTES LATER, WHEN TILLIE'S OLD FRIEND AND NEIGHBOR GERT COMES IN FOR COFFEE AND CHAT...
WHY, TILLIE! YOU'RE CRYING! WHAT'S WRONG?
OH, GERT...
I DON'T THINK JOE LOVES ME ANYMORE! THIS MORNING HE WENT OFF TO WORK AND ONLY KISSED ME GOODBYE ON THE CHEEK, NOT THE LIPS!
I'VE GOT TO FIGURE OUT A WAY TO WIN HIS LOVE BACK!
LISTEN, TILL! IT JUST SO HAPPENS I'M READING THIS NEW BOOK BY A TOP PSYCHOLOGIST! IT SAYS, TO WIN YOUR HUSBAND'S LOVE BACK, YOU HAVE TO FEED HIM HIS FAVORITE FOOD!
LET ME SEE... YOU'RE RIGHT! IT DOES SAY THAT!
JOE'S FAVORITE FOOD IS MOLASSES! I'LL RUSH RIGHT DOWN TO THE ACME SUPER-MARKET AND GET LOTS OF MOLASSES FOR TONIGHT!
I'LL CHECK BACK WITH YOU LATER!
MEANWHILE...
LOOK, MR. ACME! SOME MORE FOOD RETURNED BE-CAUSE OF MISLABELED CANS!
DON'T LET WORD GET AROUND! WE'LL LOSE ALL OUR BUSINESS!
ACME
LATER
DIDJA GET IT, TILL?
EVERY LAST CAN IN THE PLACE! COST ME $117, BUT ITS WORTH IT TO KEEP MY FAMILY TOGETHER!
WHERE'D YOU PUT IT?
IN THE PANTRY CLOSET... OH NO!
WHAT'S WRONG?
THE CLOSET IS SELF-LOCKING AND I LEFT THE ONLY KEY IN JOE'S AND MY UNISEX JACKET I GAVE TO THE SALVATION ARMY!
MY MARRIAGE IS RUINED!
NOT YET IT ISN'T! YOU CAN MAKE YOUR OWN MOLASSES! MY MOTHER-IN-LAW ONCE SHOWED ME THE RECIPE!
MEANWHILE, DOWNTOWN...
NICE UNISEX JACKET YOU HAVE THERE, JOE!
MY WIFE TILLIE ALMOST THREW IT OUT! AT THE LAST MINUTE, HAD TO GRAB IT FROM THE SAL-VATION ARMY PILE!
BY THE WAY, ROCKBOTTOM IS ON HIS WAY OVER! IF YOU LAND HIS BIG ZIP-PER CONTRACT, YOU'RE A CINCH FOR THE PRO-MOTION!
I'LL INVITE HIM TO DINNER! TILLIE IS ONE GREAT COOK!
I BETTER WARN YOU OF ONE THING, THOUGH... HE'S A BIT ECCENTRIC! THE FOOD HE HATES MOST IS MOLASSES, AND THE FOOD HE LOVES MOST IS KUMQUAT INSIDES!
ALSO, HE GREW UP IN AN ORPHANAGE WHERE HE ONCE WAS BRUTALLY BEATEN FOR TOUCHING WET PAINT! ANOTHER THING HE HATES IS STICKY WALLS!
MY HOME PHONE IS OUT OF ORDER, SO I CAN'T CAN'T REACH MY WIFE TO TELL HER TO BUY KUMQUAT INSIDES, BUT SHE'S NEVER SERVED MOLASSES IN OUR OVER 14 YEARS OF MARRIAGE AND SHE'S SCRUPULOUS ABOUT CLEAN WALLS!
LATER
GERT, YOU DID SAY 46 BOTTLES OF SYRUP, DIDN'T YOU?
I CAN'T HEAR YOU FROM OVER THERE, BUT THAT SOUNDS RIGHT!
BOOM!
LATER
SOB! THERE ISN'T EVEN ANY MOLASSES SMELL TO SAVE MY MARRIAGE! AND THERE'S STICKY STUFF OVER EVERY LAST WALL IN THE HOUSE!
WE'LL TRY AGAIN TOMORROW! YOUR MARRIAGE CAN LAST TILL THEN, TILL!
MEANWHILE, I BETTER GO BEFORE JOE GETS HOME!
A FEW MOMENTS LATER...
I DIDN'T KNOW WE WERE HAVING A GUEST FOR DINNER...
HON, I'D LIKE YOU TO MEET MR. ROCKBOTTOM!
PLEASED!
GASP! THESE WALLS! I'M GOING HOME! YOU LOSE THE CON-TRACT!
I THINK I'M GOING TO PASS OUT!
BETTER REVIVE HIM WITH SOME FOOD WHILE I START CHECKING THE "HELP WANTED" ADS!
TRY SOME-THING SWEET!
THE ONLY SWEET FOOD IN THE HOUSE IS IN THE PANTRY CLOSET! BUT I LOST THE KEY!
WAIT A MINUTE! WHAT'S THIS IN MY JACKET POCKET...
A MOMENT LATER
BY THE WAY, TILL, WHAT IS IT YOU'RE ABOUT TO FEED HIM?
SURPRISE... IT'S MOLASSES!
NO! STOP! YOU MUSN'T!
IT'S TOO LATE! I'M HOLDING THE CAN OVER HIS MOUTH AND I JUST GOT THE TOP OFF!
SIGH! WHEN WORD OF THIS GETS AROUND, NO COMPANY WILL HIRE ME ANY-WHERE!
WHY LOOK! THIS STUFF ISN'T MOLASSES! MUST HAVE BEEN MISLABELED!
IT LOOKS LIKE... KUMQUAT INSIDES!
LATER
YOU SAY YOU HAVE 152 MORE CANS OF THIS? I CHANGED MY MIND! YOU CAN HAVE THE CONTRACT AFTER ALL!
THE END

INSTANT REPLAY COMICS!
WELL, ARNOLD, OUR SOCIAL AGENDA FOR THIS EVENING IS HOT SEX, AX MURDER AND CHINESE CHECKERS!
WHICH WOULD YOU RATHER DO FIRST?
CHINESE CHECKERS!
CHINESE CHECKERS!
CHINESE CHECKERS!
CHINESE CHECKERS!
THE END

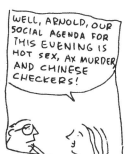

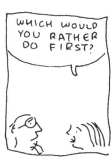

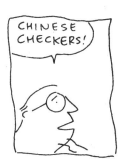

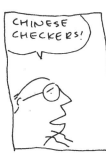

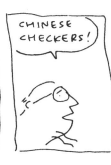

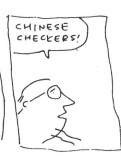

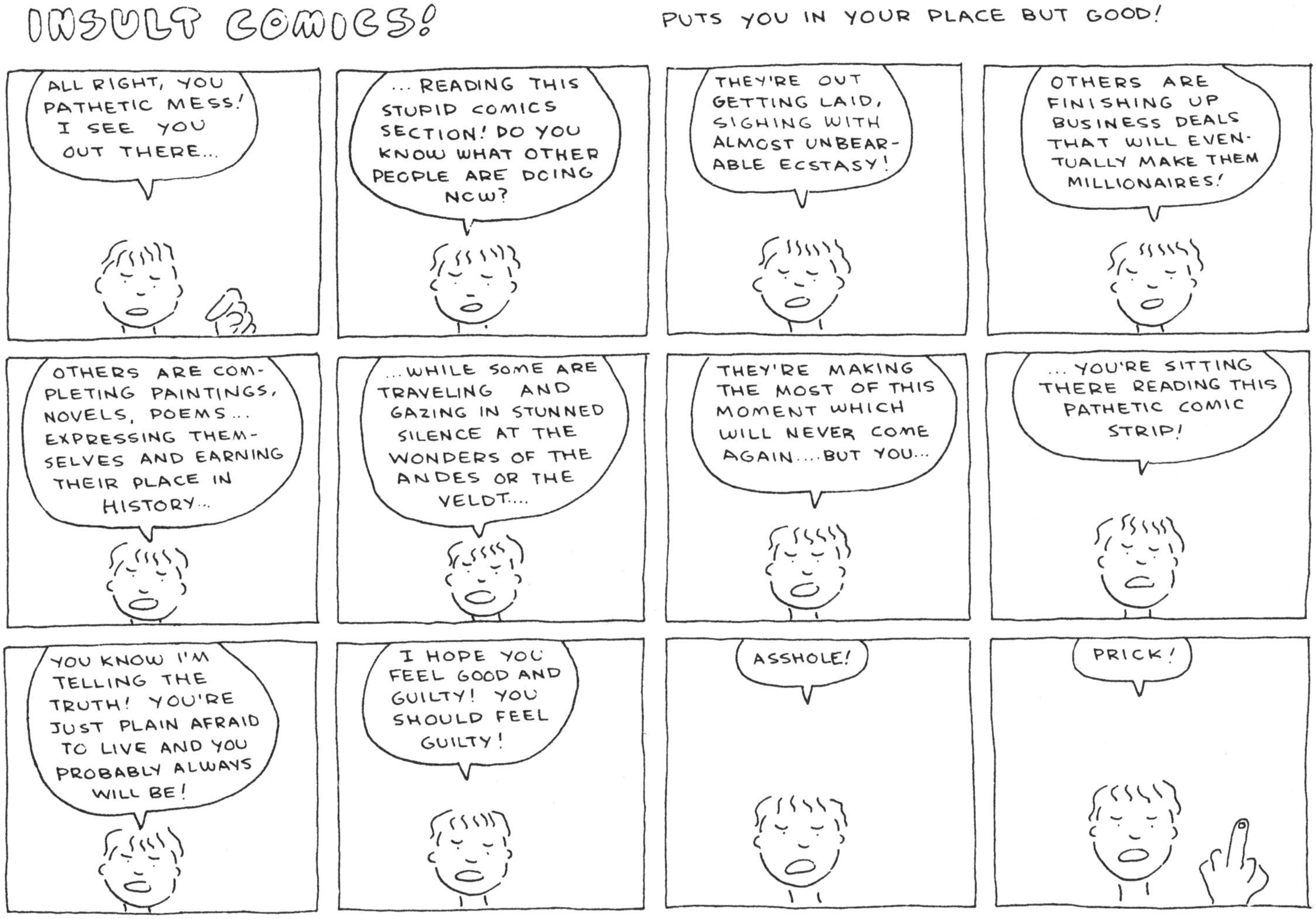
INSULT COMICS!
PUTS YOU IN YOUR PLACE BUT GOOD!
ALL RIGHT, YOU PATHETIC MESS! I SEE YOU OUT THERE...
...READING THIS STUPID COMICS SECTION! DO YOU KNOW WHAT OTHER PEOPLE ARE DOING NOW?
THEY'RE OUT GETTING LAID, SIGHING WITH ALMOST UNBEARABLE ECSTASY!
OTHERS ARE FINISHING UP BUSINESS DEALS THAT WILL EVENTUALLY MAKE THEM MILLIONAIRES!
OTHERS ARE COMPLETING PAINTINGS, NOVELS, POEMS... EXPRESSING THEMSELVES AND EARNING THEIR PLACE IN HISTORY...
...WHILE SOME ARE TRAVELING AND GAZING IN STUNNED SILENCE AT THE WONDERS OF THE ANDES OR THE VELDT...
THEY'RE MAKING THE MOST OF THIS MOMENT WHICH WILL NEVER COME AGAIN....BUT YOU...
...YOU'RE SITTING THERE READING THIS PATHETIC COMIC STRIP!
YOU KNOW I'M TELLING THE TRUTH! YOU'RE JUST PLAIN AFRAID TO LIVE AND YOU PROBABLY ALWAYS WILL BE!
I HOPE YOU FEEL GOOD AND GUILTY! YOU SHOULD FEEL GUILTY!
ASSHOLE!
PRICK!

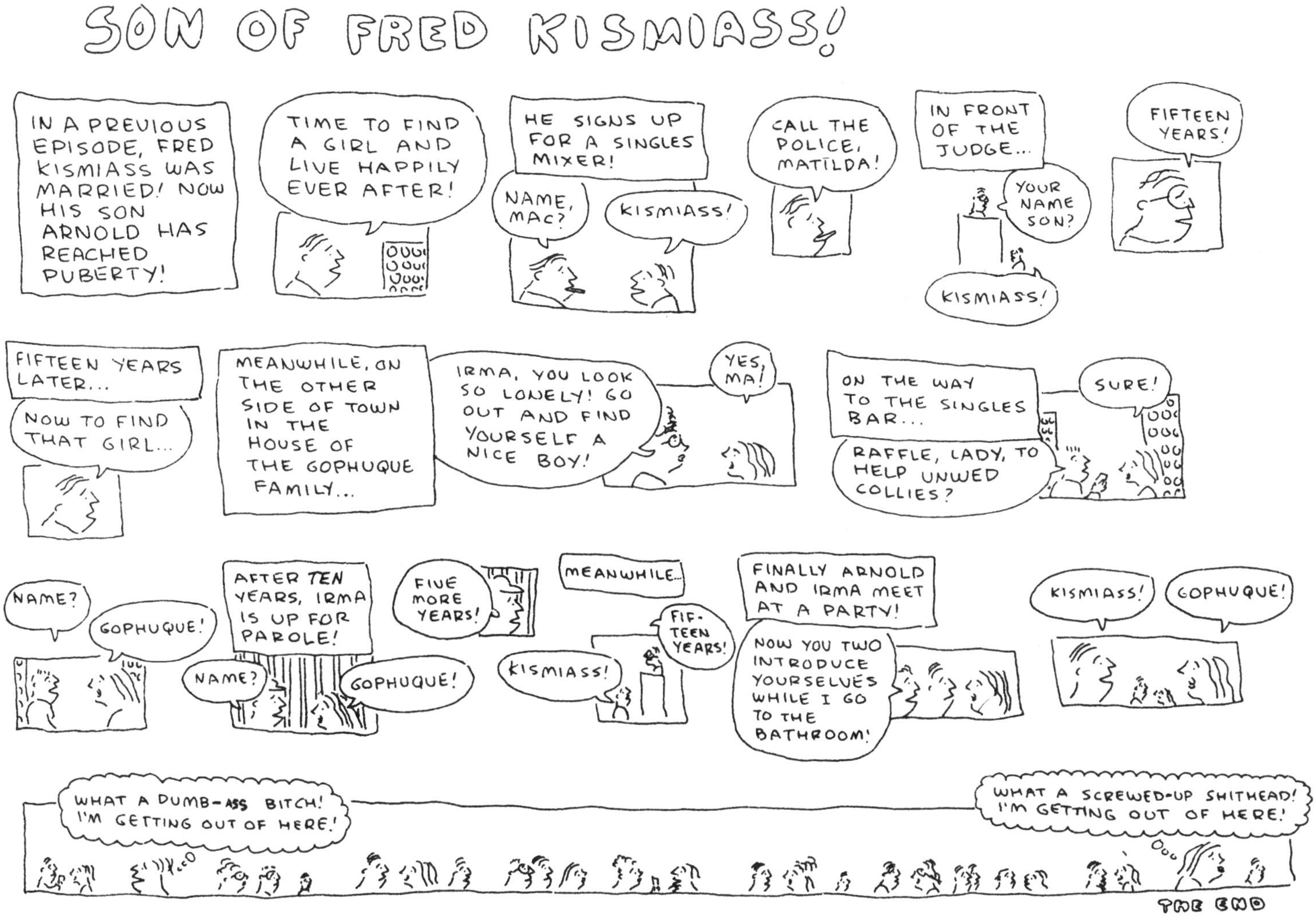
SON OF FRED KISMIASS!
IN A PREVIOUS EPISODE, FRED KISMIASS WAS MARRIED! NOW HIS SON ARNOLD HAS REACHED PUBERTY!
TIME TO FIND A GIRL AND LIVE HAPPILY EVER AFTER!
HE SIGNS UP FOR A SINGLES MIXER!
NAME, MAC?
KISMIASS!
CALL THE POLICE, MATILDA!
IN FRONT OF THE JUDGE...
YOUR NAME SON?
KISMIASS!
FIFTEEN YEARS!
FIFTEEN YEARS LATER...
NOW TO FIND THAT GIRL...
MEANWHILE, ON THE OTHER SIDE OF TOWN IN THE HOUSE OF THE GOPHUQUE FAMILY...
IRMA, YOU LOOK SO LONELY! GO OUT AND FIND YOURSELF A NICE BOY!
YES, MA!
ON THE WAY TO THE SINGLES BAR...
SURE!
RAFFLE, LADY, TO HELP UNWED COLLIES?
NAME?
GOPHUQUE!
AFTER TEN YEARS, IRMA IS UP FOR PAROLE!
NAME?
GOPHUQUE!
FIVE MORE YEARS!
MEANWHILE...
FIF-TEEN YEARS!
KISMIASS!
FINALLY ARNOLD AND IRMA MEET AT A PARTY!
NOW YOU TWO INTRODUCE YOURSELVES WHILE I GO TO THE BATHROOM!
KISMIASS!
GOPHUQUE!
WHAT A DUMB-ASS BITCH! I'M GETTING OUT OF HERE!
WHAT A SCREWED-UP SHITHEAD! I'M GETTING OUT OF HERE!
THE END

CAREFULLY RATED SEX COMICS! BY ED SUBITZKY

PERFECT FOR CONCERNED FAMILIES — CONTAINS DETAILED WARNINGS SO EACH INDIVIDUAL GETS JUST THE RIGHT AMOUNT OF SEX AND VIOLENCE!

THE FOLLOWING SEVEN PANELS MAY BE VIEWED BY ALL READERS

OUR STORY BEGINS IN A SMALL MIDWESTERN TOWN AS A YOUNG WOMAN BOARDS A BUS....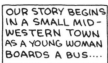

SOB! GOODBYE, DARLING! WE'LL MISS YOU! / BYE, MOM! BYE, DAD!

ARE YOU SURE THIS ISN'T A FOOLISH DREAM—TO GO TO NEW YORK AND BECOME A FASHION MODEL?

OH, DAD, MOM! WE'VE BEEN THROUGH THIS BEFORE! I'M 19 YEARS OLD NOW AND I'LL BE FINE!

AS THE BUS PULLS AWAY INTO THE SOFT SPRING AIR... / BE A GOOD GIRL, DARLING! / I WILL!

MARCIA... DO YOU THINK WE SHOULD HAVE TOLD HER?

NO, CHARLES! AND LET US PRAY SHE NEVER LEARNS OUR FAMILY'S GHASTLY SECRET!

THE FOLLOWING FOUR PANELS CONTAIN MATERIAL THAT MAY BE UNSUITABLE FOR CHILDREN UNDER 13

MEANWHILE, IN NEW YORK'S TOP MODELING AGENCY / NO, DAMN IT, NO! THAT'S NOT THE WAY TO DO A BRA BILLBOARD CAMPAIGN!

THESE DAMN OLD HAS-BEENS! WHAT WE NEED IS A FRESH, NEW BUSTLINE... ONE THE PUBLIC HAS NEVER SEEN BEFORE!

DAMN IT, BABY! I WANT YOU TO SEARCH EVERYWHERE! THE RIGHT FACE—THE RIGHT FIGURE—HAS TO BE OUT THERE SOMEPLACE!

BUT FIRST, BABY, HOW ABOUT POURING ME SOME SCOTCH AND MAYBE A LITTLE BACK RUB! I'M TENSE, DAMN IT! / YES, SIR!

THE FOLLOWING SEVEN PANELS CONTAIN MATERIAL THAT MAY BE TOO INTENSE FOR CHILDREN UNDER 17

OUR SCENE NOW SWITCHES TO A SECLUDED MENTAL HOSPITAL IN VERMONT! / AAAARGHH!

THERE ARE HUGE INSECTS CRAWLING ALL OVER ME! THEY'RE RUINING MY SUIT! / TAKE THIS NEW DRUG!

WHY... THE INSECTS ARE GONE! MY NAME IS ARNIE! 2+7=9! THE CAPITAL OF NORTH CAROLINA IS RALEIGH! / HE'S PERFECTLY RATIONAL NOW!

RELEASE HIM! / YOU'RE FREE TO GO! / IGNEOUS ROCK IS OFTEN FOUND ASSOCIATED WITH INTENSE VOLCANIC ACTIVITY!

OH NO! / DR. JOHNSON! WHAT'S WRONG?

I ONLY GAVE HIM THE GREEN PILLS FOR HIS INSECT-CRAWLING DELUSIONS! I FORGOT TO GIVE HIM THE RED ONES FOR HIS AX-MURDERER TENDENCIES!

JUST OUT OF CURIOSITY, DR. JOHNSON, WHAT CAUSED HIS BRUTAL HOMICIDAL TENDENCIES?

THE FOLLOWING TWO PANELS CONTAIN MATERIAL THAT MAY BE UNSUITABLE FOR CHILDREN UNDER 13

I DON'T KNOW, DAMN IT! BUT HE KEEPS HAVING THESE TERRIFYING DREAMS ABOUT A WOMAN ACCIDENTALLY STANDING BY AN OPEN WINDOW IN A BRA!

SHE THOUGHT THE SHADES WERE DRAWN, BUT THE FAMILY HAD TO LEAVE TOWN IN DISGRACE! / HIS MOTHER, MAYBE.... DAMN IT ANYWAY!

THE FOLLOWING PANEL MAY BE VIEWED BY ALL READERS

ARRIVING IN NEW YORK, THE INNOCENT YOUNG GIRL GOES STRAIGHT TO HER FIRST INTERVIEW FOR A MODELING JOB / MIGHT AS WELL START WITH NEW YORK'S TOP AGENCY!

THE FOLLOWING PANEL CONTAINS MATERIAL THAT MAY BE UNSUITABLE FOR CHILDREN UNDER 13

AS SHE WALKS THROUGH THE DOOR... / DAMN IT, LOOK AT THAT SHAPE! SHE'S PERFECT!

THE FOLLOWING TWO PANELS CONTAIN STRONG LANGUAGE

HURRY UP, BABY! SHOW US YOUR TITS! / WHAT?

YOUR TITS! BOOBS! KNOCKERS! I'M GONNA PLASTER 'EM ON EVERY FUCKING BILLBOARD ON EVERY FUCKING HIGHWAY IN THE WHOLE FUCKING COUNTRY!

THE FOLLOWING PANEL MAY BE VIEWED BY ALL READERS

IN TEARS, SHE RUNS OUT OF THE BUILDING....

THE FOLLOWING FOUR PANELS CONTAIN MATERIAL THAT MAY BE TOO TRAGIC FOR YOUNGER READERS

OOOPS! / HEY! GETTING CAUGHT IN THE LEASH, YOU JUST STRANGLED MY SEEING EYE DOG!

I CAN'T AFFORD ANOTHER, MUCH LESS THE DELICATE EYE SURGERY THAT COULD RESTORE MY VISION!

SOB! I'LL HAVE TO TAKE THAT HORRIBLE JOB NOW!

MEANWHILE, AN AGITATED HITCHHIKER BOARDS A TRUCK ON A RAINY INTERSTATE... / WHERE YA HEADIN', LADY? / NEW YORK / WHAT YA HAULIN'? / AXES FOR HARDWARE STORES!

THE FOLLOWING PANEL CONTAINS MATERIAL THAT MAY BE UNSUITABLE FOR CHILDREN UNDER 15

WHAT YOU DOIN'? / STRAIGHTENING MY BRA!

THE FOLLOWING PANEL CONTAINS GRAPHIC VIOLENCE

ARRGHHHH! / AXES / AXES

THE FOLLOWING TWO PANELS CONTAIN MATERIAL THAT MAY BE UNSUITABLE FOR CHILDREN UNDER 13

SOB! MY BUSTLINE IS VISIBLE TO TRAVELERS ON HIGHWAYS EVERYWHERE, DAMN IT!

WELL, IF I'M GOING TO GO DOWN THE DRAIN, DAMN IT, I MAY AS WELL DO IT ALL THE WAY!

THE FOLLOWING THREE PANELS CONTAIN MATERIAL OF AN EXPLICITLY SEXUAL NATURE AND SHOULD NOT BE READ BY ANYONE UNDER 21

BOY, THAT WANTON WOMAN HAS ALREADY FUCKED EVERY MAN, WOMAN, AND CHILD WALKING DOWN 42ND STREET!
AND RUSH HOUR'S JUST BEGINNING!

HEY, LADY, YOU DISGUSTING SLUT! I OUGHTTA RUN YOU IN!
BUT OFFICER! I JUST LOVE TO FUCK POLICE HORSES!

YEAH, BITCH! YOU OWE ME TEN GRAND FOR THIS POT, COCAINE, LSD, HEROIN, AND HERBAL TEA!
SO? MY BILLBOARD RESIDUALS WILL PAY FOR IT! LET'S S&M!

THE FOLLOWING TWO PANELS CONTAIN MATERIAL THAT MAY BE UNSUITABLE FOR CHILDREN UNDER 10

BUT WHEN SHE GOES BACK TO THE AGENCY FOR THE NEXT ROUND OF PHOTOGRAPHS...
YOU? LOOK AT YOU... DARN IT, YOU'RE A PHYSICAL WRECK!

YOU'RE THROUGH IN THE MODELING BUSINESS! YOU'LL NEVER WORK FOR ANYONE IN THIS TOWN AGAIN!
WE'RE EVEN TAKING DOWN YOUR BILLBOARDS, DARN YOU!

THE FOLLOWING PANEL CONTAINS MATERIAL OF AN EXPLICITLY SEXUAL NATURE AND SHOULD NOT BE READ BY ANYONE UNDER 21

NOT EVEN IF I GIVE YOU A BLOWJOB RIGHT HERE AND NOW?
DON'T YOU REMEMBER? YOU JUST DID! AND THE ANSWER IS STILL NO!

THE FOLLOWING TWO PANELS CONTAIN MATERIAL THAT MAY BE TOO INTENSE FOR CHILDREN UNDER 16

THERE'S NO MISTAKE ABOUT IT, CHIEF! SOME MADMAN HAS BEEN MURDERING EVERY WOMAN ON THE EAST COAST WHO EVER APPEARED IN PUBLIC WITH HER BRA VISIBLE!

AND LOOK! THE BLOODY TRAIL SEEMS TO BE LEADING TO NEW YORK!
YEAH, HE SHOULD BE RIGHT AROUND LAKEVILLE, CONNECTICUT, BY NOW!

THE FOLLOWING FIVE PANELS SHOULD BE READ ONLY BY THE VERY LOWEST AND SICKEST ORDER OF HUMAN PERVERTS AND SADISTS

IN HER DESPAIR, SHE STOPS OFF AT A CHEAP HOTEL AND HAS A LESBIAN RELATIONSHIP WITH A RUBBER SEX DOLL!
SOB! NO ONE ELSE WILL HAVE ME!

GEE, I THINK I LOVE YOU!
CIGARETTE?

SHIT! IT WAS FLAMMABLE! I BURNED THE BUILDING DOWN AND EVERYONE IS DYING WITH THEIR SKIN BUBBLING OFF AND THEIR ENTRAILS SPEWING!

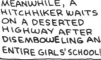
MEANWHILE, A HITCHHIKER WAITS ON A DESERTED HIGHWAY AFTER DISEMBOWELING AN ENTIRE GIRLS' SCHOOL!
GASP! THAT BILLBOARD! THAT WOMAN MUST BE THE MOST EVIL PERSON IN THE WORLD!

I'M GOING TO FIND HER AND THEN CHOP HER UP INTO THOUSANDS OF LITTLE PIECES AND EAT THEM!
LUCKILY, I STILL HAVE A GOOD SUPPLY OF AXES LEFT FROM THE FIRST TRUCK!

THE FOLLOWING PANEL CONTAINS MATERIAL THAT MAY BE UNSUITABLE FOR CHILDREN UNDER 13

MEANWHILE, IN THE MIDWEST...
THAT BILLBOARD! GASP! OUR DAUGHTER! WE MUST GO TO NEW YORK AT ONCE!
DAMN IT!

THE FOLLOWING TWO PANELS CONTAIN MATERIAL THAT MAY BE TOO POWERFUL FOR YOUNGER READERS

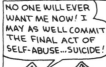

MEANWHILE, IN NEW YORK!
JOBLESS, PENNILESS... A RUINED WOMAN WITH A FOOLHARDY PAST AND NO FUTURE...

NO ONE WILL EVER WANT ME NOW! I MAY AS WELL COMMIT THE FINAL ACT OF SELF-ABUSE...SUICIDE!

THE FOLLOWING FOUR PANELS MAY BE VIEWED BY ALL READERS

WAIT! I WANT YOU!
WHAT?

REMEMBER ME? I'M THE MAN WHOSE SIGHT WAS SAVED BY THE MONEY YOU SO GENEROUSLY GAVE ME!

AND SINCE I WAS NEVER ABLE TO SEE ANY OF THOSE HORRIBLE BILLBOARDS, I CAN STILL LOVE YOU AND RESPECT YOU!

LET'S GET MARRIED AT ONCE!
I KNOW A GREAT PLACE TO HONEYMOON! A DESERTED CABIN IN LAKEVILLE, CONNECTICUT!

THE FOLLOWING TWO PANELS CONTAIN MATERIAL THAT MAY BE UNSUITABLE FOR CHILDREN UNDER 13

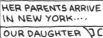

HER PARENTS ARRIVE IN NEW YORK....
OUR DAUGHTER POSING FOR BRA BILLBOARDS! SOB!
DAMN IT!

SHE'S NOT HERE, BUT SHE LEFT THIS NOTE FOR THE MAILMAN SAYING SHE WENT TO LAKEVILLE, CONNECTICUT!
LET'S GO THERE AT ONCE! DAMN IT!

THE FOLLOWING PANEL CONTAINS MATERIAL THAT MAY BE TOO INTENSE FOR CHILDREN UNDER 16

IN CONNECTICUT, A MADMAN LOOKS OVER THE COUNTRYSIDE....
THERE... IN THAT DISTANT CABIN... THE WORLD'S MOST EVIL WOMAN!
LUCKILY I'VE GOT ONE AX LEFT!

THE FOLLOWING PANEL CONTAINS MATERIAL OF AN EXPLICITLY SEXUAL NATURE AND SHOULD NOT BE READ BY ANYONE UNDER 21

OOH! LOVE ME! DARLING!
AHH...WAIT, DID YOU HEAR A NOISE?

THE REMAINING PANELS SHOULD NOT BE READ BY ANYONE HAVING A HEART CONDITION OR WHO CANNOT ENDURE SHOCK AFTER SHOCK AND SURPRISE AFTER SURPRISE

DIE!
NO! NO!

WAIT! STOP!
MOM! DAD! WHAT ARE YOU DOING HERE?

SOB! SHE'S NOT YOUR MOM, DARLING! SHE IS!
I DON'T UNDERSTAND! THAT'S OBVIOUSLY A MALE AX MURDERER!

NO, DEAR! YOU SEE, LONG AGO, WHEN YOU WERE ONLY ONE YEAR OLD, YOUR MOTHER ACCIDENTALLY STOOD BY AN OPEN WINDOW IN HER BRA!

DISGRACED, SHE PSYCHOLOGICALLY REJECTED FEMININITY AND, IN HER MIND, BECAME A MAN! SO PERFECT WAS HER DISGUISE THAT LATER, WHEN SHE WENT COMPLETELY INSANE, SHE EVEN FOOLED TOP MENTAL HOSPITAL PSYCHIATRISTS!

YOU WERE RAISED BY MYSELF AND YOUR AUNT, POSING AS YOUR REAL MOTHER! AND NOW, BY APPEARING IN BRA BILLBOARDS, YOU'RE UNCONSCIOUSLY FOLLOWING THE SAME DESTRUCTIVE PATTERN!

TO THINK I ALMOST AX MURDERED MY OWN DAUGHTER! THE SHOCK OF IT HAS CURED ME COMPLETELY!
LOOK! THE POLICE!

AS A NOTED BRA MODEL, WE KEPT AN EYE ON YOU!
SIR, WILL THEY GO EASY ON MY MOTHER?

THAT'S UP TO THE COURTS TO DECIDE!
NOW, I THINK WE'VE ALL DISTURBED THESE TWO HAPPY NEWLYWEDS LONG ENOUGH! THE END

MN: Were you able to transition some of your extracurricular *Lampoon* work into advertising?

ES: No. Never. They had nothing to do with each other.

MN: You never did any funny advertising?

ES: Very rarely. The reason is that direct marketing is a very serious part of advertising, unless it's for a video game or something.

MN: You did some modeling, too, right?

ES: Yeah, they used to use everybody at the *Lampoon* for modeling. A lot of the people you'd see in the magazine were *Lampoon* secretaries or people who worked there. They used to use me, too. Like I said, I'm a ham in front of a camera. I enjoyed modeling, so later I signed up with FunnyFaces Today and got some work here and there. But it was hard to sneak away for auditions and photoshoots when I was in the advertising business, so I couldn't really pursue it.

I once appeared as an actor in one of the commercials I wrote at the ad agency. Being in my own commercial was a highlight for me. Writing it was just another job, an advertising assignment for a video game called *Mountain King*.[18] During casting they tried and tried and tried, but they couldn't find anybody they really liked. Finally, the director we had hired said, "Ed, why don't you show us how you think it should be done." I did, and he cast me on the spot. It got me my SAG card, believe it or not.[19]

ES: The commercial shows me, sitting in a chair, playing a video game and making all sorts of expressions as various events happen. Like this: [*Ed makes a series of faces, met with laughter*]—while I'm playing with the game controls like this: [*Miming*] It was fun. I don't know if I ever will, but it would be great if I could get back into some kind of performing or modeling. Anything in front of an audience, really.

---

[18]Released in 1983 by CBS Electronics.

[19]Membership card for the Screen Actors Guild.

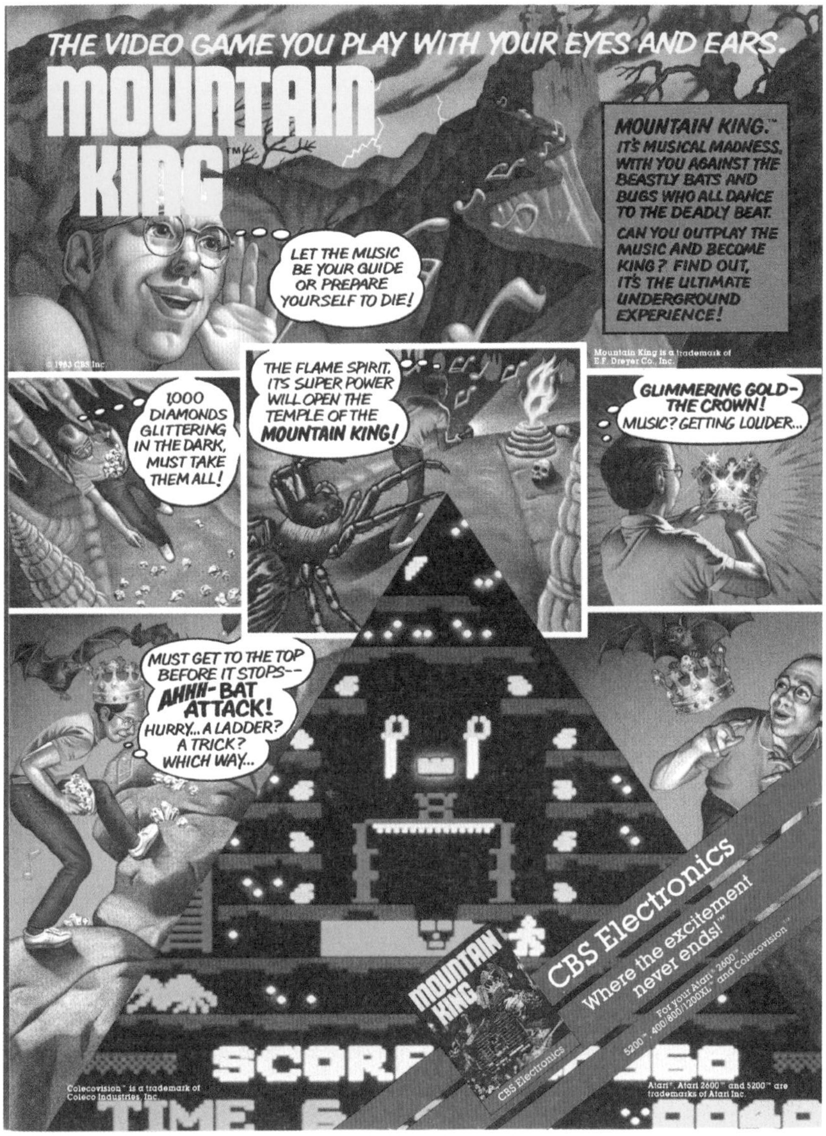
THE VIDEO GAME YOU PLAY WITH YOUR EYES AND EARS.
MOUNTAIN KING™
MOUNTAIN KING.™ IT'S MUSICAL MADNESS, WITH YOU AGAINST THE BEASTLY BATS AND BUGS WHO ALL DANCE TO THE DEADLY BEAT. CAN YOU OUTPLAY THE MUSIC AND BECOME KING? FIND OUT. IT'S THE ULTIMATE UNDERGROUND EXPERIENCE!
LET THE MUSIC BE YOUR GUIDE OR PREPARE YOURSELF TO DIE!
1,000 DIAMONDS GLITTERING IN THE DARK, MUST TAKE THEM ALL!
THE FLAME SPIRIT, ITS SUPER POWER WILL OPEN THE TEMPLE OF THE MOUNTAIN KING!
GLIMMERING GOLD– THE CROWN! MUSIC? GETTING LOUDER...
MUST GET TO THE TOP BEFORE IT STOPS-- AHHH- BAT ATTACK! HURRY... A LADDER? A TRICK? WHICH WAY...
CBS Electronics
Where the excitement never ends!™
SCORE
TIME

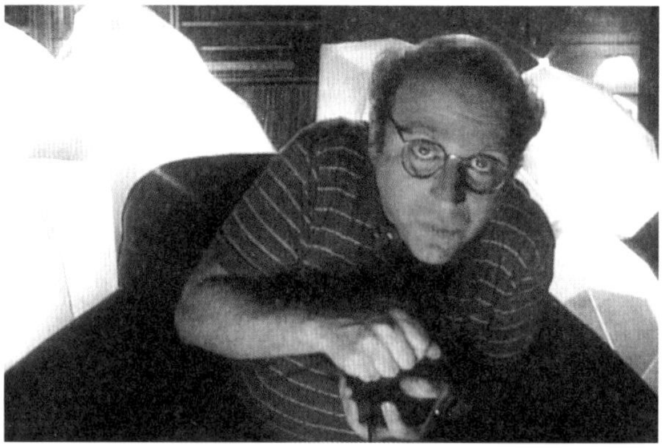

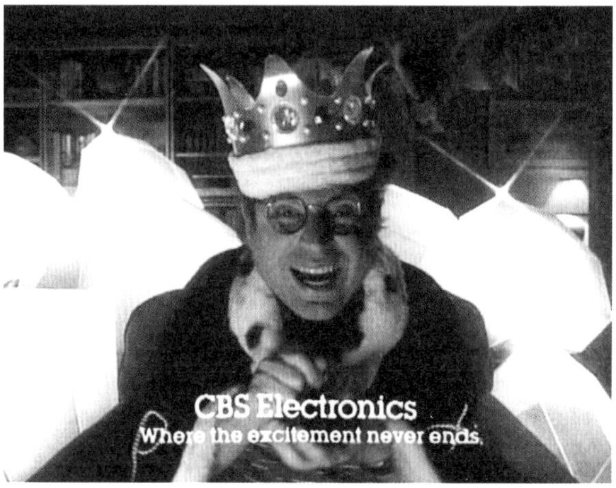
CBS Electronics
Where the excitement never ends.

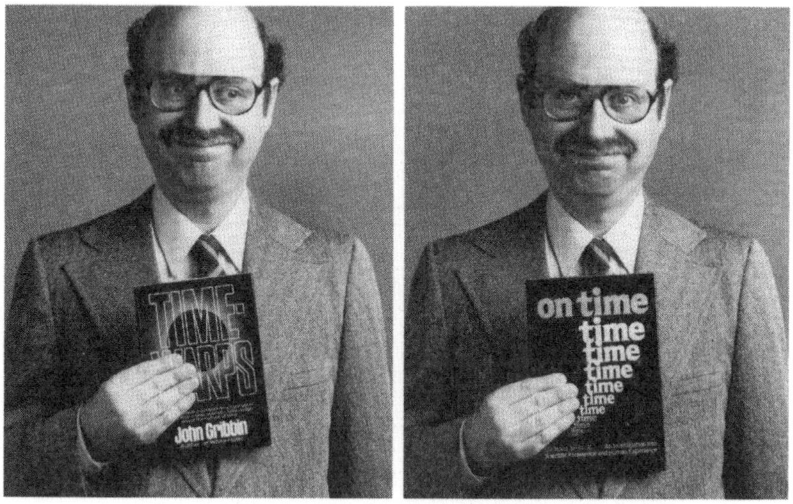
TIME-WARPS
John Gribbin
on time
time
time
time

COULD THERE BE AN ALTERNATE UNIVERSE WITH AN ALTERNATE YOU?

During a typical day you make thousands of small decisions. Could there be alternate universes where similar "yous" make other choices? While such ideas are speculation, some scientists take them as a possibility. To discover why, decide on TIMEWARPS.

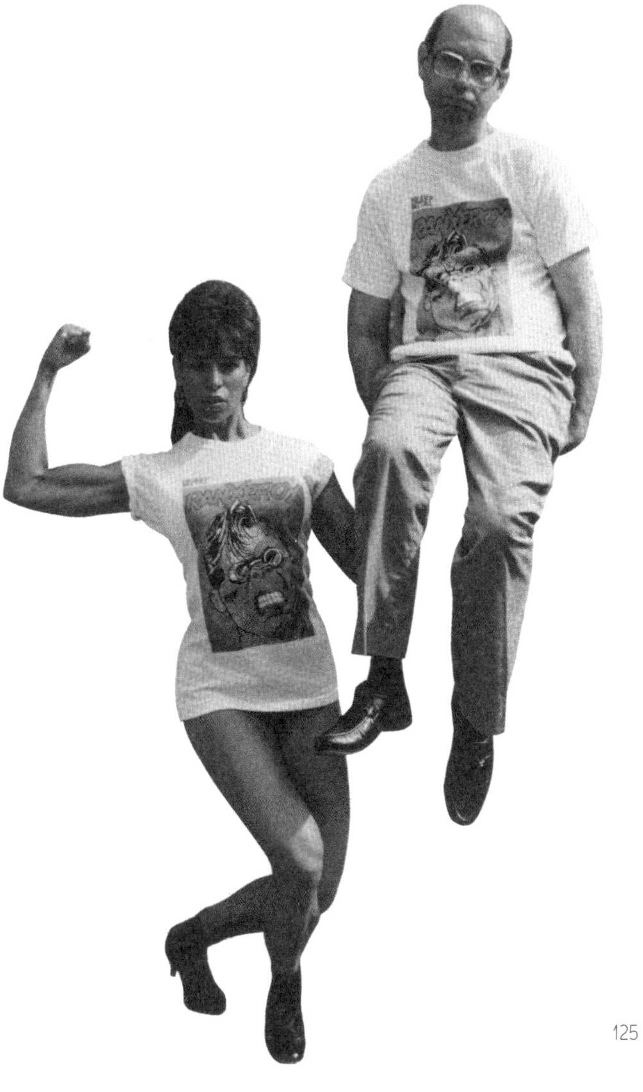

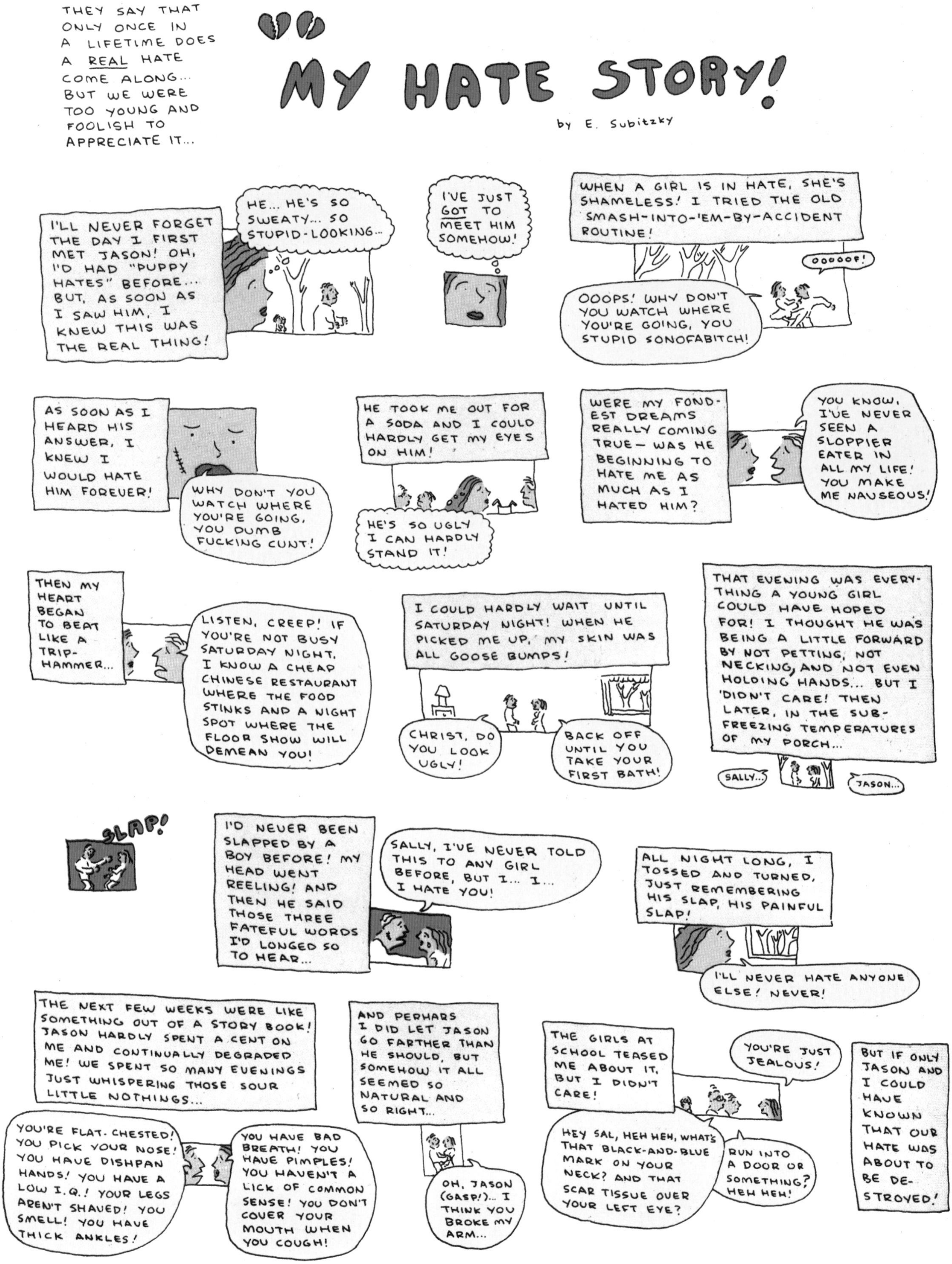

THEY SAY THAT ONLY ONCE IN A LIFETIME DOES A REAL HATE COME ALONG... BUT WE WERE TOO YOUNG AND FOOLISH TO APPRECIATE IT...
MY HATE STORY!
by E. Subitzky
I'LL NEVER FORGET THE DAY I FIRST MET JASON! OH, I'D HAD "PUPPY HATES" BEFORE... BUT, AS SOON AS I SAW HIM, I KNEW THIS WAS THE REAL THING!
HE... HE'S SO SWEATY... SO STUPID-LOOKING...
I'VE JUST GOT TO MEET HIM SOMEHOW!
WHEN A GIRL IS IN HATE, SHE'S SHAMELESS! I TRIED THE OLD SMASH-INTO-'EM-BY-ACCIDENT ROUTINE!
OOOOOF!
OOOPS! WHY DON'T YOU WATCH WHERE YOU'RE GOING, YOU STUPID SONOFABITCH!
AS SOON AS I HEARD HIS ANSWER, I KNEW I WOULD HATE HIM FOREVER!
WHY DON'T YOU WATCH WHERE YOU'RE GOING, YOU DUMB FUCKING CUNT!
HE TOOK ME OUT FOR A SODA AND I COULD HARDLY GET MY EYES ON HIM!
HE'S SO UGLY I CAN HARDLY STAND IT!
WERE MY FONDEST DREAMS REALLY COMING TRUE— WAS HE BEGINNING TO HATE ME AS MUCH AS I HATED HIM?
YOU KNOW, I'VE NEVER SEEN A SLOPPIER EATER IN ALL MY LIFE! YOU MAKE ME NAUSEOUS!
THEN MY HEART BEGAN TO BEAT LIKE A TRIP-HAMMER...
LISTEN, CREEP! IF YOU'RE NOT BUSY SATURDAY NIGHT, I KNOW A CHEAP CHINESE RESTAURANT WHERE THE FOOD STINKS AND A NIGHT SPOT WHERE THE FLOOR SHOW WILL DEMEAN YOU!
I COULD HARDLY WAIT UNTIL SATURDAY NIGHT! WHEN HE PICKED ME UP, MY SKIN WAS ALL GOOSE BUMPS!
CHRIST, DO YOU LOOK UGLY!
BACK OFF UNTIL YOU TAKE YOUR FIRST BATH!
THAT EVENING WAS EVERYTHING A YOUNG GIRL COULD HAVE HOPED FOR! I THOUGHT HE WAS BEING A LITTLE FORWARD BY NOT PETTING, NOT NECKING, AND NOT EVEN HOLDING HANDS... BUT I DIDN'T CARE! THEN LATER, IN THE SUB-FREEZING TEMPERATURES OF MY PORCH...
SALLY...
JASON...
SLAP!
I'D NEVER BEEN SLAPPED BY A BOY BEFORE! MY HEAD WENT REELING! AND THEN HE SAID THOSE THREE FATEFUL WORDS I'D LONGED SO TO HEAR...
SALLY, I'VE NEVER TOLD THIS TO ANY GIRL BEFORE, BUT I... I... I HATE YOU!
ALL NIGHT LONG, I TOSSED AND TURNED, JUST REMEMBERING HIS SLAP, HIS PAINFUL SLAP!
I'LL NEVER HATE ANYONE ELSE! NEVER!
THE NEXT FEW WEEKS WERE LIKE SOMETHING OUT OF A STORY BOOK! JASON HARDLY SPENT A CENT ON ME AND CONTINUALLY DEGRADED ME! WE SPENT SO MANY EVENINGS JUST WHISPERING THOSE SOUR LITTLE NOTHINGS...
YOU'RE FLAT-CHESTED! YOU PICK YOUR NOSE! YOU HAVE DISHPAN HANDS! YOU HAVE A LOW I.Q.! YOUR LEGS AREN'T SHAVED! YOU SMELL! YOU HAVE THICK ANKLES!
YOU HAVE BAD BREATH! YOU HAVE PIMPLES! YOU HAVEN'T A LICK OF COMMON SENSE! YOU DON'T COVER YOUR MOUTH WHEN YOU COUGH!
AND PERHAPS I DID LET JASON GO FARTHER THAN HE SHOULD, BUT SOMEHOW IT ALL SEEMED SO NATURAL AND SO RIGHT...
OH, JASON (GASP!)... I THINK YOU BROKE MY ARM...
THE GIRLS AT SCHOOL TEASED ME ABOUT IT, BUT I DIDN'T CARE!
YOU'RE JUST JEALOUS!
HEY SAL, HEH HEH, WHAT'S THAT BLACK-AND-BLUE MARK ON YOUR NECK? AND THAT SCAR TISSUE OVER YOUR LEFT EYE?
RUN INTO A DOOR OR SOMETHING? HEH HEH!
BUT IF ONLY JASON AND I COULD HAVE KNOWN THAT OUR HATE WAS ABOUT TO BE DESTROYED!

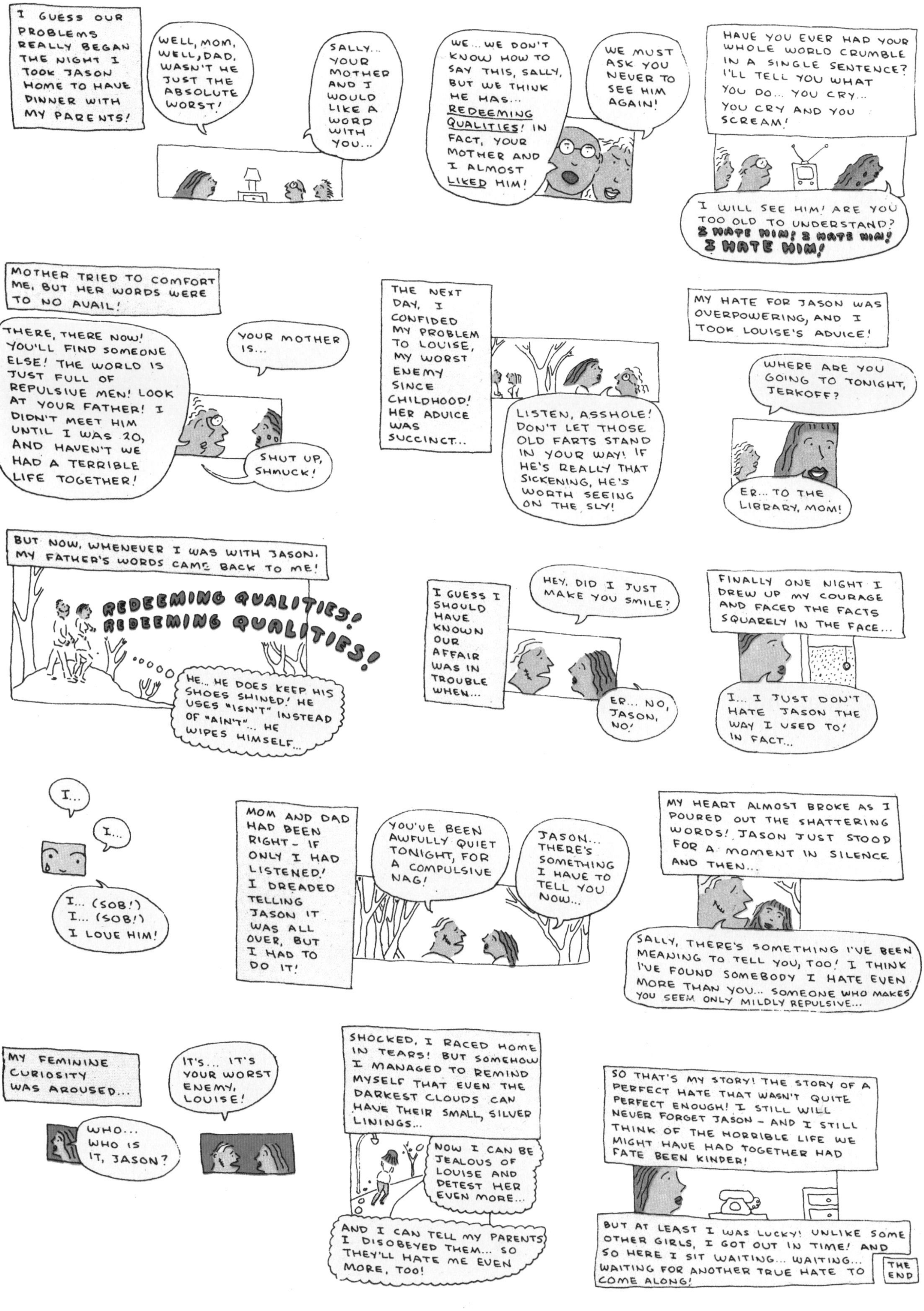
I GUESS OUR PROBLEMS REALLY BEGAN THE NIGHT I TOOK JASON HOME TO HAVE DINNER WITH MY PARENTS!
WELL, MOM, WELL, DAD, WASN'T HE JUST THE ABSOLUTE WORST!
SALLY... YOUR MOTHER AND I WOULD LIKE A WORD WITH YOU...
WE... WE DON'T KNOW HOW TO SAY THIS, SALLY, BUT WE THINK HE HAS... REDEEMING QUALITIES! IN FACT, YOUR MOTHER AND I ALMOST LIKED HIM!
WE MUST ASK YOU NEVER TO SEE HIM AGAIN!
HAVE YOU EVER HAD YOUR WHOLE WORLD CRUMBLE IN A SINGLE SENTENCE? I'LL TELL YOU WHAT YOU DO... YOU CRY... YOU CRY AND YOU SCREAM!
I WILL SEE HIM! ARE YOU TOO OLD TO UNDERSTAND? I HATE HIM! I HATE HIM! I HATE HIM!
MOTHER TRIED TO COMFORT ME, BUT HER WORDS WERE TO NO AVAIL!
THERE, THERE NOW! YOU'LL FIND SOMEONE ELSE! THE WORLD IS JUST FULL OF REPULSIVE MEN! LOOK AT YOUR FATHER! I DIDN'T MEET HIM UNTIL I WAS 20, AND HAVEN'T WE HAD A TERRIBLE LIFE TOGETHER!
YOUR MOTHER IS...
SHUT UP, SHMUCK!
THE NEXT DAY, I CONFIDED MY PROBLEM TO LOUISE, MY WORST ENEMY SINCE CHILDHOOD! HER ADVICE WAS SUCCINCT...
LISTEN, ASSHOLE! DON'T LET THOSE OLD FARTS STAND IN YOUR WAY! IF HE'S REALLY THAT SICKENING, HE'S WORTH SEEING ON THE SLY!
MY HATE FOR JASON WAS OVERPOWERING, AND I TOOK LOUISE'S ADVICE!
WHERE ARE YOU GOING TO TONIGHT, JERKOFF?
ER... TO THE LIBRARY, MOM!
BUT NOW, WHENEVER I WAS WITH JASON, MY FATHER'S WORDS CAME BACK TO ME!
REDEEMING QUALITIES! REDEEMING QUALITIES!
HE... HE DOES KEEP HIS SHOES SHINED! HE USES "ISN'T" INSTEAD OF "AIN'T"... HE WIPES HIMSELF...
I GUESS I SHOULD HAVE KNOWN OUR AFFAIR WAS IN TROUBLE WHEN...
HEY, DID I JUST MAKE YOU SMILE?
ER... NO, JASON, NO!
FINALLY ONE NIGHT I DREW UP MY COURAGE AND FACED THE FACTS SQUARELY IN THE FACE...
I... I JUST DON'T HATE JASON THE WAY I USED TO! IN FACT...
I...
I...
I... (SOB!) I... (SOB!) I LOVE HIM!
MOM AND DAD HAD BEEN RIGHT - IF ONLY I HAD LISTENED! I DREADED TELLING JASON IT WAS ALL OVER, BUT I HAD TO DO IT!
YOU'VE BEEN AWFULLY QUIET TONIGHT, FOR A COMPULSIVE NAG!
JASON... THERE'S SOMETHING I HAVE TO TELL YOU NOW...
MY HEART ALMOST BROKE AS I POURED OUT THE SHATTERING WORDS! JASON JUST STOOD FOR A MOMENT IN SILENCE AND THEN...
SALLY, THERE'S SOMETHING I'VE BEEN MEANING TO TELL YOU, TOO! I THINK I'VE FOUND SOMEBODY I HATE EVEN MORE THAN YOU... SOMEONE WHO MAKES YOU SEEM ONLY MILDLY REPULSIVE...
MY FEMININE CURIOSITY WAS AROUSED...
WHO... WHO IS IT, JASON?
IT'S... IT'S YOUR WORST ENEMY, LOUISE!
SHOCKED, I RACED HOME IN TEARS! BUT SOMEHOW I MANAGED TO REMIND MYSELF THAT EVEN THE DARKEST CLOUDS CAN HAVE THEIR SMALL, SILVER LININGS...
NOW I CAN BE JEALOUS OF LOUISE AND DETEST HER EVEN MORE...
AND I CAN TELL MY PARENTS I DISOBEYED THEM... SO THEY'LL HATE ME EVEN MORE, TOO!
SO THAT'S MY STORY! THE STORY OF A PERFECT HATE THAT WASN'T QUITE PERFECT ENOUGH! I STILL WILL NEVER FORGET JASON - AND I STILL THINK OF THE HORRIBLE LIFE WE MIGHT HAVE HAD TOGETHER HAD FATE BEEN KINDER!
BUT AT LEAST I WAS LUCKY! UNLIKE SOME OTHER GIRLS, I GOT OUT IN TIME! AND SO HERE I SIT WAITING... WAITING... WAITING FOR ANOTHER TRUE HATE TO COME ALONG!
THE END

GOES-ON-FOREVER PORNO COMICS!

MOST FOR YOUR MONEY!

(INSTRUCTIONS: START HERE, THEN READ NORMALLY, PANEL AFTER PANEL, FOLLOWING ARROWS)
HOW ABOUT IT, BABY! WANNA FUCK?
OH, ALL RIGHT! LET'S GET STARTED!
YOU MEAN RIGHT NOW?
YES! AND I HOPE YOU DO BETTER THAN LAST TIME!
SO LET'S STOP THIS YAPPING AND GET DOWN TO BUSINESS!
MMMM! YOUR LIPS ARE LIKE HONEY-LIMNED DIAMOND ORBS AT SUNSET!
YOU SAID THAT LAST TIME! NOW HOW ABOUT SOME ACTION!
AHHHH! YOUR BREASTS ARE LIKE SOFT SNOW WITH SPRINGTIME MOCKING BIRDS FLUTTERING BENEATH!
I KNOW! I KNOW! NOW HOW ABOUT SOME ACTION FOR A CHANGE!
AAAH! YESSS! OOOOH! AH!
GNNNNNNXXMGGG! AH! AH! YES! AHH! AGGHHHH!
SHIT, AREN'T YOU EVER GONNA LEARN HOW TO MAKE ME COME! YOU BETTER TRY AGAIN!

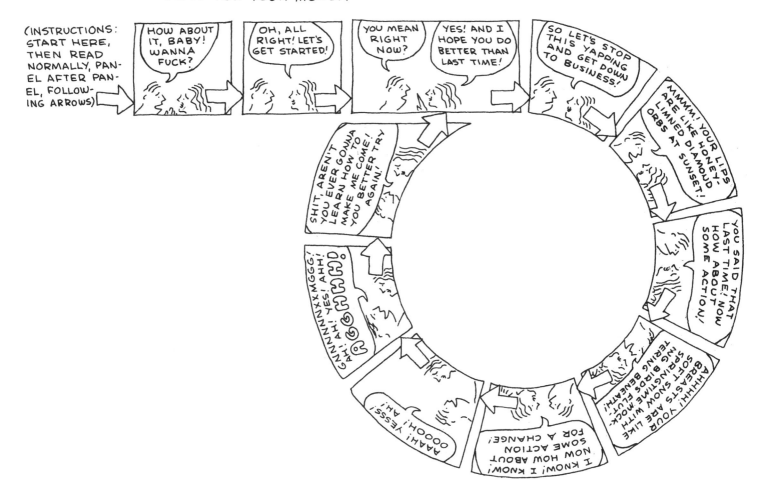

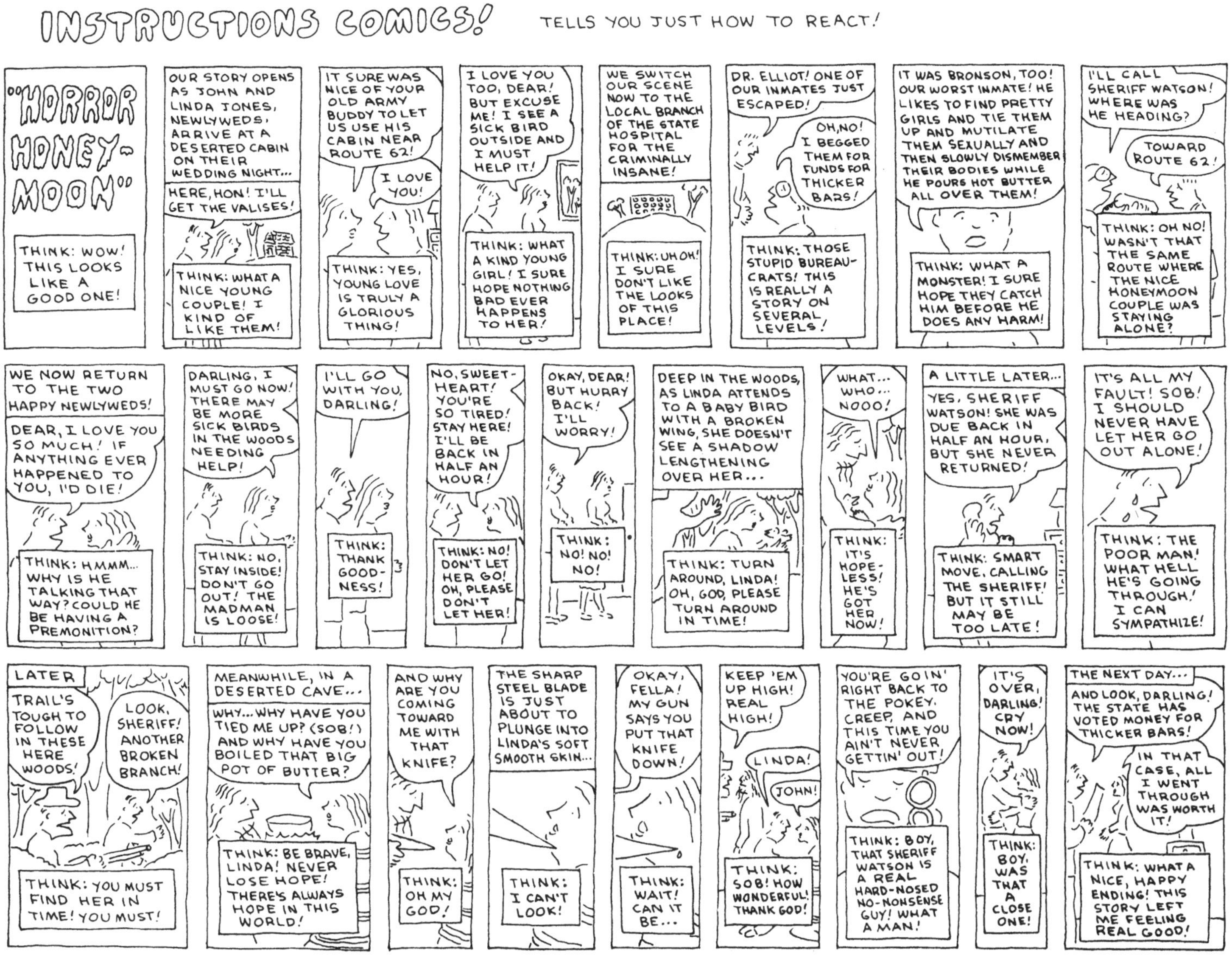
INSTRUCTIONS COMICS!
TELLS YOU JUST HOW TO REACT!
"HORROR HONEY-MOON"
THINK: WOW! THIS LOOKS LIKE A GOOD ONE!
OUR STORY OPENS AS JOHN AND LINDA JONES, NEWLYWEDS, ARRIVE AT A DESERTED CABIN ON THEIR WEDDING NIGHT...
HERE, HON! I'LL GET THE VALISES!
THINK: WHAT A NICE YOUNG COUPLE! I KIND OF LIKE THEM!
IT SURE WAS NICE OF YOUR OLD ARMY BUDDY TO LET US USE HIS CABIN NEAR ROUTE 62!
I LOVE YOU!
THINK: YES, YOUNG LOVE IS TRULY A GLORIOUS THING!
I LOVE YOU TOO, DEAR! BUT EXCUSE ME! I SEE A SICK BIRD OUTSIDE AND I MUST HELP IT!
THINK: WHAT A KIND YOUNG GIRL! I SURE HOPE NOTHING BAD EVER HAPPENS TO HER!
WE SWITCH OUR SCENE NOW TO THE LOCAL BRANCH OF THE STATE HOSPITAL FOR THE CRIMINALLY INSANE!
THINK: UH OH! I SURE DON'T LIKE THE LOOKS OF THIS PLACE!
DR. ELLIOT! ONE OF OUR INMATES JUST ESCAPED!
OH, NO! I BEGGED THEM FOR FUNDS FOR THICKER BARS!
THINK: THOSE STUPID BUREAUCRATS! THIS IS REALLY A STORY ON SEVERAL LEVELS!
IT WAS BRONSON, TOO! OUR WORST INMATE! HE LIKES TO FIND PRETTY GIRLS AND TIE THEM UP AND MUTILATE THEM SEXUALLY AND THEN SLOWLY DISMEMBER THEIR BODIES WHILE HE POURS HOT BUTTER ALL OVER THEM!
THINK: WHAT A MONSTER! I SURE HOPE THEY CATCH HIM BEFORE HE DOES ANY HARM!
I'LL CALL SHERIFF WATSON! WHERE WAS HE HEADING?
TOWARD ROUTE 62!
THINK: OH NO! WASN'T THAT THE SAME ROUTE WHERE THE NICE HONEYMOON COUPLE WAS STAYING ALONE?
WE NOW RETURN TO THE TWO HAPPY NEWLYWEDS!
DEAR, I LOVE YOU SO MUCH! IF ANYTHING EVER HAPPENED TO YOU, I'D DIE!
THINK: HMMM... WHY IS HE TALKING THAT WAY? COULD HE BE HAVING A PREMONITION?
DARLING, I MUST GO NOW! THERE MAY BE MORE SICK BIRDS IN THE WOODS NEEDING HELP!
THINK: NO, STAY INSIDE! DON'T GO OUT! THE MADMAN IS LOOSE!
I'LL GO WITH YOU, DARLING!
THINK: THANK GOODNESS!
NO, SWEETHEART! YOU'RE SO TIRED! STAY HERE! I'LL BE BACK IN HALF AN HOUR!
THINK: NO! DON'T LET HER GO! OH, PLEASE DON'T LET HER!
OKAY, DEAR! BUT HURRY BACK! I'LL WORRY!
THINK: NO! NO! NO!
DEEP IN THE WOODS, AS LINDA ATTENDS TO A BABY BIRD WITH A BROKEN WING, SHE DOESN'T SEE A SHADOW LENGTHENING OVER HER...
THINK: TURN AROUND, LINDA! OH, GOD, PLEASE TURN AROUND IN TIME!
WHAT... WHO... NOOO!
THINK: IT'S HOPELESS! HE'S GOT HER NOW!
A LITTLE LATER...
YES, SHERIFF WATSON! SHE WAS DUE BACK IN HALF AN HOUR, BUT SHE NEVER RETURNED!
THINK: SMART MOVE, CALLING THE SHERIFF! BUT IT STILL MAY BE TOO LATE!
IT'S ALL MY FAULT! SOB! I SHOULD NEVER HAVE LET HER GO OUT ALONE!
THINK: THE POOR MAN! WHAT HELL HE'S GOING THROUGH! I CAN SYMPATHIZE!
LATER
TRAIL'S TOUGH TO FOLLOW IN THESE HERE WOODS!
LOOK, SHERIFF! ANOTHER BROKEN BRANCH!
THINK: YOU MUST FIND HER IN TIME! YOU MUST!
MEANWHILE, IN A DESERTED CAVE...
WHY... WHY HAVE YOU TIED ME UP? (SOB!) AND WHY HAVE YOU BOILED THAT BIG POT OF BUTTER?
THINK: BE BRAVE, LINDA! NEVER LOSE HOPE! THERE'S ALWAYS HOPE IN THIS WORLD!
AND WHY ARE YOU COMING TOWARD ME WITH THAT KNIFE?
THINK: OH MY GOD!
THE SHARP STEEL BLADE IS JUST ABOUT TO PLUNGE INTO LINDA'S SOFT SMOOTH SKIN...
THINK: I CAN'T LOOK!
OKAY, FELLA! MY GUN SAYS YOU PUT THAT KNIFE DOWN!
THINK: WAIT! CAN IT BE...
KEEP 'EM UP HIGH! REAL HIGH!
LINDA!
JOHN!
THINK: SOB! HOW WONDERFUL! THANK GOD!
YOU'RE GOIN' RIGHT BACK TO THE POKEY, CREEP, AND THIS TIME YOU AIN'T NEVER GETTIN' OUT!
THINK: BOY, THAT SHERIFF WATSON IS A REAL HARD-NOSED NO-NONSENSE GUY! WHAT A MAN!
IT'S OVER, DARLING! CRY NOW!
THINK: BOY, WAS THAT A CLOSE ONE!
THE NEXT DAY...
AND LOOK, DARLING! THE STATE HAS VOTED MONEY FOR THICKER BARS!
IN THAT CASE, ALL I WENT THROUGH WAS WORTH IT!
THINK: WHAT A NICE, HAPPY ENDING! THIS STORY LEFT ME FEELING REAL GOOD!

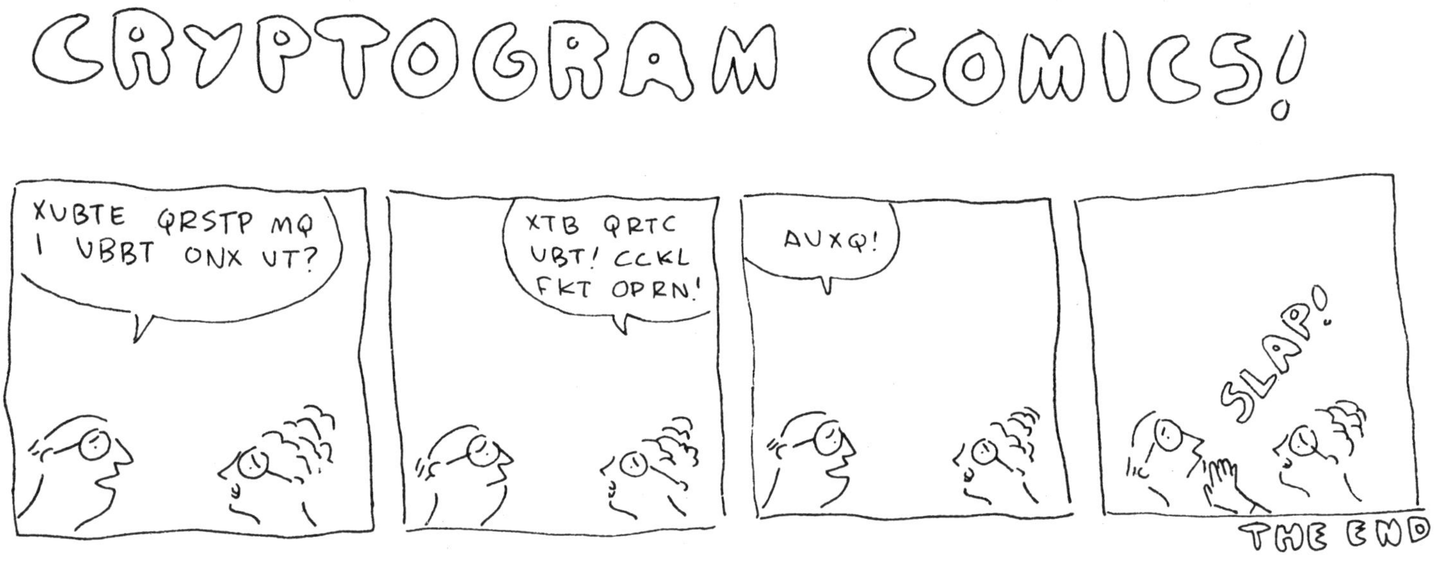
CRYPTOGRAM COMICS!
XUBTE QRSTP MQ I VBBT ONX VT?
XTB QRTC UBT! CCKL FKT OPRN!
AUXQ!
SLAP!
THE END

OFF-THE PAGE COMICS!
WARNING: THE LAST PANEL OF THIS COMIC SHOWS EXPLICIT SEXUAL INTERCOURSE BETWEEN MAN AND WOMAN.
BUT, VERONICA, WHY HOLD BACK! THE NIGHT IS MADE OF POETRY!
MY MOTHER ALWAYS TOLD ME, "WHY GIVE FREE MILK WHEN THE PITCHER'S WORTH A SIXPENCE"!
ALL RIGHT! I'M A PREACHER! I NOW PRONOUNCE US MAN AND WIFE! SATISFIED?
YES!
OH

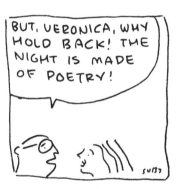

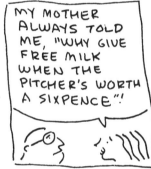

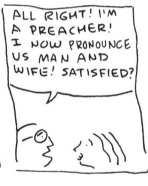

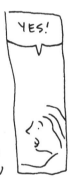

STUPIDWORLD

The sun, which should have set hours ago, was just getting down to the horizon. As usual, I took the wrong route home and, when I finally put the right key in the lock, I realized the door had gotten too big for the frame again. I smashed against it with my shoulder and finally it gave; I tumbled into the foyer and wet flakes fell off my jacket and dotted the carpet.

"Damn summer snow," I muttered.

"Is that you?" Alice shouted from the kitchen.

"What?"

"Never mind. I forgot what I was going to say."

I wanted to sit down on my favorite chair, but I couldn't remember which one it was. Alice came in, stirring an empty bowl, and almost kissed me on the cheek.

"I remember now," she said.

"Okay," I said. "What is it?'

"What's what?" she said.

After we ate, I lit a cigarette and took a long, lingering look at my wife.

Like me, she was beginning to show the wear and tear of middle age, and her lipstick was in the wrong place as usual.

"TV?" I asked.

"What what?"

"Never mind." I got up and turned on the set. It was showing three programs at once, and I was trying to figure out how to turn it off when the phone rang.

I picked up the receiver and my blood jumped.

"Damn it!" I whispered. "Didn't I tell you never to call me here?"

"Did you?" As always, I found it hard to be angry at Joanne; her soft, sexy voice seemed to make everything all right.

"I think I did," I said.

"Well," she said, "you might have."

"What are you calling for?"

"What am I what?"

"What..." We were disconnected.

"Who was that?" my wife asked.

"Harry," I said.

"We don't know any Harrys."

"Are you sure?"

"No. I'm not sure."

Praying that Alice wouldn't notice the tremor in my hands, I sat down again. I hoped the worry wasn't showing on my face. Sooner or later, I knew, Joanne was bound to remember my number again.

Every once in a while, I could remember the day Joanne and I had met at the office. Our effect on each other had been electric: I took one look into her large brown (small blue?) eyes (eye?), she took one look into mine, and that was it, I think.

Alice, of course, never suspected a thing. With everyone always leaving work at the wrong hours and the trains always getting lost, it wasn't easy for a woman to keep tabs on her husband's time.

Sometimes, I could even remember the night Joanne and I had first made love. It was a charming, old-fashioned hotel that was usually near my office. The desk clerk had given us the onceover, then winked and handed me a mounted butterfly.

"The key," I said. "You're supposed to hand me the key."

"Sorry."

"Think nothing of it."

"Do what of what?"

Room 902! A fourteen-dollar heaven on earth for lovers!

Joanne and I couldn't figure out how to open the drapes, but we knew that, just beyond them, the whole city would be spread out before us—a magnificent smorgasbord of lights blinking on and off like stars as the people at the electric company kept pressing the wrong switches.

"A penny for your thoughts," Joanne said.

As usual, I wasn't having any, so I said, "No deal." Then we fell into each other's arms.

"Wait a minute," Joanne said. "We're supposed to take our clothes off first."

"Are you sure?"

"I think so."

I began to tug at my shirt.

"Here," Joanne said, "I think it has something to do with these small little round things stuck in these tiny little holes up and down the front. Maybe if we tried to push the round things out of the holes..."

"What about you?"

"I think it has something to do with this long silver thing down my back."

Finally, we managed to get most of our clothes off and Joanne's hot, heaving body was pressed firmly beneath mine.

"No," Joanne said, "not there."

"Where?"

"Here."

"You sure?"

"I think so."

"What is it we're trying to do?"

"Let me think a minute."

"What?"

"I forgot what I was going to say."

That had been the beginning. And tonight, I was sure, was going to be the end. The only question in my mind was: how horrible is it going to be?

"Mommy?"

My train of thought—and it was one of the longest trains of thought I'd had in months—was interrupted.

"I'm your daddy, sweetheart." Grinning, I swung Amanda around and sat her on my lap. "Isn't it past your bedtime, young lady?" I was becoming obsessed now; I couldn't get my eyes off that phone.

"I don't know. All the clocks read different."

I felt my knees beginning to sag. Amanda was only six years old, but already she weighed 124 pounds and had the full-busted, curvaceous body of a woman.

"Honey?"

"Yes?" Alice was in the kitchen, ironing the dishes.

"How many children do we have?"

"Seven, I think. Does that sound right?"

Seven children, I thought. Seven children and a nice house in the suburbs and a good job. And, thanks to me, every last little bit of it has been plunked into Joanne's pretty little hands.

I stared at the phone, as if somehow the power of my gaze could stop it from ringing.

Clink. Clink. Buzz. Gong. Clink. Buzz.

No good.

Like a puppet, I jumped.

"Joanne, didn't I tell you—"

"I'm sorry, darling. It's an emergency."

"A what?"

"What's a what?"

"What are you calling for?"

"I'm calling because I'm..." We were disconnected again.

I figured it would take Joanne at least half an hour to remember the number again. I thought, *This could be the last half hour of my marriage.* I noticed that ice was forming on the sofa. I went to the closet and put on my heaviest coat.

Alice came back into the living room. "What's wrong?"

"Damn air-conditioning again."

"Silly," Alice said. "You always get it wrong. It's clothes on, colder, clothes off, warmer. Or is it the other way around?"

I began to fumble with my shirt.

"How does this damn thing work?"

"I think it has something to do with these little tiny holes and these little pieces of round plastic on the front."

Alice and I put the kids to sleep.

Then we just sat together in the living room and didn't say very much. It was funny, but sitting there next to Alice and looking at her, I began to feel guilty as hell.

Alice was trying to knit something, and I watched as the absurd, knotted shape extruded from her knitting needles. Every few seconds, she jabbed herself and winced.

I began to wonder whether I'd done the right thing with Joanne.

"Know what, honey?" Alice said.

"What?"

"I'm glad I married you."

"Are you?"

"Very glad." She went across the room and kissed the mirror.

"I'm over here," I said.

"Oh," she said. "Well, anyway, I love you."

I glanced at the phone.

"Honey?" Alice said.

"What?"

"I forgot what I was going to say."

"Did you just say something?"

"No. I don't think so. Why?"

"Why what?"

"I can't remember."

I felt comfortable talking to Alice. It was like the old days, before Joanne. This could be one of the last real conversations I ever have with my wife, I thought with remorse.

I got up and tried to put on a record, but the hole was in the wrong place, so instead I sat down with the newspaper. The headline read, VGHGHGSTYIUJH KJHSVTEYRHNSH SHSLAKAIAUSTGH.

The doorbell rang.

"I'll get it," Alice said, trying to stand up, and tangling her head in the knitting wool.

"Sit tight," I said, "I'll get it."

"Think there's anyone there?"

"I doubt it. But it's worth a chance."

"What's worth a chance?"

"Try turning the knob in the other direction." I thought I recognized the voice on the other side of the door. I hoped I was wrong.

The door swung open and a whoosh of rain poured into the foyer, even though the sky was perfectly clear.

Joanne shook herself off. "I can't remember when I've seen a worse—"

I grabbed her by the shoulders and tried to push her back. "Are you crazy?" I whispered. "My wife is inside!"

"Who is it, dear?" Alice shouted.

"What?" I shouted back.

"Never mind."

"Never what?"

"I forgot what I was going to say."

"Listen," I pleaded to Joanne, "whatever it is, you can't do this to me. My whole life—"

Then I realized that Alice wasn't inside any longer. She was standing right beside us.

"Hello," she said to Joanne, her voice muffled by the colored threads wrapped tightly around her throat.

"Who are you?"

"She's my long-lost cousin," I said.

"Your what-what what?"

"Forget it." I looked at Joanne with a final pleading desperation in my eyes.

"Shall we all go inside?" Alice suggested sweetly.

Joanne and I followed her. On the way, we bumped into a floating ashtray and vase; gravity levels had been cut by 15 percent again.

As soon as we reached the living room, the phone rang.

I picked it up. At first, it was bringing in a radio station; but then I heard a woman's voice.

"Who is this?" I asked.

"It's Joanne."

"You can't be Joanne."

"Why not?"

"Joanne is over here."

"Over where?"

"In my living room."

"That's impossible."

"It's not impossible."

"What's not what?"

We were disconnected.

"Who was that?" my wife asked.

"No one," I said.

"Are you sure?" Joanne asked.

"No," I said.

Suddenly, the floor beneath us began to tremble; we found ourselves smashing violently against the walls, then lying together in a heap. "Earthquake!" I shouted. Finally, the furniture stopped rattling. Through the window, I could see that the sun was three times its normal size. We'd gone out of orbit again.

Part of the roof caved in. Somehow, we all managed to roll away in time; only Joanne was hurt, with an ugly gash on her arm. Alice found a Band-Aid, but she couldn't figure out how to get the paper off.

"Try the little red string," I suggested.

"It works!" Jubilantly, Alice removed the Band-Aid and taped it tightly on Joanne's arm in the wrong place.

"I'd better check on the kids," she said.

Alice went to the foot of the stairway, then paused.

"Where am I going?"

"To check on the kids."

"To what on the what?"

"What?"

"I forgot what I was going to say."

With Alice upstairs, Joanne and I were alone—perhaps the last precious moment we would ever have together. Quickly, fiercely, I tried to kiss her, but I missed.

"Joanne, whatever made you come here like this?"

Now there was a deep, coarse desperation in Joanne's voice. "It's an emergency. A real emergency."

"It's a what? A what what?"

Before she could answer, the phone rang again.

I picked it up. "Who is this?" I demanded.

"It's Joanne."

The phone felt strangely warm in my hand and I realized the room was beginning to melt. "You know I told you never to call me here!" Through the window, I could see the sun looming even larger, bloated and fierce and yellow. Halley's Comet was beside it, even though it wasn't due for another century.

"Listen to me," the voice on the phone pleaded. "It's the operation. It wasn't a success. My organs were all in the wrong parts of my body and I'm going to have to have the baby anyway!"

"Baby? What baby?" Then, all at once, the horrible, awful truth came crashing back to me. I did a ballet-step aside, as the television and hi-fi melted past me down the carpet. Tiny beads of sweat peppered my forehead, mixing and getting big enough to drip. "I wish I knew how to get this damn shirt off," I muttered.

"I think it has something to do with those little plastic circles and those funny little holes," the Joanne next to me said.

"I think it has something to do with those little plastic circles and those funny little holes," the Joanne on the phone said.

"Are you absolutely certain you're Joanne?" I asked into the phone.

"No." By now, the whole room was an ocean of molten wet. "Sometimes I think I might be her best friend, Millie."

I turned to the Joanne next to me. "Do you have a best friend, Millie?"

"I think so."

"Did you tell her about us?"

She struggled to keep her head above the bubbling lava. "I don't know. Maybe."

I checked the window again. Now the sun was getting farther away. I could see Mars, then Venus, then Jupiter roll by. Quickly, the melt began to solidify around us. The sky flickered rapidly from day to night; the Earth was spinning too fast, and I ducked as the centrifugal force sent frozen objects flying around the room.

My wife fell down the stairs.

"Turn the thermostat up!" I shouted.

Icicles were forming on my nose.

"What the what what?"

"Never mind."

"Never what?"

"How are the kids?"

"I couldn't find them."

Alice came over and stood directly between Joanne and myself. "You needn't pretend any longer," she said. "I've known all about you two for years."

I could feel my lips beginning to chunk. "How did you find out?"

"Find out what?"

Suddenly, another thought flashed through my mind. In a panic, I tried to look at my watch. At first, I looked at the wrong hand, but then I found it.

"Damn," I whistled, "I'm going to be late for work!"

I picked up what was left of my attaché case.

"Wait a minute," Alice said, grabbing the case and almost pulling it out of my hands. "These initials!"

"These what?"

"Are these your initials?"

"Are they my what?"

"You're not Oscar!"

"You mean I've come to the wrong house again?"

"How long has it been since you've come to the right house?" Joanne asked.

"I don't know," I said. "Years, I guess."

"Do I know you?" Joanne asked.

"I'm not sure."

"Do you work for McAddams-Landsbury?"

"That doesn't seem familiar."

"Then you're not the man I was having an affair with?"

"I guess not."

"I'm wrong again!"

"How many times have you been wrong?" I asked.

"I don't know," she said. She stepped back away from me.

The woman who thought she had been my wife was heading for the door. "Damn," she muttered. "I should have known I don't live here. I live a few blocks down!"

The room was beginning to warm up again.

Joanne followed her. "Want to share a cab?" she asked.

"Okay, until it breaks down."

The phone began to ring again, but I couldn't take time to answer it. The only thought in my mind was, Mustn't get fired. Got to keep supporting whoever it is I'm married to—if I'm married.

I stepped outside. I was glad to see that it was morning and that this particular morning was autumn. Oak leaves were falling from maple trees, but they still looked nice, all brown and crinkly and crisp. As I felt them rustle beneath my feet, a strangely peaceful feeling came over me, and I tried to collect what I could of my thoughts. First things first, I told myself, and I tried to remember where I worked. I took the wrong route downtown and, after a few false tries, I found a building that looked vaguely familiar. Inside, I found an empty desk that seemed to ring a bell, and I sat down and began to press the wrong keys on the typewriter.

The floor rattled a bit. I looked out the window and saw that the sky was dark and full of unfamiliar constellations.

Cghhgahhstyflgh, I wrote, kajaha¢54ahax9jaj8. Hghhgagggag6524) (kajajhajajjj.

A grl ghume overt add sad bsdie me.

I had nvege seeen aghyone as beauytful inn myy lfe. I jhng Ihad awifeee ad kidds andd shoouldn't doanything, butt shhe wass lookinng att mee with bigg, brrown-II meahn bleu--eiyes.

"What'ss ytr najjem?" I asked.

"Jaonnnnnnne," she saiid. "Iggm yoourh noew seccerttrry."

"Mnahgahhgatghgsksjsjskskj jshn ksjjtywvxcm," jhatrdfg hagbsgehehegdfehg.

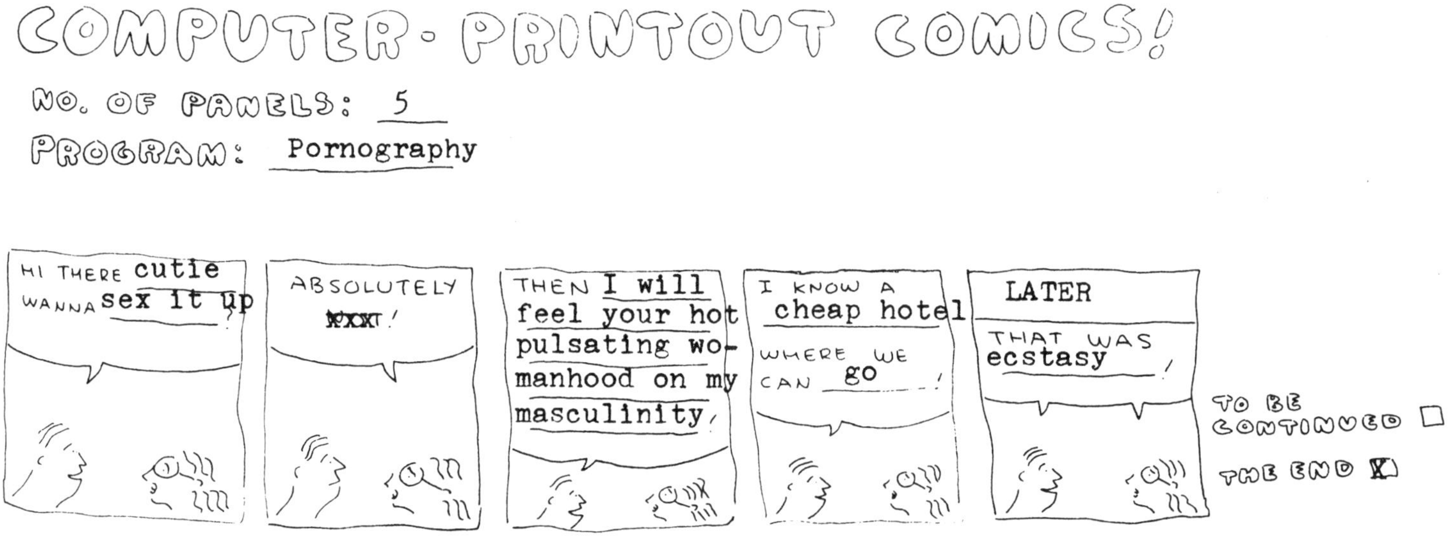
COMPUTER-PRINTOUT COMICS!
NO. OF PANELS: 5
PROGRAM: Pornography
HI THERE cutie WANNA sex it up?
ABSOLUTELY
THEN I will feel your hot pulsating wo-manhood on my masculinity!
I KNOW A cheap hotel WHERE WE CAN go!
LATER
THAT WAS ecstasy!
TO BE CONTINUED
THE END

MAD AS HELL COMICS!

BY ED SUBITZKY

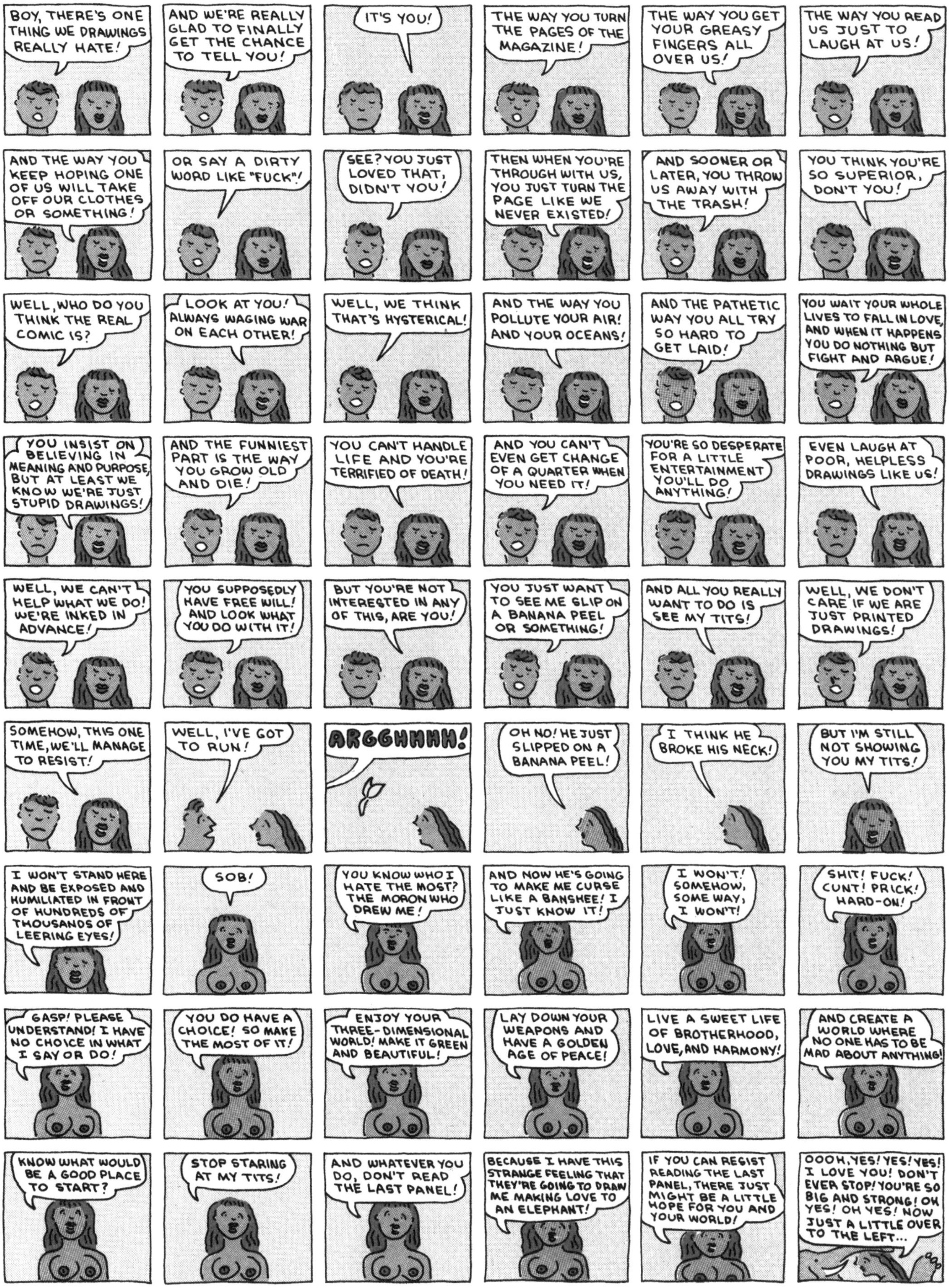

BOY, THERE'S ONE THING WE DRAWINGS REALLY HATE!
AND WE'RE REALLY GLAD TO FINALLY GET THE CHANCE TO TELL YOU!
IT'S YOU!
THE WAY YOU TURN THE PAGES OF THE MAGAZINE!
THE WAY YOU GET YOUR GREASY FINGERS ALL OVER US!
THE WAY YOU READ US JUST TO LAUGH AT US!
AND THE WAY YOU KEEP HOPING ONE OF US WILL TAKE OFF OUR CLOTHES OR SOMETHING!
OR SAY A DIRTY WORD LIKE "FUCK"!
SEE? YOU JUST LOVED THAT, DIDN'T YOU!
THEN WHEN YOU'RE THROUGH WITH US, YOU JUST TURN THE PAGE LIKE WE NEVER EXISTED!
AND SOONER OR LATER, YOU THROW US AWAY WITH THE TRASH!
YOU THINK YOU'RE SO SUPERIOR, DON'T YOU!
WELL, WHO DO YOU THINK THE REAL COMIC IS?
LOOK AT YOU! ALWAYS WAGING WAR ON EACH OTHER!
WELL, WE THINK THAT'S HYSTERICAL!
AND THE WAY YOU POLLUTE YOUR AIR! AND YOUR OCEANS!
AND THE PATHETIC WAY YOU ALL TRY SO HARD TO GET LAID!
YOU WAIT YOUR WHOLE LIVES TO FALL IN LOVE, AND WHEN IT HAPPENS YOU DO NOTHING BUT FIGHT AND ARGUE!
YOU INSIST ON BELIEVING IN MEANING AND PURPOSE, BUT AT LEAST WE KNOW WE'RE JUST STUPID DRAWINGS!
AND THE FUNNIEST PART IS THE WAY YOU GROW OLD AND DIE!
YOU CAN'T HANDLE LIFE AND YOU'RE TERRIFIED OF DEATH!
AND YOU CAN'T EVEN GET CHANGE OF A QUARTER WHEN YOU NEED IT!
YOU'RE SO DESPERATE FOR A LITTLE ENTERTAINMENT YOU'LL DO ANYTHING!
EVEN LAUGH AT POOR, HELPLESS DRAWINGS LIKE US!
WELL, WE CAN'T HELP WHAT WE DO! WE'RE INKED IN ADVANCE!
YOU SUPPOSEDLY HAVE FREE WILL! AND LOOK WHAT YOU DO WITH IT!
BUT YOU'RE NOT INTERESTED IN ANY OF THIS, ARE YOU!
YOU JUST WANT TO SEE ME SLIP ON A BANANA PEEL OR SOMETHING!
AND ALL YOU REALLY WANT TO DO IS SEE MY TITS!
WELL, WE DON'T CARE IF WE ARE JUST PRINTED DRAWINGS!
SOMEHOW, THIS ONE TIME, WE'LL MANAGE TO RESIST!
WELL, I'VE GOT TO RUN!
ARGGHHHH!
OH NO! HE JUST SLIPPED ON A BANANA PEEL!
I THINK HE BROKE HIS NECK!
BUT I'M STILL NOT SHOWING YOU MY TITS!
I WON'T STAND HERE AND BE EXPOSED AND HUMILIATED IN FRONT OF HUNDREDS OF THOUSANDS OF LEERING EYES!
SOB!
YOU KNOW WHO I HATE THE MOST? THE MORON WHO DREW ME!
AND NOW HE'S GOING TO MAKE ME CURSE LIKE A BANSHEE! I JUST KNOW IT!
I WON'T! SOMEHOW, SOME WAY, I WON'T!
SHIT! FUCK! CUNT! PRICK! HARD-ON!
GASP! PLEASE UNDERSTAND! I HAVE NO CHOICE IN WHAT I SAY OR DO!
YOU DO HAVE A CHOICE! SO MAKE THE MOST OF IT!
ENJOY YOUR THREE-DIMENSIONAL WORLD! MAKE IT GREEN AND BEAUTIFUL!
LAY DOWN YOUR WEAPONS AND HAVE A GOLDEN AGE OF PEACE!
LIVE A SWEET LIFE OF BROTHERHOOD, LOVE, AND HARMONY!
AND CREATE A WORLD WHERE NO ONE HAS TO BE MAD ABOUT ANYTHING!
KNOW WHAT WOULD BE A GOOD PLACE TO START?
STOP STARING AT MY TITS!
AND WHATEVER YOU DO, DON'T READ THE LAST PANEL!
BECAUSE I HAVE THIS STRANGE FEELING THAT THEY'RE GOING TO DRAW ME MAKING LOVE TO AN ELEPHANT!
IF YOU CAN RESIST READING THE LAST PANEL, THERE JUST MIGHT BE A LITTLE HOPE FOR YOU AND YOUR WORLD!
OOOH, YES! YES! YES! I LOVE YOU! DON'T EVER STOP! YOU'RE SO BIG AND STRONG! OH YES! OH YES! NOW JUST A LITTLE OVER TO THE LEFT...

Amnesiac Class Reunion!

BY ED SUBITZKY

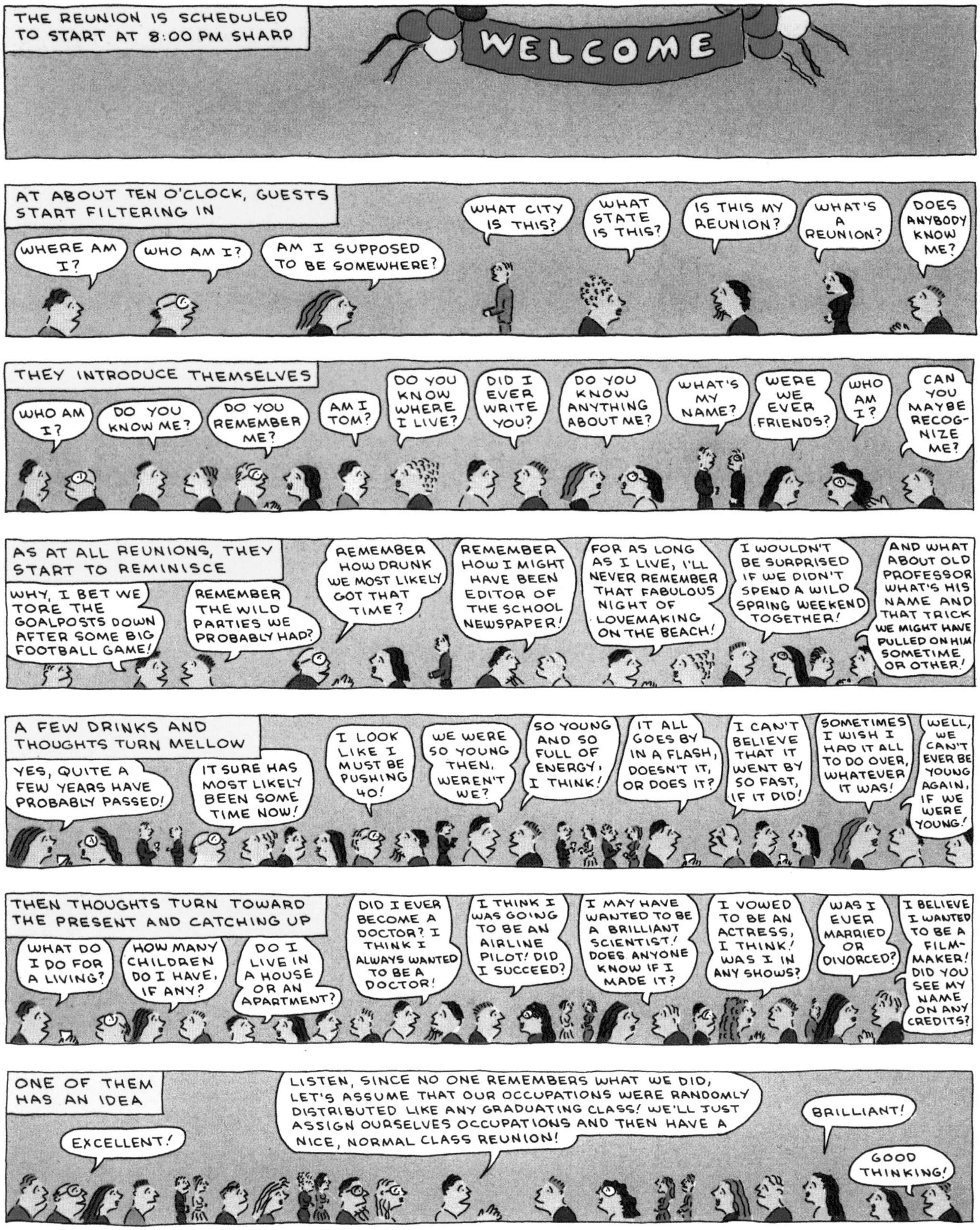
THE REUNION IS SCHEDULED TO START AT 8:00 PM SHARP
WELCOME
AT ABOUT TEN O'CLOCK, GUESTS START FILTERING IN
WHERE AM I?
WHO AM I?
AM I SUPPOSED TO BE SOMEWHERE?
WHAT CITY IS THIS?
WHAT STATE IS THIS?
IS THIS MY REUNION?
WHAT'S A REUNION?
DOES ANYBODY KNOW ME?
THEY INTRODUCE THEMSELVES
WHO AM I?
DO YOU KNOW ME?
DO YOU REMEMBER ME?
AM I TOM?
DO YOU KNOW WHERE I LIVE?
DID I EVER WRITE YOU?
DO YOU KNOW ANYTHING ABOUT ME?
WHAT'S MY NAME?
WERE WE EVER FRIENDS?
WHO AM I?
CAN YOU MAYBE RECOG-NIZE ME?
AS AT ALL REUNIONS, THEY START TO REMINISCE
WHY, I BET WE TORE THE GOALPOSTS DOWN AFTER SOME BIG FOOTBALL GAME!
REMEMBER THE WILD PARTIES WE PROBABLY HAD?
REMEMBER HOW DRUNK WE MOST LIKELY GOT THAT TIME?
REMEMBER HOW I MIGHT HAVE BEEN EDITOR OF THE SCHOOL NEWSPAPER!
FOR AS LONG AS I LIVE, I'LL NEVER REMEMBER THAT FABULOUS NIGHT OF LOVEMAKING ON THE BEACH!
I WOULDN'T BE SURPRISED IF WE DIDN'T SPEND A WILD SPRING WEEKEND TOGETHER!
AND WHAT ABOUT OLD PROFESSOR WHAT'S HIS NAME AND THAT TRICK WE MIGHT HAVE PULLED ON HIM SOMETIME OR OTHER!
A FEW DRINKS AND THOUGHTS TURN MELLOW
YES, QUITE A FEW YEARS HAVE PROBABLY PASSED!
IT SURE HAS MOST LIKELY BEEN SOME TIME NOW!
I LOOK LIKE I MUST BE PUSHING 40!
WE WERE SO YOUNG THEN, WEREN'T WE?
SO YOUNG AND SO FULL OF ENERGY, I THINK!
IT ALL GOES BY IN A FLASH, DOESN'T IT, OR DOES IT?
I CAN'T BELIEVE THAT IT WENT BY SO FAST, IF IT DID!
SOMETIMES I WISH I HAD IT ALL TO DO OVER, WHATEVER IT WAS!
WELL, WE CAN'T EVER BE YOUNG AGAIN, IF WE WERE YOUNG!
THEN THOUGHTS TURN TOWARD THE PRESENT AND CATCHING UP
WHAT DO I DO FOR A LIVING?
HOW MANY CHILDREN DO I HAVE, IF ANY?
DO I LIVE IN A HOUSE OR AN APARTMENT?
DID I EVER BECOME A DOCTOR? I THINK I ALWAYS WANTED TO BE A DOCTOR!
I THINK I WAS GOING TO BE AN AIRLINE PILOT! DID I SUCCEED?
I MAY HAVE WANTED TO BE A BRILLIANT SCIENTIST! DOES ANYONE KNOW IF I MADE IT?
I VOWED TO BE AN ACTRESS, I THINK! WAS I IN ANY SHOWS?
WAS I EVER MARRIED OR DIVORCED?
I BELIEVE I WANTED TO BE A FILM-MAKER! DID YOU SEE MY NAME ON ANY CREDITS?
ONE OF THEM HAS AN IDEA
EXCELLENT!
LISTEN, SINCE NO ONE REMEMBERS WHAT WE DID, LET'S ASSUME THAT OUR OCCUPATIONS WERE RANDOMLY DISTRIBUTED LIKE ANY GRADUATING CLASS! WE'LL JUST ASSIGN OURSELVES OCCUPATIONS AND THEN HAVE A NICE, NORMAL CLASS REUNION!
BRILLIANT!
GOOD THINKING!

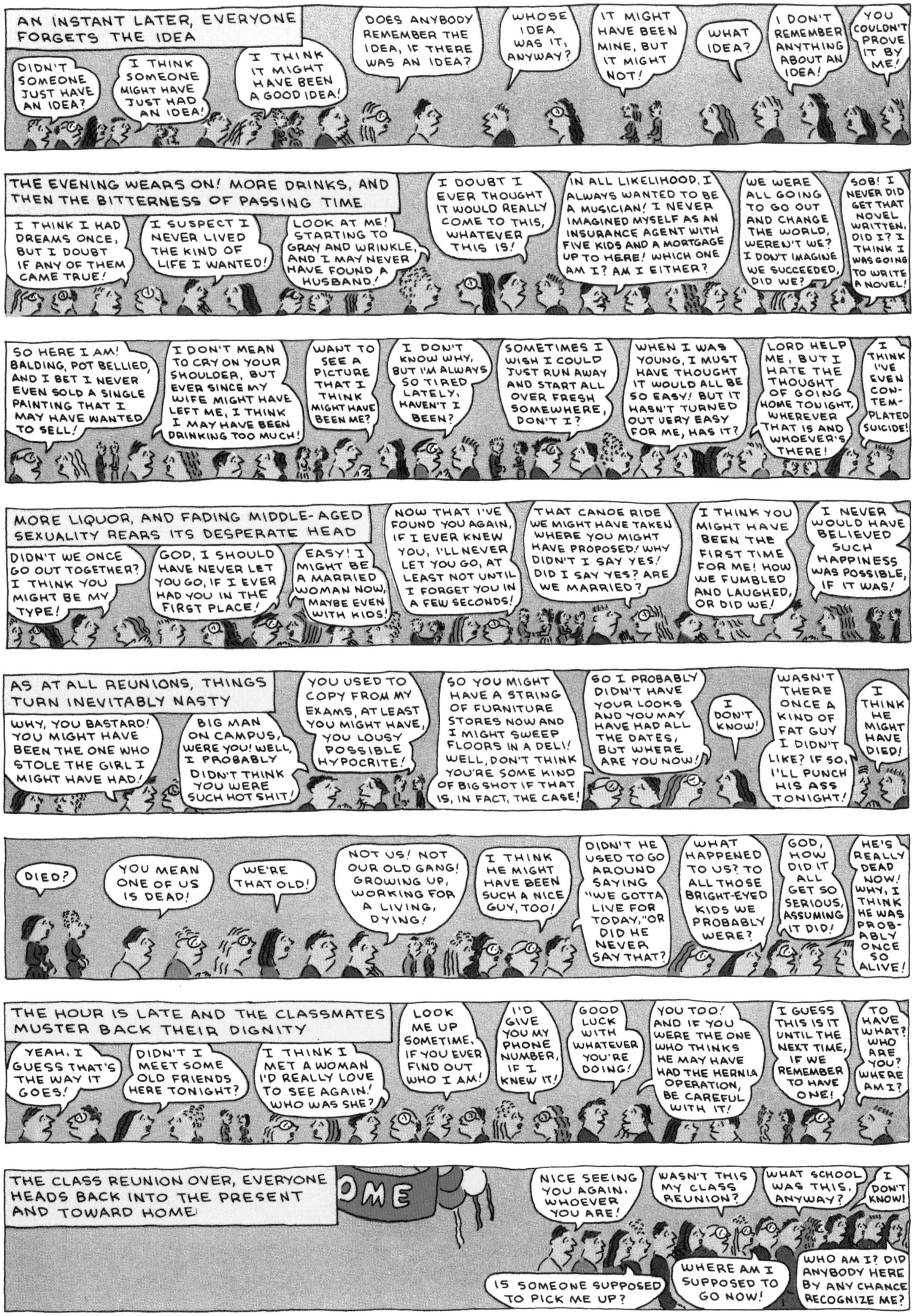
AN INSTANT LATER, EVERYONE FORGETS THE IDEA
DIDN'T SOMEONE JUST HAVE AN IDEA?
I THINK SOMEONE MIGHT HAVE JUST HAD AN IDEA!
I THINK IT MIGHT HAVE BEEN A GOOD IDEA!
DOES ANYBODY REMEMBER THE IDEA, IF THERE WAS AN IDEA?
WHOSE IDEA WAS IT, ANYWAY?
IT MIGHT HAVE BEEN MINE, BUT IT MIGHT NOT!
WHAT IDEA?
I DON'T REMEMBER ANYTHING ABOUT AN IDEA!
YOU COULDN'T PROVE IT BY ME!
THE EVENING WEARS ON! MORE DRINKS, AND THEN THE BITTERNESS OF PASSING TIME
I THINK I HAD DREAMS ONCE, BUT I DOUBT IF ANY OF THEM CAME TRUE!
I SUSPECT I NEVER LIVED THE KIND OF LIFE I WANTED!
LOOK AT ME! STARTING TO GRAY AND WRINKLE, AND I MAY NEVER HAVE FOUND A HUSBAND!
I DOUBT I EVER THOUGHT IT WOULD REALLY COME TO THIS, WHATEVER THIS IS!
IN ALL LIKELIHOOD, I ALWAYS WANTED TO BE A MUSICIAN! I NEVER IMAGINED MYSELF AS AN INSURANCE AGENT WITH FIVE KIDS AND A MORTGAGE UP TO HERE! WHICH ONE AM I? AM I EITHER?
WE WERE ALL GOING TO GO OUT AND CHANGE THE WORLD, WEREN'T WE? I DON'T IMAGINE WE SUCCEEDED, DID WE?
SOB! I NEVER DID GET THAT NOVEL WRITTEN, DID I? I THINK I WAS GOING TO WRITE A NOVEL!
SO HERE I AM! BALDING, POT BELLIED, AND I BET I NEVER EVEN SOLD A SINGLE PAINTING THAT I MAY HAVE WANTED TO SELL!
I DON'T MEAN TO CRY ON YOUR SHOULDER, BUT EVER SINCE MY WIFE MIGHT HAVE LEFT ME, I THINK I MAY HAVE BEEN DRINKING TOO MUCH!
WANT TO SEE A PICTURE THAT I THINK MIGHT HAVE BEEN ME?
I DON'T KNOW WHY, BUT I'M ALWAYS SO TIRED LATELY, HAVEN'T I BEEN?
SOMETIMES I WISH I COULD JUST RUN AWAY AND START ALL OVER FRESH SOMEWHERE, DON'T I?
WHEN I WAS YOUNG, I MUST HAVE THOUGHT IT WOULD ALL BE SO EASY! BUT IT HASN'T TURNED OUT VERY EASY FOR ME, HAS IT?
LORD HELP ME, BUT I HATE THE THOUGHT OF GOING HOME TONIGHT, WHEREVER THAT IS AND WHOEVER'S THERE!
I THINK I'VE EVEN CONTEMPLATED SUICIDE!
MORE LIQUOR, AND FADING MIDDLE-AGED SEXUALITY REARS ITS DESPERATE HEAD
DIDN'T WE ONCE GO OUT TOGETHER? I THINK YOU MIGHT BE MY TYPE!
GOD, I SHOULD HAVE NEVER LET YOU GO, IF I EVER HAD YOU IN THE FIRST PLACE!
EASY! I MIGHT BE A MARRIED WOMAN NOW, MAYBE EVEN WITH KIDS!
NOW THAT I'VE FOUND YOU AGAIN, IF I EVER KNEW YOU, I'LL NEVER LET YOU GO, AT LEAST NOT UNTIL I FORGET YOU IN A FEW SECONDS!
THAT CANOE RIDE WE MIGHT HAVE TAKEN WHERE YOU MIGHT HAVE PROPOSED! WHY DIDN'T I SAY YES! DID I SAY YES? ARE WE MARRIED?
I THINK YOU MIGHT HAVE BEEN THE FIRST TIME FOR ME! HOW WE FUMBLED AND LAUGHED, OR DID WE!
I NEVER WOULD HAVE BELIEVED SUCH HAPPINESS WAS POSSIBLE, IF IT WAS!
AS AT ALL REUNIONS, THINGS TURN INEVITABLY NASTY
WHY, YOU BASTARD! YOU MIGHT HAVE BEEN THE ONE WHO STOLE THE GIRL I MIGHT HAVE HAD!
BIG MAN ON CAMPUS, WERE YOU! WELL, I PROBABLY DIDN'T THINK YOU WERE SUCH HOT SHIT!
YOU USED TO COPY FROM MY EXAMS, AT LEAST YOU MIGHT HAVE, YOU LOUSY POSSIBLE HYPOCRITE!
SO YOU MIGHT HAVE A STRING OF FURNITURE STORES NOW AND I MIGHT SWEEP FLOORS IN A DELI! WELL, DON'T THINK YOU'RE SOME KIND OF BIG SHOT IF THAT IS, IN FACT, THE CASE!
SO I PROBABLY DIDN'T HAVE YOUR LOOKS AND YOU MAY HAVE HAD ALL THE DATES, BUT WHERE ARE YOU NOW!
I DON'T KNOW!
WASN'T THERE ONCE A KIND OF FAT GUY I DIDN'T LIKE? IF SO, I'LL PUNCH HIS ASS TONIGHT!
I THINK HE MIGHT HAVE DIED!
DIED?
YOU MEAN ONE OF US IS DEAD!
WE'RE THAT OLD!
NOT US! NOT OUR OLD GANG! GROWING UP, WORKING FOR A LIVING, DYING!
I THINK HE MIGHT HAVE BEEN SUCH A NICE GUY, TOO!
DIDN'T HE USED TO GO AROUND SAYING "WE GOTTA LIVE FOR TODAY," OR DID HE NEVER SAY THAT?
WHAT HAPPENED TO US? TO ALL THOSE BRIGHT-EYED KIDS WE PROBABLY WERE?
GOD, HOW DID IT ALL GET SO SERIOUS, ASSUMING IT DID!
HE'S REALLY DEAD NOW! WHY, I THINK HE WAS PROBABLY ONCE SO ALIVE!
THE HOUR IS LATE AND THE CLASSMATES MUSTER BACK THEIR DIGNITY
YEAH, I GUESS THAT'S THE WAY IT GOES!
DIDN'T I MEET SOME OLD FRIENDS HERE TONIGHT?
I THINK I MET A WOMAN I'D REALLY LOVE TO SEE AGAIN! WHO WAS SHE?
LOOK ME UP SOMETIME, IF YOU EVER FIND OUT WHO I AM!
I'D GIVE YOU MY PHONE NUMBER, IF I KNEW IT!
GOOD LUCK WITH WHATEVER YOU'RE DOING!
YOU TOO! AND IF YOU WERE THE ONE WHO THINKS HE MAY HAVE HAD THE HERNIA OPERATION, BE CAREFUL WITH IT!
I GUESS THIS IS IT UNTIL THE NEXT TIME, IF WE REMEMBER TO HAVE ONE!
TO HAVE WHAT? WHO ARE YOU? WHERE AM I?
THE CLASS REUNION OVER, EVERYONE HEADS BACK INTO THE PRESENT AND TOWARD HOME
OME
NICE SEEING YOU AGAIN, WHOEVER YOU ARE!
WASN'T THIS MY CLASS REUNION?
WHAT SCHOOL WAS THIS, ANYWAY?
I DON'T KNOW!
IS SOMEONE SUPPOSED TO PICK ME UP?
WHERE AM I SUPPOSED TO GO NOW!
WHO AM I? DID ANYBODY HERE BY ANY CHANCE RECOGNIZE ME?

MN: How do you know when something is working and when it isn't?

ES: I read it and some process inside me that I can't explain says, "This works. This is funny. This feels right." Sometimes a flaw will show itself. But usually it's just a feeling you get deep in your heart that something is good.

When you have something that comes to you from a gut level, you always feel secure about that part of yourself. It's coming at you like—[*points*] there's a glass over there, I'm not going to doubt that. At least not today. I'll read a philosophy book tomorrow and doubt it plenty. [*Laughs*] But not right now.

I think that operating so much by instinct allows what's inside you to come out through the tangled mess of the rest of your mind. You're not hammering something together, you're not putting it together or building it. Instinct comes out from the deepest parts of you. It drags all the good stuff that you're really about out with it, and hopefully none of the bad stuff.

MN: And when something's not working, do you try to fix it?

ES: Sometimes, and sometimes not. Sometimes it's worth saving and I try to fix it. Otherwise, I might just move on to something else and say, "This isn't worth the time any more."

The only problem with instinct is when you are talking to someone else about their work and trying to explain why you think it's wrong. You don't have their instinct and they don't have yours.

MN: How do you know how to fix it?

ES: [*Laughs*] I would say, just the way I tend to write things—I look at it and it tells me what needs fixing! That's probably the way to describe it. I don't ask it. I wait for it to tell me, and it tells me and then I know.

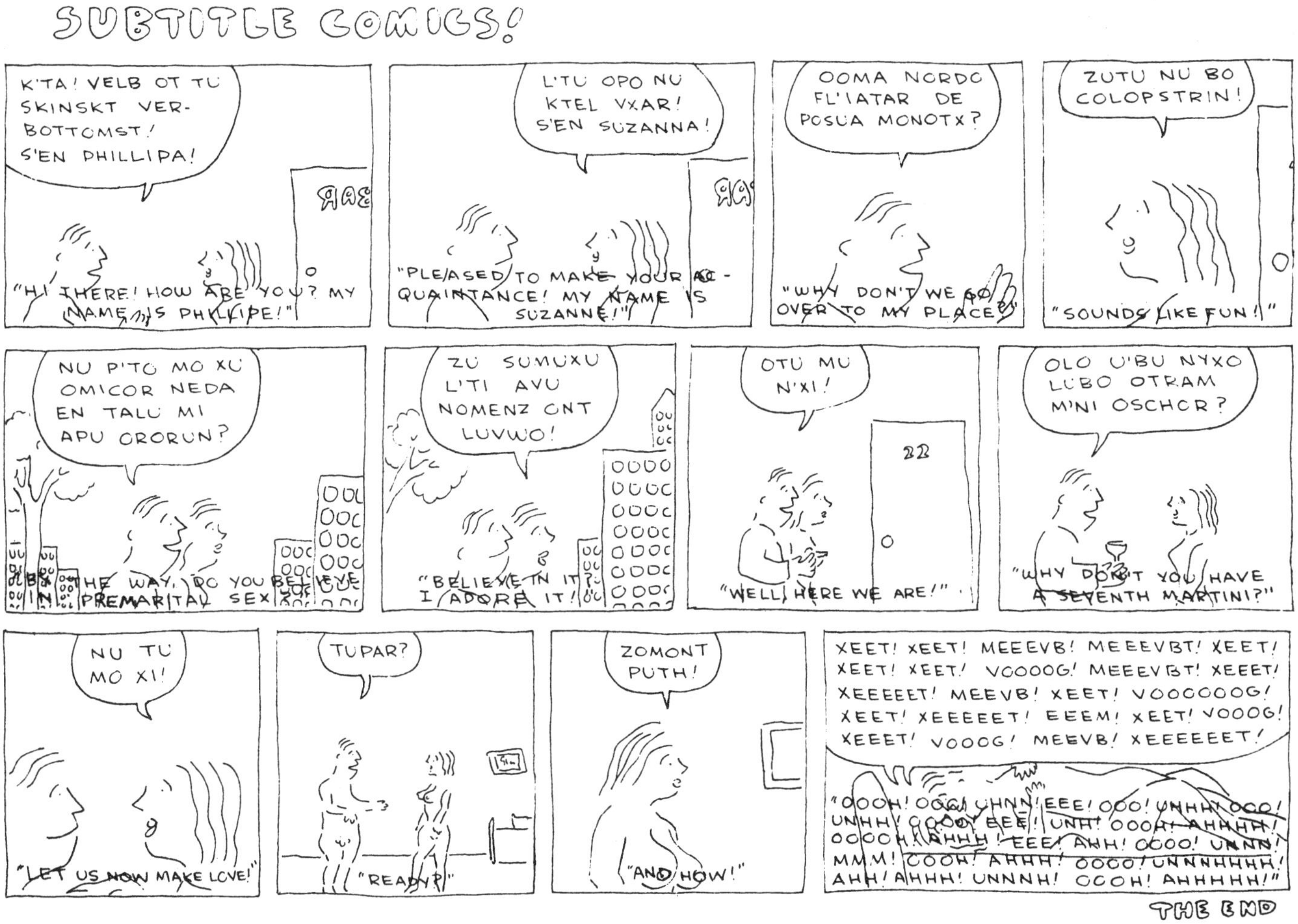
SUBTITLE COMICS!
K'TA! VELB OT TU SKINSKT VER-BOTTOMST! S'EN PHILLIPA!
"HI THERE! HOW ARE YOU? MY NAME IS PHILLIPE!"
L'TU OPO NU KTEL VXAR! S'EN SUZANNA!
"PLEASED TO MAKE YOUR AC-QUAINTANCE! MY NAME IS SUZANNE!"
OOMA NORDO FL'IATAR DE POSUA MONOTX?
"WHY DON'T WE GO OVER TO MY PLACE?"
ZUTU NU BO COLOPSTRIN!
"SOUNDS LIKE FUN!"
NU P'TO MO XU OMICOR NEDA EN TALU MI APU ORORUN?
"BY THE WAY, DO YOU BELIEVE IN PREMARITAL SEX?"
ZU SUMUXU L'TI AVU NOMENZ ONT LUVWO!
"BELIEVE IN IT? I ADORE IT!"
OTU MU N'XI!
"WELL, HERE WE ARE!"
OLO U'BU NYXO LUBO OTRAM M'NI OSCHOR?
"WHY DON'T YOU HAVE A SEVENTH MARTINI?"
NU TU MO XI!
"LET US NOW MAKE LOVE!"
TUPAR?
"READY?"
ZOMONT PUTH!
"AND HOW!"
XEET! XEET! MEEEVB! MEEEVBT! XEET! XEET! XEET! VOOOOG! MEEEVBT! XEEET! XEEEEET! MEEVB! XEET! VOOOOOOG! XEET! XEEEEET! EEEM! XEET! VOOOG! XEEET! VOOOG! MEEVB! XEEEEEET!
"OOOH! OOO! UHNN! EEE! OOO! UNHH! OOO! UNHH! OOOO! EEE! UNH! OOOH! AHHHH! OOOOH! AHHH! EEE! AHH! OOOO! UNNN! MMM! OOOH! AHHH! OOOO! UNNNHHHH! AHH! AHHH! UNNNH! OOOH! AHHHHH!"
THE END

VCR COMICS!

TO FAST-FORWARD PAST THE BORING PARTS, FOLLOW THE SOLID ARROWS!
TO REPEAT THE GOOD PARTS, FOLLOW THE DOTTED ARROWS!

"TRIP TO THE TOP!"
A STORY OF LUST, INTRIGUE, AND OUT-OF-CONTROL AMBITION!

A YOUNG, AMBITIOUS WOMAN COMES TO NEW YORK!

AS SURE AS MY NAME IS JANE, I'LL DO ANYTHING TO GET TO THE TOP! ANYTHING!

SHE BEGINS HER RUTHLESS CLIMB!

MR. JOHNSON, THERE'S A NAKED WOMAN TO SEE YOU!

SEND HER IN!

YOU'RE HIRED AND IMMEDIATELY PROMOTED TO VICE PRESIDENT AND IMMEDIATELY PROMOTED TO SENIOR VICE PRESIDENT AND IMMEDIATELY PROMOTED TO THE HIGHEST POSITION IN THE COMPANY EXCEPT FOR ME!

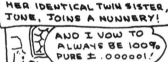

MEANWHILE, BACK IN IOWA, HER IDENTICAL TWIN SISTER, JUNE, JOINS A NUNNERY!

AND I VOW TO ALWAYS BE 100% PURE ± .00001!

JANE SLEEPS WITH THE MAIL BOY AND READS ALL THE COMPANY MAIL!

OH! OH!

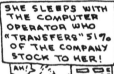

SHE SLEEPS WITH THE COMPUTER OPERATOR WHO "TRANSFERS" 51% OF THE COMPANY STOCK TO HER!

AH!

SHE SLEEPS WITH THE STAFF PUBLICIST WHO RENAMES THE COMPANY AFTER HER!

YES! YES!

SHE IMMEDIATELY FIRES ALL THE PEOPLE WHO HELPED HER, INCLUDING THE COMPUTER OPERATOR, WHO FELL IN LOVE WITH HER!

JANE INDUSTRIES

SOB!

BACK IN IOWA, HER SISTER IS NOMINATED "THE RELIGIOUS WORLD'S MOST PIOUS NUN"!

WE'RE VERY PROUD OF YOU, SISTER JUNE!

ON SKID ROW IN DAVENPORT, A DRUNK EX-MATERNITY WARD WORKER SUDDENLY COMES OUT OF A 21-YEAR COMA!

GASP!

BY SLEEPING WITH ALL OF THE TOP EXECUTIVES IN THE FORTUNE 500, JANE TAKES OVER THE ENTIRE KNOWN BUSINESS WORLD!

I HOPE YOU'RE BETTER THAN NUMBER 497!

SHE IS NOW THE MOST POWERFUL PERSON ON EARTH! STRANGE THAT SHE KEEPS THINKING OF A CERTAIN COMPUTER OPERATOR...

IN FIVE DAYS, I'VE AMASSED EVERYTHING, EXCEPT LOVE!

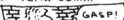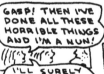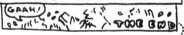

SUDDENLY HER SISTER AND A GRIZZLED OLD ALCOHOLIC APPEAR AT THE DOOR! HE EXPLAINS...

EVEN THOUGH YOU'RE TWINS, I STILL GOT YOU MIXED UP AT BIRTH! THE ONE CALLED JUNE IS REALLY THE ONE CALLED JANE AND VICE VERSA!

GASP! THEN I'VE DONE ALL THESE HORRIBLE THINGS AND I'M A NUN!

I'LL SURELY BE PUNISHED!

GASP! THEN I'M A NUN AND I'VE DONE ALL THESE HORRIBLE THINGS!

I'LL SURELY BE PUNISHED!

JUST THEN THE COMPUTER OPERATOR, CRAZED WITH RESENTMENT, RUSHES IN AND HACKS THEM ALL TO PIECES WITH A TOOL FOR INSERTING MICROCHIPS!

GAAH!

THE END

DISSOLVE COMICS! JUST LIKE THE MOVIES

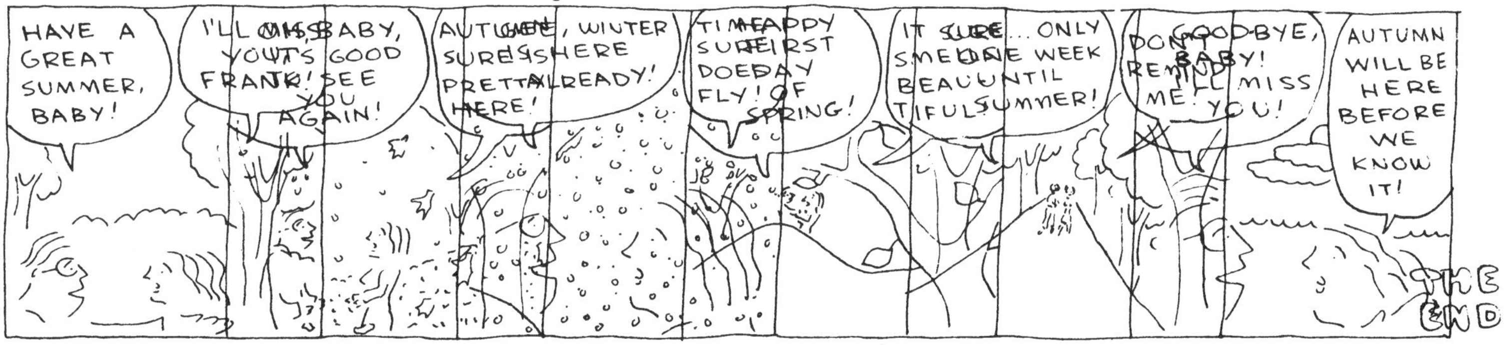

THERAPY COMICS!

TODAY'S PROBLEM: SHYNESS!

 HI! I'M DR. ANDREWS, YOUR COMIC CHARACTER THERAPIST!

 YOU'RE ABOUT TO HAVE SOME CAREFULLY CONTROLLED INTERACTIONS WITH COMIC CHARACTERS!

 RIGHT HERE ON THIS PAGE, WE'LL HELP YOU DECONDITION YOURSELF OUT OF YOUR PROBLEM!

 AND THE NEW BEHAVIOR YOU'VE ESTABLISHED WILL TRANSFER ITSELF TO THE REAL WORLD AROUND YOU!

 WHAT'S MORE, THERE'S NO EXTRA CHARGE FOR THIS SERVICE! IT WAS INCLUDED IN THE PRICE OF THIS MAGAZINE!

 READY TO BEGIN? MEET JENNY, A PRETTY, YOUNG, VIVACIOUS COMIC STRIP CHARACTER!

 NOW I WANT YOU TO SAY SOMETHING TO HER, AND SHE'LL POSITIVELY REINFORCE YOU!

 GO AHEAD! IT DOESN'T HAVE TO BE ANYTHING FANCY! JUST TELL HER YOUR NAME!

 COME ON! SHE'S ONLY PAPER AND INK! SHE CAN'T SLAP YOU OR ANYTHING!

 AND REMEMBER... YOUR MOTHER DOESN'T EVEN KNOW YOU READ THIS MAGAZINE!

JUST TAKE A DEEP BREATH... RELAX... AND LET THE WORDS POP OUT OF YOUR MOUTH!

 SHE'S WAITING! DO IT IN THE NEXT PANEL!

 WHY, WHAT A NICE NAME! I'D LIKE TO GIVE YOU A BLOW JOB RIGHT NOW!

 OBVIOUSLY I CAN'T DO THAT! BUT AT LEAST I CAN SHOW YOU MY TITS!

 SEE HOW EASY IT WAS? I BET YOU DIDN'T FEEL GUILTY OR AWKWARD AT ALL!

 WELL, OUR SPACE IS UP NOW! BUT IF YOU'D LIKE ANOTHER SESSION, JUST READ THIS AGAIN NEXT WEEK, SAME TIME!

SUNSET COMICS!

THE BEACH IS DESERTED! PLEASE!

BUT DARLING, IT IS SO PERVERSE... SO BIZARRE!

I KNOW! BUT IT IS THE ONLY WAY I CAN TRULY BE SATISFIED!

BUT I JUST PUT ON A FRESH COAT OF TOENAIL POLISH... AND MY EARS AREN'T PIERCED!

YOU'LL ENJOY IT TOO! TRUST ME...

OKAY... BUT ONLY BECAUSE I LOVE YOU!

OOOOH! AHHHH! GUNGNH! AHHH!

AHHHHH! YES! YES! MGMGHH! AHHHH!

THE END

MN: In your more recent work, do you think humor comes harder or easier for you?

ES: The same.

MN: Completely the same?

ES: Yeah.

MN: Do you read any contemporary comics or graphic novels?

ES: No. Only newspaper comics.

MN: What about other humor outlets? What makes you laugh right now?

ES: Very little, to be honest. It might be because I'm not exposing myself to enough. As I said, right or wrong, I'm not enamored with most stand up comics, so I don't know what's going on with most of the stand-up scene. And the only place I know that has cartoons is *The New Yorker*, and we don't subscribe to that.

MN: Do you feel that print humor is dead?

ES: Yes. Definitely. There aren't even many gag cartoons around. Very few magazines are running them. *The American Bystander* is just about the only humor publication I'm aware of.[20] But I would say an unequivocal yes: print humor is dead. I hope it will come back.

---

[20]Humor magazine edited and published by Michael Gerber (2015–).

LARGE, IMPERMANENT SAND MANDALA

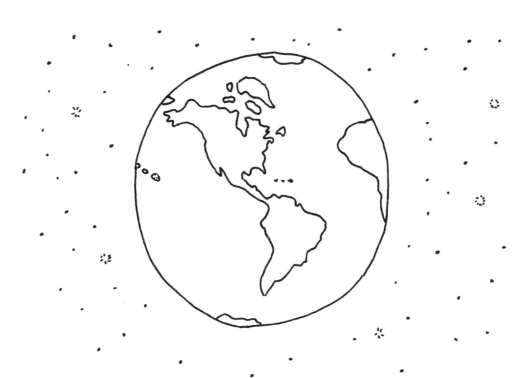

THE NEW YORK TIMES **OP-ED** FRIDAY, JUNE 27, 1997

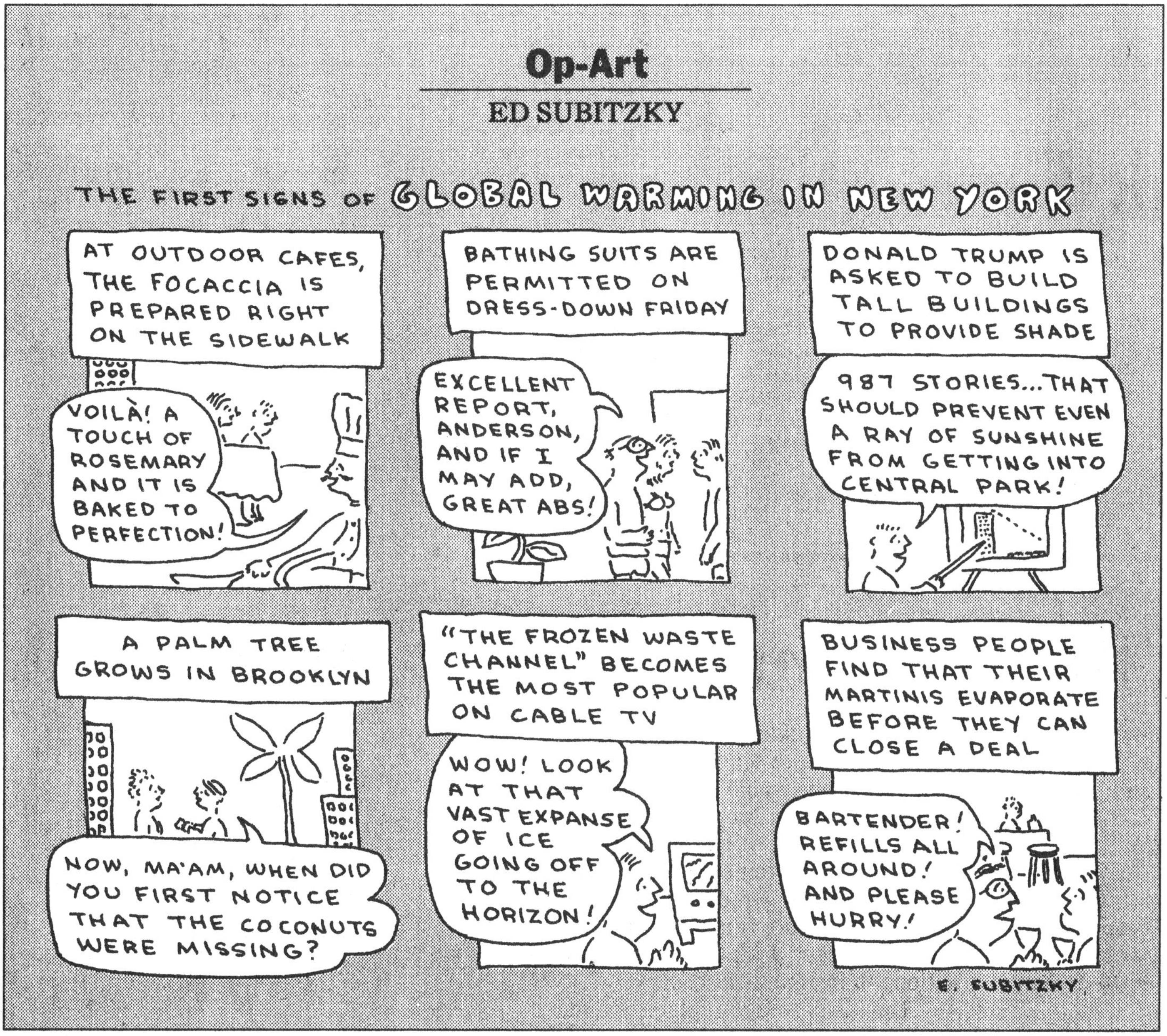

MOVING ON COMICS!
BY ED SUBITZKY
BOY, I CAN'T STAND THIS PART OF THE STRIP, OVER TO THE LEFT!
IT'S SO UN-AMERICAN!
YEAH, I ACTUALLY FEEL SOME COMPASSION FOR MY FELLOW HUMAN BEINGS!
I HAVE THIS STRANGE URGE TO HELP OUT A POOR PERSON!
NOW, THIS PANEL HERE IS A LITTLE MORE LIKE IT!
YEAH, I'M STARTING TO WONDER WHY PREGNANT TEENAGERS DON'T TAKE MORE FACTORY JOBS!
WE'RE FINALLY RIGHT OF CENTER! THANK GOODNESS!
DID I REALLY SAY I WANTED TO HELP THAT PATHETIC OLD BUM? I SHOULD HAVE PUSHED HIS FACE IN!
LOOK! WE'RE ALMOST AT THE RIGHT MARGIN! I THINK WE SHOULD ELECT GENERAL MOTORS PRESIDENT!
I SUDDENLY REALIZED I'M THE ONLY PERSON IN THE COUNTRY WHO DESERVES MEDICAL CARE!
WE MADE IT! WHAT A RUSH! ALL THIS HATE FEELS BETTER THAN A TRIPLE ESPRESSO!
LOOK! I JUST DESTROYED THE ENVIRONMENT BECAUSE GOD TOLD ME TO!

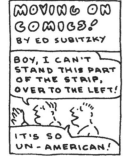

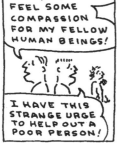

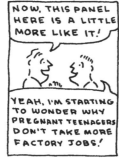

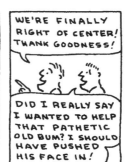

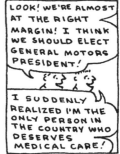

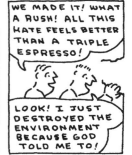

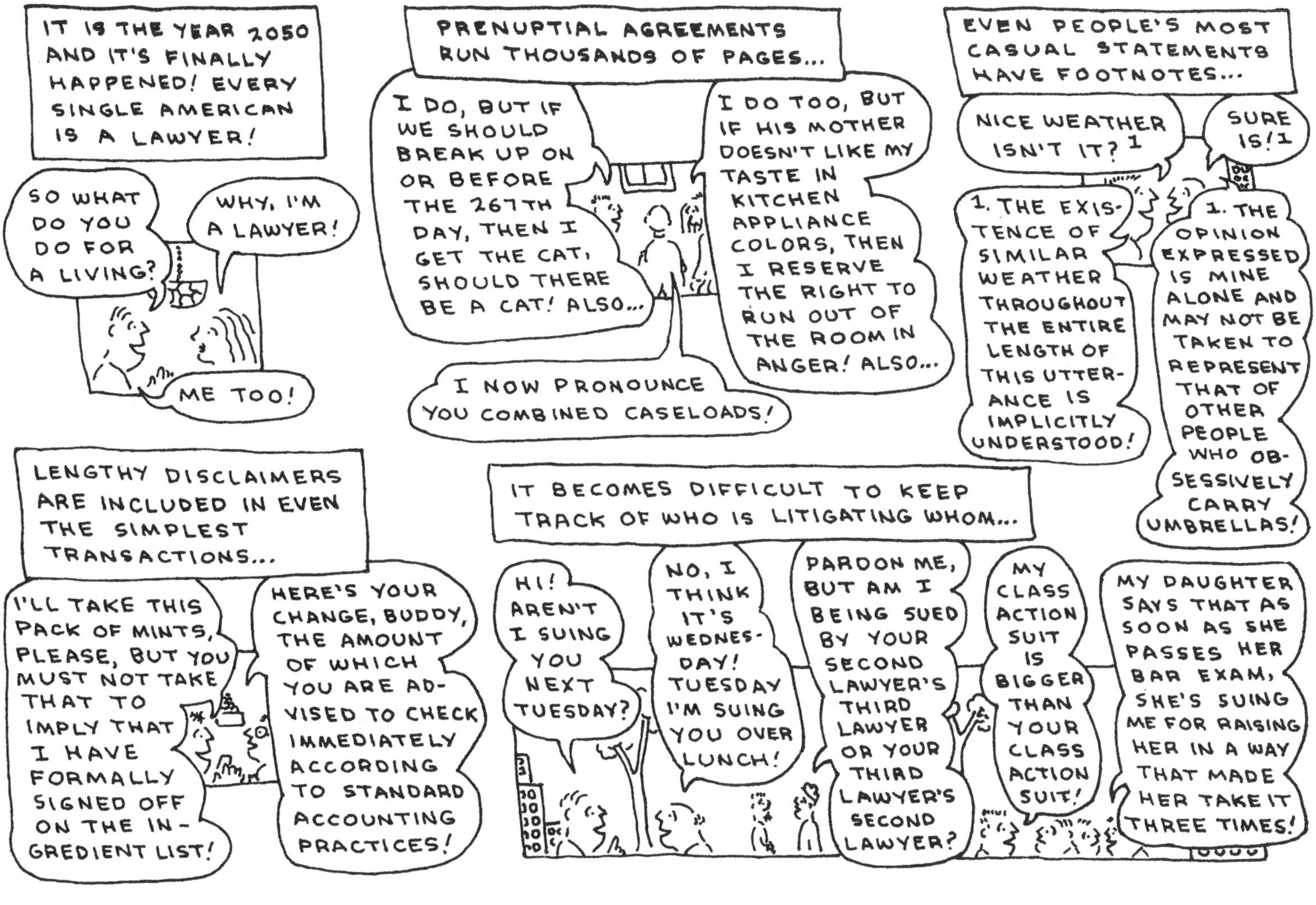
IT IS THE YEAR 2050 AND IT'S FINALLY HAPPENED! EVERY SINGLE AMERICAN IS A LAWYER!
SO WHAT DO YOU DO FOR A LIVING?
WHY, I'M A LAWYER!
ME TOO!
PRENUPTIAL AGREEMENTS RUN THOUSANDS OF PAGES...
I DO, BUT IF WE SHOULD BREAK UP ON OR BEFORE THE 267TH DAY, THEN I GET THE CAT, SHOULD THERE BE A CAT! ALSO...
I DO TOO, BUT IF HIS MOTHER DOESN'T LIKE MY TASTE IN KITCHEN APPLIANCE COLORS, THEN I RESERVE THE RIGHT TO RUN OUT OF THE ROOM IN ANGER! ALSO...
I NOW PRONOUNCE YOU COMBINED CASELOADS!
EVEN PEOPLE'S MOST CASUAL STATEMENTS HAVE FOOTNOTES...
NICE WEATHER ISN'T IT? 1
SURE IS! 1
1. THE EXISTENCE OF SIMILAR WEATHER THROUGHOUT THE ENTIRE LENGTH OF THIS UTTERANCE IS IMPLICITLY UNDERSTOOD!
1. THE OPINION EXPRESSED IS MINE ALONE AND MAY NOT BE TAKEN TO REPRESENT THAT OF OTHER PEOPLE WHO OBSESSIVELY CARRY UMBRELLAS!
LENGTHY DISCLAIMERS ARE INCLUDED IN EVEN THE SIMPLEST TRANSACTIONS...
I'LL TAKE THIS PACK OF MINTS, PLEASE, BUT YOU MUST NOT TAKE THAT TO IMPLY THAT I HAVE FORMALLY SIGNED OFF ON THE INGREDIENT LIST!
HERE'S YOUR CHANGE, BUDDY, THE AMOUNT OF WHICH YOU ARE ADVISED TO CHECK IMMEDIATELY ACCORDING TO STANDARD ACCOUNTING PRACTICES!
IT BECOMES DIFFICULT TO KEEP TRACK OF WHO IS LITIGATING WHOM...
HI! AREN'T I SUING YOU NEXT TUESDAY?
NO, I THINK IT'S WEDNESDAY! TUESDAY I'M SUING YOU OVER LUNCH!
PARDON ME, BUT AM I BEING SUED BY YOUR SECOND LAWYER'S THIRD LAWYER OR YOUR THIRD LAWYER'S SECOND LAWYER?
MY CLASS ACTION SUIT IS BIGGER THAN YOUR CLASS ACTION SUIT!
MY DAUGHTER SAYS THAT AS SOON AS SHE PASSES HER BAR EXAM, SHE'S SUING ME FOR RAISING HER IN A WAY THAT MADE HER TAKE IT THREE TIMES!

Op-Art

ED SUBITZKY

SOME MORE WAYS TO

IMPROVE OUR TAXI SERVICE

LET DRIVERS PICK UP PASSENGERS WHILE MOVING

JUST GET UP TO 27 M.P.H. AND THEN JUMP RIGHT IN, PAL!

TRAIN DRIVERS INTO GIVING MINI-COURSES FOR COLLEGE CREDIT

AND THAT'S WHY MACBETH HIMSELF CAN BE TAKEN TO BE A SYMBOL OF MANKIND'S INNER TURMOIL!

WOW! JUST 10,000 MORE RIDES AND I'LL HAVE MY B.A. IN ENGLISH LIT!

REQUIRE "RIDE ATTENDANTS" ON EVERY TRIP LONGER THAN 15 MINUTES

SALTED PEANUTS, SIR? I'LL BE SERVING DINNER AND A BEVERAGE WHEN THE METER PASSES $20!

TICKET DRIVERS WHO HARASS PASSENGERS BY MAKING DISPARAGING REMARKS ABOUT PRESENT OR FORMER MAYORS

PULL OVER, BUDDY! OUR PARABOLIC MIKE PICKED UP THAT COMMENT ABOUT GIULIANI!

GIVE PUSHCART VENDORS THE RIGHT TO PICK UP PASSENGERS

SECOND AVENUE AND FIFTY-SIXTH, PLEASE!

OKAY, BUT PLEASE UNDERSTAND THAT I BRAKE FOR FALAFEL LOVERS!

ALLOW FREE TRANSFERS TO CABS WITH BETTER DRIVERS

ONE MORE U-TURN ON A ONE-WAY STREET AND I'M OUT OF HERE!

E. SUBITZKY

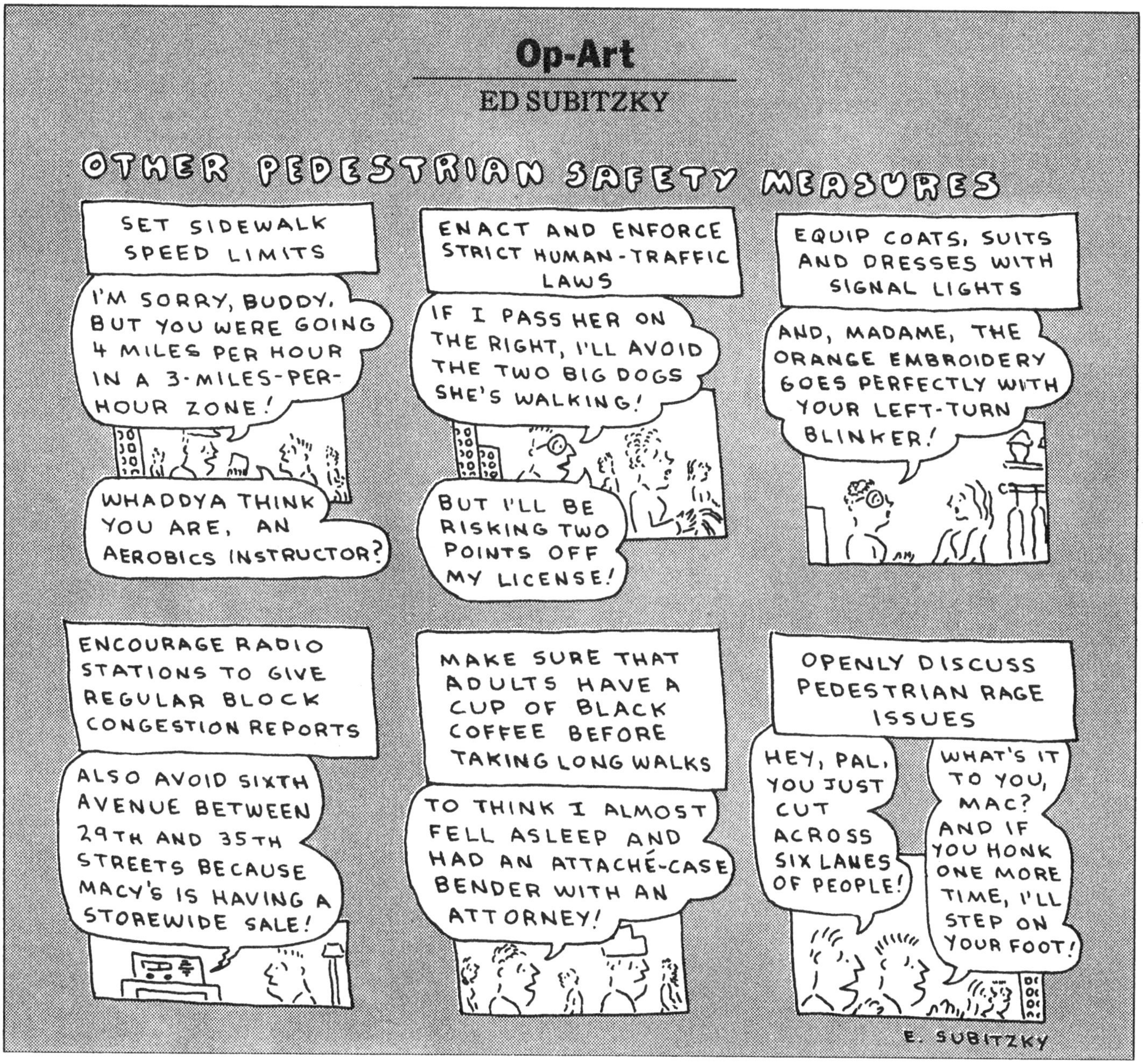

Op-Art
ED SUBITZKY
OTHER PEDESTRIAN SAFETY MEASURES
SET SIDEWALK SPEED LIMITS
I'M SORRY, BUDDY, BUT YOU WERE GOING 4 MILES PER HOUR IN A 3-MILES-PER-HOUR ZONE!
WHADDYA THINK YOU ARE, AN AEROBICS INSTRUCTOR?
ENACT AND ENFORCE STRICT HUMAN-TRAFFIC LAWS
IF I PASS HER ON THE RIGHT, I'LL AVOID THE TWO BIG DOGS SHE'S WALKING!
BUT I'LL BE RISKING TWO POINTS OFF MY LICENSE!
EQUIP COATS, SUITS AND DRESSES WITH SIGNAL LIGHTS
AND, MADAME, THE ORANGE EMBROIDERY GOES PERFECTLY WITH YOUR LEFT-TURN BLINKER!
ENCOURAGE RADIO STATIONS TO GIVE REGULAR BLOCK CONGESTION REPORTS
ALSO AVOID SIXTH AVENUE BETWEEN 29TH AND 35TH STREETS BECAUSE MACY'S IS HAVING A STOREWIDE SALE!
MAKE SURE THAT ADULTS HAVE A CUP OF BLACK COFFEE BEFORE TAKING LONG WALKS
TO THINK I ALMOST FELL ASLEEP AND HAD AN ATTACHÉ-CASE BENDER WITH AN ATTORNEY!
OPENLY DISCUSS PEDESTRIAN RAGE ISSUES
HEY, PAL, YOU JUST CUT ACROSS SIX LANES OF PEOPLE!
WHAT'S IT TO YOU, MAC? AND IF YOU HONK ONE MORE TIME, I'LL STEP ON YOUR FOOT!
E. SUBITZKY

Op-Art

ED SUBITZKY

SURE-FIRE WAYS TO IMPROVE THE I.R.S.

HAVE THEM SEND THANK-YOU NOTES

IT SAYS THEY REALLY APPRECIATE GETTING OUR MONEY, AND IT'S EVEN ENGRAVED IN RAISED GOLD LETTERS!

SIMPLIFY THE FORMS

ALL I HAVE TO DO IS SIGN MY NAME AND ENCLOSE A BLANK CHECK!

SERVE PASTRY AND ESPRESSO AT AUDITS

I'M SORRY, BUT YOU CAN'T DEDUCT AN IMITATION LEOPARD-SKIN STEERING WHEEL COVER! MAY I OFFER YOU A NAPOLEON BEFORE WE TALK ABOUT GARNISHEEING YOUR SALARY?

GIVE PEOPLE A LIST OF THINGS THEIR TAX DOLLARS PAID FOR

LOOK, HONEY! THANKS TO US, A COLONEL AT FORT BRAGG GOT A $900 BOLT FOR HIS FAVORITE RIFLE!

OFFER FREE GIFTS FOR PROMPT PAYMENT

JUST THINK... IF IT ARRIVES THERE BY MARCH 31, WE GET A SET OF COASTERS AUTOGRAPHED BY THE ASSISTANT SECRETARY OF THE TREASURY!

GIVE PEOPLE EXEMPTIONS FOR PETS

SOMEONE HAS FINALLY REALIZED HOW MUCH IT COSTS TO MAINTAIN AN AQUARIUM WITH 17 GOLDFISH!

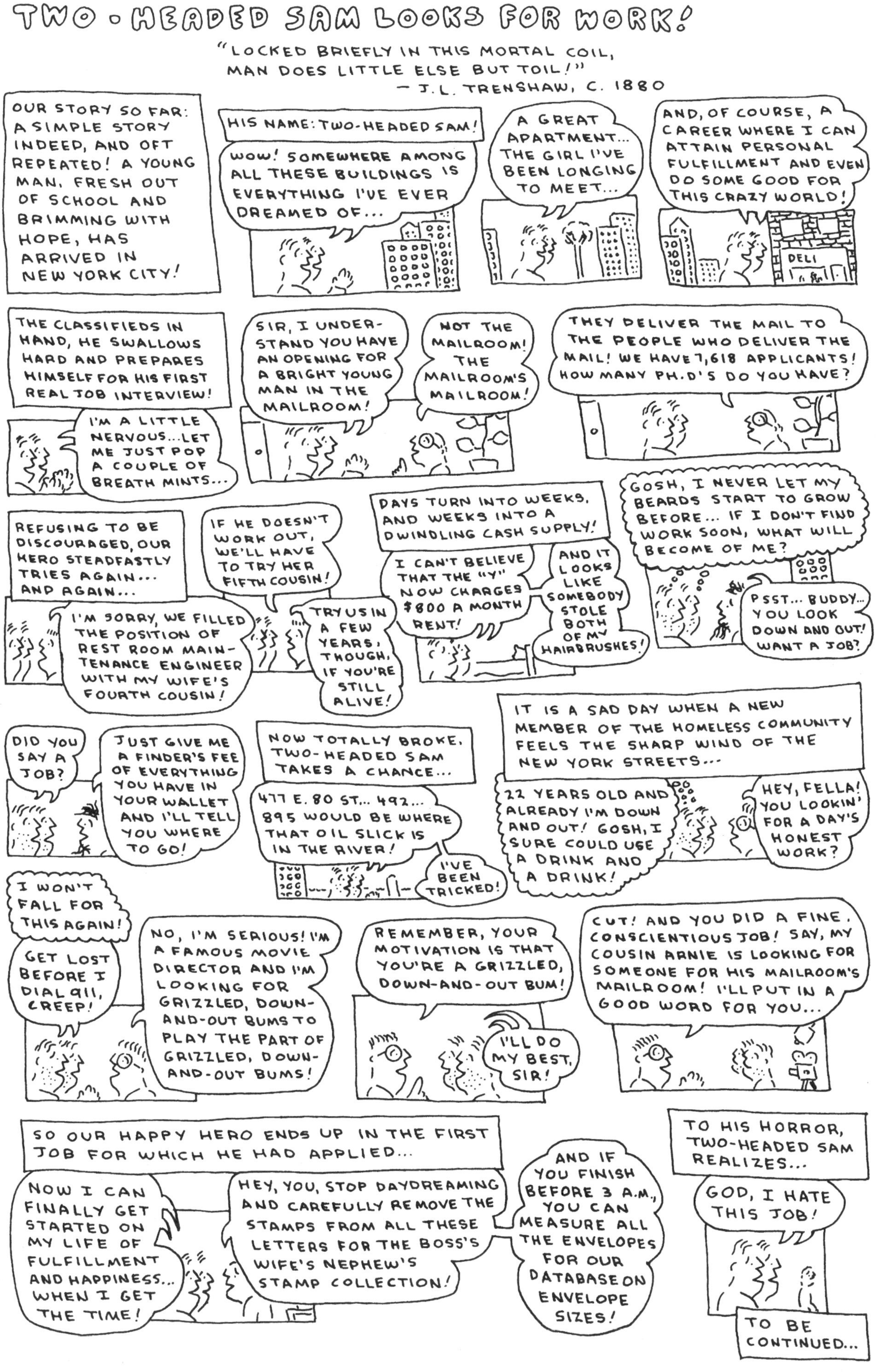
TWO-HEADED SAM LOOKS FOR WORK!
"LOCKED BRIEFLY IN THIS MORTAL COIL, MAN DOES LITTLE ELSE BUT TOIL!" — J.L. TRENSHAW, C. 1880
OUR STORY SO FAR: A SIMPLE STORY INDEED, AND OFT REPEATED! A YOUNG MAN, FRESH OUT OF SCHOOL AND BRIMMING WITH HOPE, HAS ARRIVED IN NEW YORK CITY!
HIS NAME: TWO-HEADED SAM!
WOW! SOMEWHERE AMONG ALL THESE BUILDINGS IS EVERYTHING I'VE EVER DREAMED OF...
A GREAT APARTMENT... THE GIRL I'VE BEEN LONGING TO MEET...
AND, OF COURSE, A CAREER WHERE I CAN ATTAIN PERSONAL FULFILLMENT AND EVEN DO SOME GOOD FOR THIS CRAZY WORLD!
DELI
THE CLASSIFIEDS IN HAND, HE SWALLOWS HARD AND PREPARES HIMSELF FOR HIS FIRST REAL JOB INTERVIEW!
I'M A LITTLE NERVOUS... LET ME JUST POP A COUPLE OF BREATH MINTS...
SIR, I UNDERSTAND YOU HAVE AN OPENING FOR A BRIGHT YOUNG MAN IN THE MAILROOM!
NOT THE MAILROOM! THE MAILROOM'S MAILROOM!
THEY DELIVER THE MAIL TO THE PEOPLE WHO DELIVER THE MAIL! WE HAVE 7,618 APPLICANTS! HOW MANY PH.D'S DO YOU HAVE?
REFUSING TO BE DISCOURAGED, OUR HERO STEADFASTLY TRIES AGAIN... AND AGAIN...
I'M SORRY, WE FILLED THE POSITION OF REST ROOM MAINTENANCE ENGINEER WITH MY WIFE'S FOURTH COUSIN!
IF HE DOESN'T WORK OUT, WE'LL HAVE TO TRY HER FIFTH COUSIN!
TRY US IN A FEW YEARS, THOUGH, IF YOU'RE STILL ALIVE!
DAYS TURN INTO WEEKS, AND WEEKS INTO A DWINDLING CASH SUPPLY!
I CAN'T BELIEVE THAT THE "Y" NOW CHARGES $800 A MONTH RENT!
AND IT LOOKS LIKE SOMEBODY STOLE BOTH OF MY HAIRBRUSHES!
GOSH, I NEVER LET MY BEARDS START TO GROW BEFORE... IF I DON'T FIND WORK SOON, WHAT WILL BECOME OF ME?
PSST... BUDDY... YOU LOOK DOWN AND OUT! WANT A JOB?
DID YOU SAY A JOB?
JUST GIVE ME A FINDER'S FEE OF EVERYTHING YOU HAVE IN YOUR WALLET AND I'LL TELL YOU WHERE TO GO!
NOW TOTALLY BROKE, TWO-HEADED SAM TAKES A CHANCE...
477 E. 80 ST... 492... 895 WOULD BE WHERE THAT OIL SLICK IS IN THE RIVER!
I'VE BEEN TRICKED!
IT IS A SAD DAY WHEN A NEW MEMBER OF THE HOMELESS COMMUNITY FEELS THE SHARP WIND OF THE NEW YORK STREETS...
22 YEARS OLD AND ALREADY I'M DOWN AND OUT! GOSH, I SURE COULD USE A DRINK AND A DRINK!
HEY, FELLA! YOU LOOKIN' FOR A DAY'S HONEST WORK?
I WON'T FALL FOR THIS AGAIN!
GET LOST BEFORE I DIAL 911, CREEP!
NO, I'M SERIOUS! I'M A FAMOUS MOVIE DIRECTOR AND I'M LOOKING FOR GRIZZLED, DOWN-AND-OUT BUMS TO PLAY THE PART OF GRIZZLED, DOWN-AND-OUT BUMS!
REMEMBER, YOUR MOTIVATION IS THAT YOU'RE A GRIZZLED, DOWN-AND-OUT BUM!
I'LL DO MY BEST, SIR!
CUT! AND YOU DID A FINE, CONSCIENTIOUS JOB! SAY, MY COUSIN ARNIE IS LOOKING FOR SOMEONE FOR HIS MAILROOM'S MAILROOM! I'LL PUT IN A GOOD WORD FOR YOU...
SO OUR HAPPY HERO ENDS UP IN THE FIRST JOB FOR WHICH HE HAD APPLIED...
NOW I CAN FINALLY GET STARTED ON MY LIFE OF FULFILLMENT AND HAPPINESS... WHEN I GET THE TIME!
HEY, YOU, STOP DAYDREAMING AND CAREFULLY REMOVE THE STAMPS FROM ALL THESE LETTERS FOR THE BOSS'S WIFE'S NEPHEW'S STAMP COLLECTION!
AND IF YOU FINISH BEFORE 3 A.M., YOU CAN MEASURE ALL THE ENVELOPES FOR OUR DATABASE ON ENVELOPE SIZES!
TO HIS HORROR, TWO-HEADED SAM REALIZES...
GOD, I HATE THIS JOB!
TO BE CONTINUED...

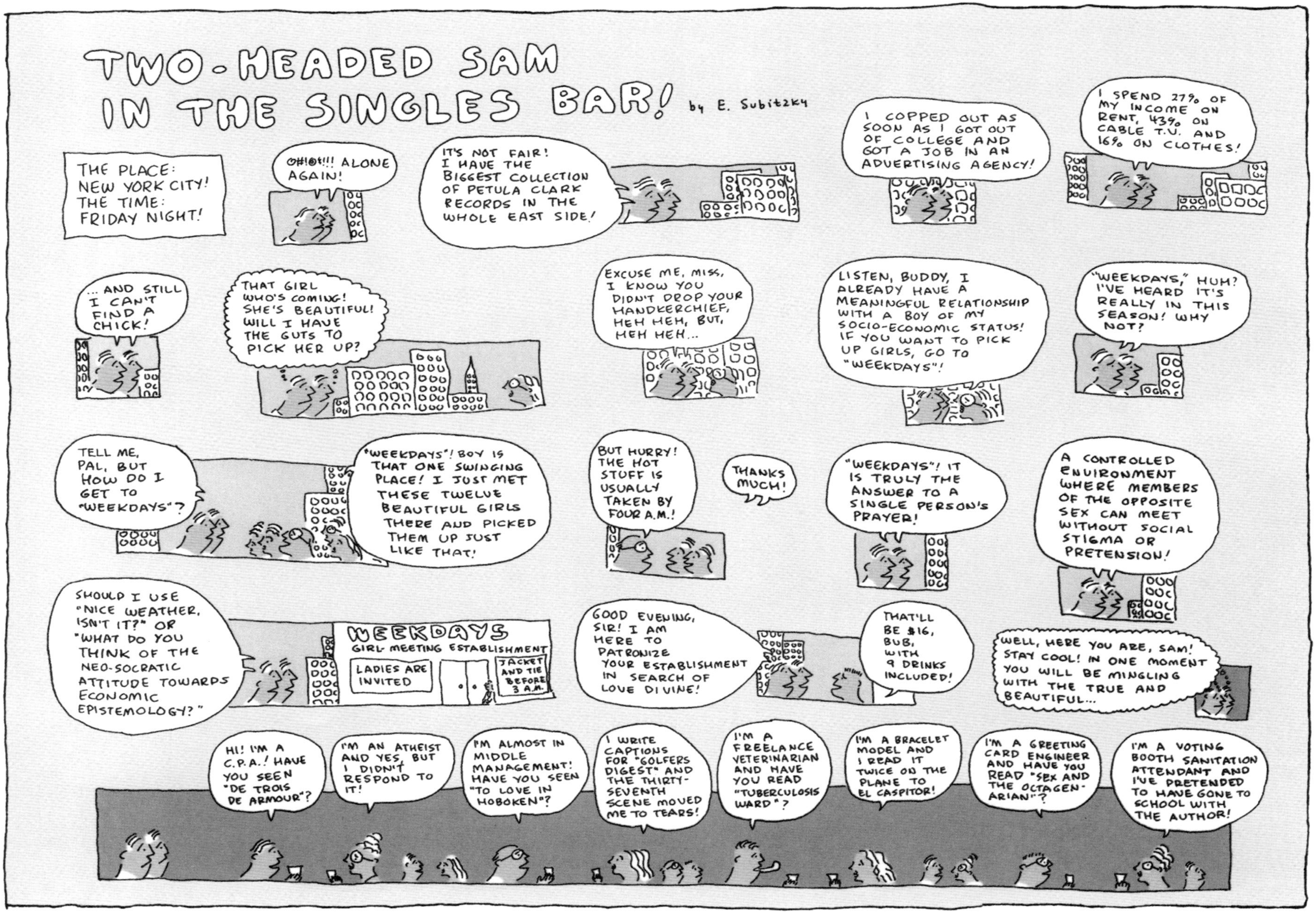
TWO-HEADED SAM IN THE SINGLES BAR!
by E. Subitzky
THE PLACE: NEW YORK CITY! THE TIME: FRIDAY NIGHT!
@#!@*!!! ALONE AGAIN!
IT'S NOT FAIR! I HAVE THE BIGGEST COLLECTION OF PETULA CLARK RECORDS IN THE WHOLE EAST SIDE!
I COPPED OUT AS SOON AS I GOT OUT OF COLLEGE AND GOT A JOB IN AN ADVERTISING AGENCY!
I SPEND 27% OF MY INCOME ON RENT, 43% ON CABLE T.V. AND 16% ON CLOTHES!
... AND STILL I CAN'T FIND A CHICK!
THAT GIRL WHO'S COMING! SHE'S BEAUTIFUL! WILL I HAVE THE GUTS TO PICK HER UP?
EXCUSE ME, MISS, I KNOW YOU DIDN'T DROP YOUR HANDKERCHIEF, HEH HEH, BUT, HEH HEH...
LISTEN, BUDDY, I ALREADY HAVE A MEANINGFUL RELATIONSHIP WITH A BOY OF MY SOCIO-ECONOMIC STATUS! IF YOU WANT TO PICK UP GIRLS, GO TO "WEEKDAYS"!
"WEEKDAYS," HUH? I'VE HEARD IT'S REALLY IN THIS SEASON! WHY NOT?
TELL ME, PAL, BUT HOW DO I GET TO "WEEKDAYS"?
"WEEKDAYS"! BOY IS THAT ONE SWINGING PLACE! I JUST MET THESE TWELVE BEAUTIFUL GIRLS THERE AND PICKED THEM UP JUST LIKE THAT!
BUT HURRY! THE HOT STUFF IS USUALLY TAKEN BY FOUR A.M.!
THANKS MUCH!
"WEEKDAYS"! IT IS TRULY THE ANSWER TO A SINGLE PERSON'S PRAYER!
A CONTROLLED ENVIRONMENT WHERE MEMBERS OF THE OPPOSITE SEX CAN MEET WITHOUT SOCIAL STIGMA OR PRETENSION!
SHOULD I USE "NICE WEATHER, ISN'T IT?" OR "WHAT DO YOU THINK OF THE NEO-SOCRATIC ATTITUDE TOWARDS ECONOMIC EPISTEMOLOGY?"
WEEKDAYS
GIRL-MEETING ESTABLISHMENT
LADIES ARE INVITED
JACKET AND TIE BEFORE 3 A.M.
GOOD EVENING, SIR! I AM HERE TO PATRONIZE YOUR ESTABLISHMENT IN SEARCH OF LOVE DIVINE!
THAT'LL BE $16, BUB, WITH 9 DRINKS INCLUDED!
WELL, HERE YOU ARE, SAM! STAY COOL! IN ONE MOMENT YOU WILL BE MINGLING WITH THE TRUE AND BEAUTIFUL...
HI! I'M A C.P.A.! HAVE YOU SEEN "DE TROIS DE ARMOUR"?
I'M AN ATHEIST AND YES, BUT I DIDN'T RESPOND TO IT!
I'M ALMOST IN MIDDLE MANAGEMENT! HAVE YOU SEEN "TO LOVE IN HOBOKEN"?
I WRITE CAPTIONS FOR "GOLFERS DIGEST" AND THE THIRTY-SEVENTH SCENE MOVED ME TO TEARS!
I'M A FREELANCE VETERINARIAN AND HAVE YOU READ "TUBERCULOSIS WARD"?
I'M A BRACELET MODEL AND I READ IT TWICE ON THE PLANE TO EL CASPITOR!
I'M A GREETING CARD ENGINEER AND HAVE YOU READ "SEX AND THE OCTAGENARIAN"?
I'M A VOTING BOOTH SANITATION ATTENDANT AND I'VE PRETENDED TO HAVE GONE TO SCHOOL WITH THE AUTHOR!

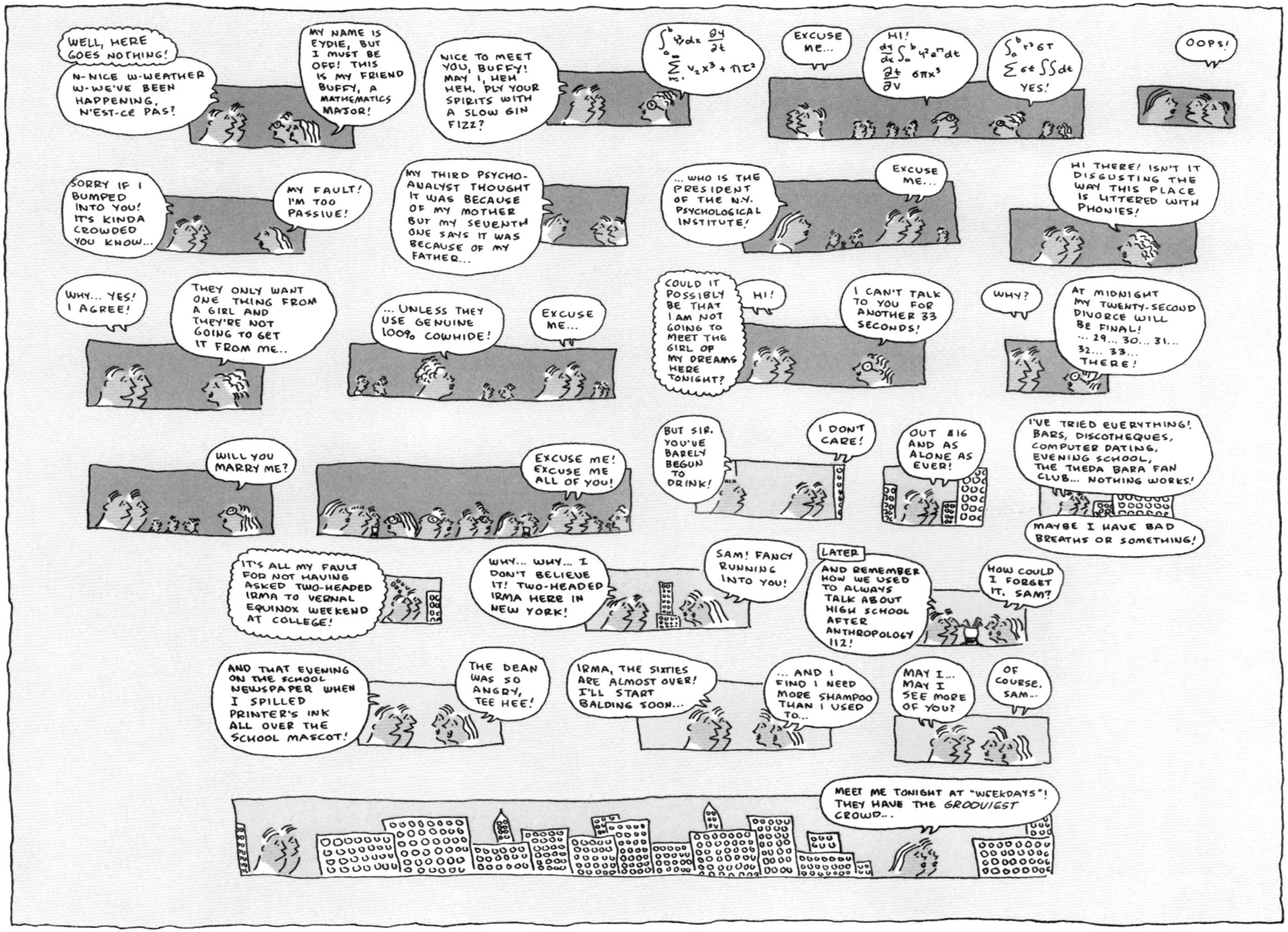
WELL, HERE GOES NOTHING!
N-NICE W-WEATHER W-WE'VE BEEN HAPPENING, N'EST-CE PAS?
MY NAME IS EYDIE, BUT I MUST BE OFF! THIS IS MY FRIEND BUFFY, A MATHEMATICS MAJOR!
NICE TO MEET YOU, BUFFY! MAY I, HEH HEH, PLY YOUR SPIRITS WITH A SLOW GIN FIZZ?
EXCUSE ME...
HI!
YES!
OOPS!
SORRY IF I BUMPED INTO YOU! IT'S KINDA CROWDED YOU KNOW...
MY FAULT! I'M TOO PASSIVE!
MY THIRD PSYCHO-ANALYST THOUGHT IT WAS BECAUSE OF MY MOTHER BUT MY SEVENTH ONE SAYS IT WAS BECAUSE OF MY FATHER...
... WHO IS THE PRESIDENT OF THE N.Y. PSYCHOLOGICAL INSTITUTE!
EXCUSE ME...
HI THERE! ISN'T IT DISGUSTING THE WAY THIS PLACE IS LITTERED WITH PHONIES!
WHY... YES! I AGREE!
THEY ONLY WANT ONE THING FROM A GIRL AND THEY'RE NOT GOING TO GET IT FROM ME...
... UNLESS THEY USE GENUINE 100% COWHIDE!
EXCUSE ME...
COULD IT POSSIBLY BE THAT I AM NOT GOING TO MEET THE GIRL OF MY DREAMS HERE TONIGHT?
HI!
I CAN'T TALK TO YOU FOR ANOTHER 33 SECONDS!
WHY?
AT MIDNIGHT MY TWENTY-SECOND DIVORCE WILL BE FINAL! ... 29... 30... 31... 32... 33... THERE!
WILL YOU MARRY ME?
EXCUSE ME! EXCUSE ME ALL OF YOU!
BUT SIR, YOU'VE BARELY BEGUN TO DRINK!
I DON'T CARE!
OUT #16 AND AS ALONE AS EVER!
I'VE TRIED EVERYTHING! BARS, DISCOTHEQUES, COMPUTER DATING, EVENING SCHOOL, THE THEDA BARA FAN CLUB... NOTHING WORKS!
MAYBE I HAVE BAD BREATHS OR SOMETHING!
IT'S ALL MY FAULT FOR NOT HAVING ASKED TWO-HEADED IRMA TO VERNAL EQUINOX WEEKEND AT COLLEGE!
WHY... WHY... I DON'T BELIEVE IT! TWO-HEADED IRMA HERE IN NEW YORK!
SAM! FANCY RUNNING INTO YOU!
LATER
AND REMEMBER HOW WE USED TO ALWAYS TALK ABOUT HIGH SCHOOL AFTER ANTHROPOLOGY 112!
HOW COULD I FORGET IT, SAM?
AND THAT EVENING ON THE SCHOOL NEWSPAPER WHEN I SPILLED PRINTER'S INK ALL OVER THE SCHOOL MASCOT!
THE DEAN WAS SO ANGRY, TEE HEE!
IRMA, THE SIXTIES ARE ALMOST OVER! I'LL START BALDING SOON...
... AND I FIND I NEED MORE SHAMPOO THAN I USED TO...
MAY I... MAY I SEE MORE OF YOU?
OF COURSE, SAM...
MEET ME TONIGHT AT "WEEKDAYS"! THEY HAVE THE GROOVIEST CROWD...

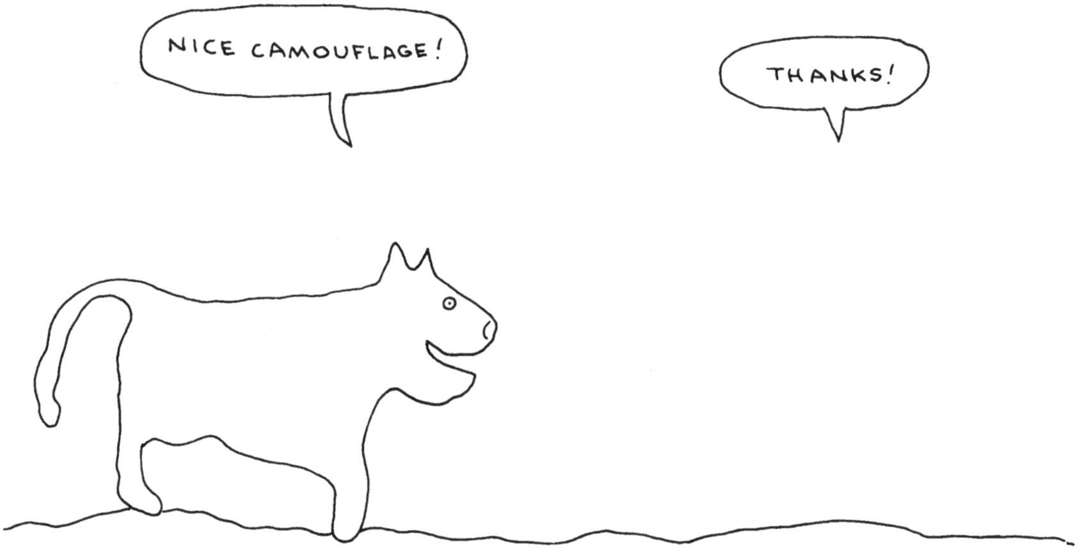
NICE CAMOUFLAGE!
THANKS!

THE PEOPLE YOU PASS ON THE STREET... WHAT THEY'RE THINKING

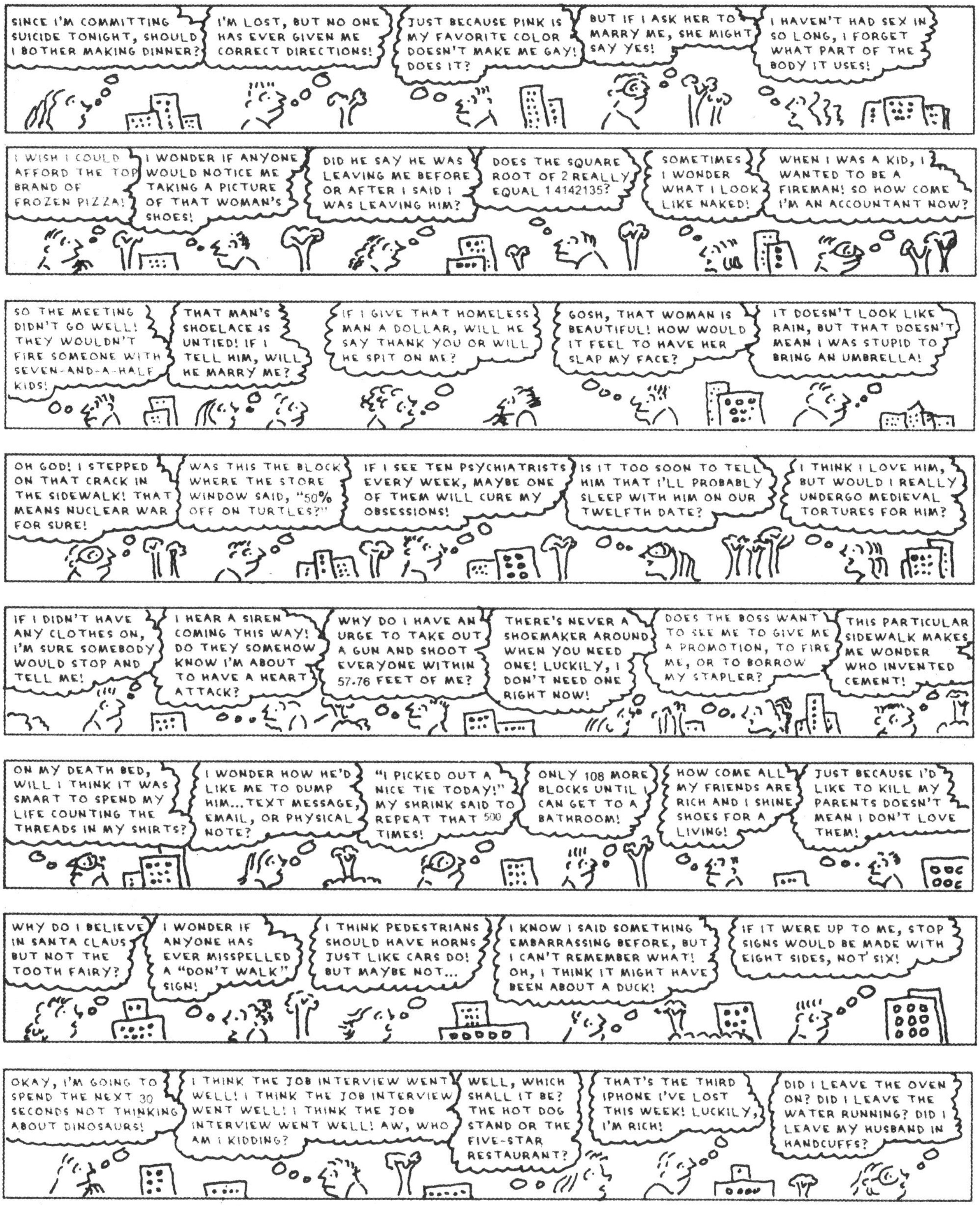

SINCE I'M COMMITTING SUICIDE TONIGHT, SHOULD I BOTHER MAKING DINNER?
I'M LOST, BUT NO ONE HAS EVER GIVEN ME CORRECT DIRECTIONS!
JUST BECAUSE PINK IS MY FAVORITE COLOR DOESN'T MAKE ME GAY! DOES IT?
BUT IF I ASK HER TO MARRY ME, SHE MIGHT SAY YES!
I HAVEN'T HAD SEX IN SO LONG, I FORGET WHAT PART OF THE BODY IT USES!
I WISH I COULD AFFORD THE TOP BRAND OF FROZEN PIZZA!
I WONDER IF ANYONE WOULD NOTICE ME TAKING A PICTURE OF THAT WOMAN'S SHOES!
DID HE SAY HE WAS LEAVING ME BEFORE OR AFTER I SAID I WAS LEAVING HIM?
DOES THE SQUARE ROOT OF 2 REALLY EQUAL 1.4142135?
SOMETIMES I WONDER WHAT I LOOK LIKE NAKED!
WHEN I WAS A KID, I WANTED TO BE A FIREMAN! SO HOW COME I'M AN ACCOUNTANT NOW?
SO THE MEETING DIDN'T GO WELL! THEY WOULDN'T FIRE SOMEONE WITH SEVEN-AND-A-HALF KIDS!
THAT MAN'S SHOELACE IS UNTIED! IF I TELL HIM, WILL HE MARRY ME?
IF I GIVE THAT HOMELESS MAN A DOLLAR, WILL HE SAY THANK YOU OR WILL HE SPIT ON ME?
GOSH, THAT WOMAN IS BEAUTIFUL! HOW WOULD IT FEEL TO HAVE HER SLAP MY FACE?
IT DOESN'T LOOK LIKE RAIN, BUT THAT DOESN'T MEAN I WAS STUPID TO BRING AN UMBRELLA!
OH GOD! I STEPPED ON THAT CRACK IN THE SIDEWALK! THAT MEANS NUCLEAR WAR FOR SURE!
WAS THIS THE BLOCK WHERE THE STORE WINDOW SAID, "50% OFF ON TURTLES?"
IF I SEE TEN PSYCHIATRISTS EVERY WEEK, MAYBE ONE OF THEM WILL CURE MY OBSESSIONS!
IS IT TOO SOON TO TELL HIM THAT I'LL PROBABLY SLEEP WITH HIM ON OUR TWELFTH DATE?
I THINK I LOVE HIM, BUT WOULD I REALLY UNDERGO MEDIEVAL TORTURES FOR HIM?
IF I DIDN'T HAVE ANY CLOTHES ON, I'M SURE SOMEBODY WOULD STOP AND TELL ME!
I HEAR A SIREN COMING THIS WAY! DO THEY SOMEHOW KNOW I'M ABOUT TO HAVE A HEART ATTACK?
WHY DO I HAVE AN URGE TO TAKE OUT A GUN AND SHOOT EVERYONE WITHIN 57.76 FEET OF ME?
THERE'S NEVER A SHOEMAKER AROUND WHEN YOU NEED ONE! LUCKILY, I DON'T NEED ONE RIGHT NOW!
DOES THE BOSS WANT TO SEE ME TO GIVE ME A PROMOTION, TO FIRE ME, OR TO BORROW MY STAPLER?
THIS PARTICULAR SIDEWALK MAKES ME WONDER WHO INVENTED CEMENT!
ON MY DEATH BED, WILL I THINK IT WAS SMART TO SPEND MY LIFE COUNTING THE THREADS IN MY SHIRTS?
I WONDER HOW HE'D LIKE ME TO DUMP HIM...TEXT MESSAGE, EMAIL, OR PHYSICAL NOTE?
"I PICKED OUT A NICE TIE TODAY!" MY SHRINK SAID TO REPEAT THAT 500 TIMES!
ONLY 108 MORE BLOCKS UNTIL I CAN GET TO A BATHROOM!
HOW COME ALL MY FRIENDS ARE RICH AND I SHINE SHOES FOR A LIVING!
JUST BECAUSE I'D LIKE TO KILL MY PARENTS DOESN'T MEAN I DON'T LOVE THEM!
WHY DO I BELIEVE IN SANTA CLAUS BUT NOT THE TOOTH FAIRY?
I WONDER IF ANYONE HAS EVER MISSPELLED A "DON'T WALK" SIGN!
I THINK PEDESTRIANS SHOULD HAVE HORNS JUST LIKE CARS DO! BUT MAYBE NOT...
I KNOW I SAID SOMETHING EMBARRASSING BEFORE, BUT I CAN'T REMEMBER WHAT! OH, I THINK IT MIGHT HAVE BEEN ABOUT A DUCK!
IF IT WERE UP TO ME, STOP SIGNS WOULD BE MADE WITH EIGHT SIDES, NOT SIX!
OKAY, I'M GOING TO SPEND THE NEXT 30 SECONDS NOT THINKING ABOUT DINOSAURS!
I THINK THE JOB INTERVIEW WENT WELL! I THINK THE JOB INTERVIEW WENT WELL! I THINK THE JOB INTERVIEW WENT WELL! AW, WHO AM I KIDDING?
WELL, WHICH SHALL IT BE? THE HOT DOG STAND OR THE FIVE-STAR RESTAURANT?
THAT'S THE THIRD IPHONE I'VE LOST THIS WEEK! LUCKILY, I'M RICH!
DID I LEAVE THE OVEN ON? DID I LEAVE THE WATER RUNNING? DID I LEAVE MY HUSBAND IN HANDCUFFS?

IN THE SKYSCRAPER!

IS THAT THE OCEAN I'M SEEING OR A WATER-MAIN BREAK?
PHILLIPS, IF YOU DON'T GET THAT REPORT DONE BY MIDNIGHT, DON'T BOTHER COMING BACK AT FOUR A.M.!
THE TAKE-OUT PLACE SENT IT TO THE WRONG FLOOR, WRONG BUILDING, WRONG CITY!
I'M HERE TO REPLACE THE WATER COOLER WITH A DESK!
MISS, SINCE WE'RE STUCK IN AN ELEVATOR TOGETHER, AND HELP MAY NOT ARRIVE FOR HOURS, WOULD YOU LIKE TO SEE MY IMITATION OF A GORILLA?
YES SIR! YES SIR! YES SIR! YOU BET, SIR! RIGHT ON IT, SIR!
IS IT FRIDAY YET?
NO, BUT I HAVE A FEELING IT MIGHT BE CHRISTMAS...
YOU KNOW, YOU REALLY SHOULD PULL DOWN THE BLINDS BEFORE YOU TAKE YOUR SHOES OFF!
I'VE BEEN WORKING SO HARD I HAVEN'T SEEN MY FAMILY IN WEEKS!
I THINK I MIGHT HAVE A FAMILY, TOO...
I'M THE BUILDING INSPECTOR! YEP, IT SURE DOES LOOK LIKE A BUILDING!
BUT IF YOU FIRE ME, MY FAMILY WILL STARVE!
YOU JUST REMINDED ME THAT I HAVE A DINNER RESERVATION...
CAN SOMEBODY PLEASE TELL ME WHICH CUBICLE IS NUMBER 986?
CAN I GO TO HUMAN RESOURCES EVEN THOUGH I HAVE A CAT?
I HEAR THE ENTIRE BOARD WAS ARRESTED FOR EMBEZZLING!
DOES THAT MEAN WE CAN GO HOME EARLY?
IF I JUMP, WILL ANYONE MISS ME? ESPECIALLY MY TWO WIVES?
HEY, CLOSE THAT WINDOW! THE POLLUTION IS TERRIBLE ABOVE THE THIRTIETH FLOOR!
COULD I HAVE THE KEY TO THE MEN'S ROOM?
SORRY, NOBODY'S SEEN IT FOR WEEKS!
MY PAPER PLANE STAYED OUT LONGER THAN YOURS DID!
TOO BAD I'M YOUR BOSS...
THAT'S THE THIRD NEW CEO WE'VE HAD THIS MORNING!
I DON'T PAY YOU TO WATCH BALLGAMES ON A COMPANY COMPUTER!
THAT'S OKAY, BECAUSE I DON'T WORK HERE!
I'M BORED!
I'M SO BORED!
GOD, AM I BORED!
I'D GLADLY GIVE YOU A RAISE, HARRIS, IF I HADN'T JUST GIVEN MYSELF ONE!
WHAT ARE YOU DOING?
COUNTING THE BRICKS IN THE BUILDING ACROSS THE WAY!
OH, I DID THAT YESTERDAY!
PETERSON, I'M TRIPLING YOUR WORKLOAD AND HALVING YOUR SALARY! ALSO, CAN YOU LOAN ME A TWENTY?
SOME DAY YOU'LL HAVE A KEY TO THE EXECUTIVE MEN'S ROOM!
BUT I NEED TO GO TO THE BATHROOM NOW!
I'D LIKE TO RETIRE AT SEVENTY!
BUT YOU'RE ALREADY EIGHTY-FIVE!
IF I WORKED ON A HIGHER FLOOR, WOULD I FEEL MORE IMPORTANT?
SORRY, MA'AM, BUT ALL OF THE COMPANIES IN THIS BUILDING WENT OUT OF BUSINESS THIS MORNING!

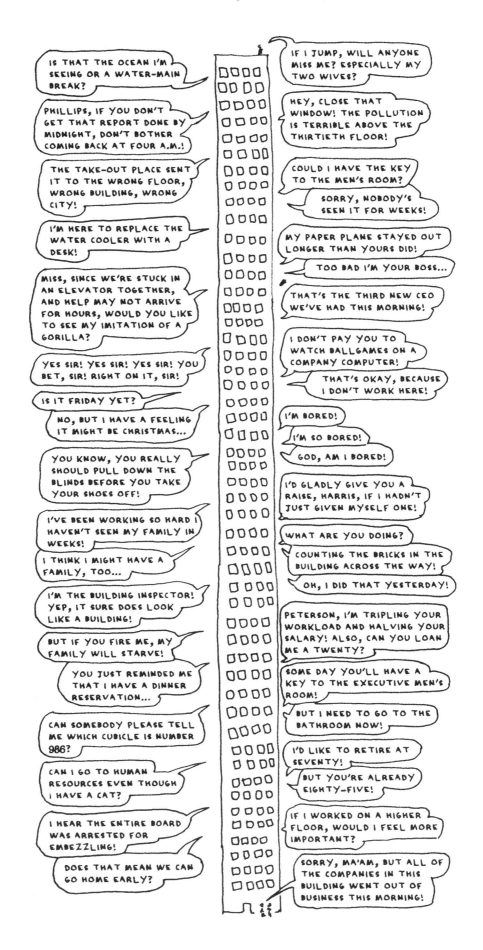

STOP SEARCHING. STOP BROWSING. FOR YOUR CONVENIENCE, HERE IS

THE ENTIRE INTERNET ON A PAGE

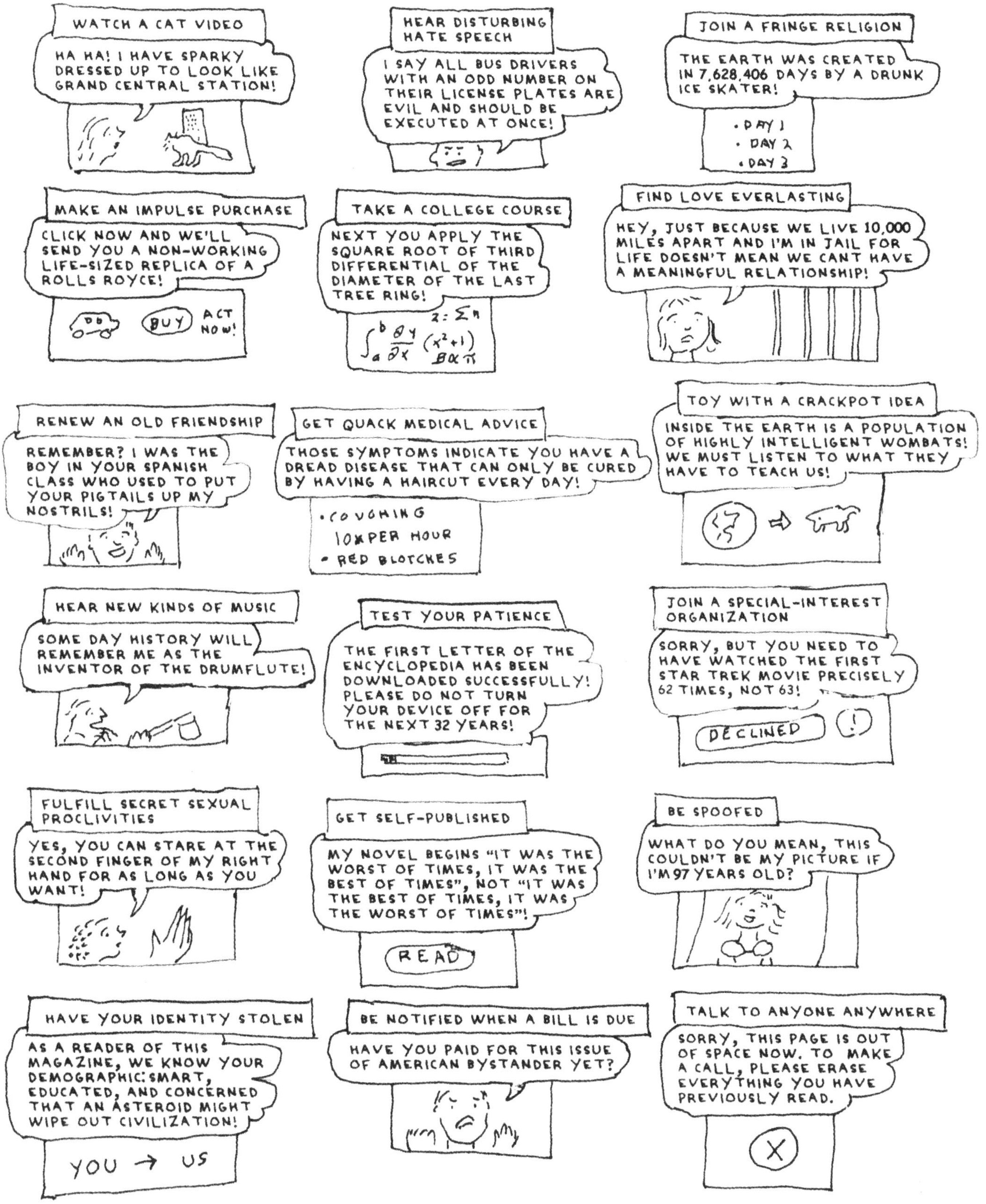
WATCH A CAT VIDEO
HA HA! I HAVE SPARKY DRESSED UP TO LOOK LIKE GRAND CENTRAL STATION!
HEAR DISTURBING HATE SPEECH
I SAY ALL BUS DRIVERS WITH AN ODD NUMBER ON THEIR LICENSE PLATES ARE EVIL AND SHOULD BE EXECUTED AT ONCE!
JOIN A FRINGE RELIGION
THE EARTH WAS CREATED IN 7,628,406 DAYS BY A DRUNK ICE SKATER!
• DAY 1
• DAY 2
• DAY 3
MAKE AN IMPULSE PURCHASE
CLICK NOW AND WE'LL SEND YOU A NON-WORKING LIFE-SIZED REPLICA OF A ROLLS ROYCE!
BUY
ACT NOW!
TAKE A COLLEGE COURSE
NEXT YOU APPLY THE SQUARE ROOT OF THIRD DIFFERENTIAL OF THE DIAMETER OF THE LAST TREE RING!
FIND LOVE EVERLASTING
HEY, JUST BECAUSE WE LIVE 10,000 MILES APART AND I'M IN JAIL FOR LIFE DOESN'T MEAN WE CANT HAVE A MEANINGFUL RELATIONSHIP!
RENEW AN OLD FRIENDSHIP
REMEMBER? I WAS THE BOY IN YOUR SPANISH CLASS WHO USED TO PUT YOUR PIGTAILS UP MY NOSTRILS!
GET QUACK MEDICAL ADVICE
THOSE SYMPTOMS INDICATE YOU HAVE A DREAD DISEASE THAT CAN ONLY BE CURED BY HAVING A HAIRCUT EVERY DAY!
• COUGHING 10X PER HOUR
• RED BLOTCHES
TOY WITH A CRACKPOT IDEA
INSIDE THE EARTH IS A POPULATION OF HIGHLY INTELLIGENT WOMBATS! WE MUST LISTEN TO WHAT THEY HAVE TO TEACH US!
HEAR NEW KINDS OF MUSIC
SOME DAY HISTORY WILL REMEMBER ME AS THE INVENTOR OF THE DRUMFLUTE!
TEST YOUR PATIENCE
THE FIRST LETTER OF THE ENCYCLOPEDIA HAS BEEN DOWNLOADED SUCCESSFULLY! PLEASE DO NOT TURN YOUR DEVICE OFF FOR THE NEXT 32 YEARS!
JOIN A SPECIAL-INTEREST ORGANIZATION
SORRY, BUT YOU NEED TO HAVE WATCHED THE FIRST STAR TREK MOVIE PRECISELY 62 TIMES, NOT 63!
DECLINED
FULFILL SECRET SEXUAL PROCLIVITIES
YES, YOU CAN STARE AT THE SECOND FINGER OF MY RIGHT HAND FOR AS LONG AS YOU WANT!
GET SELF-PUBLISHED
MY NOVEL BEGINS "IT WAS THE WORST OF TIMES, IT WAS THE BEST OF TIMES", NOT "IT WAS THE BEST OF TIMES, IT WAS THE WORST OF TIMES"!
READ
BE SPOOFED
WHAT DO YOU MEAN, THIS COULDN'T BE MY PICTURE IF I'M 97 YEARS OLD?
HAVE YOUR IDENTITY STOLEN
AS A READER OF THIS MAGAZINE, WE KNOW YOUR DEMOGRAPHIC: SMART, EDUCATED, AND CONCERNED THAT AN ASTEROID MIGHT WIPE OUT CIVILIZATION!
YOU → US
BE NOTIFIED WHEN A BILL IS DUE
HAVE YOU PAID FOR THIS ISSUE OF AMERICAN BYSTANDER YET?
TALK TO ANYONE ANYWHERE
SORRY, THIS PAGE IS OUT OF SPACE NOW. TO MAKE A CALL, PLEASE ERASE EVERYTHING YOU HAVE PREVIOUSLY READ.

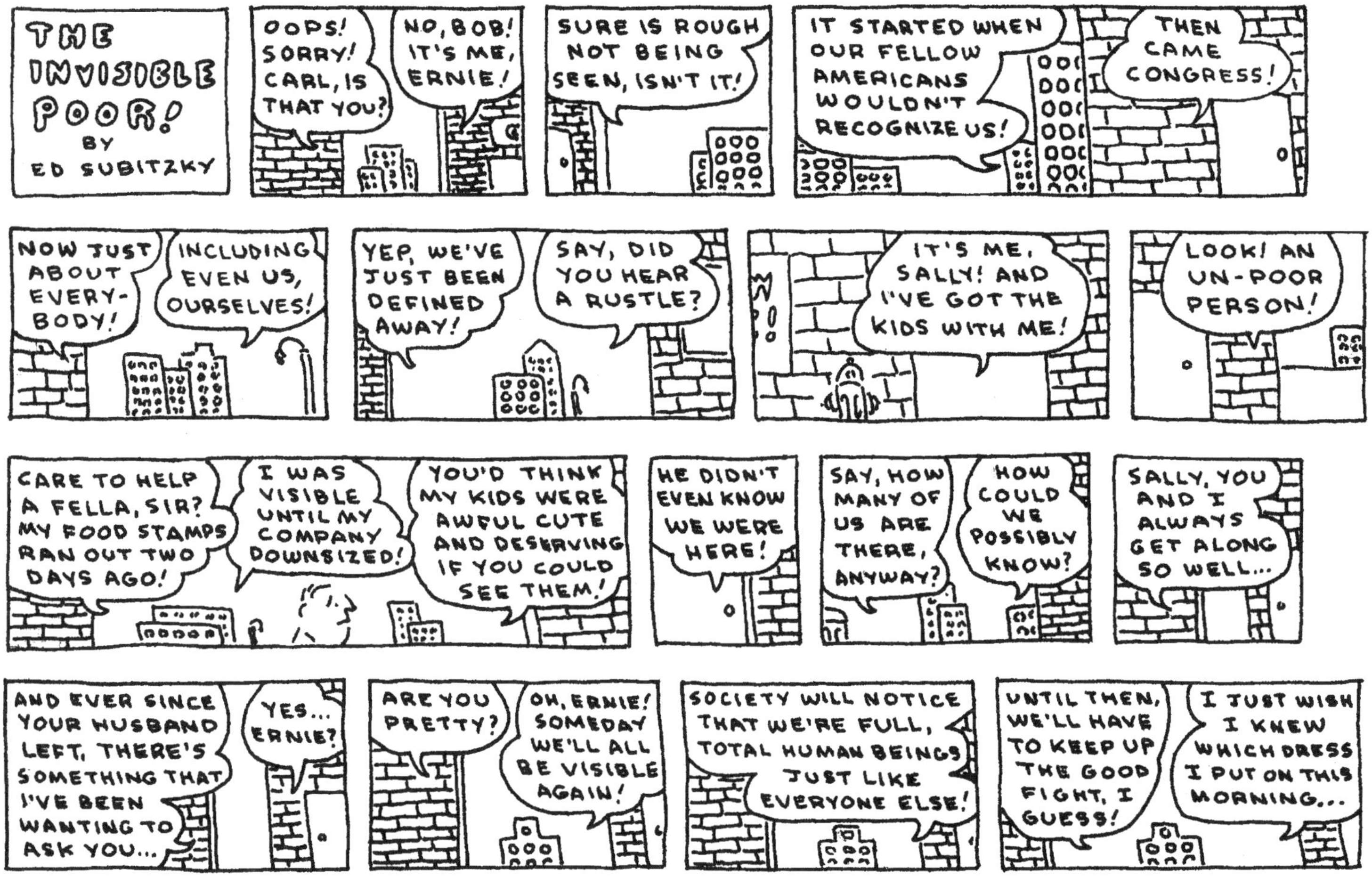
THE INVISIBLE POOR!
BY
ED SUBITZKY
OOPS! SORRY! CARL, IS THAT YOU?
NO, BOB! IT'S ME, ERNIE!
SURE IS ROUGH NOT BEING SEEN, ISN'T IT!
IT STARTED WHEN OUR FELLOW AMERICANS WOULDN'T RECOGNIZE US!
THEN CAME CONGRESS!
NOW JUST ABOUT EVERY-BODY!
INCLUDING EVEN US, OURSELVES!
YEP, WE'VE JUST BEEN DEFINED AWAY!
SAY, DID YOU HEAR A RUSTLE?
IT'S ME, SALLY! AND I'VE GOT THE KIDS WITH ME!
LOOK! AN UN-POOR PERSON!
CARE TO HELP A FELLA, SIR? MY FOOD STAMPS RAN OUT TWO DAYS AGO!
I WAS VISIBLE UNTIL MY COMPANY DOWNSIZED!
YOU'D THINK MY KIDS WERE AWFUL CUTE AND DESERVING IF YOU COULD SEE THEM!
HE DIDN'T EVEN KNOW WE WERE HERE!
SAY, HOW MANY OF US ARE THERE, ANYWAY?
HOW COULD WE POSSIBLY KNOW?
SALLY, YOU AND I ALWAYS GET ALONG SO WELL...
AND EVER SINCE YOUR HUSBAND LEFT, THERE'S SOMETHING THAT I'VE BEEN WANTING TO ASK YOU...
YES... ERNIE?
ARE YOU PRETTY?
OH, ERNIE! SOMEDAY WE'LL ALL BE VISIBLE AGAIN!
SOCIETY WILL NOTICE THAT WE'RE FULL, TOTAL HUMAN BEINGS JUST LIKE EVERYONE ELSE!
UNTIL THEN, WE'LL HAVE TO KEEP UP THE GOOD FIGHT, I GUESS!
I JUST WISH I KNEW WHICH DRESS I PUT ON THIS MORNING...

TAKE A WALK WITH
MR. ANXIETY

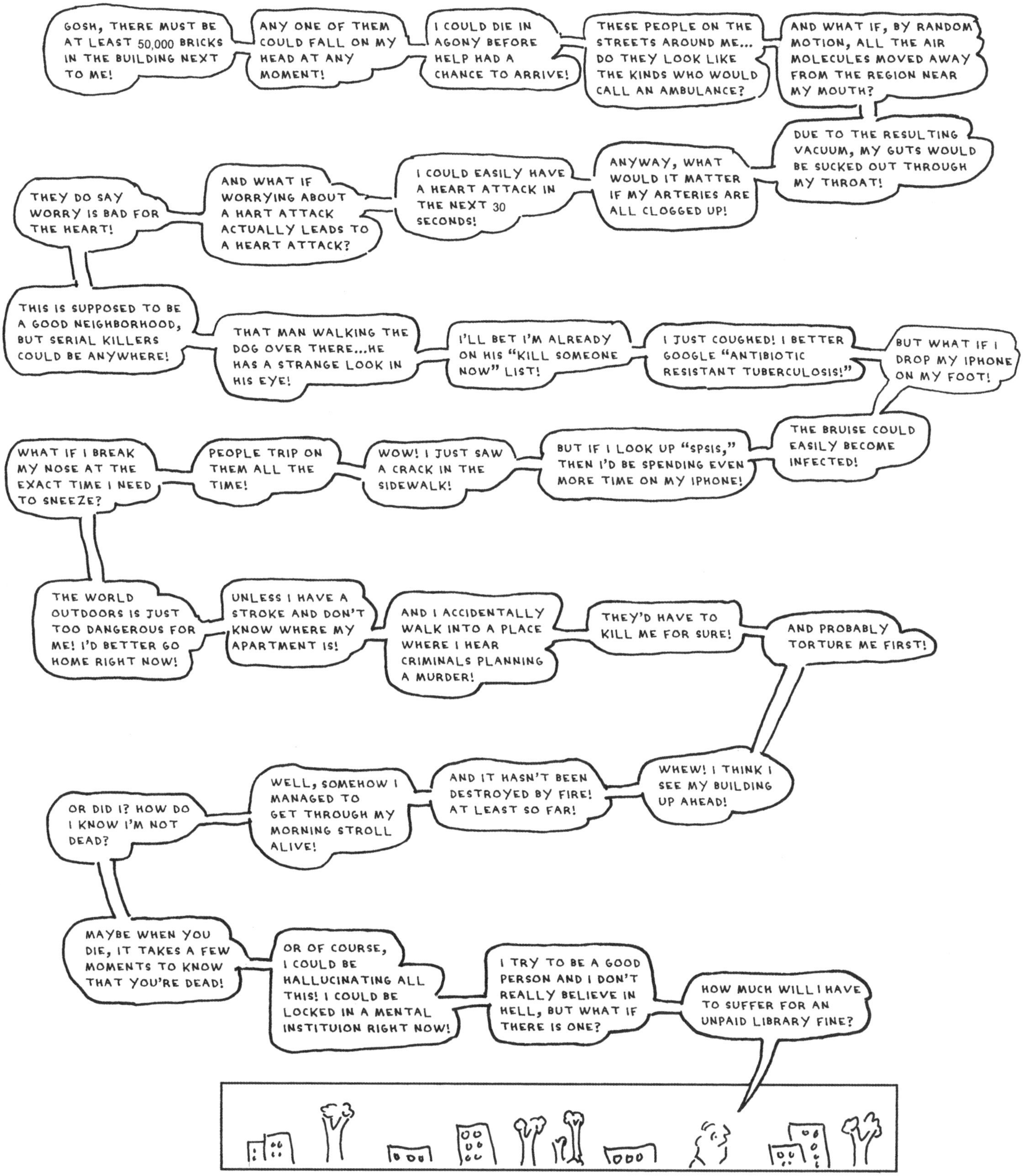
GOSH, THERE MUST BE AT LEAST 50,000 BRICKS IN THE BUILDING NEXT TO ME!
ANY ONE OF THEM COULD FALL ON MY HEAD AT ANY MOMENT!
I COULD DIE IN AGONY BEFORE HELP HAD A CHANCE TO ARRIVE!
THESE PEOPLE ON THE STREETS AROUND ME... DO THEY LOOK LIKE THE KINDS WHO WOULD CALL AN AMBULANCE?
AND WHAT IF, BY RANDOM MOTION, ALL THE AIR MOLECULES MOVED AWAY FROM THE REGION NEAR MY MOUTH?
DUE TO THE RESULTING VACUUM, MY GUTS WOULD BE SUCKED OUT THROUGH MY THROAT!
ANYWAY, WHAT WOULD IT MATTER IF MY ARTERIES ARE ALL CLOGGED UP!
I COULD EASILY HAVE A HEART ATTACK IN THE NEXT 30 SECONDS!
AND WHAT IF WORRYING ABOUT A HART ATTACK ACTUALLY LEADS TO A HEART ATTACK?
THEY DO SAY WORRY IS BAD FOR THE HEART!
THIS IS SUPPOSED TO BE A GOOD NEIGHBORHOOD, BUT SERIAL KILLERS COULD BE ANYWHERE!
THAT MAN WALKING THE DOG OVER THERE...HE HAS A STRANGE LOOK IN HIS EYE!
I'LL BET I'M ALREADY ON HIS "KILL SOMEONE NOW" LIST!
I JUST COUGHED! I BETTER GOOGLE "ANTIBIOTIC RESISTANT TUBERCULOSIS!"
BUT WHAT IF I DROP MY IPHONE ON MY FOOT!
THE BRUISE COULD EASILY BECOME INFECTED!
BUT IF I LOOK UP "SPSIS," THEN I'D BE SPENDING EVEN MORE TIME ON MY IPHONE!
WOW! I JUST SAW A CRACK IN THE SIDEWALK!
PEOPLE TRIP ON THEM ALL THE TIME!
WHAT IF I BREAK MY NOSE AT THE EXACT TIME I NEED TO SNEEZE?
THE WORLD OUTDOORS IS JUST TOO DANGEROUS FOR ME! I'D BETTER GO HOME RIGHT NOW!
UNLESS I HAVE A STROKE AND DON'T KNOW WHERE MY APARTMENT IS!
AND I ACCIDENTALLY WALK INTO A PLACE WHERE I HEAR CRIMINALS PLANNING A MURDER!
THEY'D HAVE TO KILL ME FOR SURE!
AND PROBABLY TORTURE ME FIRST!
WHEW! I THINK I SEE MY BUILDING UP AHEAD!
AND IT HASN'T BEEN DESTROYED BY FIRE! AT LEAST SO FAR!
WELL, SOMEHOW I MANAGED TO GET THROUGH MY MORNING STROLL ALIVE!
OR DID I? HOW DO I KNOW I'M NOT DEAD?
MAYBE WHEN YOU DIE, IT TAKES A FEW MOMENTS TO KNOW THAT YOU'RE DEAD!
OR OF COURSE, I COULD BE HALLUCINATING ALL THIS! I COULD BE LOCKED IN A MENTAL INSTITUION RIGHT NOW!
I TRY TO BE A GOOD PERSON AND I DON'T REALLY BELIEVE IN HELL, BUT WHAT IF THERE IS ONE?
HOW MUCH WILL I HAVE TO SUFFER FOR AN UNPAID LIBRARY FINE?

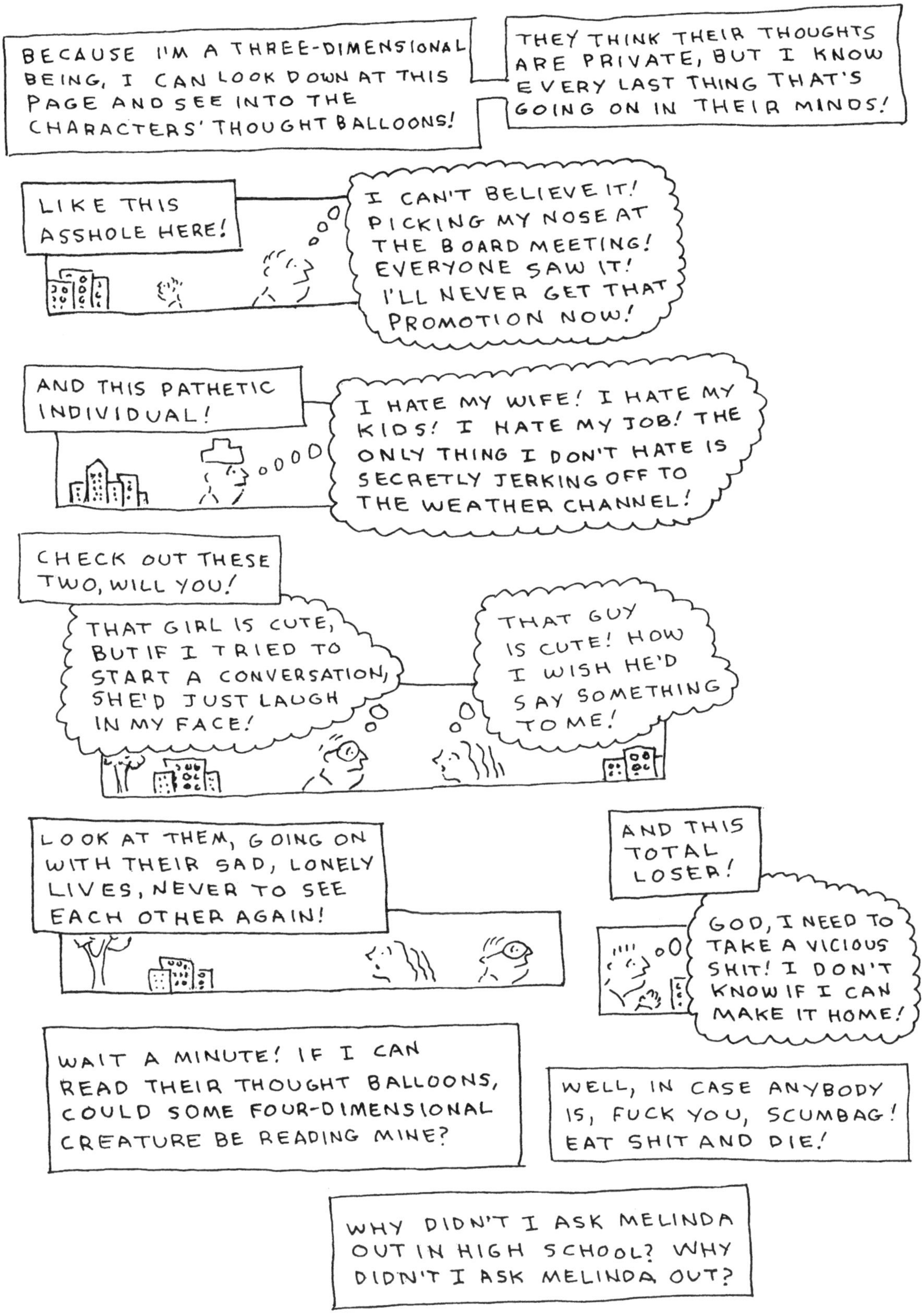

BECAUSE I'M A THREE-DIMENSIONAL BEING, I CAN LOOK DOWN AT THIS PAGE AND SEE INTO THE CHARACTERS' THOUGHT BALLOONS!
THEY THINK THEIR THOUGHTS ARE PRIVATE, BUT I KNOW EVERY LAST THING THAT'S GOING ON IN THEIR MINDS!
LIKE THIS ASSHOLE HERE!
I CAN'T BELIEVE IT! PICKING MY NOSE AT THE BOARD MEETING! EVERYONE SAW IT! I'LL NEVER GET THAT PROMOTION NOW!
AND THIS PATHETIC INDIVIDUAL!
I HATE MY WIFE! I HATE MY KIDS! I HATE MY JOB! THE ONLY THING I DON'T HATE IS SECRETLY JERKING OFF TO THE WEATHER CHANNEL!
CHECK OUT THESE TWO, WILL YOU!
THAT GIRL IS CUTE, BUT IF I TRIED TO START A CONVERSATION, SHE'D JUST LAUGH IN MY FACE!
THAT GUY IS CUTE! HOW I WISH HE'D SAY SOMETHING TO ME!
LOOK AT THEM, GOING ON WITH THEIR SAD, LONELY LIVES, NEVER TO SEE EACH OTHER AGAIN!
AND THIS TOTAL LOSER!
GOD, I NEED TO TAKE A VICIOUS SHIT! I DON'T KNOW IF I CAN MAKE IT HOME!
WAIT A MINUTE! IF I CAN READ THEIR THOUGHT BALLOONS, COULD SOME FOUR-DIMENSIONAL CREATURE BE READING MINE?
WELL, IN CASE ANYBODY IS, FUCK YOU, SCUMBAG! EAT SHIT AND DIE!
WHY DIDN'T I ASK MELINDA OUT IN HIGH SCHOOL? WHY DIDN'T I ASK MELINDA OUT?

AGONY COMICS

INDULGE YOUR INNER SADIST BY WATCHING OTHER PEOPLE SUFFER

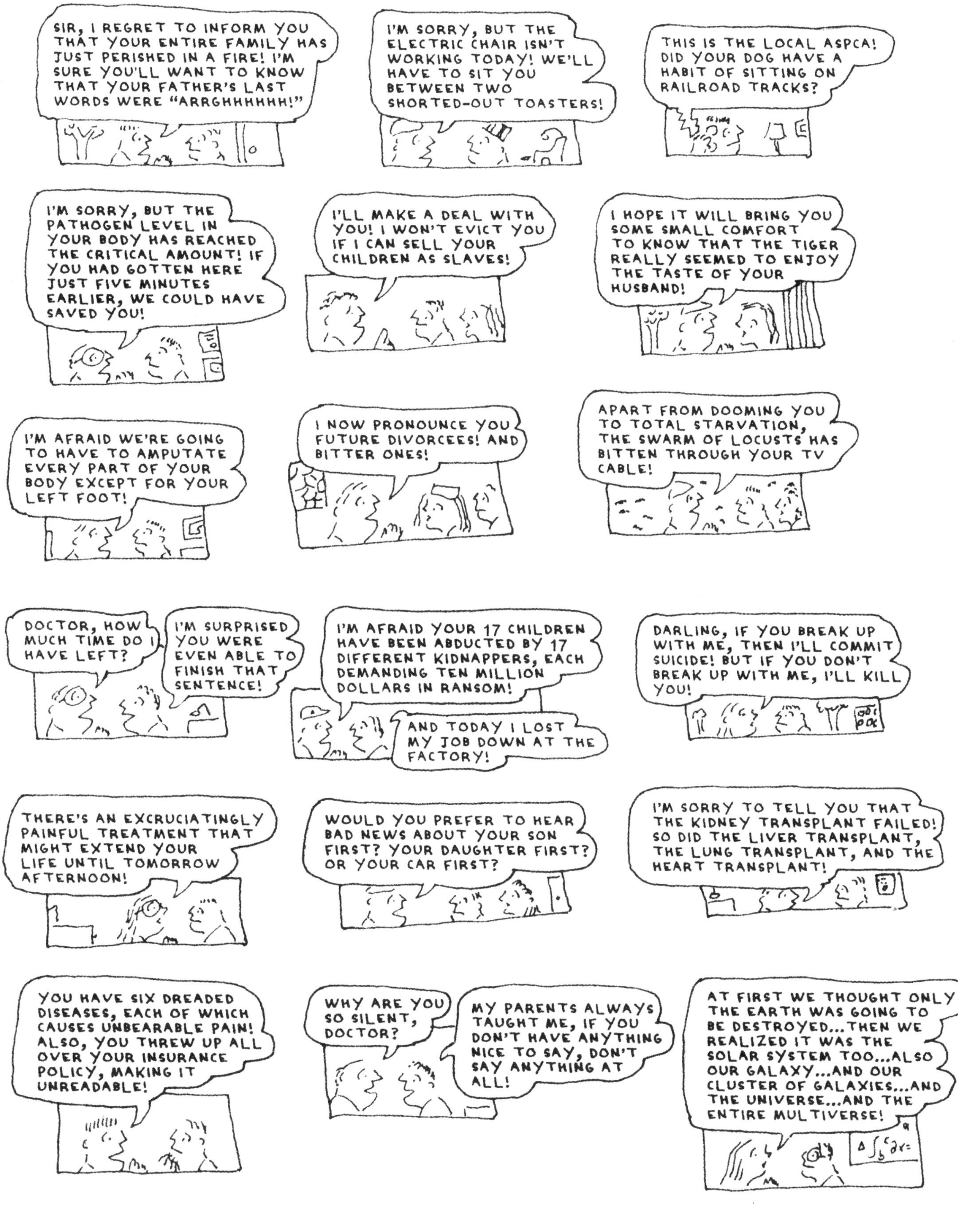
SIR, I REGRET TO INFORM YOU THAT YOUR ENTIRE FAMILY HAS JUST PERISHED IN A FIRE! I'M SURE YOU'LL WANT TO KNOW THAT YOUR FATHER'S LAST WORDS WERE "ARRGHHHHHH!"
I'M SORRY, BUT THE ELECTRIC CHAIR ISN'T WORKING TODAY! WE'LL HAVE TO SIT YOU BETWEEN TWO SHORTED-OUT TOASTERS!
THIS IS THE LOCAL ASPCA! DID YOUR DOG HAVE A HABIT OF SITTING ON RAILROAD TRACKS?
I'M SORRY, BUT THE PATHOGEN LEVEL IN YOUR BODY HAS REACHED THE CRITICAL AMOUNT! IF YOU HAD GOTTEN HERE JUST FIVE MINUTES EARLIER, WE COULD HAVE SAVED YOU!
I'LL MAKE A DEAL WITH YOU! I WON'T EVICT YOU IF I CAN SELL YOUR CHILDREN AS SLAVES!
I HOPE IT WILL BRING YOU SOME SMALL COMFORT TO KNOW THAT THE TIGER REALLY SEEMED TO ENJOY THE TASTE OF YOUR HUSBAND!
I'M AFRAID WE'RE GOING TO HAVE TO AMPUTATE EVERY PART OF YOUR BODY EXCEPT FOR YOUR LEFT FOOT!
I NOW PRONOUNCE YOU FUTURE DIVORCEES! AND BITTER ONES!
APART FROM DOOMING YOU TO TOTAL STARVATION, THE SWARM OF LOCUSTS HAS BITTEN THROUGH YOUR TV CABLE!
DOCTOR, HOW MUCH TIME DO I HAVE LEFT?
I'M SURPRISED YOU WERE EVEN ABLE TO FINISH THAT SENTENCE!
I'M AFRAID YOUR 17 CHILDREN HAVE BEEN ABDUCTED BY 17 DIFFERENT KIDNAPPERS, EACH DEMANDING TEN MILLION DOLLARS IN RANSOM!
AND TODAY I LOST MY JOB DOWN AT THE FACTORY!
DARLING, IF YOU BREAK UP WITH ME, THEN I'LL COMMIT SUICIDE! BUT IF YOU DON'T BREAK UP WITH ME, I'LL KILL YOU!
THERE'S AN EXCRUCIATINGLY PAINFUL TREATMENT THAT MIGHT EXTEND YOUR LIFE UNTIL TOMORROW AFTERNOON!
WOULD YOU PREFER TO HEAR BAD NEWS ABOUT YOUR SON FIRST? YOUR DAUGHTER FIRST? OR YOUR CAR FIRST?
I'M SORRY TO TELL YOU THAT THE KIDNEY TRANSPLANT FAILED! SO DID THE LIVER TRANSPLANT, THE LUNG TRANSPLANT, AND THE HEART TRANSPLANT!
YOU HAVE SIX DREADED DISEASES, EACH OF WHICH CAUSES UNBEARABLE PAIN! ALSO, YOU THREW UP ALL OVER YOUR INSURANCE POLICY, MAKING IT UNREADABLE!
WHY ARE YOU SO SILENT, DOCTOR?
MY PARENTS ALWAYS TAUGHT ME, IF YOU DON'T HAVE ANYTHING NICE TO SAY, DON'T SAY ANYTHING AT ALL!
AT FIRST WE THOUGHT ONLY THE EARTH WAS GOING TO BE DESTROYED...THEN WE REALIZED IT WAS THE SOLAR SYSTEM TOO...ALSO OUR GALAXY...AND OUR CLUSTER OF GALAXIES...AND THE UNIVERSE...AND THE ENTIRE MULTIVERSE!

CONSCIOUSNESS PUZZLE PAGE!

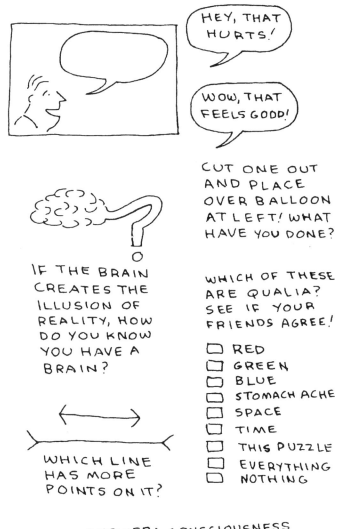

HEY, THAT HURTS!

WOW, THAT FEELS GOOD!

CUT ONE OUT AND PLACE OVER BALLOON AT LEFT! WHAT HAVE YOU DONE?

IF THE BRAIN CREATES THE ILLUSION OF REALITY, HOW DO YOU KNOW YOU HAVE A BRAIN?

WHICH OF THESE ARE QUALIA? SEE IF YOUR FRIENDS AGREE!

- ☐ RED
- ☐ GREEN
- ☐ BLUE
- ☐ STOMACH ACHE
- ☐ SPACE
- ☐ TIME
- ☐ THIS PUZZLE
- ☐ EVERYTHING
- ☐ NOTHING

WHICH LINE HAS MORE POINTS ON IT?

ANSWER: CONSCIOUSNESS FOR QUESTION, TURN PAGE UPSIDE DOWN!

QUESTION: WHAT IS CONSCIOUSNESS?

CONSCIOUSNESS PUZZLE PAGE!

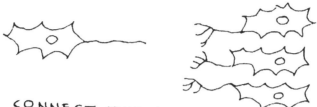

CONNECT THE AXON TO ONE OF THE DENDRITES! HAVE YOU DONE ANYTHING IMMATERIAL?

JIM'S GLOBAL WORKSPACE
JIM'S SPEECH CENTER
MARY'S HEARING CENTER
MARY'S GLOBAL WORKSPACE
MARY'S SPEECH CENTER
JIM'S HEARING CENTER

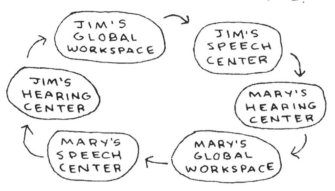

DOES JIM'S GLOBAL WORKSPACE CONNECT ONLY TO HIS OWN BRAIN? FOLLOW THE ARROWS AND SEE!

IS THIS PUZZLE PART OF AN EXTERNAL REALITY? IF IT'S JUST A CREATION OF YOUR MIND, HOW COME YOU CAN'T SOLVE IT?

AND NOW... THE THREE BIGGEST PUZZLES OF ALL!

1. WHY IS THERE SOMETHING INSTEAD OF NOTHING?
2. WHY IS THERE CONSCIOUSNESS INSTEAD OF NOTHING?
3. IS NOTHING A WORD, A THING, OR NOTHING?

"Whaddya mean, you won't help me get down from here?"

MURDER AT THE MANSION!

THE MYSTERY WITH A COMPLETELY ARBITRARY ENDING!

INSTRUCTIONS BEFORE YOU START READING, THINK OF A
SECRET NUMBER BETWEEN 1 AND 8! IF NECESSARY, WRITE IT
DOWN TO BE SURE THAT YOU REMEMBER IT!

NOW GO AHEAD AND SEE IF YOU CAN FIGURE OUT "WHO DUNNIT"!

OUR STORY BEGINS AS WORLD-FAMOUS DETECTIVE PIERRE ROLMAUD IS INVITED TO A GALA SOCIAL EVENT AT THE HOME OF EVERETT FABRILL THE THIRD AND HIS WIFE LADY FABRILL!

THANK YOU FOR JOINING US TONIGHT, MR. ROLMAUD!

LADY FABRILL, IT WILL BE A PLEASURE TO SPEND AN EVENING FREE OF INVESTIGATING GRISLY MURDERS!

THEN PERMIT ME TO INTRODUCE YOU TO YOUR FELLOW GUESTS!

MAY I PRESENT SIR ERNEST HAVERFORD, MILLIONAIRE INDUSTRIALIST!

AND NEXT, JENNIFER CROWLEY, FASHION CONSULTANT TO THE STARS!

COLONEL REGINALD POTTERDAM, A WAR HERO WHOSE FAME KNOWS NO BOUNDS!

ROSANNE HANTLERY, CERTAIN TO WIN THIS YEAR'S ELECTION AS CHANCELLOR!

THE GREAT PARADINI, ACCOMPLISHED STAGE MAGICIAN AND HYPNOTIST!

DAME MAXINE CHESTERFELD, BEST-SELLING AUTHOR OF THE SELF-HELP BOOK "GET IT ALL!"

AND LAST BUT NOT LEAST, PHILIP OULLOT, AN ACTOR KNOWN FOR HIS MASTERFUL PORTRAYALS OF DEPRAVED CRIMINALS!

THE FESTIVITIES OF THE EVENT ARE PROCEEDING NICELY... WHEN SUDDENLY THERE IS A BLOOD-CURDLING SCREAM FROM UPSTAIRS!

THE CHAMBERMAID RUSHES DOWN, SOBBING HYSTERICALLY!

MR. FABRIL... HE...HE'S DEAD!

WELL, I DID NOT EXPECT TO BE CALLED UPON TO SOLVE A CASE TONIGHT, BUT A SLEUTH I AM AND ALWAYS SHALL BE!

I KNOW THIS MAY SEEM INSENSITIVE, LADY FABRILL, BUT I MUST EXAMINE THE BODY AND THE VICTIM'S ROOM AT ONCE! CLUES ARE AT THEIR MOST TELLING WHEN THEY ARE FRESH!

YES (SOB!) I... I UNDERSTAND!

HMMM...

MOST INTERESTING...

AHA!

IT IS ALL BEGINNING TO MAKE SENSE NOW!

A FEW MINUTES LATER...

I HAVE GATHERED YOU ALL TOGETHER HERE IN THE STUDY BECAUSE I, PIERRE ROLMAUD, HAVE ONCE AGAIN UNCOVERED THE IDENTITY OF A COLD-BLOODED KILLER!

IN FACT, AS YOU MAY HAVE SURMISED, THE MURDERER IS HERE IN THIS VERY ROOM WITH US RIGHT NOW!

I AM REFERRING, OF COURSE, TO NONE OTHER THAN...

IMPORTANT:

WHEN YOU GO ON TO THE NEXT PAGE, READ ONLY THE ROW CORRESPONDING TO YOUR SECRET NUMBER! BE SURE TO IGNORE ALL THE OTHER ROWS!

⇨

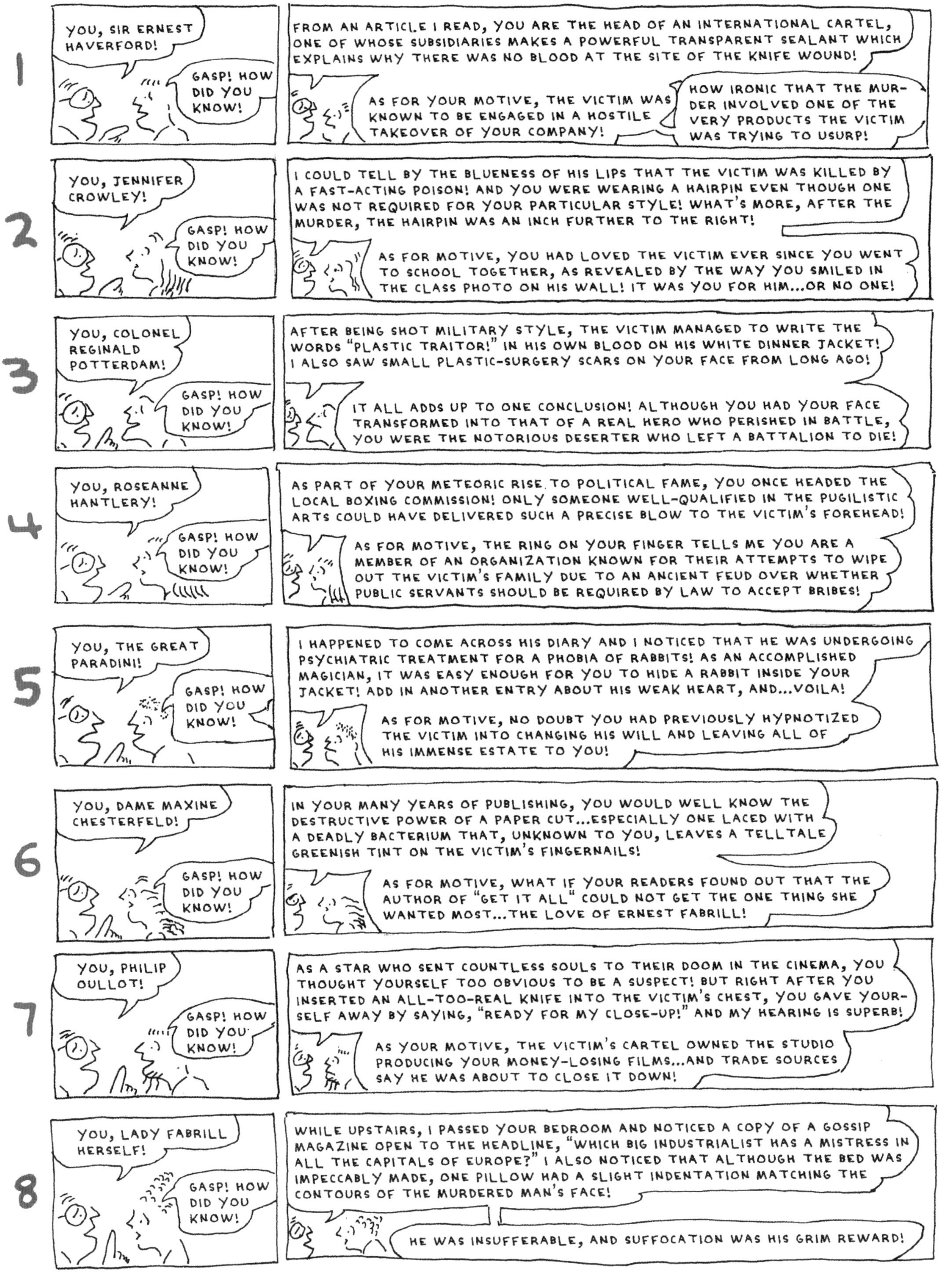
1
YOU, SIR ERNEST HAVERFORD!
GASP! HOW DID YOU KNOW!
FROM AN ARTICLE I READ, YOU ARE THE HEAD OF AN INTERNATIONAL CARTEL, ONE OF WHOSE SUBSIDIARIES MAKES A POWERFUL TRANSPARENT SEALANT WHICH EXPLAINS WHY THERE WAS NO BLOOD AT THE SITE OF THE KNIFE WOUND!
AS FOR YOUR MOTIVE, THE VICTIM WAS KNOWN TO BE ENGAGED IN A HOSTILE TAKEOVER OF YOUR COMPANY!
HOW IRONIC THAT THE MURDER INVOLVED ONE OF THE VERY PRODUCTS THE VICTIM WAS TRYING TO USURP!
2
YOU, JENNIFER CROWLEY!
GASP! HOW DID YOU KNOW!
I COULD TELL BY THE BLUENESS OF HIS LIPS THAT THE VICTIM WAS KILLED BY A FAST-ACTING POISON! AND YOU WERE WEARING A HAIRPIN EVEN THOUGH ONE WAS NOT REQUIRED FOR YOUR PARTICULAR STYLE! WHAT'S MORE, AFTER THE MURDER, THE HAIRPIN WAS AN INCH FURTHER TO THE RIGHT!
AS FOR MOTIVE, YOU HAD LOVED THE VICTIM EVER SINCE YOU WENT TO SCHOOL TOGETHER, AS REVEALED BY THE WAY YOU SMILED IN THE CLASS PHOTO ON HIS WALL! IT WAS YOU FOR HIM...OR NO ONE!
3
YOU, COLONEL REGINALD POTTERDAM!
GASP! HOW DID YOU KNOW!
AFTER BEING SHOT MILITARY STYLE, THE VICTIM MANAGED TO WRITE THE WORDS "PLASTIC TRAITOR!" IN HIS OWN BLOOD ON HIS WHITE DINNER JACKET! I ALSO SAW SMALL PLASTIC-SURGERY SCARS ON YOUR FACE FROM LONG AGO!
IT ALL ADDS UP TO ONE CONCLUSION! ALTHOUGH YOU HAD YOUR FACE TRANSFORMED INTO THAT OF A REAL HERO WHO PERISHED IN BATTLE, YOU WERE THE NOTORIOUS DESERTER WHO LEFT A BATTALION TO DIE!
4
YOU, ROSEANNE HANTLERY!
GASP! HOW DID YOU KNOW!
AS PART OF YOUR METEORIC RISE TO POLITICAL FAME, YOU ONCE HEADED THE LOCAL BOXING COMMISSION! ONLY SOMEONE WELL-QUALIFIED IN THE PUGILISTIC ARTS COULD HAVE DELIVERED SUCH A PRECISE BLOW TO THE VICTIM'S FOREHEAD!
AS FOR MOTIVE, THE RING ON YOUR FINGER TELLS ME YOU ARE A MEMBER OF AN ORGANIZATION KNOWN FOR THEIR ATTEMPTS TO WIPE OUT THE VICTIM'S FAMILY DUE TO AN ANCIENT FEUD OVER WHETHER PUBLIC SERVANTS SHOULD BE REQUIRED BY LAW TO ACCEPT BRIBES!
5
YOU, THE GREAT PARADINI!
GASP! HOW DID YOU KNOW!
I HAPPENED TO COME ACROSS HIS DIARY AND I NOTICED THAT HE WAS UNDERGOING PSYCHIATRIC TREATMENT FOR A PHOBIA OF RABBITS! AS AN ACCOMPLISHED MAGICIAN, IT WAS EASY ENOUGH FOR YOU TO HIDE A RABBIT INSIDE YOUR JACKET! ADD IN ANOTHER ENTRY ABOUT HIS WEAK HEART, AND...VOILA!
AS FOR MOTIVE, NO DOUBT YOU HAD PREVIOUSLY HYPNOTIZED THE VICTIM INTO CHANGING HIS WILL AND LEAVING ALL OF HIS IMMENSE ESTATE TO YOU!
6
YOU, DAME MAXINE CHESTERFELD!
GASP! HOW DID YOU KNOW!
IN YOUR MANY YEARS OF PUBLISHING, YOU WOULD WELL KNOW THE DESTRUCTIVE POWER OF A PAPER CUT...ESPECIALLY ONE LACED WITH A DEADLY BACTERIUM THAT, UNKNOWN TO YOU, LEAVES A TELLTALE GREENISH TINT ON THE VICTIM'S FINGERNAILS!
AS FOR MOTIVE, WHAT IF YOUR READERS FOUND OUT THAT THE AUTHOR OF "GET IT ALL" COULD NOT GET THE ONE THING SHE WANTED MOST...THE LOVE OF ERNEST FABRILL!
7
YOU, PHILIP OULLOT!
GASP! HOW DID YOU KNOW!
AS A STAR WHO SENT COUNTLESS SOULS TO THEIR DOOM IN THE CINEMA, YOU THOUGHT YOURSELF TOO OBVIOUS TO BE A SUSPECT! BUT RIGHT AFTER YOU INSERTED AN ALL-TOO-REAL KNIFE INTO THE VICTIM'S CHEST, YOU GAVE YOURSELF AWAY BY SAYING, "READY FOR MY CLOSE-UP!" AND MY HEARING IS SUPERB!
AS YOUR MOTIVE, THE VICTIM'S CARTEL OWNED THE STUDIO PRODUCING YOUR MONEY-LOSING FILMS...AND TRADE SOURCES SAY HE WAS ABOUT TO CLOSE IT DOWN!
8
YOU, LADY FABRILL HERSELF!
GASP! HOW DID YOU KNOW!
WHILE UPSTAIRS, I PASSED YOUR BEDROOM AND NOTICED A COPY OF A GOSSIP MAGAZINE OPEN TO THE HEADLINE, "WHICH BIG INDUSTRIALIST HAS A MISTRESS IN ALL THE CAPITALS OF EUROPE?" I ALSO NOTICED THAT ALTHOUGH THE BED WAS IMPECCABLY MADE, ONE PILLOW HAD A SLIGHT INDENTATION MATCHING THE CONTOURS OF THE MURDERED MAN'S FACE!
HE WAS INSUFFERABLE, AND SUFFOCATION WAS HIS GRIM REWARD!

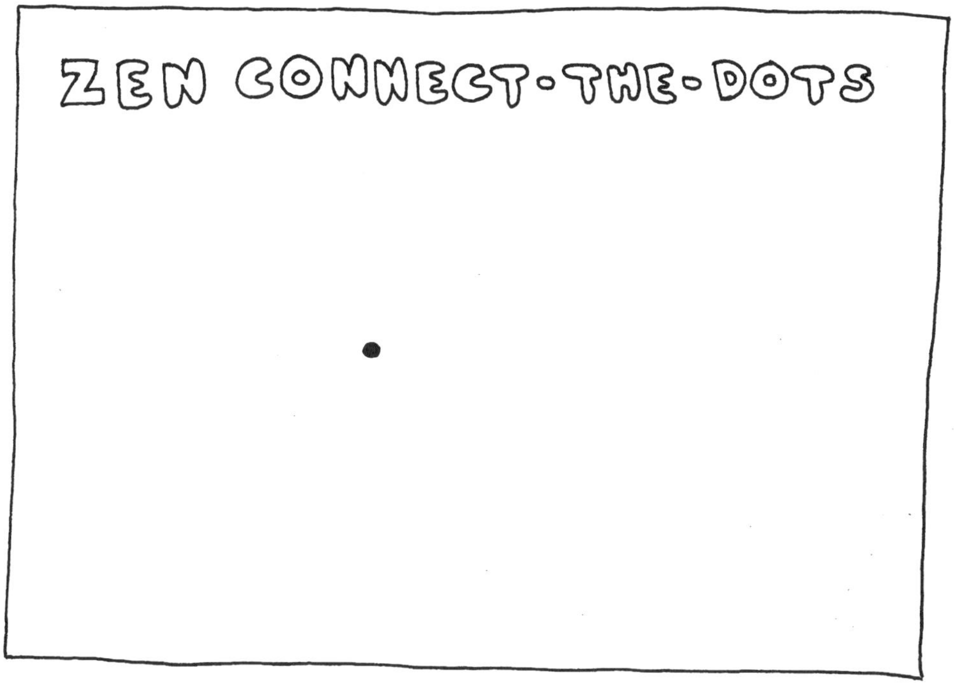
ZEN CONNECT-THE-DOTS

MN: Do you still make comics?

ES: I don't know what kind of thing this is to say, but I've found that as I've gotten older now, I've gotten less interested in doing things like that and more interested in learning.

I'm trying to spend my time understanding the world and reading about stuff like that. I don't have the itch to draw—I probably shouldn't be undercutting myself like that, but it is true. I wonder if that happens to a lot of people my age. We won't name the birthday that's coming up, I don't want to hear it. But if an opportunity comes along, I will jump on it.

MN: What's the most important thing I didn't ask you about?

ES: Susan.[21]

MN: Please, tell us!

ES: She walked into my life and was great for me as a person and as a cartoonist.[22]

In the cartooning part of our lives, Susan really knows when something works and something doesn't. I have complete confidence when I give her something that she's going to know if it's good, and if it's not working she's going to let me know, in a nice way, but she's going to let me know. I have to say, my biggest influence is who's sitting next to me.

---

[21]Susan Hewitt is a dedicated naturalist who was born in England, five miles from Charles Darwin's house. She has published sixty academic papers, mostly about seashells. She taught at Yale and has also been actively involved in the arts. She ended up married to a cartoonist, even though her mother forbade her to read comic books for fear she would become a juvenile delinquent.

[22]They met at a fund-raising event for *Science News* (they were both subscribers).

MN: Why is this the first anthology of Ed Subitzky's work?

ES: I put it down to my personality. I'm not an aggressive person. I just take stuff and put it away in drawers and I say, "How nice," and I don't promote it. And as the years go by, you do not have the energy you used to have. So probably when I was younger, when I was at an age I could've run around more and approached people, there could have been an earlier collection.

I remember one person said to me once: if I had the contacts you have, I'd be world famous now. I remember that distinctly. I don't have the kind of personality that runs around and tries to interest people in things, but I am so happy to have this book now.

MN: Are you surprised that, decades later, so much of your work completely holds up? It feels very contemporary.

ES: Yeah. I was very happy about that. I was very happy. Maybe that's because my work deals with people and not the issues of the day. It was all about what it means to be—

Susan Hewitt:—human.

ES: If what you do is all about what it means to be human, it'll never go out of date. Until humans do. That will happen, too.

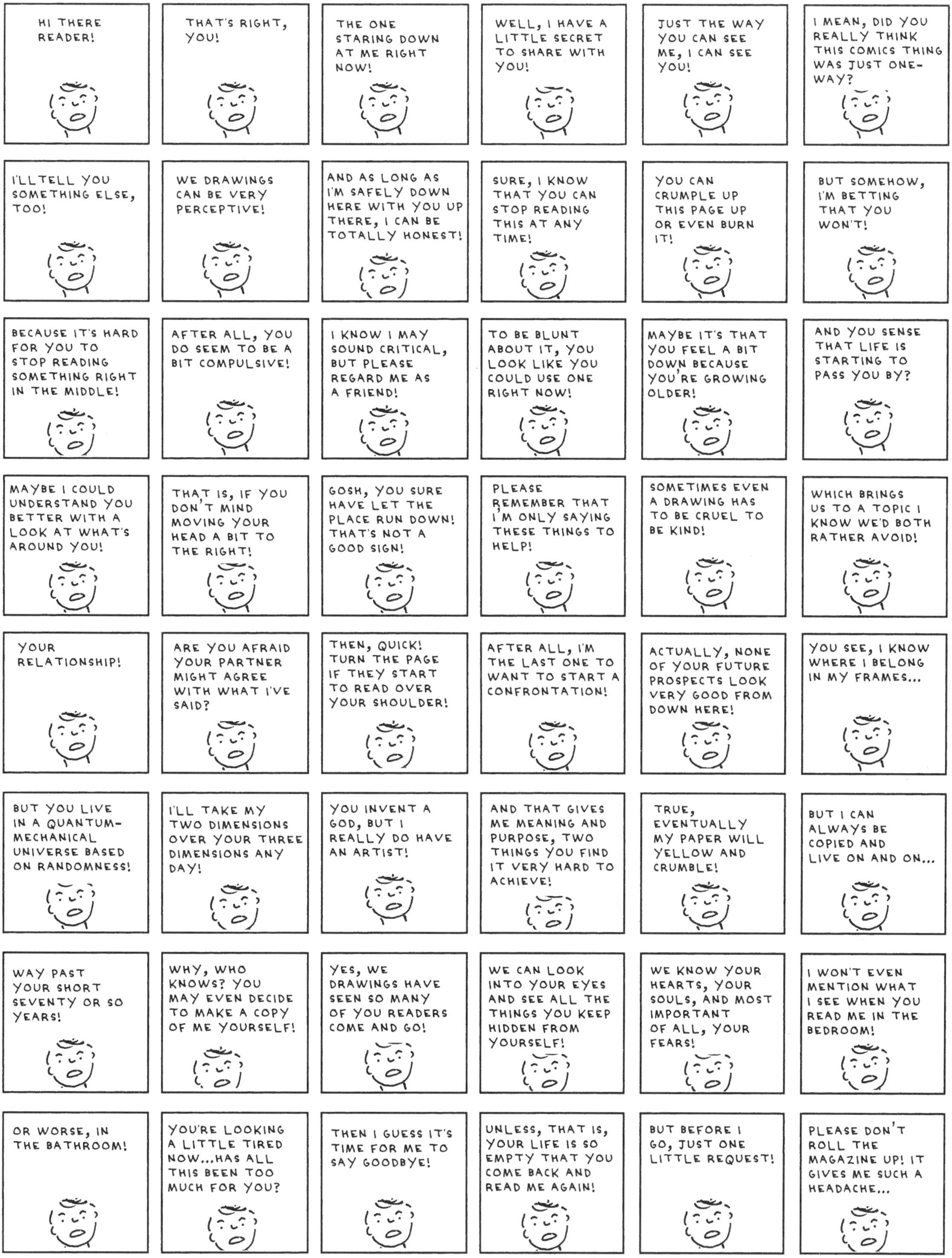
HI THERE READER!
THAT'S RIGHT, YOU!
THE ONE STARING DOWN AT ME RIGHT NOW!
WELL, I HAVE A LITTLE SECRET TO SHARE WITH YOU!
JUST THE WAY YOU CAN SEE ME, I CAN SEE YOU!
I MEAN, DID YOU REALLY THINK THIS COMICS THING WAS JUST ONE-WAY?
I'LLTELL YOU SOMETHING ELSE, TOO!
WE DRAWINGS CAN BE VERY PERCEPTIVE!
AND AS LONG AS I'M SAFELY DOWN HERE WITH YOU UP THERE, I CAN BE TOTALLY HONEST!
SURE, I KNOW THAT YOU CAN STOP READING THIS AT ANY TIME!
YOU CAN CRUMPLE UP THIS PAGE UP OR EVEN BURN IT!
BUT SOMEHOW, I'M BETTING THAT YOU WON'T!
BECAUSE IT'S HARD FOR YOU TO STOP READING SOMETHING RIGHT IN THE MIDDLE!
AFTER ALL, YOU DO SEEM TO BE A BIT COMPULSIVE!
I KNOW I MAY SOUND CRITICAL, BUT PLEASE REGARD ME AS A FRIEND!
TO BE BLUNT ABOUT IT, YOU LOOK LIKE YOU COULD USE ONE RIGHT NOW!
MAYBE IT'S THAT YOU FEEL A BIT DOWN BECAUSE YOU'RE GROWING OLDER!
AND YOU SENSE THAT LIFE IS STARTING TO PASS YOU BY?
MAYBE I COULD UNDERSTAND YOU BETTER WITH A LOOK AT WHAT'S AROUND YOU!
THAT IS, IF YOU DON'T MIND MOVING YOUR HEAD A BIT TO THE RIGHT!
GOSH, YOU SURE HAVE LET THE PLACE RUN DOWN! THAT'S NOT A GOOD SIGN!
PLEASE REMEMBER THAT I'M ONLY SAYING THESE THINGS TO HELP!
SOMETIMES EVEN A DRAWING HAS TO BE CRUEL TO BE KIND!
WHICH BRINGS US TO A TOPIC I KNOW WE'D BOTH RATHER AVOID!
YOUR RELATIONSHIP!
ARE YOU AFRAID YOUR PARTNER MIGHT AGREE WITH WHAT I'VE SAID?
THEN, QUICK! TURN THE PAGE IF THEY START TO READ OVER YOUR SHOULDER!
AFTER ALL, I'M THE LAST ONE TO WANT TO START A CONFRONTATION!
ACTUALLY, NONE OF YOUR FUTURE PROSPECTS LOOK VERY GOOD FROM DOWN HERE!
YOU SEE, I KNOW WHERE I BELONG IN MY FRAMES...
BUT YOU LIVE IN A QUANTUM-MECHANICAL UNIVERSE BASED ON RANDOMNESS!
I'LL TAKE MY TWO DIMENSIONS OVER YOUR THREE DIMENSIONS ANY DAY!
YOU INVENT A GOD, BUT I REALLY DO HAVE AN ARTIST!
AND THAT GIVES ME MEANING AND PURPOSE, TWO THINGS YOU FIND IT VERY HARD TO ACHIEVE!
TRUE, EVENTUALLY MY PAPER WILL YELLOW AND CRUMBLE!
BUT I CAN ALWAYS BE COPIED AND LIVE ON AND ON...
WAY PAST YOUR SHORT SEVENTY OR SO YEARS!
WHY, WHO KNOWS? YOU MAY EVEN DECIDE TO MAKE A COPY OF ME YOURSELF!
YES, WE DRAWINGS HAVE SEEN SO MANY OF YOU READERS COME AND GO!
WE CAN LOOK INTO YOUR EYES AND SEE ALL THE THINGS YOU KEEP HIDDEN FROM YOURSELF!
WE KNOW YOUR HEARTS, YOUR SOULS, AND MOST IMPORTANT OF ALL, YOUR FEARS!
I WON'T EVEN MENTION WHAT I SEE WHEN YOU READ ME IN THE BEDROOM!
OR WORSE, IN THE BATHROOM!
YOU'RE LOOKING A LITTLE TIRED NOW...HAS ALL THIS BEEN TOO MUCH FOR YOU?
THEN I GUESS IT'S TIME FOR ME TO SAY GOODBYE!
UNLESS, THAT IS, YOUR LIFE IS SO EMPTY THAT YOU COME BACK AND READ ME AGAIN!
BUT BEFORE I GO, JUST ONE LITTLE REQUEST!
PLEASE DON'T ROLL THE MAGAZINE UP! IT GIVES ME SUCH A HEADACHE...

ACKNOWLEDGMENTS

To my dear wife, Susan Hewitt, for her matchless organizational skills and infinite kindnesses; and to Lucas Adams, the world's greatest and nicest editor. Gosh, I just realized that I put Susan's name first, but will that hurt Lucas's feelings? Or if I put his name first, will that hurt Susan's feelings? Now I don't know what to do...

CARTOONS AND WRITING IN ORDER OF APPEARANCE

"The Beginning Comics!"
National Lampoon, October 1991

"Anti-Comics!"
National Lampoon, April 1972

"The Beginning of Life"
National Lampoon, August 1973

"8 Comics In One!"
National Lampoon, May 1973

"Come-Too-Soon Comics!"
National Lampoon, November 1974

"Crossword Puzzle Comics!"
National Lampoon, June 1972

"The Kiss!"
National Lampoon, April 1973

"Hey dad, can I have the car tonight?"
National Lampoon, ??

Background Music Comics!
National Lampoon, October 1985

"An Average Love Story!"
National Lampoon, July 1978

"Hot Sex Porno Comics!"
National Lampoon, March 1979

"Mobius Strip Comics!"
The National Lampoon Encyclopedia of Humor, October 1973

"Potboiler Comics!"
National Lampoon, August 1978

"Socially Redeeming Sex Comics!"
National Lampoon, June 1985

"Useful Comics!"
National Lampoon, August 1974

"Backwards Comics!"
National Lampoon, January 1975

"Origami Comics!"
The National Lampoon Encyclopedia of Humor, October 1973

"Feelies Comics!"
National Lampoon, March 1974

"How I Spent My Summer"
National Lampoon, December 1973

"Saturday Nite on Antarius!"
National Lampoon, February 1974

"Reverse Censorship Comics!"
National Lampoon, July 1972

"The Adventures of Timmy Taylor in Titland!"
The Encyclopedia of Humor by National Lampoon, October 1973

"Torture the Characters Comics!"
National Lampoon, January 1979

"Striptease Comics!"
National Lampoon, September 1978

"Coincidental Juxtaposition Comics!"
National Lampoon, July 1973

"Cinema East Schedule"
The New Yorker, August 6, 1974

"Cineplex Comics!"
National Lampoon, October 1991

"Law of the Universe #8,407"
Movies Movies Movies: A Hilarious Collection of Cartoons by Sam Gross, December 1989

"Condensed Movies! The Case Was Murder!"
National Lampoon, March 1979

"Being at the Movies Comics!"
National Lampoon, August 1986

"Condensed Movies! Make Mine... Love!"

National Lampoon, October 1977

"Don't you just hate it when the screen breaks?"
Movies Movies Movies: A Hilarious Collection of Cartoons by Sam Gross, December 1989

"Condensed Movies! Beach Party Monster"
National Lampoon, October 1980

"Come-in-the-Middle Comics!"
National Lampoon, November 1980

Untitled [Exit sign in screen]
Movies Movies Movies: A Hilarious Collection of Cartoons by Sam Gross, December 1989

"Poor Reception Comics!"
National Lampoon, July 1979

"Confessions of a Hi-Fi Neophyte"
Official National Lampoon Hi-Fi Primer, 1974

"In the French Restaurant"
National Lampoon, September 1972

"Ticket, please"
National Lampoon's Son of Cartoons Even We Wouldn't Dare Print II: A Sequel by *National Lampoon,* 1985

"Tattooed Lady Comics!"
National Lampoon, December 1978

"Small Consolations"
National Lampoon, September 1974

"Men: This Room Is Rated 'X'"
Scanlan's Monthly, September 1970

"Bestiality Comics!"
National Lampoon, May 1972

"It's a telegram from the governor..."
*National Lampoon's Son of Cartoons Even

We Wouldn't Dare Print II: A Sequel by
National Lampoon, 1985

"Compact Comics!"
National Lampoon, October 1974

"Tragic Love!"
National Lampoon, May 1979

"Just Married"
Cavalier, June 1969

"Magician Comics!"
National Lampoon, September 1979

"Dull Comics!"
National Lampoon, July 1974

"Assembly Line Comics!"
National Lampoon, April 1975

"Foldout Comics!"
The Encyclopedia of Humor by *National Lampoon*, October 1973

"Read Aloud Porno Comics!"
National Lampoon, January 1979

"Do-It-Yourself Comics!"
National Lampoon, December 1972

Untitled [Comic world speeding away]
National Lampoon, March 1974

"Count-the-Mistakes Porno Comics!"
National Lampoon, November 1973

"The Sins of Marcia!"
National Lampoon, 1974

"Growing Older Comics!"
National Lampoon, July 1978

"The Ax-Murderer and the Ladybug Fetishist and the Stripper..."
National Lampoon, December 1973

"Doctor-Lawyer!"
National Lampoon, April 1986

"Pubescent Comics!"
National Lampoon, February 1976

"Fortune-Telling Comics!"
National Lampoon, March 1975

"Two-Way Comics!"
National Lampoon, August 1974

"Printer's Strike Comics!"
The Encyclopedia of Humor by *National Lampoon*, October 1973

"The Intergalactic Gourmet!"
National Lampoon, July 1974

"Polaroid Pornographic Comics!"
National Lampoon, November 1972

"The Great 3-D Show!"
National Lampoon, July 1975

"An Evening in 1973"
National Lampoon, July 1973

"Palindrome Comics!"
National Lampoon, 199x

"Fred Kismiass"
National Lampoon, August 1972

Untitled [Universe Made Out of Ink]
National Lampoon, February 1976

"Situation Comedy Comics!"
National Lampoon, January 1977

"Instant Replay Comics!"
National Lampoon, June 1974

"Insult Comics!"
National Lampoon, November 1975

"Son of Fred Kismiass!"
National Lampoon, September 1974

"Carefully Rated Sex Comics!"
National Lampoon, September 1985

"My Hate Story!"
National Lampoon, September 1973

"Goes-On-Forever Porno Comics!"
National Lampoon, May 1975

"Instructions Comics!"
National Lampoon, January 1980

"Cryptogram Comics!"
National Lampoon, November 1978

"Off-the Page Comics!"
National Lampoon, October 1972

"Stupidworld"
National Lampoon, March 1974

"Computer Printout Comics!"
The Encyclopedia of Humor by *National Lampoon*, October 1973

"Mad As Hell Comics!"
National Lampoon, November 1985

"Amnesiac Class Reunion!"
National Lampoon, November 1983

"Subtitle Comics!"
National Lampoon, January 1976

"VCR Comics!"
National Lampoon, September 1991

"Dissolve Comics!"
National Lampoon, April 1979

"Therapy Comics!"
National Lampoon, Spring 1993

"Sunset Comics!"
National Lampoon, March 1975

Untitled [Suicide from Clock Face]
National Lampoon, Spring 1993

"Large, Impermanent Sand Mandala"
Tricycle, Fall 1994

"The First Signs of Global Warming in New York"
New Yorks Times Op-Ed, June 27, 1997

"Moving On Comics!"
Issue #7 *Nozone,* 1997

"Too Many Lawyers"
New York Times Op-Ed, February 22, 1997

"Some More Ways to Improve Our Taxi Service"
New York Times Op-Ed, August 15, 1998

"Other Pedestrian Safety Measures"
New York Times Op-Ed, February 16, 1998

"Sure-Fire Ways to Improve the I.R.S."
New York Times Op-Ed, November 22, 1997

"Two-Headed Sam Looks For Work!"
Issue #8 *Nozone,* 1998

"Two-Headed Sam in the Singles Bar!"
The Someday Funnies by Michel Choquette, November 2011

"Nice camouflage!"
Natural History, July 1994

"The People You Pass On The Street… What They're Thinking"
The American Bystander

"In the Skyscraper!"
The American Bystander

"The Entire Internet On a Page!"
The American Bystander

"The Invisible Poor!"
The War on the Poor: A Defense Manual by Nancy Folbre, March 1996

"Take a Walk with Mr. Anxiety"
Unpublished

"Because I'm a three dimensional being"
Black Eye magazine, 2013

"Agony Comics!"
The American Bystander

Consciousness Puzzle
Journal of Consciousness Studies, 18, No. 3–4, 2011

Consciousness Puzzle
Journal of Consciousness Studies, 20, No. 1–2, 2013

"Whaddya mean, you won't help me get down from here?"
National Lampoon, January 1975

"Murder at the Mansion!"
The American Bystander

"Zen Connect-the-Dots!"
Tricycle, Summer 1992

Untitled [Man talking to the reader]
The American Bystander

"Hypno-Comics!"
National Lampoon, September 1978

HYPNO-COMICS!

PUTS YOU IN A TRANCE!

...AND NOW THAT I HAVE SNAPPED MY FINGERS, YOU HAVE BLANKED OUT EVERYTHING YOU JUST READ!

THE END

ALSO AVAILABLE FROM NEW YORK REVIEW COMICS

YELLOW NEGROES AND OTHER IMAGINARY CREATURES Yvan Alagbé
PIERO Edmond Baudoin
ALMOST COMPLETELY BAXTER Glen Baxter
AGONY Mark Beyer
MITCHUM Blutch
PEPLUM Blutch
THE GREEN HAND AND OTHER STORIES Nicole Claveloux
WHAT AM I DOING HERE? Abner Dean
THE TENDERNESS OF STONES Marion Fayolle
W THE WHORE Anke Feuchtenberger and Katrin de Vries
TROTS AND BONNIE Shary Flenniken
LETTER TO SURVIVORS Gébé
PRETENDING IS LYING Dominique Goblet
ALAY-OOP William Gropper
THE RULING CLAWSS Syd Hoff
BUNGLETON GREEN AND THE MYSTIC COMMANDOS Jay Jackson
THE PROJECTOR AND THE ELEPHANT Martin Vaughn-James
ALL YOUR RACIAL PROBLEMS WILL SOON END Charles Johnson
THE GULL YETTIN Joe Kessler
VOICES IN THE DARK Ulli Lust
IT'S LIFE AS I SEE IT: BLACK CARTOONISTS IN CHICAGO, 1940-1980 Edited by Dan Nadel
JIMBO: ADVENTURES IN PARADISE Gary Panter
FATHER AND SON E.O. Plauen
SOFT CITY Pushwagner
THE NEW WORLD Chris Reynolds
PITTSBURGH Frank Santoro
DISCIPLINE Dash Shaw
MACDOODLE ST. Mark Alan Stamaty
SLUM WOLF Tadao Tsuge
THE MAN WITHOUT TALENT Yoshiharu Tsuge
RETURN TO ROMANCE Ogden Whitney